Writing National Histories

Historical writing has been associated with the process of nation-building across Europe since the concept of the modern nation was first formulated during the American and French Revolutions at the close of the eighteenth century. *Writing National Histories* examines comparatively how the writing of history by individuals and groups, historians, politicians and journalists, has been used to 'legitimate' the nation-state, focusing on the nation-building of the nineteenth century and the subsequent struggle to defend the nation-state against socialist, communist and Catholic internationalism in the modern era. Covering four countries in Western Europe, the book includes discussion of:

- history as legitimation in post-revolutionary France
- unity and confederation in the Italian Risorgimento
- German historians as critics of Prussian conservatism
- right-wing history writing in France between the wars
- British historiography from Macaulay to Trevelyan
- the search for national identity in the reunified Germany

Stefan Berger is Senior Lecturer in German history at the University of Wales, Cardiff, where **Mark Donovan** lectures in Italian politics and **Kevin Passmore** lectures in modern European history.

Writing National Histories

Western Europe since 1800

Stefan Berger, Mark Donovan and Kevin Passmore

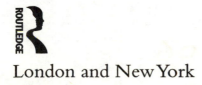

London and New York

First published 1999
by Routledge
11 New Fetter Lane, London EC4P 4EE

Simultaneously published in the USA and Canada
by Routledge
29 West 35th Street, New York, NY 10001

Typeset in Bembo by Routledge
Printed and bound in Great Britain by Creative Print and Design
(Wales), Ebbw Vale

British Library Cataloguing in Publication Data
A catalogue record for this book is available from the British Library

Library of Congress Cataloging in Publication Data
Berger, Stefan.
Writing national histories: Western Europe since 1800 / Stefan Berger,
Mark Donovan, and Kevin Passmore.
p. cm.
Includes bibliographical references and index.
alk. paper
1. Europe, Western — Historiography. 2. Europe—History—
1789–1996—Historiography. 3. Europe—History—20th century
—Historiography. I. Donovan, Mark. II. Passmore, Kevin.
III. Title.
D352.9.B47 1999
940.2'8—dc21 98–21825
CIP

ISBN 0–415–16426–5 (hbk)
ISBN 0–415–16427–3 (pbk)

This book is dedicated to Georg G. Iggers

Contents

Contributors

Patrick Bahners is a journalist with the *Frankfurter Allgemeine Zeitung*. He has published widely on British and German historiography, and is currently completing a Ph.D. on Ranke and Macaulay in comparative perspective.

Stefan Berger, is Senior Lecturer in German History at the University of Wales, Cardiff. He has published numerous books and articles on comparative labour history and historiography, including *The Search for Normality. National Identity and Historical Consciousness in Germany since 1800*, Berghahn (1997).

Martin Clark is Reader in the Department of Politics, University of Edinburgh. He has published widely on various aspects of modern Italy and an updated second edition of his *Modern Italy, 1871–1996* has been published by Longman (1996).

Ceri Crossley is Professor of Nineteenth-Century French Studies at the University of Birmingham. He is the author of *French Historians and Romanticism*, Routledge (1993), and has written books on Edgar Quinet and Alfred de Musset.

Mark Donovan is Lecturer in the School of European Studies at the University of Wales, Cardiff, where he specialises in Italian government and politics. He has recently edited *Italy*, Dartmouth (1998), a two-volume reader, and co-edited, with David Broughton, *Changing Party Systems in Western Europe*, Pinter (1998).

Hugo Frey is Associate Lecturer in European Studies and a Ph.D. research student at the University of Surrey. His dissertation focuses on ideological currents in the French historiography of the Occupation.

Mary Fulbrook, Professor of History at University College London, has published extensively on German history and related fields. She has recently completed *The Myth of German National Identity after the Holocaust* for Polity Press (1998), and is writing a book on historical theory.

Bertram M. Gordon is the Frederick A. Rice Professor of History at Mills

College in Oakland, California. He is the author of *Collaborationism in France during the Second World War*, Cornell University Press (1980) and the editor of *The Historical Dictionary of World War II France*, Greenwood Press (1998).

Georg Iggers has recently retired as Professor of History at the State University of New York at Buffalo. He has published widely in Western European and American historiography, including *The German Conception of History* (3rd edition 1988).

Julian Jackson is Reader in Modern History at University College, Swansea. He has published books and articles on French history in the twentieth century, and his *Occupied France* will shortly be published by Oxford University Press.

Stuart Jones is Lecturer in History at the University of Manchester. He is the author of *The French State in Question: Public Law and Political Argument in the Third Republic*, Cambridge University Press (1993).

Peter Lambert, Lecturer in Modern European History at the University of Wales, Aberystwyth, has published widely on German historiography. He is currently completing a book about German historians since 1914 for Cambridge University Press.

Carl Levy lectures in European Politics at Goldsmiths College, London. His chief publications are: *Socialism and the Intelligentsia, 1870–1914*, Routledge and Kegan Paul (1988), *Italian Regionalism*, Berg (1996) and, with V. Symes and J. Littlewood, *The Future of Europe*, Macmillan (1997).

Mauro Moretti has been a researcher in contemporary history at the Scuola Normale Superiore, Pisa, since 1981. His publications focus on the history of Italian culture since unification, on Italy's university and educational system, and on aspects of nineteenth-century European historiography.

Philip Morgan is Head of the Department of European Studies in the School of European Languages and Cultures at the University of Hull where he lectures in nineteenth- and twentieth-century European history. He has recently published *Italian Fascism, 1919–1945*, Macmillan (1995).

Kevin Passmore is Lecturer in History at the University of Wales, Cardiff. He is the author of *From Liberalism to Fascism: the Right in a French Province, 1928–1939*, Cambridge University Press (1997).

Hans Schleier, recently retired Professor of History at the University of Halle, has published extensively on German historiography including *Die bürgerliche deutsche Geschichtsschreibung der Weimarer Republik*, Akademie Verlag (1974).

Peter Schöttler, Directeur de Recherche at the CNRS, Paris, has written extensively on French historiography and has a particular interest in the

Annales. He has recently edited *Geschichtesschreibung als Legitimationswissen-schaft*, Suhrkamp (1997).

Benedikt Stuchtey is Research Fellow at the German Historical Institute in London. He is a specialist on Anglo-Irish historiography and has published *Historisches Denken und politische Kritik im Werk eines anglo-irischen Gelehrten des 19. Jahrhunderts*, Vandenhoeck & Ruprecht (1997).

Martin Thom is a freelance translator and author based in Cambridge. His most recent publications are *Republics, Nations and Tribes*, Verso (1995) and 'City, Region and Nation: Carlo Cattaneo and the "Making" of Italy', in *Citizenship Studies* (forthcoming).

Alastair Thompson, Lecturer in Twentieth-Century European History at the University of Durham, has published widely on Wilhelmine Germany. His *The Strange Survival of German Liberalism* will appear shortly from Oxford University Press.

Roberto Vivarelli has been Professor of Contemporary History at the Scuola Normale Superiore, Pisa, since 1986. He specialises in Italian and European history. He has published two volumes on the origins of fascism (Istituto Italiano per gli Studi Storici 1967 and Il Mulino 1991) and a third is in progress.

Preface

This book arises from a conference, entitled *Apologias for the Nation-State*, held at the University of Wales, Cardiff, on 9–11 April 1996. The intention of the organisers was to examine comparatively the manner in which the writing of history has been used to 'legitimate' the nation-state, in the double sense of substantialising it as the 'natural' principle of political organisation, and of making it the subject and object of historical development. We were also interested in exploring the nature and importance of calls to 'renationalise' the pasts of Britain, France, Germany and Italy. Our focus is therefore upon 'establishment' history – that which participated in the nation-building of the nineteenth century, and which struggled to defend the nation-state against socialist, communist and Catholic internationalism in the century and a half that followed. The reader will therefore find relatively little material on left-wing nationalisms, which usually sought to supersede the nation-state, even where they endeavoured to exploit the potential of nationalism for the purpose of mass mobilisation. For the same reason university history has been privileged, 'amateur' history – that is history written by historians not employed in universities – usually enters into discussion only where it has been written by conservative and wealthy figures.

The editors are indebted to Adrian Lyttleton, Roger Magraw and Hans Mommsen for their brilliant summing up of the themes of the conference in the concluding 'round table'. The editors would also like to thank the four anonymous readers of the initial book proposal, and the final manuscript, as well as the following institutions which sponsored the conference and hence made possible the present volume: the German History Society, the School of European Studies and the School of History and Archaeology at the University of Wales, Cardiff, the British Academy, the German Academic Exchange Service, the Elizabeth Barker Foundation, the Association for the Study of Modern Italy, the Association for the Study of Modern and Contemporary France, L'Ambassade de France and the Royal Historical Society. Enormous gratitude is also due to Amanda Attwood who assisted with the administration of the conference, and to Anett Pförtner who helped with the preparation of the final manuscript. Finally, the editors would like to thank Heather McCallum, at Routledge, who supported the project and provided valuable comments and suggestions.

Part I
Comparative perspectives

1 Apologias for the nation–state in Western Europe since 1800[1]

Stefan Berger with Mark Donovan and Kevin Passmore

Historical writing has been connected to the process of nation-building across Europe ever since the concept of the modern nation was first formulated in the American and French Revolutions of the late-eighteenth century. The links between historiography and nationalism so far have often been investigated within their respective national contexts. Whilst this research has undoubtedly yielded important results, the predominance of the national paradigm tended to overlook the common European dimension of historiographic nationalism. The ambition of this volume is to contribute to a Europeanisation of historical studies by comparing traditions of historical writing in Britain, France, Germany and Italy, i.e. in four core countries of Western Europe.[2]

Apart from its historiographical ambitions, the present volume also has a rather haunting contemporary relevance. All four countries discussed here have witnessed attempts to renationalise their respective national identities in the 1980s and 1990s. The most recent attempts to construct and reaffirm the belea-guered principle of the sovereign nation-state are clearly related to a deep-seated sense of crisis. The collapse of the 'First Republic' in Italy, reunifi-cation in Germany, the debates about the place of Vichy in French history and not the least the political aim of achieving 'ever closer union' in Europe by means of currency union have all heightened a sense of national identities being under threat. In 1980s Britain, Margaret Thatcher and like-minded historians most blatantly attempted to dictate a return to national(ist) history and Victorian values through school curricula and conservative research agendas.[3] In view of all these diverse strategies for renationalising identities across Western Europe, it seems particularly important to place current debates within the long tradition of close links between the writing of history and the complex process of 'becoming national'. Hence this book aims to draw atten-tion to the origins and limits of historiographical nationalism as well as to the many contestations, changes and often violent ruptures of historical conscious-ness in nineteenth- and twentieth-century Western Europe.

History writing was, however, only one way in which historical conscious-ness was expressed. The writing of academic texts had an influence, above all, amongst a university-trained elite. There were other expressions of historical consciousness which were far more popular. One just has to think of the diverse ways in which national days of remembrance and festivals were celebrated across Europe, or of the institutionalisation of national holidays, monuments and symbols, or the popularity of historical novels, or the increasing influence of the mass media (newspapers, radio and television) throughout the nineteenth and twentieth centuries. Whilst the writing and reading of academic history books has remained to a very large extent the pastime of elites, the political mobilisation of the masses has by and large relied on different means to achieve their integration into nation-states.

The professionalisation and objectivisation of historical writing

The nineteenth century witnessed the increasing professionalisation of historical writing and the rigorous application of methodological ground rules. It evolved, first of all, within the reformed German university system and was adopted in France, Italy and Britain at some point during the second-half of the nineteenth century. It provided the basis for a self-confident and exclusive self-understanding of the historical profession which now began to distinguish sharply between 'professional historians' and 'dilettantes'. The writing of history became more and more a scientific (*wissenschaftlich*) exercise, while less importance was attached to the literary merits of an historical work. Yet these methodological ground rules, in particular the ones to do with the handling of and critical approach towards archival source material (*Quellenkritik*), were by no means invented by German historians at the end of the eighteenth century. Much of it had been good practice amongst historians ever since Thucydides and the beginnings of historical enquiry and analysis in early antiquity. Nor were such methodological ground rules particularly successful in preventing the continued legitimatory use of historical writings. To the contrary, in Germany most mainstream historians were soon demanding that the historian had to be partisan (*parteilich*), and that they should take a stance in the contemporary political battles. At the same time they also insisted that their politics had no influence on their scholarliness and in particular on their objectivity as scholars. The precise relationship between politics and scholarliness has been the focus of much debate, as historians, and social scientists more generally, grapple with the problem of value judgements and their impact on choice of topics, on the interpretative frameworks adopted, on the rhetorical strategies pursued and on the emotive tone of writing employed.[4] When Marc Bloch admitted to his own patriotism as a value judgement and at the same time insisted that this should have no influence on his scholarly work, he made an important step in the direction of disqualifying nationalist prejudice in transnational historiographical discourses. However, such strict separation between politics and scholarliness has been a standard rhetorical device amongst nineteenth- and twentieth-century historians. It is arguable that Bloch's objectivism represents an unattainable idealisation of scholarliness, that was often little more than a useful concept in the institutional and political power struggles amongst historians which had much to do with career opportunities and access to funding.

Seen in this light, the new emphasis on 'history as an objective science' (*Wissenschaft*) and on 'rational discourse' was rapidly becoming the new metaphysics of historical text production.[5] Within its pretences, a plethora of mythopoeic concepts structured very diverse historical interpretations. Take for example the notion of the *Volk* in the works of Fritz Rörig. It was a highly ambivalent but nevertheless guiding concept which could be attached to both democratic and racialist interpretations of German history. As such it could be used as foundational myths in historical writings legitimating democratic, fascist and communist regimes in Germany. Or, in the case of Italian historiography, an obvious example is provided by the history of the Resistance to Mussolini. This was a crucial foundational myth which underpinned the self-understanding of all parties in Italy's First Republic (except the neofascist MSI), but was especially important for the identity of the Italian left. In France, Gaullist historical consciousness post-1945 operated within an understanding of French history which divided the past neatly into periods of ascent and decline. Finally, British historians of the dominant Whig tradition have constructed various myths surrounding the development of the parliamentary prerogative. This in turn enabled them to stake out a special 'civilising' mission in the world with reference to Britain having established the 'mother of parliaments'. Where Whiggism, the Gaullist historians, the historians of the Italian Resistance and Fritz Rörig would no doubt claim that their histories were based on 'scientific objectivity', they in fact provided 'scientifically' legitimated foundational myths for contemporary definitions of their respective nation-states.

If all four historiographies attempted to contribute to and influence the nation-building processes in the nineteenth and twentieth centuries, the obvious question emerges: can we identify common themes in those attempts to shape the national historical consciousness? And, on the other hand, what was specific about those attempts? As for the latter, Italian historians, for example, had to come to terms with the role of the papacy in Italian history. For French historians, the Revolution of 1789, significantly adorned with the adjective 'great' in many historical accounts, was an unrivalled foundational myth in a way that it was not for British, Italian or German historians, despite its impact on all European nation-states. The systematic racialisation of historical discourses in Germany in the form of *Volksgeschichte*, especially after the defeat of the nation-state in 1918, seems to find no real parallel in other West European historiographies. British historiography's concern for the centuries of unparalleled global naval and military triumph was peculiar to the historians of the island nation.

With regard to common themes across the different national traditions, there is an obvious celebration of cultural identity and superiority in both Germany and Italy which stands in stark contrast to the more political identities constructed in France and Britain. Thus in France the idea of the political citizen (*citoyen*) formed the basis of national cohesion, whereas in Britain it was the identification of the nation with the development of a parliamentary tradition which widely came to be seen as epicentre of the national identity. Whilst a pro-parliamentary historiography in Britain was necessarily an anti-absolutist and anti-Stuart historiography, and whilst in France Republican Jacobinism was to marginalise a Royalist historiography on the political right over much of the past two centuries, in Italy and Germany there emerged an unashamedly apologetic historiography of the ruling houses. These dynasties were perceived as the founders of their modern nation-states and their history was written as that of a long vocation for the unification of their respective nation-states. The Hohenzollerns in Germany and the House of Savoy in Italy were described by scores of historians in the late-nineteenth and early-twentieth centuries as the saviours of the German and Italian nation-state respectively. By contrast, the only claim to fame of the Hanoverians in much of English constitutional history was that they reconciled the British monarchy with the predominance of parliament. A number of common themes also characterised the extreme right-wing historiography of the interwar period. These included, under the fascist regimes, a renewed interest in war and military history in Italy and Germany. In both countries, leading historians propagated the idea that the nation had found its true self through fascism, and there was a distinct tendency to glorify the peasantry as the basis of a 'healthy' nation-state.

Whilst the politicisation of historiography in the name of the national interest could be intense, there were periods when historians withdrew from explicit political intervention and emphasised the 'objective', 'disinterested' and 'scientific' nature of their professional endeavours. Yet, as the examples of neo-Rankeanism in late nineteenth-century Germany or post-Risorgimento historiography in Italy demonstrate, historical texts remained loaded with political meaning. It was simply impossible to write any history with the contemporary politics left out. Professional historians, whether historist,[6] Hegelian, Marxist or postmodernist, were never able to avoid the question of politics.

If the nation-state stood at the centre of much historical investigation in the nineteenth century, historians focused especially on the role of the state in the making of the nations. Yet in the first-half of the twentieth century, historians began to explore societal issues, often within more or less contested national parameters. In France in particular the interwar period saw the breakthrough of social history in the form of the *Annales*.[7] One of the foremost Italian historians of the interwar period, Gioacchino Volpe, had fascist sympathies and was writing histories in which much attention was given to social history. In Britain the writing of social history can be traced to the endeavours of the Hammonds, the Webbs, G.D.H. Cole and R.H. Tawney.[8] It was only in Germany that social history failed to establish itself within the profession thanks to a much publicised debate between Karl Lamprecht and virtually the rest of the historical establishment in the 1890s. Although there clearly were other issues which played an important role (notably the tighter control exercised by both state and profession over recruitment to academic positions), it is hard to avoid the impression that it was no mere accident that (for a long time) social history was weakest in the one country which (of the four) had the strongest state and the least representative government.

In Britain a nineteenth-century state-centred history could (and sometimes did) take account of the people and societal issues because the people were both ideologically, through the idea of 'virtual representation',[9] and practically, through the growing participation via the 1832 and 1867 franchise extensions, regarded as a central part of that national history. The people were represented by the central institution of the nation: parliament, which defended the liberty and constitution of the entire nation. British historians in a sense underwrote the progressive constitutional and electoral reform of the nineteenth century. In France, although women did not get the vote until after 1945, the early mobilisation of the adult male population in elections formed a major impetus for historians to concern themselves with the people (or at least the male half). And even before that, much of French Enlightenment historiography was oppositional in the sense that it undermined the traditional foundations of the *ancien régime*. Furthermore, it was of considerable importance that an enlarged public sphere emerged earlier in Britain and France than in Germany. This meant that French and British historians wrote for a broader public and had much closer ties to the publishing market. The huge English-language book market, especially, maintained very strong ties between historical writing and the market-orientation of historical texts, up to the present day. Only in Germany was there a powerful state run by an Imperial government not accountable to parliament and administered by a highly efficient state bureaucracy with its own elitist ethos. Here, the universities and university historians existed first and foremost to train future civil servants, e.g. servants of the state. And the historians became the undisputed upholders of the existing idea of the state. Many of them served the Prussian state directly, i.e. Niebuhr as Ambassador to the Vatican or Ranke as official 'historiographer of the Prussian state'. The loyalty of an increasing number of professional historians, in line with general public opinion, moved from Prussia towards the German Reich from the 1860s onwards. Yet whilst conservative Prussianism was widely regarded as an expression of narrow sectional interests, the idea of the general state interest was maintained. The only difference was that it now came to be identified with Germany rather than Prussia. For Ranke and subsequent generations of German historians, service to the state – be it to the Prussian or the German one – meant service to God (as the states were, in Ranke's view, 'ideas of God', *Gedanken Gottes*). Hence the state could not be criticised. There could not even be a meaningful dialogue between the state and its servants. The only possible attitude towards the state was one of obedience and worship. Nowhere else in Western Europe was there so little government and so much state. Nowhere else were the people regarded so much as subjects and so little as citizens. Social history had a hard time getting established in such a political context. In fact, the exploration of societal issues in Germany found expression through racialist *Volksgeschichte* after 1918. And it was not until the 1950s and 1960s that a variant of social history comparable to the *Annales* school in France emerged in West Germany. Even then, it is a matter of contentious debate how much German social history owed to the indigenous *Volksgeschichte* and how much it tried to catch up with the kind of social history practised in other Western European nation-states.[10]

However, the turn to social history did not mean the abandonment of an earlier national commitment. The hyper-nationalism of *Volksgeschichte* as well as the national commitment of the doyens of social history in the Federal Republic, Theodor Schieder and Werner Conze, demonstrate the continuities of the national tradition in non-state-centred historical writings.[11] In France, the intense patriotism of one of the leading figures of the *Annales* school, Marc Bloch, points in a similar direction. And in Britain, much has been written about the essential Englishness of the Webbs, or, for that matter, of a later key figure in the writing of English social history, E.P. Thompson. In Italy, the social history championed and practised by Volpe went hand in hand with a firm commitment to the Italian state. Even earlier, the first generation of professional university historians were employed precisely to write 'official histories' and to present all other historical possibilities as 'deviations', 'withdrawals' or 'mistaken routes'. And in France's Third Republic, historians enjoyed an excellent reputation amongst a wider public precisely because they were regarded as the knights of the Holy Grail of the national heritage. A school textbook like the 'petit Lavisse' influenced the historical consciousness of generations of French schoolchildren.[12]

The institutionalisation of professional history-writing in the nineteenth century and its close links with the task of nation-building led to relatively high levels of conformity amongst professional historians. The state, which wielded considerable powers over the appointment and promotion of 'professional' historians at the universities and research institutes, often had a clear idea of which histories and historians it wanted to promote.[13] However, the degrees of conformity encouraged by such state intervention differed quite substantially. They seemed to have been strongest in nineteenth-century Germany where literally a handful of professors controlled the *cursus honorum* leading to academic titles and careers. In France and Britain, academic historians were able to move in and out of the historical profession much more freely than in Germany, where a greater degree of professionalisation also meant: once a historian always a historian. In the western democracies, it was frequently the case that historians such as Macaulay, Cousin and Guizot, moved into politics or some other position in the public life of the nation or vice versa, from politics and public life into the universities. At the same time the university systems in France and Britain were both far less significant and prestigious in comparison with their German counterpart. Especially in Britain, the 'German mandarins' never really found any equivalent.[14] It is very striking, too, how much more lenient the Italian fascist state was in its control of the historical profession compared to the National Socialist *Gleichschaltung*. Liberals like Croce or social democrats such as the brothers Rosselli most certainly would not have had a place in German universities in the Third Reich.[15] At the same time it is also amazing how willingly the overwhelming majority of German historians accepted a legitimatory role in the service of the Nazi regime, and how they combined their traditional understanding of the writing of history with support for the political dictatorship. There was no need for historians in Germany to take sides in any kind of 'war of manifestoes' like that which divided the Italian profession in 1925. In their methodologies, as in their politics, the German profession showed a remarkable continuity despite the fact that there were new developments such as the strengthening of *Volksgeschichte* after 1933. The First World War, and in particular Germany's defeat in 1918, was crucial here. The national principle seemed weakened and disgraced by the military defeat and historians were looking towards something stronger to replace it. The *völkisch* concepts which became popular also amongst professional German historians after 1918 filled that gap. *Volksgeschichte* with its racialist overtones had few parallels in France and Italy. These nations, both on the victorious side in 1918, had developed their own brand of social history well before 1914.

Yet, overall, the relative absence of a genuinely fascist historiography in Germany, Italy and France is striking. Undoubtedly there were some new concepts and ideas, more so in Germany than in Italy or France, but there was a remarkable continuity in the history departments of all three countries. The historical professions in all three countries were remarkably successful in defending their institutional autonomy against the interventions of the fascist state, and notions of objectivity – whilst never detaching political meaning from scholarly research agendas – could prevent historians in all three countries from the worst excesses of apologetic history-writing in the service of fascist regimes.

History-writing and its political context

With the rise of nationalisms across nineteenth-century Europe, there was an increasing essentialising of alleged 'national characteristics' in all four countries discussed in this volume. Much of British historiography was concerned with demonstrating the civilisatory progress achieved by Britain through its championing of liberty and constitutional values, and through its long and continuous parliamentary tradition. French historians also came to perceive their nation as the champion of '*liberté, egalité, fraternité*'. The slogan of the French Revolution of 1789 symbolised the fact that it was in France that the Third Estate had, for the first time, truly become the nation. In Germany, it was the notion of the superiority of German culture, and of German scholarship in particular, which lay at the heart of the nationalist discourse of the nineteenth century. In Italy that discourse was often connected to the celebration of the country's ancient culture and the tradition of its medieval city-states. The construction of 'national characters' in the historiographical discourse of nineteenth-century Western Europe tended to attribute 'eternal' characteristics' to the nations.

Furthermore, all national histories showed a remarkable zeal in demonstrating the uniqueness of their particular nation-state, leading to a historiography of special paths which often obscured the common characteristics of the European heritage. Thus, Whig historians in Britain put in a claim for the unique tradition of liberal parliamentarism, whereas French historians tended to stress the singular significance of the 'Great Revolution'. German historians were concerned with the fact that it was not politics which brought true liberation to the individual self, but, rather, that the powerful state was to protect the innermost search of the individual for true fulfilment of his (rarely her) potential. This was the *machtgeschützte Innerlichkeit* celebrated by Thomas Mann in his notorious defence of the authoritarian Imperial German state against Weimar democracy in 1918.[16] And in Italian historiography there were frequent references to the singularity of the Italian national character which could be traced back to the great 'civilising mission' of ancient Rome – interpreted as the birthplace of a civilised European society.

All of these claims to uniqueness were connected to the notion that one's own nation was superior to other nations. The tradition of liberty and progress made Britain a better nation than others and justified their 'civilising mission' in the Empire. French historians could lay claim to a universal mission in spreading their revolutionary values, whilst for their German counterparts, true culture, in opposition to shallow Western European civilisation, could only be represented by Germans. And in Italy the singularity of the *comuni* and the celebration of early Etruscan civilisation could lead to notions of Italian national superiority even in someone as cosmopolitan as Carlo Cattaneo. In the age of Imperialism, the construction of such national 'civilising missions' served a particular purpose – that of extending the power of the European nation-states across the globe.

Moreover, ideas of national uniqueness and superiority were almost always defined in contrast to negative counter-examples of nations that were somehow inferior. The celebration of German culture included the denigration of Western European civilisation (*Kultur* versus *Zivilisation*) as well as Slav 'barbarity'. British notions of 'progress' were connected to the perceptions of others, including Ireland and most continental countries, as 'backward'. It is striking that in a multi-national state such as Britain, the histories of Ireland, Scotland and Wales could be marginalised for such a long period of time, and that the terms 'England' and 'Britain' should have become almost synonymous. The championing of ancient Rome in Italy often meant little respect for Germanic and Celtic cultures. And the revolutionary tradition in France made all other nation-states sideshows to the real progress of humanity which could, of course, only take place in and with France. The construction of specific national continuities always entailed the repression of others, both outside and within one's own nation-state.

Almost all of these constructed continuities, rooted in the past, created national teleologies designed to legitimate the present and prevent future change. They read national histories backward to arrive at foundational dates for their respective national histories. Thus, for example, the Magna Carta (1215) came to be seen as starting the long parliamentary tradition in Britain, the ancient Roman Empire was perceived as the precursor to the Italian nation-state, and the Holy Roman Empire and the idea of the Reich played a large role in the self-definition of the German nation-state. Thus 1688 and/or 1832 for Britain, 1789 for France, 1861 for Italy and 1871 for Germany mark important foundational dates connected to the creation of foundational myths which were in themselves always contested by rival mythologies.

None of the national historiographies discussed in this book were characterised by complete unity of purpose. Their narrative strategies and their politics were hotly contested, and in the *longue durée* one can usefully distinguish between, on the one hand, the writing of history as legitimation of existing political systems, and, on the other, the writing of oppositional history which aimed at undermining the dominant versions of the national narratives. No doubt the birth of the modern party systems in the last-third of the nineteenth century and the competing national-popular mobilisations by different political parties contributed a great deal to the pluralisation of competing historical discourses. Time and again, legitimatory historical writings tended to deny the possibility of historical change, and time and again they were refuted by historical developments. Whether we take the bourgeois-liberal historians of the post-revolutionary period in France or the historical discourses in the two Germanies post 1949, attempts to arrest historical change proved futile in every national context throughout the nineteenth and twentieth centuries.

Alternative historical discourses of both left and right were able to challenge the dominant national discourses with differing success. So, for example, in nineteenth-century Italy, Cattaneo put federalism before nationalism and liberty before unity, thereby opposing both Mazzinian nationalism and the idea of the Piedmontese vocation. And in the second-half of the nineteenth century, Taine wrote largely against attempts by 'official' French historians such as Lavisse to legitimate the Third Republic. Antifascists like Marc Bloch in France and the Rosselli brothers in Italy attempted to formulate an alternative, left-wing patriotism to the dominant nationalism in the interwar period.

When fascist attempts to portray their own movements as the pinnacle of the national tradition went up in smoke at the end of the Second World War, all forms of nationalism were seriously threatened. In the post-1945 period many European states faced what amounted to their worst crisis of national identity. Eventually, this crisis led, almost everywhere in Western Europe, to the recognition of the need to pluralise national discourses. The break with the national tradition of history-writing was greatest in nations with home-grown fascist governments, i.e. Italy and Germany. Yet in France and Italy the myths of the Resistance provided, for a long time, a vantage point from which an attempt could be made to salvage the nation by reformulating the old dichotomies between good patriotism and bad nationalism. In Britain, which was never occupied and where, thus, collaboration with fascism never was much of an issue (except for the Channel Islands), there was least soul-searching after 1945. The Second World War was very widely perceived as the nation's 'finest hour' and, if anything, the fact that Britain for a long time was the only nation willing to stand up to the fascist threat strengthened an apparently unproblematic national identity. In Britain, any subsequent crisis of national identity probably had more to do with the rise of Scottish and (to a much more limited extent) Welsh nationalism from the 1960s than with the memory of the Second World War.

The crisis of the national principle contributed to an increasing Europeanisation and comparativisation of historical writing after 1945. The emergence of a specific Euro-historiography is a development with enormous potential but it is also fraught with new problems. It transcends the narrow national limitations of the traditional historiographies and begins to question the notions of 'national character' and of the 'uniqueness' of national experiences. But it also brings the danger of new ideological closures, of erecting new borders and building new boundaries. It encourages the vilification of non-European nations and cultures (as one sees in the debates about the Islamic world and Islamic fundamentalism in Western Europe). It can lead to the constitution of a homogenised 'European path' which is then perceived as superior to other non-European experiences. Europe has been for a very long time an ambiguous and multi-faceted phenomenon, as several contributions to this volume impressively underline. It was an ideological weapon in the armour of the Nazis, as they conjured up a phantasmagoric unity of the European occident against the forces of 'Asian Bolshevism'. Whilst the concept of Europe was usurped by the Nazis in the later stages of the Second World War, it was equally used by Italian antifascists such as Rosselli to counter the narrow nationalism propagated by the Mussolini government in the 1930s. In the Cold War, 'Europe' once again became an important ideological justification for a series of political, economic and military alliances in Western Europe directed against the evil 'enemy' of communism behind the 'Iron Curtain' (an expression coined not by Churchill, as is widely believed, but by Joseph Goebbels).[17] And in the post-Cold War era since 1989, 'Europe' has, for some, become synonymous with the demise of the traditional nation-states and the creation of an ahistorical, bureaucratic superstate which is not democratically legitimised by its people. Others predict the renewed Balkanisation of Europe despite further moves to 'ever closer union' in Europe, especially the allegedly all-important move to a common European currency. Hence 'Europe' has for a very long time been a multifaceted concept which has served many masters and a multitude of often conflicting purposes.

There was no simple 'death' of the national idea in the post-Second World

War era. The 1980s and 1990s witnessed a renaissance of neo-nationalist movements on the political right and a new national discourse of the political centre which is focused on the alleged 'normality' of national feeling and identity in Europe. However, contemporary debates on national identities have taken place under very different political circumstances. In Germany they were connected to the surprising re-emergence of a powerful, united nation-state following the breakdown of the communist regime in the GDR. In Italy, the political crisis brought with it the threat of the dissolution of the nation-state by a powerful northern secessionist movement, the *Lega Nord*. In France, the bicentenary of the French Revolution and the discovery of 'memory' as a new historiographical subject have led to a variety of reaffirmations and reappropriations of the republican-Jacobin legacy.

The experiences of historians in all four nation-states in the nineteenth and twentieth centuries reveal the fallacies and dangers of any attempt to provide historical legitimacy to forms of national identity. Historians today would do well not to continue the unholy alliance with governments and states in constructing diverse forms of national identity, but rather to show up these identities as multi-faceted, fragile, contested and continually in a state of making and remaking. Furthermore, the very term 'identity' needs to be scrutinised as an incantation of unity and uniformity. The more frequently it is used, the more likely it is a symptom for a deeply divided society. In questioning the conceptual validity of identity politics and in de-essentialising the concept of national identity (and, not least, in asking who benefits from the propagation of national identity!), historians help to prevent the spread of nationalism and instead contribute to rising levels of tolerance of 'the other' in all Western European societies.

Notes

1 I would like to thank Heiko Feldner for his valuable comments on a draft version of this introduction. Any remaining errors are, of course, entirely my own.

2 For the strong connections between historical writing and nation-building in Eastern Europe see Dennis Deletant and Harry Hanak (eds) *Historians as Nation-Builders: Central and South-East Europe*, London, Macmillan, 1988. No similar volume exists on Western Europe.

3 Harvey J. Kaye, 'The Use and Abuse of the Past: The New Right and the Crisis of History', in Ralph Miliband, Leo Panitch and John Saville (eds) *The Socialist Register 1987*, London, 1987, pp. 332–64.

4 For a comparative perspective on the relationship between 'scholarliness' and politics in different national contexts see Heiner Timmermann (ed.) *Geschichtsschreibung zwischen Wissenschaft und Politik. Deutschland – Frankreich – Polen im 19. und 20. Jahrhundert*, Saarbrücken, Dadder, 1987. For the social sciences see also Peter Wagner, *Sozialwissenschaften und Staat. Frankreich, Italien und Deutschland 1870–1980*, Frankfurt am Main, Campus, 1990.

5 I am particularly grateful here to Heiko Feldner who drew my attention to the fact that the concern for 'professionalisation' amongst early-nineteenth-century historians can be described in terms of the 'new metaphysics' of rationalised historical discourse. Feldner will discuss this further in the Ph.D. he is currently

writing at the University of Wales, Cardiff, provisionally entitled: 'New Scientificity in German Historiography around 1800: A Case Study of Karl Dietrich Hüllmann'.

6 See ch. 20, endnote 5, p. 261.

7 For a comparative perspective on the breakthrough to social history – or lack of it – in the United States, France and Germany see Georg G. Iggers, 'Social History, the Social Sciences and Political Culture, 1890–1914. An International Perspective', *Tel Aviver Jahrbuch für deutsche Geschichte*, 1987, vol. 17, pp. 117–34.

8 Specifically on Tawney see Anthony Wright, *Richard H. Tawney*, Manchester, Manchester University Press, 1987.

9 For the idea of 'virtual representation' see A.H. Birch, *Representative and Responsible Government. An Essay on the British Constitution*, London, George Allen & Unwin, 1964.

10 See, for example, the contrasting views of Winfried Schulze, *Deutsche Geschichtswissenschaft nach 1945*, Munich, dtv, 1993, pp. 281ff., who sees much continuity, and Jürgen Kocka, 'Ideological Regression and Methodological Innovation: Historiography and the Social Sciences in the 1930s and 1940s', in: *History and Memory*, vol. 2, 1990, pp. 130–8, who points out that *Volksgeschichte* was so discredited by its racism and flawed with methodological weaknesses that it remained without much influence after 1945. The best study on the topic is Willi Oberkrome, *Volksgeschichte*, Göttingen, Vandenhoeck & Ruprecht, 1993.

11 Götz Aly, 'Rückwärtsgewandte Propheten. Willige Historiker – Bemerkungen in eigener Sache', in idem, *Macht – Geist – Wahn. Kontinuitäten deutschen Denkens*, Berlin, Argon, 1997, pp. 153–83.

12 Pierre Nora, 'Ernest Lavisse: son Rôle dans la Formation du Sentiment National', *Revue Historique*, 1962, vol. 228, pp. 73–106. See also the intriguing comparison between what politicians expected of university historians in France and Germany in Christian Simon, *Staat und Geschichtswissenschaft in Deutschland und Frankreich, 1871–1914*, 2 vols, Bern, 1988, especially vol. 1, pp. 262ff.

13 The state is, of course, not a historical agent as such. For each historical era it would therefore be vital to ask who is the state!

14 Fritz K. Ringer, *The Decline of the German Mandarins: The German Academic Community, 1890–1933*, Cambridge, MA, Harvard University Press, 1969.

15 Although it should be noted that the Rosellis were finally condemned by tribunal in 1927 and assassinated by Mussolini's henchmen. The tolerance of Italian fascism clearly had its own very narrow limits.

16 Thomas Mann, 'Betrachtungen eines Unpolitischen' (1918), in: *idem, Reden, Essays, Aufsätze*, vol. 2: *1914–1918*, Berlin, Aufbau, 1983, especially pp. 267ff. on the relationship between the educated middle classes in Germany (*Bürgerlichkeit*) and politics.

17 Wolfgang Benz, *Potsdam 1945. Besatzungsherrschaft und Neuaufbau im Vier-Zonen-Deutschland*, 2nd edn, Munich, dtv, 1992, p. 82.

2 Nationalism and historiography, 1789–1996

The German example in historical perspective

Georg G. Iggers

A great deal has been published in recent years on the topic of nationalism. The present essay is not intended as a review of this literature. I shall restrict myself to examining the changing role of nationalism in German historiography within the context of major trends in other Western countries, particularly the United States, France, and Italy.

Opinions have long been divided as to the origins and age of nationalism. Nineteenth-century historians in France, Great Britain, Italy and Germany traced national consciousness into the distant past. Michelet projected the French nation into the Middle Ages. For Droysen and Sybel, Prussia, almost from the beginning, pursued a national purpose. Luther to them appeared as a national prophet. For Kleist and Fichte German nationality was born in the Teutoburg forest. More recent writers (e.g. Benedict Anderson, Eric Hobsbawm, Ernest Gellner and William Pfaff) have argued against the notion that nations have grown out of history. Instead they have viewed them as 'imagined communities',[1] the conscious creations of intellectuals and politicians. For Anderson they have filled the vacuum created in early modern times by the destruction of an international community held together by religious faith. Nationalism is now widely seen as the product of the French Revolution which, by sweeping away old corporate institutions and establishing the notion of popular sovereignty, laid the foundations of national identity.

A key to an understanding of how a nation conceives itself is contained in the way it remembers aspects of its past or chooses not to remember them. July 4 in the United States and July 14 in France are obvious examples of the former. April 25, the Day of Liberation, recently introduced in Italy to commemorate the struggle of the *Resistenza* in the years 1943 to 1945, is another example, as is Martin Luther King's birthday in the United States. The observance and non-observance in Germany of two recent anniversaries is illuminating. The foundation of the German Empire on 18 January 1871, which was widely celebrated not only in Imperial Germany but also in the Weimar Republic, received virtually no mention, on its one hundred and twenty-fifth anniversary, in the German media in 1996. By contrast the national holiday commemorating the adoption of the Weimar constitution in 1919 inspired only an embattled minority during the Weimar Republic which continued to identify itself as the *Deutsche Reich*. There was no attempt to give republican names to such institutions as the Kaiser Wilhelm Institute (now the Max Planck Institute) or the Friedrich Wilhelm University of Berlin (now the Humboldt University). The election of Field Marshal Paul von Hindenburg to the German presidency in 1925 is indicative of the continuity. The observances in 1995 of the end of the War involved a conscious attempt to redefine the German national community by distancing it from the past, not only from the Nazi period but also from the political traditions and outlooks which preceded it. Already in 1971, on the one hundredth anniversary of the foundation of Imperial Germany, Federal President Gustav Heinemann in a speech on the occasion had made it clear that he did not consider the Federal Republic of Germany to be a continuation of Bismarck's *Reich*; that the Federal Republic instead must identify itself with the democratic heritage of 1848, not with the autocratic and militaristic ethos of 1871 which led to disaster. By 1996 the memory of the *Reichsgründung* had been quietly laid to rest. On the other hand, the fiftieth anniversary on 8 May 1995, of the end of the Second World War and the liberation of the concentration camps which preceded it, received considerable attention. The Holocaust now plays an important role in the self-definition of the Germans: a negative definition but also one which involves the affirmation of new values. The end of the War was thus understood by a majority of Germans not only as a liberation from nazism but also as a conscious expression of belonging to a democratic Western world. The bombing of Dresden in February 1945 too was remembered very differently in 1995 than it had been in the Adenauer era when Germans saw themselves primarily as the victims of bombing, occupation and expulsion. While the observances stressed its senseless brutality, they also placed it emphatically in the context of total war begun by the Nazis with the support of much of the German population.

I would like to occupy a middle position in this essay between two interpretations of German nationalism. The first interpretation, championed by conservative German nationalists since the nineteenth century and taken up in recent decades by critics of German nationalism, asserted that there was a fundamental difference between German and West European nationalism. While conservatives asserted the superiority of the German conception of the nation, their critics maintained that Germany had followed a dangerous *Sonderweg* which deviated from a democratic norm. The second interpretation denied that there was a German exceptionalism and viewed German nationalism within the context of European nationalism, maintaining that the excesses of German nationalism had their sources not in peculiarly German traditions but in a modern mass-culture common to Western societies with its roots in the French Revolution. The first interpretation, espoused since the early nineteenth century by thinkers politically as diverse as J.G. Fichte, J.G. Droysen, Ernst Troeltsch, Thomas Mann, Helmut Plessner, Hans-Ulrich Wehler and most recently in reply to the calls for a reform of the citizenship law by the Christian Democratic politician Wolfgang Schäuble, maintained a fundamental difference between a German and Western idea of the nation. While the Western conception of the nation, they argued, rested on a revolutionary experience and a set of political ideas, the German definition of who was a German was still defined in the Basic Law of the Federal Republic of Germany of 1949 in terms of biological descent. Thus one could become a Frenchman or an American through naturalisation by embracing the political ethos of the national community; it was much more difficult, if not impossible, to become a German.

In fact, however, the distinction between the two types of nationalism is much more complex. Elements of universalism also had a place in German historical thought and ethnocentrism played a role in Western forms of national identity. At all times there were competing conceptions of national identity and history in all European nations and in North America, although undoubtedly an ethnocentric notion, focusing on a powerful, expansionist state, played a decisive role in German thinking and historiography from well before 1848 until well after 1945. But then ethnocentric notions also played a role in American expansion at the expense of Native Americans and Mexicans in the nineteenth century and in French, British, Belgian and Dutch colonialism. German nationalism too originally incorporated important elements of the democratic ethos of the French Revolution. It is tragic that the development of liberalism and democracy in Germany from its beginnings in the so-called War of Liberation was deeply intertwined with an ethnocentrism with much stronger racist, xenophobic and anti-Semitic components than, for example, its Italian counterpart in the Risorgimento. In contrast the Prussian state as it had emerged in the eighteenth century had seen itself as a political community in which ethnic Germans, Poles, Masurians, Lithuanians and to a limited extent Jews, could view themselves as citizens, although the concept of citizenship was very imperfectly developed. Similar concepts of political community, defined in terms of dynastic loyalty or, in the case of the free cities, local patriotism, rather than in ethnic terms, existed in other German states. The Hapsburg monarchy, of course, is a prime example besides Prussia of a state calling forth loyalty transcending ethnic lines. It is also tragic that the revolt against absolutism and the call for a more popularly based government from the War of Liberation contained a strongly ethnophobic and expansionist component. The strident calls for hatred against the French, the bloodthirsty calls for military encounters, as in Arndt's poem, *Der Gott, ders Eisen wachsen ließ*, contrast with the much more muted calls for resistance and liberation of Mazzini. Yet German nationalism was by no means unique in its aggressive tone. We must remember that it was the supposedly moderate French revolutionary government which in 1792 plunged Europe into war and which did not give civic liberty to the Alsatian Jews or emancipate the slaves overseas until the Jacobins did so.

In 1848 liberals and particularly democrats, last but not least Karl Marx, were more outspoken opponents of Slav strivings for autonomy than were the conservatives, and were willing to risk a general European war. Marx, in fact, called for a revolutionary world war against England and Russia. After the failure of the 1848 Revolution, liberals increasingly relied on the Hohenzollern monarchy to pursue nationalistic aims and to maintain social stability at the expense of their liberal convictions, and the monarchy increasingly relied on the liberals to solidify its position. The history of the capitulation of the liberals in 1866 on the army issue is well known and need not be repeated here. Bismarck in turn made concessions to the liberals which did not seriously lessen the authority of the monarchy. With the introduction of universal male suffrage in the elections for the Reichstag he correctly perceived the nationalistic aspirations of the masses which legitimised his charismatic dictatorship.

In Imperial Germany the liberals not only took over the political values of the conservatives, including the ethos and mystique of an aristocratic and military society, but the conservatives took over the nationalist and expansionist aspirations of the liberals. A major portion of the liberals, the National Liberals, were comfortable with the incomplete democratisation of Germany because of their fear of the emergent working-class movement and their consequent willingness to rely on a strong state. The conservatives in turn were increasingly converted to the nationalistic values of mainstream German liberalism, although it should be stressed that there was a liberal minority which remained dissatisfied with the concessions made to Bismarck in 1866 and with the Antisocialist law in 1878 and which also sought international reconciliation, particularly with England. The radicalisation which took place in Imperial Germany, particularly after the accession of Wilhelm II, cannot, of course, be seen as a purely German phenomenon. It reflected the atmosphere of the time in an age of rapid industrialisation and imperialism in which social Darwinian ideas occupied an important role. The xenophobia with its anti-French, anti-Slav, and anti-Semitic components which had occupied a crucial place in the ideology of pre-1848 nationalism now became part of an outlook essential elements of which were shared by Prussian conservatives and national liberals. Earlier notions of ethnicity as elements of conflicts between nations were increasingly reinforced by a biologistic racism, particularly in the treatment of Slav populations at home and non-white populations abroad. If the Prussian conception of the state before 1848, for which legitimacy rested in the dynasty and not in the population at large, had transcended ethnic identities, the new Prussian monarchy after 1871 was emphatically German, also in an ethnic sense, as the citizenship law of 1913 demonstrated. Yet its basically ethnic and expansionistic nationalism, with its stress on military power, was also taken over by political intellectuals like Max Weber and Friedrich Naumann who wished to democratise the monarchy by integrating the working class into the Imperial political system. The extent to which even the latter shared the nationalist aspirations of the general German population was demonstrated in the support which the Social Democrats gave the war in 1914.

Where do the historians fit in here? There is a striking paradox between their professional ethos and their political commitment. The period which we have been discussing is also the time when history became a professional discipline, generally in Europe, in the United States and Japan, following German models of scholarship, generally one or two generations after this process had begun in Germany. Professionalisation meant that historical research and writing were to be conducted by persons who were technically trained. History, Droysen proclaimed, was to be raised to the 'rank of a science'.[2] To be sure, this science, as he explained, was to be an interpretative science searching for meaning, not an empirical one seeking to establish laws. Although fundamentally different in its aims from the natural sciences, it resembled them in several ways. It called for a rigorous methodology and it also called for a strict, value-free (in Ranke's words *unpartheisch* – impartial) approach.[3] The task of the historian, Ranke wrote in the famous passage in the preface to his first major work, was not to judge but 'to show how things actually occurred' (*wie es eigentlich gewesen*).[4] The historians, as they constituted themselves into a discipline, thus took over much of the *habitus*, the life and work style of the scientists in the natural and mathematical sciences, which had emerged as clearly defined disciplines much earlier. Insisting on objectivity, historians as professional scholars could speak with an air of authority with which the older literature could not.

At the same time, virtually all of the important German historians of the nineteenth century, Dahlmann, Gervinus, Droysen, Sybel, Baumgarten, Treitschke, Mommsen, but also Ranke, were politically involved and understood the political function of their scholarship. This was also true of French historians such as Guizot, de Tocqueville and Thiers, who not only espoused political positions in their writings, but, even more than their German colleagues, occupied powerful political posts. Sybel, who had been trained in Ranke's seminar and who founded the *Historische Zeitschrift*, the journal of the new discipline which defined itself as a science, emphatically proclaimed that the historian must not be impartial but must have a definite political viewpoint. The only way to explain this apparent contradiction is in terms of the theological presuppositions which guided their historical and historiographical thought. Thus Ranke, Sybel and Droysen were all convinced that divine will, in Ranke's words 'the finger of God',[5] gave history direction and meaning. As Ranke explained in his inaugural address on the affinity of politics and history, a historical approach makes it possible to understand the objective forces which operate in the world. Thus, while they rejected the schematism of Hegel's philosophy of history, they nevertheless maintained the conviction that history was a meaningfully unfolding process. In the final analysis, despite their philosophical idealism, their concept of objective truth and partisanship was not very different from the Marxist or the Marxist-Leninist conception of *Parteilichkeit* which also assumed the congruence of scientific inquiry and political convictions.

Thus the new scientific school was, from the start, politically oriented and propagandistic. The students of Ranke, who was still a good European, formed the core of the so-called Prussian School which merged allegiance to the

Hohenzollern dynasty with a notion of popular participation and German nationalism. The Prussia which had transcended national lines was now Germanised. The Prussian historians were not manipulated by the state; until 1848 they were even in opposition. But they were never revolutionaries, least of all did they want a repetition of the French Revolution on German soil. They abhorred disorder and wanted reforms which would guarantee the security and prosperity of the solid *Bürgertum*. They were not directly controlled or manipulated by the state. In fact the Prussian universities as they were reformed by Wilhelm von Humboldt in the aftermath of Prussia's initial defeat by Napoleon guaranteed a greater degree of autonomy for research and teaching than universities in France or most other non-English speaking countries. Yet there were mechanisms of selection which guaranteed an immense degree of conformity among the professoriate, particularly after 1848. A small number of mentors, beginning with Ranke, controlled university appointments, a sort of old boys' network, which guaranteed that the chair holders came from a similar social background, were Protestants, and represented a common political outlook. Dissidence, as the persecution of a democratically oriented historian like Gervinus after 1848 and the campaign against Lamprecht in the 1890s showed, was difficult. Conformity was demanded not only in political views but also in methodological approaches. At the heart of the methodology of the scientific school was the philological examination of documents. The historian was to go into the archives, itself a worthy thing. But historians like Droysen, Sybel and Treitschke and a host of their less well known colleagues, went into the archives with preconceived answers which they sought to document. They saw themselves in the service of the Hohenzollern dynasty as the guarantor of a *bürgerlich* order and a powerful Germ[...] [t]hey created historical myths such as in Droysen's history of Prussia w[...]ed Prussia already in the Middle Ages with a German mission.

The [...], established by blood and iron with the ardent sup[...]s, reflected the compromise of the latter with the d[...]es. Historians and intellectuals played a key role in the [...] [t]his order. Among them Sybel and Treitschke moved away [...] their earlier moderate liberalism to social conservatism and in [...] Treitschke to an outspoken anti-Semitism. Not all historians [...] this route. Hermann Baumgarten and Theodor Mommsen, who had or[...]lly supported Bismarck, expressed serious concerns when Bismarck after 1878 broke with the liberals. Mommsen in his testament of 1899 expressed his sorrow that in Imperial Germany it was no longer possible to be a citizen (*Bürger*) in any meaningful way.[6] Because the degree of professionalisation among historians was so much more advanced in Germany than in other countries, the place of non-academic historians, who, particularly in France but also elsewhere, occupied an important role in the literary reviews, was much more limited. But non-historians too participated in the creation of a national consciousness and of national myths. Felix Dahn's glorification of the early Germans who assailed the Roman Empire is an example. But monuments too bolstered myths of a Germanic past, from the *Hermannsdenkmal* commemorating Arminius' defeat of the Romans, to the *Kyffhäuserdenkmal* calling forth a sleeping Frederick Barbarossa ready some day to save the German nation, and to the *Völkerschlachtsdenkmal*, dedicated in Leipzig in 1913 commemorating the supposed popular uprising against the French in 1813.

In 1914 virtually all German intellectuals, including the historians, rallied to the flag. This was not surprising and had its counterpart in France and German-speaking Austria. In England and Italy and, after 1917, in the United States there were a few dissenting voices. What, however, distinguished the public statements of the German intellectuals, including that of thinkers like Ernst Troeltsch and Friedrich Meinecke who were not entirely uncritical of the direction in which the Wilhelminian Empire was moving, was their attempt to define a specific German ideology, distinct from and superior to that of the West. A pronouncement by German historians and social philosophers in the volume *Deutschland und der Weltkrieg*, edited by Otto Hintze, who himself belonged rather to the moderate-wing, contrasted the German ideas of 1914, in which individual freedom was embedded into a monarchical political order which stood above diverse interests, with the anarchic, democratic ideas of 1789 which placed special interests above the community. In the literature which followed a whole set of stereotypes were bandied about to distinguish a superior German world from an inferior undifferentiated Western one. German *Kultur* was contrasted with Western *Zivilisation*, the depth of German *Bildung* with the superficiality of Western culture, a Western political and philosophical tradition of immutable natural law with the historical perspective of the Germans.

The historical outlook of Imperial Germany persisted in the Weimar Republic where it was further radicalised. The historians who had dominated the profession before 1918 continued to do so. A very small number of established historians, most notably Friedrich Meinecke, the editor of the *Historische Zeitschrift*, supported the Republic not because they were republicans, but because they saw no alternative other than a revolution of the right which they abhorred as much as that of the left. But even Meinecke continued to maintain the superiority of German intellectual traditions over those of the West and saw in the German form of historism the highest point achieved in the understanding of things human. Historism, he reiterated, had freed German thought from the heritage of natural law and natural rights which had dominated Western political thought since Roman times.

[...] ion held by the historians who dominated the [...] the 1920s by a new group of historians, sociolo- [...] ght to replace the concentration on the state [...] *Volk* as a racial community. The proponents of the new *Volksgeschichte* sought to recapture the everyday life of the common people. But their history of the common people differed sharply from that of Marxist historiography as well as from that of non-Marxist historians like Karl

Lamprecht. They wished to extend the borders of Germany beyond those of the 'small-German' (*kleindeutsch*) Empire of 1871, with Prussia as its core, to include all ethnic Germans in Europe. Their focus was not modern industrial society but pre-modern agrarian society. There was thus a close affinity between the ideology of *Volksgeschichte* and that of the Nazis. In fact almost without exception the practitioners of *Volksgeschichte* joined the Nazi movement. It is striking that the established historians, who at the turn of the century had so vigorously fought the attempts by Karl Lamprecht to extend the scope of history from politics to society and culture, were able to accept them. But then they agreed on a broad number of points: the rejection of the Weimar Republic, its replacement by a strong authoritarian state, the revision of Versailles and with it the pursuit of an expansive foreign policy particularly in the East. While the historical profession had opposed Lamprecht because they feared that social history would open the doors to the political left, they had no such fears of the new *Volksgeschichte*. Moreover most members of the profession were able to coexist well with the Nazis. The few dissident historians were purged in 1933. And while the Nazis made half-hearted attempts to establish *Volksgeschichte*, they left the established historians largely undisturbed because of the consensus which existed with them on the political issues which mattered to the Nazis.

German historiography did not, initially, alter in 1945. Fewer persons were replaced than in 1933 which had seen the dismissal of the small number of mostly young historians who had viewed the German past critically and were committed to democratic values. None of the latter returned to Germany except for visiting appointments and none was particularly encouraged to return. The exception was Hans Rothfels, a key spokesman before 1933 for an expansive German policy in the East, who had left Germany reluctantly as late as 1939 because of his Jewish ancestry. With Gerhard Ritter, certainly the most powerful German historian until the mid-1960s, Rothfels defended the basic soundness of Prussian–German traditions and, like Friedrich Meinecke, held not a lack of democracy but an excess of democracy as responsible for the Nazi catastrophe. For Ritter not Prussian traditions, which shaped the political consciousness of the men and women of 20 July 1944, but the heritage of the French Revolution with its mobilisation of the masses, provided the intellectual heritage of National Socialism. Meinecke regarded Hitler's appointment as chancellor on 30 January 1933 as a *Zufall* (chance occurrence) with deep roots in European, but not specifically in German, traditions; and, although condemning Nazi atrocities, he, like Gerhard Ritter, expressed an 'understanding' for anti-Semitism. *Volksgeschichte*, now cleansed of its racial vocabulary and transformed into a form of modern social history,[7] turned to the industrial world but continued to work with a concept of community which avoided notions of social conflict and class.

It was only in the 1960s that a fundamental reorientation took place in Germany. There are several reasons for this. An overarching reason is the changed international situation of the Cold War, in which West Germany found itself as part of the Atlantic defence system. This situation made the blanket rejection of the West insupportable. Nevertheless many, particularly Catholic, historians in the 1950s did not identify with democratic values, but rather affirmed their belief in the conservative heritage of a Christian occident (*christliches Abendland*)[8] in the battle against communism, the ultimate evil. By the 1960s two factors have to have been considered: one is the appearance of a generation, born too late to have participated in the Nazi regime as adults, which received its higher education in the Federal Republic. The other is a fundamental structural change. Germany was not only a country which, in the nineteenth century, had undergone rapid industrialisation, but, also one in which older economic and social patterns and the political attitudes which accompanied them coexisted. Modernisation created tensions everywhere, even in countries like the United States which had not known corporatist or aristocratic institutions. These tensions were undoubtedly more pronounced in Germany than in countries like France where the pace of economic modernisation was slower, or in the United States where older institutions and attitudes were weaker. Beginning with the currency reform (the introduction of the Deutsche Mark in 1948), West Germany was rapidly transformed into a modern consumer society, part of a global economy. It is in this period that a democratic ethos established itself in the Federal Republic.

All this led to a re-examination of the nation. A decisive contribution to this discussion was made in 1961 by Fritz Fischer's investigation of German responsibility for the outbreak of the First World War. The important thing was not that he broke the taboo which since the Treaty of Versailles had forbidden German historians to acknowledge a special German responsibility for the outbreak of the war, but that he attempted to show a structural and ideological continuity from an incompletely democratised Germany in the nineteenth century to the Nazi drive for hegemony. Concern with the incomplete political modernisation of Germany was taken up by a group of younger German historians, including Hans-Ulrich Wehler, Jürgen Kocka, Hans Mommsen, Wolfgang Mommsen and others. A democratic ethos now began to replace the older forms of authoritarian nationalism. Nevertheless, the older conceptions of what constituted the German nation remained alive in the expellee movements and in the attempts of historians in the historians' controversy (*Historikerstreit*) to divest the German past of responsibility for the enormities which took place between 1933 and 1945. But this tradition of nationalism was increasingly replaced by what Jürgen Habermas has called a constitutional patriotism (*Verfassungspatriotismus*), which viewed the political community not in terms of ethnic belonging but of shared political and social institutions and attitudes. This shared community was not a *Volksgemeinschaft* but the Federal Republic of Germany as a democratic, open society, integrated into a broader European and Atlantic community.

Yet Germans were far yet from a consensus on this redefinition of German national identity and its relation to the past. In some ways the observations of the fortieth anniversary of the end of the Second World War in 1985 were symbolic of the split in German consciousness. On 5 May 1985, Chancellor Kohl, accompanied by President Reagan, visited, on the same day, a military cemetery at Bitburg in which members of the Waffen-SS were also buried and the Bergen Belsen concentration camp, thus bestowing the soldiers who had fought and killed for the Nazi regime the same recognition as the victims of the regime. The Nazi episode, it appeared, was now to be relegated to history once and for all. Three days later on the actual anniversary, Federal President Weizsäcker in his speech reminded the nation that Germans could not escape responsibility for their past. The reluctance of many Germans to accept this responsibility led to the *Historikerstreit* in 1986 and 1987 in which Ernst Nolte, supported by other historians, sought to relativise and historicise the Holocaust by comparing it to the mass killings under Stalin and Pol Pot. But in retrospect the historians who stressed the special elements in the German past and in German nationalism which made national socialism and its practice of genocide possible, and in important ways unique, appeared to have won broader support.

Ernst Nolte, and his disciple Rainer Zitelmann, have propagated the extreme and in my view untenable position that the Holocaust must be seen primarily as a German reaction to Bolshevism. They have, however, remained marginal with almost no foothold in the universities. It is nevertheless worrisome that they found a willing publisher in the Ullstein Verlag which also commissioned one of their closest allies, Karlheinz Weißmann, to write the volume on the years 1933 to 1945 in the *Propyläen History of Germany*. In the meantime, however, Zittelmann has been replaced as editor and the Weißmann volume has since been withdrawn. It is further disturbing that Ullstein and Klett-Cotta, one of the largest publishers of textbooks, have published works maintaining that Hitler launched a preventive war against the Soviet Union to forestall a Soviet attack. It is also disturbing that the respectable *Frankfurter Allgemeine Zeitung* has frequently been sympathetic to these views. At the universities themselves conservative historians like Hans-Peter Schwarz, Klaus Hildebrand, Michael Wolffsohn and the late Thomas Nipperdey, called for an explicit renationalisation of German identity in the face of contemporary trends to postnationalism even before 1989. Yet I believe that these are minority positions and that the years since 1989, if anything, have seen a strengthened identification with Europe.

How do the conceptions of national identity in the historiography of other countries differ from that of Germany? In both France and the United States, from the late-nineteenth until well into the twentieth century, two different national identities coexisted. For one the nation was built upon common political institutions and attitudes essentially republican if not always democratic in nature with origins in a successful revolution against arbitrary authority. The other defined the nation in ethnic or even racial terms, as Gallic in France or Nordic and Protestant in the United States. But the republican and democratic traditions, particularly in France, also placed a high value on the military and glorified expansion. The monuments and streets of Paris reflect a bellicose picture of the past in which autocrats like Richelieu and Napoleon have their place in a national pantheon. A socialist like Jean Jaurès sought to break through these patterns of narrow nationalistic and militaristic attitudes and was assassinated on the eve of the First World War. And side by side with the republican tradition there existed throughout the nineteenth century, and until 1945, a xenophobic, anti-Semitic orientation which, as Maurice Barrès's novel *Les Déracinés* demonstrates, employs a language not very different from that of *Blut und Boden* in Germany. In the United States, the Know Nothing Movement of the mid-nineteenth century and the Ku-Klux-Klan after the Civil War were always at the margins of American political society but many of their attitudes, the belief not only in the superiority of the white race but more specifically that of Nordics, were part of the mainstream. The treatment of blacks, Native Americans and Asians and the immigration law of the 1920s reflect this. The professionalisation of the historical discipline in the 1870s and 1880s not only followed German models of scholarship but created a historical myth which saw the origins of American liberty in the primeval forests of Teutonic Northern Europe.

Nevertheless there were also marked differences between the mainstreams of French and American historical thought and that of Germany. In the background there stood different national myths and symbols; Revolution in the case of both France and the United States, in that of Germany the so-called War of Liberation under dynastic leadership. The Revolutions in France and in the United States were viewed in republican and universalistic terms, although it must not be forgotten that the French Revolution was embedded in a tradition which had its roots in the expansionism of Louis XIV and which identified with Napoleon. But in Germany the myth of the War of Liberation built upon German exclusiveness and hatred of the French. French historiography spanned a much broader political spectrum in the nineteenth century than did German historiography. The university at no point occupied the same significance in French public life that it did in Germany and thus was unable to enforce the same ideological conformity. Within the university a relatively high degree of conformity existed, but it was predominantly republican and laic. Unlike the German university, the French university also included a fair number of Jews. There could not have been a Dreyfus Affair in Germany because no Jew was likely to have been included in the general staff. Moreover, the outcome of the Affair strengthened the Republic. Although historians in both countries participated actively in political life, in France historians mostly outside the academy, from Guizot to Tocqueville and Thiers, actually repeatedly occupied leading positions in the state. Professionalisation was less all-inclusive than in Germany; nevertheless it too played a political role, this time in defence of republican traditions.

The relation of Italian historiography to nationalism diverges from the French and American as well as the German traditions we have described. A survey of recent literature, including the chapters in this volume, reflects a broad consensus that a sense of national identity emerged much more slowly and incompletely in Italy than it did in France, Germany or the United States. Regionalism played a significant role into the twentieth century and as the *Lega Nord* suggests is still very much alive today. Both the Catholic church and the organised working class movement viewed the nationalism of the Risorgimento with considerable reserve. While German historians have stressed the relative backwardness of Germany in developing democratic institutions corresponding to a modern society, students of Italian nationalism have pointed at the social and economic backwardness of Italy. Thus in their view, the Risorgimento rested on a much narrower social basis, encompassing a small urban and agrarian elite, than did German nationalism. The restricted suffrage prevented broadly based participation in the political process until at least 1912. Observers concur that it was only the First World War and the fascist era which mobilised nationalism on a broad basis. The collapse of fascism led to a reaction against any form of hypernationalism.

Mazzini's nationalism, with its optimistic faith that the self-determination of democratically constituted nations would guarantee international harmony, bore greater similarities in its cosmopolitan aspects to the democratic nationalism in France and the United States than to the ethnically orientated nationalism dominant in Germany until well after the Second World War. But Mazzini too, in his later years, accepted the notion of Italy as a great power extending its economic and cultural sway across the Mediterranean which became a key element in the *Realpolitik* of the pre-1914 liberal governments which led to Italy's entry into the war. It must be noted that the professionalisation of historical studies proceeded much more slowly in Italy than in Germany, France or the United States, and that most of the actual research was carried out by local associations of bureaucrats, archivists and history aficionados who dealt with history as learned dilettantes. The First World War encouraged historians to look for the roots of the national state in the Italian past. Nationalism as a distinct right-wing political movement was best exemplified by Gioacchino Volpe who in the fascist era sought a common Italian identity from the Middle Ages to the twentieth century in his *L'Italia in cammino* but from a perspective very different from that of Benedetto Croce and Gaetano Salvemini, who reaffirmed the Enlightenment ethos of pre-fascist liberalism.

After 1945 Italian historians had to come to terms with their national past as did German historians. The Italians had never broken as radically with liberal, democratic values as the Germans and could see in the Resistance of 1943–5 elements of an alternative form of national identity. The Risorgimento was now seen at once positively in its cosmopolitan and emancipatory understanding of nationalism, and critically in respect to its narrow class basis. The disillusionment with the nation and the opening to a broader European identity, which has marked German historical thought since the 1960s, was shared by many Italian historians. Roberto Vivarelli in his contribution to this volume has pointed to 'a real gulf between the generation of historians active before the War and the one which emerged after 1945'. 'The older generation,' he continues, 'viewed with great anxiety the decline of a national tradition which they felt as their own; the new generation was looking in different directions'.[9] This appears as a general European phenomenon, even if it is most pronounced in Germany and Italy. In both countries it involves a critical confrontation with the national past, in Italy a stronger turn to regional history.

By the turn of the twentieth century the narrow constraints of the supposedly scientific approach to history were challenged in almost all countries of the Western world, from Russia and Rumania to the United States. It was generally felt that the almost exclusive focus on politics and international affairs did not do justice to the changed circumstances of industrialising societies in an age of democratisation. Moreover there was a broad consensus that history must not only narrate but also analyse, and that the critical examination of documents must be combined with analytic concepts derived from the social sciences, particularly economics and sociology. Karl Lamprecht in Germany, Henri Berr in France, Henri Pirenne in Belgium, Frederick Jackson Turner and Charles Beard in the United States initiated the discussions which led to reorientations in historical writing. But only in Germany was there a concerted rejection of the new approaches to social history, in part, as suggested above, for political reasons. The new directions in social history also involved the rethinking of the role of nationality in historical writing. Lamprecht here played a contradictory role. In his controversial *German History* (1891–1912) he combined a highly speculative theory of historical laws of development, reminiscent of positivism, with a conception of a German *Volksgeist* deeply rooted in romanticism. But more lasting was his interest in a comprehensive history of a region which, proceeding from a geographic setting, examined many aspects of life from economics and social structure to politics, culture and religion. Generally the new approaches to social history, particularly in France, moved from a primary occupation with the nation to an in-depth examination of a region or a comparative study of aspects of social, economic, political or mental structures on an international plane. The *Annales* went in this direction. On the one hand there are the great works spanning large areas of the world: Marc Bloch's *Feudal Society*, Pierre Vilar's *Séville et l'Atlantique* and Fernand Braudel's *The Mediterranean*; on the other hand there are the hosts of regional studies, beginning with Lucien Febvre's thesis of 1911 on the Franche-Comté during the Reformation. Braudel's last great work, *The Identity of France* (1984–6), indeed deals with France, but not as a centralised political entity but as a pluralism of regions over the centuries. It is this diversity and the constant integration of immigrants which in Braudel's view gives France its distinct character.

The American development is different but ultimately also leads away from the traditional conception of a unitary nation. The so-called New or Progressive Historians initiated an approach to American history which focused on culture and society. Charles Beard's *Economic Interpretation of the Constitution* (1913) introduced a very critical note reminiscent of Marx to the analysis of American politics. The Cold War of the 1950s witnessed a rebirth of American nationalism and emphasis on an American exceptionalism marked by political consensus and a social equality lacking in Europe. As Michael Harrington pointed out in his *The Other America* (1962), this glorification of consensus and of an 'end of ideology'[10] overlooks the deep social divisions which mark America. The civil rights movement of the 1960s and the opposition to the Vietnam war led to a critical stocktaking which revealed a society marked by social inequality, racial discrimination and sexism at home, and by imperialism abroad. The nation indivisible under God turned out to be very divisible and very divided. A new historiography increasingly emphasised these divisions between races, genders, life styles. Strikingly, the Museum of American History in Washington in its permanent exhibition now portrays American history of the last four hundred years no longer as the history of one homogenous people but in terms of the interaction of at least three different ethnicities, the Hispanic and Native American cultures of the Southwest, the mainstream Anglo-American culture of the East, and the African American heritage.

Returning to Germany, one is struck by the movement away from the older nationalism to a growing identification with a broader European community. This identification with Europe may even be stronger in Germany than in almost any other European country. This essay thus concludes on a relatively optimistic note. On the other hand one should not ignore the persistence of older nationalistic traditions worldwide. Moreover, the four countries we have examined, which are by no means immune to these traditions, are representative of only a small affluent part of the Atlantic world. In retrospect professional historians have too often participated in the construction of national myths; their task now as honest scholars must be to dismantle these myths.

Notes

1 Benedict Anderson, *Imagined Communities. Reflections on the Origins and Spread of Nationalism*, London, Verso Editions/NLB, 1983.
2 See Johann Gustav Droysen, 'Erhebung der Geschichte zum Rang einer Wissenschaft' in *idem*, *Historik* (ed.) Peter Leyh, Stuttgart-Bad Cannstadt, Fromann-Kolzbog, 1977, pp. 451–69.
3 See Ranke, 'On the Character of Historical Science', in Georg G. Iggers and Konrad Von Moltke (eds) *Leopold von Ranke. The Theory and Practice of History*, Indianapolis, Bobbs-Merrill, 1973, p. 38.
4 Ranke, 'Preface' to the first edition of his *Histories of the Latin and Germanic Nations*, p. 137.
5 Leopold von Ranke, *Sämtliche Werke*, Leipzig, Duncker und Humblot, 1869–70, vol. 53/54, pp. 665–6.
6 See 'Testamentklausel von 1899', in Alfred Heuss, *Theodor Mommsen und das neunzehnte Jahrhundert*, Stuttgart, F. Steiner, 1996, p. 282.
7 See Winfried Schulze, *Deutsche Geschichtswissenschaft nach 1945*, Munich, Oldenbourg, 1989, pp. 254–65.
8 See ibid., pp. 266–80.

9 Vivarelli, below, p.231.

10 Daniel Bell, *The End of Ideology. On the Exhaustion of Political Ideas in the Fifties*, Glencoe, IL, 1960.

Further reading

The early seminal works on the history of nationalism are those of Carlton Hayes, *The Historical Evolution of Modern Nationalism*, New York, 1931, and Hans Kohn, *Nationalism. Its Meaning and History*, New York, 1942. Another early work is Karl Deutsch, *Nationalism and Social Communication: An Inquiry into the Foundations of Nationality*, Cambridge, MA, 1953. In recent years a large number of works have appeared on nationalism of which Benedict Anderson, *Imagined Communities. Reflections on the Origins and Spread of Nationalism*, London, Verso, 1983, dealing with nationalism as a modern phenomenon which spread from the European to the non-European world, caused the most intense discussions. Along similar comparative lines see Eric J. Hobsbawm, *Nations and Nationalism Since 1780*, New York, 1990; Ernest Gellner, *Nations and Nationalism*, Oxford, 1988; and William Pfaff, *The Wrath of Nations. Civilisation and the Furies of Nationalism*, New York, 1993. There exists no comprehensive comparative study of nationalism and historiography nor for that matter a comprehensive comparative history of historiography. For the nineteenth century, still informative but cumulative and encyclopaedic rather than analytical, is George P. Gooch, *History and Historians in the Nineteenth Century*, London, 1913. On nationalism in German historiography see Georg G. Iggers, *The German Conception of History: The National Tradition of Historical Thought from Herder to the Present*, 2nd edn, Middleton, CT, 1983.

3 Literature, liberty and life of the nation

British historiography from Macaulay to Trevelyan[1]

Benedikt Stuchtey

'English history from 1688 to the French Revolution', wrote Thomas Babington Macaulay (1800–59) in 1841, 'is even to educated people almost a "terra incognita". [...] The materials for an amusing narrative are immense. I shall not be satisfied unless I produce something which shall for a few days supersede the last fashionable novel on the tables of young ladies'.[2] Indeed, Macaulay's best-selling *History of England from the Accession of James II* (5 vols) became one of the most acclaimed and popular English history books ever. With more than 140,000 sets of the *History* sold in Britain alone, Macaulay reached a reading public that was already well educated and able to catch his political and moral messages. His fame came to supersede that of the earlier literary giants, David Hume and Edward Gibbon. But while the latter covered larger spans of history, Macaulay's merits lie in his in-depth studies and the expansiveness of his detailed and diligent analysis. Walter Bagehot (1826–77), author of the classic liberal *English Constitution* (1867), criticised this, from the academic point of view, as a defect of the *History* claiming that 'you rarely come across anything which is not decided'. On the other hand, Lord Melbourne, in whose cabinet Macaulay served, is reported to have said that he wished he could be 'as cocksure about anything as Macaulay is about everything'.[3]

Although Macaulay's political career and even his elevation to the peerage in 1857 may not have been as central to his life as his intellectual activities, his *History* and certainly his *Essays* would have been different without, for example, his celebrated speeches in the House of Commons.[4] In fact, many of the essays have the tone and style of speeches. In this respect Macaulay was a great admirer of Edmund Burke's oratorical qualities.[5] Burke, together with Macaulay, played a major role for British historiography in laying the intellectual and methodological ground for dealing with the past; consequently, Lord Acton (1834–1902) described Burke as having been the 'first of our historians'.[6]

This essay is concerned with the extent to which British historians from Lord Macaulay to G.M. Trevelyan dealt with the 'nation', a pattern, as the present volume demonstrates, so central to historical traditions in France, Italy and Germany. Three points will be made. First, the literary character of British historical writing, the nineteenth-century emphasis on narrative rather than analysis, played an important role in popularising historical accounts. Second, the concentration in the works of British historians on topics such as civilisation, progress, liberty, the constitution and parliament is striking. Third, the 'nation' was mirrored in the great picture-gallery of the collected biographies, the writing of biographies being a typically British tradition. Certainly these aspects were closely interconnected.

The Gladstonian intellectual John Morley (1838–1923) once remarked that Macaulay's *Essays* formed a textbook, that they 'have done more than any other writings of this generation to settle the direction of men's historical interest and curiosity', that they could be seen, at home and in the colonies, 'on every shelf between Shakespeare and the Bible'.[7] Although flattered by this success when Macaulay learned that many readers found his *History* as entertaining as a novel, he denied 'that a book like mine is to be regarded as written for female boarding schools. I open a school for men: I teach the causes of national prosperity and decay'.[8] This was the educational idea of history, and here was the background to what Herbert Butterfield (1900–79) later famously despised as the myth of the 'The Whig Interpretation of History'.[9] British historiography in the nineteenth century and well into the twentieth century could not cast off this Whiggish national heritage, and even quite recently its pros and cons have been debated again.[10] It was essentially based on a set of values with which the party identified (abolition of the slave trade, emancipation of Catholics, popular education, etc.). Macaulay declared himself in favour of this programme in his speech to the electors at Edinburgh in May 1839, describing the virtues of the Whigs 'for the cause of human freedom and of human happiness'.[11] Despite his original intention to write the history of the century and a half from 1688 to 1832, Macaulay's *History* covered only seventeen years and concluded with the death of William in 1702. The seventeenth century was a great period of struggle for power between monarchy, aristocracy and parliament. It is therefore of central relevance to the works of both conservative and Marxist historians to the present day. The study of the rise of the gentry, the Revolution and the Civil War, the character of the rebellion in 1641, and also the execution of the king in 1649, were at the heart of historiographical interest.[12]

The great national achievement was, in Macaulay's opinion, the development of a libertarian parliamentary tradition reaching back to Magna Carta and culminating in the Glorious Revolution of 1688. The 'glorious' aspect of this revolution was that it was not revolutionary, and it was very much the fear provoked by Chartism and the European revolutions of 1848 that motivated Macaulay to write a historical account that described how political extremes could be balanced. Reform at the right time would make revolution unnecessary and serve national stability. This was to become the political creed of the Whigs in the nineteenth century.[13] Macaulay did not condemn the French Revolution, the event of extremes. Indeed, he referred to it repeatedly in his *Essays*, and even saw some of its beneficial aspects. But he deplored its excesses. Going back to the late-seventeenth century, Macaulay contrasted the

French Revolution with the significance of King William III. Macaulay considered William III's influence, taking his Dutch background into account, first in its European rather than English dimension, and second in the relatively peaceful outcome of the Glorious Revolution.[14] Here, the particular success story of the English people had a universal aspect, and (from this self-confident perspective) it was not only a cause for envy and admiration by neighbouring states, but to the benefit of the civilised world that England had enjoyed parliamentary liberty so much longer than any other country: 'That great battle was fought for no single generation, for no single land. The destinies of the human race were staked on the same cast with the freedom of the English people'.[15] Macaulay said this in his very first essay to the 'Edinburgh Review', a homage to Milton the poet and an apology for Milton the politician who sympathised with the revolt against the Stuart monarchs. The struggle for English liberties had acquired a European dimension with the coronation of William III. Parliament served the Protestant and national unfolding of the country and disclosed the inner meaning of its history. Ultimately the English historian could only express thankfulness for his country's divine destiny, for its uniqueness, the privilege of having been spared the consequences of a revolution such as the French.

Concerning the admiration of England by continental historians, an important German reflection on seventeenth-century English history came from Friedrich Christoph Dahlmann (1785–1860). His idea of the constitutional monarchy was based on his idealised model of English political continuity and a parliamentary balance which, according to Dahlmann, England owed to William III. The drawing of historical models and the political engagement of the intellectual during the Hanoverian constitutional controversy of 1837 well complemented each other. Dahlmann later became one of the leading figures in the Paulskirche of 1848, when his account of English history was reprinted for the fifth time.[16] A second example of nineteenth-century German Anglophilia is Ranke's *Englische Geschichte* (1859–68), probably the most famous contemporary German attempt to write English history. Its author is regarded as the indisputable pillar of German historicism, and was also quite close to Whiggish historiographical principles. Ranke developed the same idea of continuity.[17] The major difference between the 'Whig interpretation' and rising German historicism, however, lay in their political aspirations. Macaulay's history was teleological, seeing history as culminating in the present. German historicism also tried to forecast the future from the process of the past.[18] But the great and topical European dates of 1793, 1861 and 1871, to which French, Italian, and German historians could refer as starting points for a new history of their respective nations, did not have the same resonance in England. In the perspective of the 'Whig historians' the Reform Bill of 1832 marked the crucial outcome of *liberty*, the final result of what had been initiated with the Glorious Revolution of 1688. If, therefore, the progress of history culminated in the present, it was the present that supplied the standard for judging the past.[19]

This Whig interpretation was essentially a complacent account of success; a contemplative story of a people that approved its past and present. When Macaulay claimed that 'The history of England is emphatically the history of progress',[20] he was thinking of one continuous line of English civilisation from the Domesday Book to the Reform Act. Behind this idea lay the concept of an English *Sonderweg* resting on the 'ancient constitution', a reflection at least as much of a national as a cultural conviction of English civilisatory superiority.[21] By emphasising the qualities of liberty and progress, Macaulay envisaged only a straightforward national attitude that painted English history in black and white: because the Protestants were good the Catholics had to be bad; the conflict of the Roundheads versus the Cavaliers was essentially the same as the struggle between defenders and opponents of the Reform Bill. The historical antipodes formed moral antitheses, too, and in any case it was clear where Macaulay believed light and darkness to be. The self-righteous certainty of superiority in the present world was not based on the Rankean belief that every period was immediate to God, but on the desire to explain and judge the world in terms of predisposition. In this respect the *Sonderweg* was not British, but essentially English, differing from European as well as Scottish and Irish developments, and in this regard Macaulay was much less sceptical about the future than Hume and Gibbon, for example, had been. The history of the nation and the progress of civilisation had become two sides of the same coin. But the blessings of civilisation, later to be strongly questioned by Thomas Carlyle (1795–1881), had disadvantages which Macaulay did not conceal: although the victory of cultivation over barbarism was a constant theme in the *History* and in his *Essays*, Macaulay, the poet of the 'Lays of Ancient Rome', acknowledged that the loss of romanticism and poetry was a high price to pay for the age of reason and science.[22] To this extent the historiographical nationalism of the Whig interpretation was a rational, less romantic undertaking than that of continental historians.

In contrast, Scotland, particularly the agrarian society of the Highlands, stood for cultural backwardness, a problem which was put into both a broader colonial context and that of Anglicisation. Henry Thomas Buckle (1821–62) picked up the Scottish problem in *The History of Civilization in England* (1857, 1861), where he presented a somewhat sociological approach to Scotland's past.[23] It is striking that many books by British historians in the nineteenth century refer to 'England' in their title, but, as in the case of Buckle, for example, they nonetheless deal with France, Spain, Scotland and other countries. This was probably to show England's superiority and singularity. On the other hand, Tom Nairn has pointed out that although there was a distinguished Scottish intelligentsia in the late-eighteenth century, there was no influential Scottish nationalist movement. This may partly be because of an effective Anglicisation of the Lowlands, partly because of an intellectual migration to the south and to London.[24] The 'Englishness' of English history so often addressed by historians was manifested as a mere construction which ignored intercultural connections, the influences of other nations on England, and intellectual transfers. Most obviously, the imperial throne had not been filled by an English dynasty since the eleventh century, but by Welsh, Scottish, Dutch and German families.[25] Buckle paid tribute to the Scottish contribution to British civilisation by describing Scotland's impressive literary and scientific achievements. Scotland's alleged 'backwardness', however, essentially concerned the religious aspects, the strong role of the clerics and the Kirk of Scotland which, retaining its ancient power, had not given way to modern notions such as liberty and toleration. The Whiggish perspective of a successful national development, however, was based on the very belief in the triumph of secular interests over ecclesiastical ones. Here, 'secularism' as the outcome of Protestantism had a political meaning.

An even bigger dilemma for the Whig model of political-religious progress was presented by Ireland, whose history was one neither of national nor of civilisatory success. Rather, Irish history was identified with Catholicism, the enemy of *liberty*, which had been overcome in the English Civil War, or by 1688 at the latest. Thus the victory of Protestantism as a reflection of 'providential history' was the backbone of the English national sense of mission, both in the British Isles and in the world: the making of an English identity as a cultural programme. A belief in the liberal tradition (this being a guarantee for the security of property) which was increasingly seen as a more or less secular one and beyond religious values, was the basis for the political use of history,[26] and it effectively integrated early-nineteenth-century radicalism as well as late-nineteenth-century democracy into the traditional thinking. Interestingly, during the course of the nineteenth century, intellectuals moved from the Macaulayan historical concept of a 'national tradition' towards one of a 'national character' which, in its emphasis on timeless moral values, became basically ahistorical.[27]

During and after the First World War the Whig interpretation was seriously tested. For obvious reasons, Ireland and some of the less glorious aspects of British Imperialism could not play a major role in the nation's self-congratulatory historiography. Macaulay himself clearly saw Ireland's miserable political, social and economic plight as the result of English misgovernment. He regarded it as a scandal that poverty, hunger and emigration were the dominant factors of Irish life, within the borders of what he thought the most civilised people in the world, the British. The history of English civilisation as a special nineteenth-century form of the history of the nation also had its shortcomings, but although these were admitted, they were not dealt with extensively. An Anglocentric view of history remained, despite its practical and moral problems, the prevailing one, and the Irish problem was ignored rather than confronted, so that the Victorian optimism could stay intact. For many Englishmen, Ireland became a politically and morally live issue only towards the end of the nineteenth century, with the burning question of Home Rule, and from then on it could no longer easily be ignored by intellectuals in general. Yet it was avoided by most historians in particular, partly, perhaps, because of methodological difficulties, partly because of the ignorance of Ireland of those – and they were the majority – who wanted to follow an explicitly national approach according to the Whig philosophy. The Anglocentric perspective characteristic of Whig historians could be overcome only by a multinational approach. The fact that Irish history, both in its British and Imperial contexts and on its own, received little attention from English historians during the nineteenth and a good deal of the twentieth centuries was fatal and contributed to the many misunderstandings between the two islands which finally led to the partition of Ireland. Surely politicians could not ignore the Irish factor for British politics. Here W.E. Gladstone is the most prominent example. The discussion about Irish Home Rule in the 1880s reflected constitutional, civilising and, of course, national issues and brought back the idea of a relatively independent Irish parliament comparable to that which Henry Grattan had founded in 1782. This discussion brought Gladstone into contact with William E.H. Lecky (1838–1903), of whom Gladstone said that 'he carefully and completely dovetailed the affairs of Ireland into English history'.[28]

Lecky was the only historian before 1916 who treated the Irish problem as a crucial part of British history in a precise and unprejudiced manner. Lecky's relationship with Irish history was a special and peculiar one, as his place in the Protestant Ascendancy cut him off from the people and culture of the country in which he was born. While identification with Catholic nationalism was entirely impossible for him, Lecky advocated Ireland's case by devoting 43 per cent of his *History of England in the Eighteenth Century* (1878–90) to its history. By bringing England, Ireland, Scotland and the major European, American and other colonial events into one narrative, Lecky made their interconnections and their responsibilities for each other from a British perspective clear. He thus showed that the Whig history of the 'winners' (England) could not be written without the history of the 'losers' (Ireland). [29]

When Lecky wrote of Ireland's history as an 'invaluable study of morbid anatomy',[30] he meant that the history of the conquered and politically less successful people had the advantage of being instructive for the study of the history of national development as such: 'much of its interest lies in the evidence it furnishes of the moral effects of bad laws, and of a vicious social condition'.[31]

The historiographical background of Lecky's *History* lies in James Anthony Froude's (1818–94) highly problematic book *The English in Ireland in the Eighteenth Century*, which he published in three volumes from 1872 to 1874. Here Froude, the disciple of Carlyle, the defender of the anti-Catholic penal code, the advocate of High Church principles and a strong, centralised state power, claimed that the Irish were unfit to have a national government, and that they had well deserved Cromwell's military dictatorship. The 1641 Rebellion had shown, in Froude's view, that Ireland was not part of British civilisation and that its people had not understood that the message of Protestantism was a national, English one. While Macaulay had looked to the

Revolution of 1688, Froude's foundation for England's national and international glory was the political success of the Reformation. Froude's massive *History of England from the Fall of Wolsey to the Defeat of the Spanish Armada* (1856–70) in twelve volumes was an apologia for the developing nation-state par excellence: this nation had proved its strength in 1588 with the military and moral victory of Protestantism over Catholicism. As the 'leading promoter of the imperialist excitement',[32] Froude saw Ireland's Home Rule movement as posing a danger to British unity. Therefore he justified England's superiority by pointing to Ireland's dependency, declaring that it was the duty of the inferior part to accept that it had to be governed. Carlyle's saying that 'might is right' was unreservedly seconded by Froude.

Lecky reacted to all this by writing two severe and angry reviews defending the peculiarity of Irish history and its educational value, and demanding a fair historiographical assessment without which reconciliation between the two countries would be impossible. Lecky wanted the history of the British nation to be placed into a moralist dimension, underlining the importance of the mutual understanding of the different traditions that form its common history. Otherwise, he said, history's function would be 'to stand by the scaffold and curse the victims as they pass'.[33] The obvious victims in this context would be Scotland and Ireland. In his reviews of Froude's book Lecky stressed two significant though very different periods of Irish history. With great admiration he described Ireland's early medieval civilisation that was only destroyed in the age of Elizabeth I; second, he pointed to Henry Grattan's parliament of 1782 which was a renewed expression of an Irish nationalism distinct from English nationalism (and from the nationalism of Ireland's Catholic population). In Gladstone's view it was the perfect model for moderate Home Rule.[34]

The Whig interpretation's emphasis on *liberty*, which for a long time and particularly since the Union had not been applicable to Ireland, would, via Gladstone's advocacy of Home Rule, finally also be applied to Ireland. Thus 1782 could be regarded as an Irish version (following the American one of 1776) of the very English event of 1688.

However, Lecky, vehemently disagreed with such utilisation of history for political ends. His definition of parliamentary liberty was rooted in an eighteenth-century aristocratic, landed definition of property, which he considered would be endangered if Home Rule were granted. According to Lecky, the lesson to be learned from Ireland's failed historical experience was not to confer power where it would certainly be misused, that is, to weaken those pillars of the social order on which Lecky's concepts of liberty and progress ultimately depended, and which benefited the British nation as a whole.[35] Therefore Lecky did not share Gladstone's opposition to the landed interest. The limits of historical analogy met at the frontier of the definition of property.

John Robert Seeley (1834–95), one of the fiercest critics of Macaulayan literary history – a tradition which Lecky followed, and an advocate of a new history as a 'school of statesmanship', found fault with exactly this when he formulated a programme which sought to take the place of *liberty*. Seeley criticised historians who specialised in the eighteenth century for dealing too much with parliamentary history and the struggle for constitutional liberty: 'They do not perceive that in that century the history of England is not in England but in America and Asia'.[36] Seeley regarded the *Empire* as the leading factor in English history, and he never tired of repeating in his book how important he thought the Imperial experience, including loss and defeat such as in North America, was for the political, economic, social and even moral constitution of England. It needs to be remembered, however, that it was less the history of the Empire than that of British expansionism, the process of the British people colonising the world, that interested British historians at the time of imperialism. Seeley, Froude and others regarded the colonies as no more than an extension of England; from their Anglocentric viewpoint they did not study indigenous traditions, but were concerned only with the impact of British civilisation abroad.

As Seeley saw the appropriation and possession of colonies as the basis of England's survival, he advocated the central function of the state and the role of individuals in it. An admirer of Baron Heinrich vom Stein's statesmanship (in 1878 Seeley published a three-volume biography of the famous early-nineteenth-century Prussian reformer), he regarded instrumentalising a knowledge of the past, with special regard to the second Empire, as a moral outcome of the study of English history.[37] History was the *Magistra Vitae* teaching a moderate English nationalism. To refer again to Froude, the Empire perfectly met the expectations placed on 'Englishness'. In fact, the Empire represented England beyond her shores carrying the same political values and promising a good future for the motherland: 'We want land on which to plant English families where they may thrive and multiply without ceasing to be Englishmen. The land lies ready to our hand'.[38]

Just as Macaulay's *History of England* and *Essays* had been of enormous cultural and educational value in the middle of the nineteenth century, so by the end of the century Seeley's *Expansion of England* and Froude's essays on imperialism had not only become best-sellers as well, but were also of extraordinary political influence. Yet these historians could not be more different. Macaulay and Seeley mark clearly two decisive periods of English historical writing. The first was a time of literary historiography, still in the shadow of the Enlightenment, represented in particular by Hume, Gibbon, Robertson and Ferguson. It lasted until about 1860. The second was a time of professionalisation, scientific history and increasing politicisation of history from about 1870, now under the influence of, for example, German historicism.[39] After Carlyle, Seeley was certainly the most Germanophile British historian in the nineteenth century.

But in an age of national success, imperial expansion, industrialisation, social modernisation, wealth and political stability, the history of the nation was perceived as part of, if not to a certain extent identical with, world history. In Morley's opinion 'the history of the world ought to go before the history of England'.[40] The process of civilisation and the world's evolution moved to the centre of intellectual interest. Charles Darwin's intellectual influence acquired greater significance than the legacy of the French Revolution.[41] Behind this confidence in progress stood the assurance of a reality that gave cause for political optimism. The message had important psychological aspects, it was 'a report on contemporary history'.[42] The emerging British conception of world history was permeated by the notion of 'Englishness', and historiography continued to serve political purposes, even if more covertly than in other European countries. Furthermore the optimism of the Victorian historians actually meant that there was little questioning of their methodological standing. That is why a considerable number of British historians in the late-nineteenth century still found it acceptable to follow the tradition of 'philosophical history' once created by Hume and Macaulay. In this view history was more than the mere record of the past; it had a moral dimension which could best be revealed and understood by studying the life of the people and not only the transactions of sovereigns and armies. Lecky's subtle intention in this respect was soon detected: 'It is a history of the English people rather than what is usually called a history of England'.[43]

It seems to have been no more difficult to write a state-orientated, national history of Britain than it was the case in France, Italy or Germany. The self-conscious British attitude towards *liberty* was really anything but a nationalist position which did not accept, or was less aware of its ideological character, an awareness which provoked debates about methods and historiographical aims so common in the discipline in other countries. In contrast to such central and politically minded German historians such as Heinrich von Sybel and Heinrich von Treitschke, a British historian writing a 'history of England' directed to the national needs of the present was embarking on a less outspoken and allegedly more moderate undertaking. Yet Seeley's ambition to educate statesmen through history was no exception. And with the advent of William Stubbs (1829–1901), the Tory and High Church representative among English historians, and Regius Professor in Oxford from 1866, Britain entered the European tradition of intellectual nationalism, of scholarly and professionalised research, the editing of medieval documents and the studying of institutions. In general, the study of the medieval constitution gained much significance for the nineteenth-century historiographical discourse. The editing of records from the national heritage allowed British historiography to catch up in terms of professionalisation and the university teaching of history. Moreover, here as in Germany, in the work of the *Monumenta Germaniae historica*, for example, the process of editing national documents implicitly introduced patriotism into the profession.

The central institution for Stubbs was the British parliament. He focused on the growth of its power as one of the major themes of constitutional history, thus disregarding the function of the monarchy. Clearly Stubbs was impressed by parliament's triumph in the nineteenth century, and although he called for a value-free historical assessment he could not deny that he himself was affected by contemporary national politics.[44] It is no surprise that Stubbs, too, was strongly influenced by Edmund Burke (and the German '*Historische Recht-sschule*'). In fact, his *Constitutional History of England in its Origins and Development* (1874–78) could be called 'the most fully realised embodiment of English, Burkean political ideas'.[45] Again there is a reference to the Whig tradition, which Stubbs pushed back to Magna Carta, when the nation had achieved a unity between the Saxon and the Norman elements in its constitution.

Macaulay's teleological view had required a subject which was responsible for historical development and change. Stubbs now looked for the roots of this order. He reconstructed the origins of the constitution and investigated the preconditions of its organism. His idea of English history returned to the notion of providence and destiny with all its philosophical, moral and national implications. The moral aspect, first, reflected Macaulay's contempt for James II: Stubbs sternly disapproved of King John's reign in the early thirteenth century. Henry Hallam (1777–1859), whose *Constitutional History* (1827) was one of the early if not really successful attempts to emancipate British histori-ography from Hume's influence, had already strongly criticised the Stuarts for their attempt to break with parliamentary tradition. The national aspect, second, can be seen in Stubbs's notion of the growth of institutions from their elementary stage at local level to their parliamentary embodiment on a national scale. The construction of the libertarian element of English history was at the same time the birth of the English *Sonderweg*. Consequently many British historians, Stubbs prominent among them, were occupied with the question of why their country's path was so different, and why it was so difficult to find parallels.

The third outstanding constitutional historian after Stubbs was doubtlessly Frederic William Maitland (1850–1906). Apart from his *Constitutional History of England*, a collection of lectures on the law from 1066 to his time, Maitland's other major work is his *History of English Law before the Time of Edward I* (1895), in which he attached much importance to the time of the Norman kings. The nation's libertarian origins lay even further back than 1215; they dated from the Norman conquest. Like Stubbs, Maitland brought the highest reputation to medieval studies through his numerous editorial projects but, unlike Stubbs, he emphasised the social side of law. Maitland drew attention to a different interpretation of the medieval parliament: that it had not been an assembly of the representatives of the estates, but essentially a royal court of law. Maitland's great late-twentieth-century admirer, Geoffrey Elton, developed this interpretation, seeing the history of England as the history of the English state with its fulfilment in the Empire. And according to Elton the rise of parliament was less central to English *liberty* than a strong monarchy, whose authority controlled political reform and even its own gradual loss of power.[46]

Finally, in the year of his death, Maitland picked up a very English tradition, the writing of biographies, in his study of his friend Leslie Stephen (1832–1904), father of Virginia Woolf.[47] Stephen, one of the last of the generation of Victorian 'men of letters', is well known for his classic *History of English Thought in the Eighteenth Century* (1876), in which he pleaded for greater appreciation for this century, before Lecky's *History* supported this cause. Moreover, Stephen achieved a lasting impact on historical scholarship by founding the *Dictionary of National Biography* (1885 ff.). He edited twenty-six volumes by 1891 and wrote 378 articles himself. By painting the nation's history through the portraits of many of its leading exponents Stephen enormously popularised a general comprehension of English history and a common pride in it. The National Portrait Gallery, founded in London in 1856, was perfectly complemented by the *Dictionary*, and second by the 'English Men of Letters' series which Stephen inaugurated in 1878 with his biography of Samuel Johnson. It is noteworthy that Johnson's life had already served a similar function in 1791 when James Boswell had invented the biography as a national genre.[48] The sixty-three volumes and the almost 30,000 entries of the first edition of the *Dictionary* became the official national memory. Its intention was a 'scientific' assessment of the national story of tradition and progress, and thus a positivist abandonment of romantic 'hero–worship'.[49] Yet Stephen's programme had parallels with Carlyle's *On Heroes and Hero Worship* (1840). Although he certainly did not share its passionate Clio con Brio, the similarity between their elitisms is obvious when looking at the distinguished names in the *Dictionary*.

Carlyle, with Samuel Taylor Coleridge, had a prominent position among the Germanophile British intellectuals during the nineteenth century. Morley compared him with Rousseau, both in political and philosophical matters.[50] Carlyle's dictum was that history is biography, the life of the people of the nation.[51] The biographical approach to history had always enjoyed high esteem and popularity in England. Macaulay became famous with his 'Biographical Essays' (1857), Lecky started his career with a collection called 'Leaders of Public Opinion in Ireland' (1861), and among Froude's essays the best are on Homer, Spinoza and Thomas Becket. Nonetheless Carlyle's biographical method had become old-fashioned. His conservative reaction against democracy and rationalism and his dislike of modern science were certainly not appreciated by all intellectuals at the end of the century. History, in Carlyle's opinion, still served a literary and a moral, not a scholarly purpose. As a result he closed ranks with Walter Scott and this literary Macaulayan heritage rather than, for example, with Lord Acton. On the other hand, whilst Carlyle, the Scotsman and admirer of Goethe and Frederick the Great, established a basic critique of the Industrial Revolution, his Nietzschian prophecy of a national decline because of capitalism and the crisis of liberty was a powerful call for more puritanism, political authoritarianism and national coherence. It comes as no surprise, then, that his personal hero was Oliver Cromwell. Seeley's attempt to replace *liberty* with *empire* as the new pattern of English history could also profit from Carlyle whose ideas of the superiority of the British nation, its commitment to rule, power and love of work fitted well into the Imperial philosophy.

According to Rosemary Jann, the increasing professionalisation and scientification of history in Britain towards the end of the nineteenth century did not heavily affect the literary tradition.[52] New historical-critical methods of Edward A. Freeman (1823–92) and Samuel R. Gardiner (1829–1902),[53] and later the revolutionary interpretations of Lewis Namier (1888–1960), were popular, but they could not claim to be the only possible way of describing the past. The tradition of 'amateur' historical writing continued strongly and claimed, as it were, that the didactic function of history to interpret rather than to research was better fulfilled when written in a literary, even dramatic style.

The most famous representative of the old-fashioned strand of historiography was George Macaulay Trevelyan (1876–1962). Born in the year when his father published the 'Life and Letters of Lord Macaulay', Trevelyan was probably the last Whig historian, and he brought the heritage of his great-uncle to an end. His short and not very impressive debate with John Bagnell Bury about 'The Science of History' was quickly won by Trevelyan who rediscovered Clio as a 'muse'.[54] Apparently more than any other twentieth-century historian, Trevelyan combined all three aspects addressed in this essay – literature, liberty and life – in his work. He still regarded his subject as a dramatic story that taught men to be good citizens, and saw in the heroes of the past examples for the present. He tried to interpret the whole account rather than present detailed research: in a word, he stood for a literary history which believed in the libertarian tradition of England exemplified by extraordinary personalities. His aesthetic commitment in his presentation could be traced back to the impact of Shakespeare and the historical novel, and of the Earl of Clarendon (1609–74). The latter's celebrated *History of the Rebellion and Civil Wars in England* (1702–4), which may be called England's first great historical work, also achieved the highest literary quality. Trevelyan followed this example, which was adhered to equally by conservatives like himself and by Marxists. To write effectively about the nation was the task of an author who knew how to catch the popular mood and bring history to the people, whose presentation of the past was a narrative art, and who naturally identified with social values that formed the background of the 'nation'. The viewpoint could only be elitist. Trevelyan fulfilled these conditions very well. As the descendant of an old family, for him the writing of English history also meant, to a certain extent, writing about his own roots.[55]

Trevelyan's *British History in the Nineteenth Century* (1922) and his *History of England* (1926) met a post-First World War romantic patriotism among the people. He brought together a Victorian concern for social matters with a cultural pessimism which feared that 'English' values such as common sense, toleration and the liberal institutions were endangered by the impact of twentieth-century mass society. In his classic, best-selling work, *English Social History: A Survey of Six Centuries* (1944), a book that was designed as a contribution to the war effort, Trevelyan patriotically and nostalgically described a 'Paradise Lost' in which the aristocracy, once so powerful in the age between Chaucer and Queen Victoria, was declining. He therefore tried to revive the

moral and ethical values which he thought so well represented in the tradition
of his country, but so poorly lived by in his own time. History had the task of
instructing people and providing them with inspiring ideas, and articulating the
Whig belief in progress – and of doing all this in an entertaining way. Because
history was a drama, the lives of individuals were the best vehicle for conveying
lessons. Here Trevelyan was following the Carlylian example. But whereas
Carlyle praised military despots, Trevelyan looked to men who fought for
liberty: *The Life of John Bright* (1913), *Lord Grey of the Reform Bill* (1920).

Trevelyan followed comfortably in Macaulay's nineteenth-century footsteps. Perhaps he knew that few other historians after him could or would do
the same, that the Whig model was incapable of explaining the world in the
face of two world wars and the fall of the British Empire. One of the very
few exceptions might be the statesman and – among British historians – so far
only recipient of the Nobel prize for literature (in 1953), Winston Churchill
(1874–1965). Churchill's descriptions of the world wars are dominated by
Britain's motive in fighting for justice and liberty, by democracy, and by the
stability of the state thanks to a strong military power.[56] His *History of the
English-speaking Peoples* (1956–8), with its strong literary claims and emphasis
on the role of influential individuals, may be called one of the last products of
the Whig tradition. Once again, liberty and law are presented as the pillars of
the English nation; once again, despite Churchill's consciousness of the weakness of historical reconstruction, history is instrumentalised as the political
guardian of the present and the future.

But generally, after the Second World War, this historical version of the
nation became academically controversial. Universal history that tried to
interpret the world using patterns different from those hitherto applied
became fashionable, although certainly not the rule. Arnold Toynbee's
(1889–1975) *Study of History* in twelve volumes which he published between
1934 and 1961 made its author one of the most famous and celebrated British
historians in the second-half of the twentieth century. He shifted the national-
civilisatory model towards a progressive 'universal church' (according to the
idea of *Heilsgeschichte*) finally resulting in a 'world-state'. Thus Toynbee strove
for an ecumenical perspective by comparing the world's leading civilisations,
thereby paying his tribute to the modern age of globalisation.[57] Although
severely criticised by professional historians, partly because of his closeness to
Oswald Spengler's philosophy, Toynbee's merits include his advocacy of a
universal historical viewpoint and the overcoming of, first of all, the dominant
Eurocentric perspective, and second, the tendency towards specialisation. This
also plays a significant role in the assessment of the development of international historiography after decolonisation.

More recently British historiography, under the impact of the multinational character of the British Isles, has seen that in the aftermath of Trevelyan
a national, Whig viewpoint of the past is no longer academically acceptable
and actually no longer feasible. As early as in 1975 J.G.A. Pocock drew attention to the problem that for too long history in the British Isles had been

dominated by a 'Little Englandism' which does not give enough weight to Ireland, Scotland and Wales. Only by demonstrating historical connections and interdependences can British history really be understood. Apart from its historiographical importance, this approach has a highly methodological significance.[58] Yet critics of this idea see the danger that historical Anglicisation of the British Isles means that an Anglocentric historiography cannot be avoided. But English historical dominance probably needs to be accepted before a model can be established that takes all parts of the common history equally into account and that does not, by favouring the common heritage, neglect fundamental differences, reflected, for example, in sources written in three Celtic languages, in Latin and English. English Whig historiography, once so strong in the period between Macaulay and Trevelyan, seems finally to have been overcome. At a time of political fragmentation and constitutional devolution in the British Isles it may, however, have a chance of revival, at least in England.

Notes

1 I would like to thank the editors of this volume for their helpful comments on this article; any remaining errors are, of course, my own.
2 T.B. Macaulay to Macvey Napier, 5 November 1841, in Thomas Pinney (ed.) *Selected Letters of Thomas Babington Macaulay*, Cambridge, Cambridge University Press, 1982, p. 183.
3 Both quotes from Charles Firth, *A Commentary on Macaulay's History of England*, London, Frank Cass, 1964, p. 54; see also Peter Gay, *Style in History*, New York, W.W. Norton, 1988, pp. 97–138.
4 That Macaulay was primarily an essayist, also essentially in his 'History of England', has recently been pointed out by P.R. Ghosh, 'Macaulay and the Heritage of the Enlightenment', *English Historical Review*, 1997, vol. 112, pp. 358–95.
5 Cf. for example T.B. Macaulay, 'Warren Hastings', in *idem*, *Critical and Historical Essays, Contributed to the Edinburgh Review*, 5 vols, Leipzig, Bernhard Tauchnitz 1850, vol. iv, pp. 213–349; on E. Burke's influence on Whig historians see Conor Cruise O'Brien, *The Great Melody: A Thematic Biography and Commented Anthology of Edmund Burke*, London, Minerva, 1993, p. xxxvi.
6 Quoted from Herbert Butterfield, *Man on his Past: The Study of the History of Historical Scholarship*, Cambridge, Cambridge University Press, 1955, p. 68.
7 John Morley, *Critical Miscellanies*, 3 vols, London, Macmillan, 1909, vol. iii, p. 296.
8 T.B. Macaulay to an unidentified recipient, 31 March 1849, in Pinney, *Selected Letters*, p. 234.
9 Herbert Butterfield, *The Whig Interpretation of History*, London, W.W. Norton, 1965 (first published in 1931).
10 Adrian Wilson and T.G. Ashplant, 'Whig History and Present-Centred History', *Historical Journal*, 1988, vol. 31, pp. 1–16.
11 George Otto Trevelyan, *The Life and Letters of Lord Macaulay*, 2 vols, London, Longmans, Green & Co. 1876, vol. ii, p. 63.
12 Ronald Hutton, 'Revisionism in Britain', in Michael Bentley (ed.) *Companion to Historiography*, London, Routledge, 1997, pp. 377–91. P.B.M. Blaas, *Continuity and Anachronism: Parliamentary and Constitutional Development in Whig Historiography and in the Anti-Whig Reaction between 1890 and 1930*, The Hague, Martinus Nijhoff, 1978, pp. 196–239.

3 For this cf. Joseph Hamburger, *Macaulay and the Whig Tradition*, Chicago, Chicago University Press, 1976.

14 See Macaulay's review of Hallam's 'Constitutional History of England from the Accession of Henry VII to the Death of George II' (1827), in *idem, Critical and Historical Essays*, vol. i, pp. 109–209.

15 Macaulay in his essay on Milton (1824), in ibid. pp. 1–59, quote pp. 29–30.

16 Friedrich Christoph Dahlmann, *Geschichte der Englischen Revolution*, Leipzig, Weidmann 1844, 5th edn 1848; cf. Wilhelm Bleek's Introduction to his new edition of *Friedrich Christoph Dahlmann: 'Die Politik'*, Frankfurt am Main, Insel 1997.

17 Rudolf Vierhaus, 'Die Idee der Kontinuität im historiographischen Werk Leopold von Rankes', in W.J. Mommsen (ed.) *Leopold von Ranke und die moderne Geschichtswissenschaft*, Stuttgart, Klett-Cotta, 1988, pp. 166–75.

18 Cf. Jürgen Osterhammel, 'Epochen der britischen Geschichtsschreibung', in Wolfgang Küttler, Jörn Rüsen, Ernst Schulin (eds) *Geschichtsdiskurs*, vol. 1: *Grundlagen und Methoden der Historiographiegeschichte*, Frankfurt am Main, Fischer 1993, pp. 157–88, here p. 172.

19 Cf. Pieter Geyl, *Debates with Historians*, London, Fontana, 1962 (first published in 1955), pp. 37ff.

20 Thomas Babington Macaulay, 'Sir James Mackintosh's History of the Revolution', in *idem, Critical and Historical Essays*, vol. ii, p. 298.

21 See Bernd Weisbrod, 'Der englische 'Sonderweg' in der neueren Geschichte', *Geschichte und Gesellschaft*, 1990, vol. 16, pp. 233–52, especially pp. 248ff.

22 John Clive, *Macaulay: The Shaping of the Historian*, Cambridge Mass., Harvard University Press, 1987 pp. 77ff.

23 See Eckhardt Fuchs, *Henry Thomas Buckle. Geschichtsschreibung und Positivismus in England und Deutschland*, Leipzig, Leipziger Universitätsverlag, 1994, especially pp. 214ff.

24 Tom Nairn, *The Break-Up of Britain*, London, NLB, 1977.

25 Benedict Anderson, *Imagined Communities. Reflections on the Origin and Spread of Nationalism*, London, Verso, 1983, p. 83.

26 O. Anderson, 'The Political Uses of History in Mid-19th Century England', *Past and Present*, 1967, vol. 36, pp. 87–105.

27 On the idea of 'character' see Stefan Collini, *Public Moralists. Political Thought and Intellectual Life in Britain, 1850–1930*, Oxford, Oxford University Press, 1991, pp. 91–118.

28 W.E. Gladstone, 'Lessons of Irish History in the Eighteenth Century', in James Bryce (ed.) *Handbook of Home Rule*, London, Kegan Paul, Trends and Co. 1887, pp. 262–80, here p. 263.

29 See Benedikt Stuchtey, *W.E.H. Lecky (1838–1903). Historisches Denken und politisches Urteilen eines anglo-irischen Gelehrten*, Göttingen, Vandenhoeck and Ruprecht, 1997, pp. 168–211.

30 W.E.H. Lecky, 'Ireland in the Light of History', in Elisabeth Lecky (ed.) *Historical and Political Essays*, London, Longmans Green and Co., 1908, p. 68.

31 W.E.H. Lecky, *History of England in the Eighteenth Century*, London, Longmans, Green & Co. 1878, vol. ii, p. 379.

32 J.W. Burrow, *A Liberal Descent: Victorian Historians and the English Past*, Cambridge, Cambridge University Press, 1981, p. 231.

33 Lecky, 'Mr. Froude's (1873)', p. 247.

34 W.E. Gladstone, 'Lecky's History of England in the Eighteenth Century', *Nineteenth Century*, 1887, vol. xxi, no. 124, pp. 919–36.

35 Lecky, *History of England*, vol. viii, p. 551–2.

36 John Robert Seeley, *The Expansion of England. Two courses of Lectures*, London, Macmillan, 1911 (first published in 1883), p. 10.

37 Deborah Wormell, *Sir John Seeley and the Uses of History*, Cambridge, Cambridge University Press, 1980, pp. 75–109.

38 James Anthony Froude, 'England and Her Colonies', in *idem*, *Short Studies on Great Subjects*, 4 vols, London, Longmans, Green & Co., 1900, vol. ii, pp. 180–216, quote pp. 208–9.

39 Klaus Dockhorn, *Der deutsche Historismus in England. Ein Beitrag zur Geistesgeschichte des 19. Jahrhunderts*, Göttingen, Vandenhoeck and Ruprecht, 1950; C.E. McClelland, *The German Historians and England*, Cambridge, Cambridge University Press, 1971.

40 Morley, *Critical Miscellanies*, vol. iii, p. 10.

41 John W. Burrow, *Evolution and Society. A Study in Victorian Social Theory*, Cambridge, Cambridge University Press, 1966; Hedva Ben-Israel, however, established some relevant interconnections: *English Historians on the French Revolution*, Cambridge, Cambridge University Press, 1968.

42 Gay, *Style in History*, p. 131.

43 *The Tablet* li, no. 1973, 2 February 1878, pp. 138–9.

44 James Campbell, *Stubbs and the English State* (The Stenton Lecture 1987), Reading, University of Reading, 1989; Burrow, *A Liberal Descent* pp. 97–154, especially pp. 126ff.

45 Burrow, *A Liberal Descent*, p. 131.

46 Geoffrey Elton, *The English*, Oxford, Blackwell, 1992.

47 F.W. Maitland, *The Life and Letters of Leslie Stephen*, London, Duckworth, 1906.

48 Osterhammel, 'Epochen der britischen Geschichtsschreibung', p. 166; Macaulay, too, devoted himself to Samuel Johnson, see his *Biographical Essays*, Leipzig, Bernhard Tauchnitz 1857, pp. 139–83.

49 See Noel Annan, *Leslie Stephen: The Godless Victorian*, London, Weidenfeld and Nicolson, 1984, especially pp. 82 ff.

50 John Morley, *Critical Miscellanies*, vol. i, 1904, pp. 135–201, especially pp. 147ff.

51 Fritz Stern (ed.) *The Varieties of History. From Voltaire to the Present*, London, Thames and Hudson, 1957, pp. 90–107.

52 Rosemary Jann, *The Art and Science of Victorian History*, Columbus, OH, Ohio State University Press, 1985, pp. 216ff.

53 E.A. Freeman, *History of the Norman Conquest of England*, 6 vols, Oxford, Oxford University Press, 1867–79; S.R. Gardiner, *History of England from the Accession of James I to the Outbreak of the Civil War*, 10 vols, London, Longmans, Green & Co. 1863–84.

54 The debate is documented in Stern (ed.) *Varieties of History*, pp. 209–45.

55 J.M. Hernon, 'The Last Whig Historian and Consensus History: George Macaulay Trevelyan, 1876–1962', *American Historical Review*, 1976, vol. lxxxi, pp. 66–97; David Cannadine, *G.M. Trevelyan. A Life in History*, London, Fontana Press, 1993.

56 Winston Churchill, *The World Crisis*, 6 vols, London, T. Butterworth, 1923–7; *idem*, *The Second World War*, 6 vols, London, Cassell, 1948–54.

57 Marvin Perry, *Arnold Toynbee and the Western Tradition*, New York, Peter Lang, 1996, especially pp. 89ff.

58 J.G.A. Pocock, 'British History: A Plea for a New Subject', *Journal of Modern History*, 1975, vol. 47, pp. 601–28.

Further reading

The classic book on British historians is by John Kenyon, *The History Men. The Historical Profession in England since the Renaissance*, London, Weidenfeld and Nicolson, 1983, second edition 1993. This study is particularly strong on Victorian England and highlights not only the major figures but also many lesser known historians well into the late-twentieth century. A good introduction to some standard works of British historiography from Walter Raleigh to Lewis Namier is given by J.R. Hale's anthology *The Evolution of British Historiography*, London, Macmillan, 1967. The outstanding expert in the field is certainly John W. Burrow, whose many books should be the basis for any dealings with the subject; among the most significant are *A Liberal Descent. Victorian Historians and the English Past*, Cambridge, Cambridge University Press, 1981, and *Whigs and Liberals. Continuity and Change in English Political Thought*, Oxford, Oxford University Press, 1988, both of which concentrate on the nineteenth century, the latter explaining the eighteenth-century antecedents, such as the Scottish Enlightenment, of the concept of the Whig tradition. Stefan Collini's study *Public Moralists. Political thought and intellectual life in Britain, 1850–1930*, Oxford, Oxford University Press, 1991, is a path-breaking and wide-ranging account of the Victorian and early twentieth-century intelligentsia, its crucial role in political debates, the setting of moral values and images of national cultural identity; here historians occupied a central position. Reba N. Soffer shows in her book *Discipline and Power. The University, History, and the Making of an English Elite, 1870–1930*, Stanford, Stanford University Press, 1994, how the study of history influenced as well as reflected intellectual, but also emotional-patriotic needs, and how the identification with the national tradition shaped the ethos of students who graduated from Oxbridge in order to choose careers in public service, the professions etc. and even business. The topic of the emerging professionalisation of history in the course of the later nineteenth century has given rise to many interesting studies, for example Rosemary Jann, *The Art and Science of Victorian History*, New York, Columbia University Press, 1985, Peter Slee, *Learning and a Liberal Education: The Study of Modern History in the Universities of Oxford, Cambridge and Manchester, 1800–1914*, Manchester, Manchester University Press, 1986, and Philippa Levine, *The Amateur and the Professional: Antiquarians, Historians and Archaeologists in Victorian England, 1838–1886*, Cambridge, Cambridge University Press, 1986. A critical account is offered by Christopher Parker, who in his *The English Historical Tradition since 1850*, Edinburgh, Edinburgh University Press, 1990, argues that English historiography has been a reactionary craft which has not accepted or even been aware of its ideological character. Two excellent demonstrations that the very British tradition of historical biography is as alive as ever, are, to give only examples relating to the figures that start and end this essay, John Clive's book *Macaulay: The Shaping of the Historian*, Cambridge, MA, Harvard University Press, 1987, and David Cannadine's scholarly account of *G.M. Trevelyan. A Life in History*, London, Fontana, 1993. Some leading British scholars after the Second World War are sympathetically portrayed in Walter L. Arnstein (ed.) *Recent Historians of Great Britain. Essays on the Post-1945 Generation*, Iowa, Iowa State University Press, 1990, some of whom, for example Christopher Hill and E.P. Thompson, also are the subject of lengthy chapters in Harvey J. Kaye's classic and very informative work *The British Marxist Historians. An Introductory Analysis*, London, Macmillan, 1995 (first published 1984).

Part II

The age of bourgeois revolution

In the nineteenth century, almost everywhere in Europe, an increasingly powerful bourgeoisie threatened a variety of *ancien régimes*. Although this challenge often resulted in compromises between old feudal elites and the *homini novi* of the industrial age, the interpretation of the past proved nevertheless to be a contested terrain where battles for political power and prestige were fought out. With the increasing professionalisation of historical research and the establishment of state-funded universities, the ability of particular states and governments to influence the historical narratives grew, and the links between nation-building and historiography were strengthened. The writing of history became an exercise legitimating the existing political system and its representatives.

As Ceri Crossley argues in his chapter on France, there was no difficulty in finding a vantage point from which to write French national history in the first half of the nineteenth century. During the Restoration and the July Monarchy, the Revolution and its consequences formed the point of departure from which historians attempted (with varying degrees of success) to establish the legitimacy of the post-revolutionary nation-state. Those histories endorsed specific governments and policies and sought to demonstrate to the French that they belonged to a progressive community which had remained essentially the same through the vicissitudes of historical change. Historical writing, as Crossley demonstrates, validated society and confirmed the nation as the site of the promised reconciliation between individual will and collective purpose.

Patrick Bahners, in contrast, shows that Ranke had immense difficulties in finding in the German past any of the colossal confrontations, momentous events or timeless institutions which gave a clear structure to his histories of particular states. In his *German History in the Age of the Reformation*, published between 1839 and 1847, Ranke located the German national character in the spiritual sphere. In his view, the German nation was characterised by having acquired a universal spiritual mission, in which German scholarship and the modern spirit of free inquiry occupied a central place. Thus, Bahners concludes, if there was nationalism in Ranke's 'German History', it was characterised by enlightened universalism.

The contested nature of nationality is also central in Martin Thom's chapter on the Italian Risorgimento. Thom focuses on historians like Carlo Cattaneo and Cesare Balbo who attempted to construct the idea of the Italian nation-state around the principle of confederation. Yet at the same time the thought of Balbo was guided by an essentially romantic — indeed, Christian-romantic — providentialism and a mystical subsumption of the city and region into the nation. By contrast, Cattaneo remained largely unaffected by the organicist teleologies inherent in romantic and Schlegelian concepts of the tribe-nation.

4 History as a principle of legitimation in France (1820–48)

Ceri Crossley

Nineteenth-century France was faced with the task of coming to terms with the Revolution and its consequences. The present essay aims to describe some of the ways in which the turn to history which characterised French intellectual life between the 1820s and the 1840s represented an attempt to establish the legitimacy of the post-revolutionary nation-state. My focus is on the liberal historians, especially Augustin Thierry (1795–1856) and François Guizot (1787–1874). By grounding political authority on a new interpretation of history the intellectuals of the 1820s and 1830s validated the bourgeois nation-state. They confirmed the nation as the prime site of belonging, as the location of the sense of identity. Henceforward, they hoped, Frenchmen would be united in their awareness of a past which moved in accordance with historical laws and actualised the intentions of divine providence. Their argument suggested that the sense of belonging which history provided might constitute an alternative to participatory politics on the one hand and to authoritarian Catholicism on the other. However, the liberal historical project was always potentially unstable since it valorised a rediscovered national past – whose content was conflict and struggle – in order to offer validation to the bourgeois state conceived as a homogeneous space within which individual enterprise could peacefully flourish. In other words the liberal historians celebrated the heroism of the collective past but sought in the present to contain the passionate and potentially destructive energies of the masses. They self-consciously wrote a form of history which was informed by the painful gain in knowledge which the experience of the Revolution had brought. Their texts justified 1789 but repudiated 1793. The underlying issue with which I am concerned is the way in which the liberals' use of history in support of the bourgeois nation represented an attempt to reconcile post-revolutionary individualism with a redefined sense of social belonging.

After 1815 liberals in France sought to develop a politics of compromise which expanded the centre ground. Their aim was to lay to rest the conflicts generated by the Revolution and thus ensure stability and preserve national unity. They turned to history because out of the national past they were able to fashion an ideology which supported *both* individual rights and a sense of communal belonging. In his seminal study, *The Political Uses of History*, Stanley Mellon described how, during the Restoration, the French national past was reinterpreted in order to endorse the ascension of the middle classes.[1] Looking back on the 1820s from the vantage point of the 1840s, Augustin Thierry's elder brother Amédée (1797–1873) summed up what had been at stake during the Restoration. In his view the liberal history of those years represented an exploration of the national psyche, a necessary redefinition of identity: 'At that time we were at the centre of the crusade which founded and popularised the reform of history in France. [...] It was as if the *patrie* itself was actively interested in the research which was being undertaken into [national life]'.[2] In the writings of François Guizot and Augustin Thierry the past was reinterpreted as a grand narrative of national purpose and the Revolution was defended as the legitimate culmination of a long process of struggle. The new liberal history was both a ground of meaning and a foundation for action since, while it validated the politics of compromise, the conditions of its fulfilment only appeared to be fully present after the July Revolution of 1830. Indeed the liberal historians who came to prominence during the Restoration generally viewed the July regime as the concluding moment in French history. Henceforward, in their view, essential individual rights would be protected while the constitutional monarchy would act as a necessary unifying power. Social oneness appeared finally to have been achieved. In their histories liberals described the development of the forces which bound the nation together. They celebrated the rise of the communes and traced the development of an individualistic, entrepreneurial spirit which was often in conflict with the forces of privilege and arbitrary rule. In their view the July Monarchy was the logical outcome of the general movement of French history.

In the 1820s and 1830s the challenge for the supporters of the bourgeois nation-state was to find a way of disentangling post-Enlightenment liberalism from aspects of pre-Revolutionary liberalism. In its initial period the French Revolution had sought to actualise the programme of the liberal Enlightenment: the replacement of a regime whose legitimacy rested upon divine right by a new form of social organisation which drew its authority from the people and which acted in accordance with the dictates of reason. Liberal discourse affirmed the primacy of the individual and asserted the capacity of individuals to come together and create a new social world, free of the legal inequalities, prejudices and injustices of the old order. The Revolution in its early phase can legitimately be viewed as the opening up of a secular space. The Universal Declaration of the Rights of Man and the abrogation of feudal privileges on the night of 4 August 1789 signalled the dismantling of religiously-founded social and political power. This process in turn enabled the emergence of centres of individual power which served private desires and projects. The rational consent of individuals expressed through the voice of their representatives became the new legitimating principle, albeit linked, until 1792, with the fading prestige of royal sovereignty. However, the course followed by the Revolution, its descent into repression and violence in the name of virtue profoundly compromised the ideals of the liberal Enlightenment.

Critics on the right damned all individualism on the grounds that it bore the seeds of authoritarian Jacobinism. Counter-revolutionary thinkers held that the spirit of unrestrained freedom of enquiry advocated by the philosophers of liberalism was co-extensive with an arrogant individualism and this, they believed, was responsible for dissolving social ties and plunging French society into chaos. The Catholic reaction rejected the notion that humans could construct a social world, draw up constitutions, possess natural rights. Their prescription was clear: a return to religion, order and hierarchy. This meant that henceforward society would have priority over the individual, that submission to authority would replace the free activity of the critical intellect. Liberal individualism was viewed as a sinful misuse of the divine power which rightfully resided within social reality. Society, divinely instituted, was held to be prior to the constitution of its members. Society had the status of a given, a primitive fact of nature which defined social obligations and relationships. The true aim which power sought to achieve was the conservation of social order. The revolutionaries were castigated for distributing power among atomised autonomous selves. According to Félicité de Lamennais (1782–1854) this dispersal of power, this shredding of authority possessed its own momentum of destruction. The unrestrained exercise of individual reason produced tyranny, sexual violence and ultimately cannibalism. In the final analysis, wrote Lamennais, 'love of self produces love of murder'.[3] According to critics such as Lamennais the revolutionary struggle to overcome historical determinations did not so much actualise freedom as establish a tragic distance between separated egos. The contending individual wills then sought domination over one another in an unrelenting effort to overcome their own corrupting isolation.

What immediately strikes the modern reader is the uncompromising nature of this critique. Counter-revolutionary thinkers such as Joseph de Maistre (1753–1821), Louis de Bonald (1754–1840) and the young Lamennais made no attempt to discriminate between the spirit of 1789 and that of militant Jacobinism. To them it was self-evident that revolutionary individualism was a consequence of Enlightenment liberalism which was itself an extension of the Protestant notion of freedom of conscience. Such counter-revolutionary critics felt under no obligation to achieve balance or fairness. Indeed, anti-liberals were blatantly unfair in the way in which they attacked Locke and Hume whom they held to be responsible for formulating a philosophical individualism which denied value to society.[4] In their polemics they chose to ignore the degree to which the eighteenth-century liberalism which they branded as antisocial in fact accepted that humans by their very nature aspired to forms of communal life. They elected to leave on one side the extent to which the eighteenth century developed notions of sympathy, benevolence and self-sacrifice. And yet, while there can be no doubt that the counter-revolutionaries produced a caricature of their opponents' position, their arguments proved highly influential.

The fact that the counter-revolutionary onslaught on individualism was taken so seriously can largely be explained by the temper of the times. The Terror had made plain to all that the Revolution had failed to integrate emancipated selves into community. The Republic had used coercion to force citizens to be free, to choose between liberty or death. Post-revolutionary liberals had to come to terms with the savage reality of Jacobin authoritarianism and explain its emergence. Nineteenth-century liberals were not democrats. They feared the unruly passions of the mob and needed no persuasion that it was the emergence of self-enclosed individuals which had produced an atomised society which in turn had allowed the dictatorship of the Terror to take hold. They recognised the threat that the seemingly purposeless character of subjective freedom posed to collective life. Did subjective autonomy and the pursuit of private interest inevitably conflict with the aim of constructing a cohesive community of moral subjects? Was it possible for the individual ego to acknowledge an identity of essence with the social understood as the site within which ethical freedom was actualised? However, while nineteenth-century liberals distrusted the excesses of democratic populism and were willing to look afresh at aspects of Enlightenment thought they held fast to the notion that reason was the power which legitimated the modern world of representative government, religious toleration, freedom of the press and individual rights. In their view human reason, unaided, was able to discover truths concerning society and nature. Nineteenth-century liberals recognised the threat which extreme forms of individualism constituted for the well-being of society but they rejected the aggressive anti-individualism which was the hallmark of the counter-revolutionary agenda.

Liberals were conscious of how seductive reactionary theories of human belonging could be. Their aim was to demonstrate that individualism was compatible with cohesive models of human association. They argued that parliamentary forms of government were admirable because they gave space to individual freedom but nonetheless preserved social cohesion. The ideal state imagined by liberals did more than endorse private relations between individuals. It presupposed a national community united around certain core values. Guizot, for example, held that the aim of politics was to represent reason, not the will of the people. He viewed representative government as a unifying force which organised ideas of truth and justice which were distributed unequally throughout the population: 'it is a question of [...] concentrating, of realising public reason and public morality and summoning them to occupy power'.[5] On the one hand popular sovereignty was repudiated but on the other it was evident that there could be no return to traditional hierarchies and anti-individual theocratic models. However, political theory alone was deemed insufficient to provide legitimation for the post-revolutionary liberal order. Liberals were suspicious of political theory. They blamed the errors of the Revolution on the Enlightenment's preoccupation with abstract political thought at the expense of historical knowledge.

They criticised the revolutionaries for paying inadequate attention to the complex interplay of forces which sustained social life. Guizot summed up the liberal position when he observed that political reality could never fully be grasped without reference to history: 'The institutions of a people cannot properly be understood without knowledge of its history'.[6] Henceforward a reassessment of the collective past was held to be a prerequisite for the construction of a stable and cohesive nation.

Instead of proclaiming universal abstract rights, nineteenth–century liberals turned to the study of history which in their view progressively disclosed a series of truths. They attempted to reconcile the individual with society by rewriting national history as a progressive narrative which both legitimated subjective autonomy *and* guaranteed collective cohesion. Liberal romanticism forged new myths of collective identity which endeavoured to lend meaning, purpose and direction to individual lives, to restore a sense of belonging to isolated selves which had been severed from their ontological moorings within the political and social order of the *ancien régime*. Indeed the phenomenon of romanticism itself, often associated with the idea of individualism, can perhaps more accurately be approached in relation to the struggle made by the post-revolutionary world to reassemble community, to reconstruct the social bond. The turn to history meant in effect that the new public space of the liberal state was founded on a new hermeneutics, on the reading and interpretation of the text of history. Liberal historians such as Guizot and Thierry did more than reforge links with the national past. History was called upon to fulfil an integrative function, demonstrating to individuals that they belonged to a community which somehow remained the same despite being embroiled within the dynamic processes of historical change over the centuries. History validated society or, more accurately, history confirmed the bourgeois nation as the site of the promised reconciliation between individual will and collective purpose. Counter-revolutionary models of belonging ascribed primacy to the social over the individual. Liberal nationalism provided a different model of community according to which individuals were bound together by their awareness of a shared past. History held up a mirror within which individuals recognised themselves and had confirmed their sense of a common national identity.

The turn to history thus provided the liberal nation with an alternative to the theocratic ideal according to which society was held together by submission to an unchanging, divinely instituted authority. However, it would be erroneous to suppose that liberals excluded God from their work or presented history in exclusively human terms. Much of their work was built upon a bedrock of metaphysical idealism. In the 1820s the philosopher Victor Cousin (1792–1867) and his disciples understood history in terms of the outworking within time of Absolute Spirit which had initially externalised itself in the form of material nature. History had meaning for Cousin because it corresponded to the Absolute's journey to self-knowledge. Liberal historians were generally of a philosophical bent and tended to view history in terms of the progressive actualisation of reason, justice and freedom, ideas which were identified with the manifestation of the divine. God was not banished but his active presence was reinterpreted and described in new ways. For liberals this had the great advantage of allowing them both to endorse individualism and implicitly sacralise collective life – a combination quite inconceivable to those who believed in the counter-revolutionary model of social cohesion. In the eyes of liberals humans made history in collaboration with a God who was at one with the progressive unfolding of freedom, reason and justice. Through the mediation of history individualism was reconciled with collective purpose. At the heart of history liberals placed the development of conscious-ness and the growth of moral autonomy: world history told of the progressive victory of self over non-self, the increasing mastery of matter by mind. Western bourgeois values were held to be superior and to have a universal relevance. At the same time, however, history was understood in relation to the development of collective entities. World history took the form of a spatial movement from the Orient to Europe. European history told of the forma-tion of nations whose dynamic drew its force from the ascension of the Third Estate whose role in the grand scheme of things was to advance individual and collective freedoms. The Third Estate was the agent for the realisation of national oneness.

Liberal history validated bourgeois freedoms while at the same time drawing attention to the central role played by France. Guizot asserted that only in France had the Third Estate truly become the nation. Liberal histo-rians grasped the nettle of justifying 1789 but took care to insert the Revolution within a broader history of struggle going back to the Middle Ages. In this way, while the Revolution stood as the culmination of a provi-dentially authorised process, it lost something of its unsettlingly unique significance. Liberals concluded that the actualisation of the rational nation-state had effectively been postponed until 1830. In their view the constitutional arrangements of the July Monarchy marked the re-establishment of the essen-tial alliance between the French people who built the nation and the monarch which acted as a power preserving unity. In their writings the liberal historians furnished citizens with a coherent narrative of national develop-ment according to which struggle and pain found their resolution in the balanced politics of the bourgeois nation. History described the slow emer-gence of a stable, unified and homogeneous national community. When Augustin Thierry looked back over the preceding seven centuries he felt able to discern within French history a reassuring spirit of unity and continuity: 'one nation and one monarchy, bound to one another, modified together'.[7]

Liberal history reappropriated the past as a weapon to be used against the counter-revolutionaries. However, with the advent of the July Monarchy it seemed as if the desired reconciliation between freedom and order had been achieved. The liberal historians confirmed the legitimacy of the new regime by providing explanations and justifications which combined the pseudo-scientific with the pseudo-religious: according to Augustin Thierry the mysterious but continuous elevation of the Third Estate was nothing less than the providential law which governed French history. After July 1830 the task for liberal history became the endorsement of the ruling order. Guizot's lectures delivered during the Restoration were reprinted. Augustin Thierry worked on his study of the rise of the Third Estate. Liberal history articulated the difficult reconciliation of change and continuity within the public presentation of national memory. Political rights were restricted but liberal history offered to its readers a surrogate form of participation, a different sense of belonging: French unity was preserved and French identity was affirmed because citizens appeared to give assent to the general truths which were disclosed by history and actualised by the nation. The government of Louis Philippe took steps to organise research into the national past and to provide official support for the publication of texts and documents. At the same time leading Restoration liberals such as Cousin and Guizot moved from teaching positions to ministerial posts.

However, the liberals seriously underestimated the power of the revolutionary past to invest present reality. Their historical scheme validated the constitutional monarchy as the form of government which brought about the resolution of conflict, the achievement of balance, the victory of reason. But all of this bore little resemblance to French social reality in the 1830s and 1840s. Numerous commentators were struck by the alienation and the social divisions produced by industrialism and economic liberalism. The liberal nation was clearly failing to foster unity, cohesion and a sense of belonging. Left-wing critics of the liberal order returned to the notion of the law as a depersonalised power emanating from the general will of the people. They refused to accept that July 1830 marked an ending. For them the Revolution remained the founding moment of political modernity. In the wake of July 1830 liberal history's objective was to justify and consolidate present reality. Republican history developed a different project. It looked to the future and sought to mobilise collective energies in order to actualise the unfulfilled promise of the Revolution. Jules Michelet (1798–1874) revived the revolutionary aspiration to fraternity as a challenge to the fragmented and antagonistic society of the July Monarchy. The credibility of the liberal interpretation of history ultimately rested on the ability of the bourgeois monarchy to resist disintegration and overcome opposition. However, the Revolution of February 1848 demonstrated that the supposedly providentially-endorsed balance achieved by the constitutional monarchy did not after all represent an ending. In the wake of the February Revolution doubt entered the soul of Augustin Thierry. His political faith crumbled.[8] He no longer felt secure in his understanding of the French past. The February Revolution dramatically demonstrated the unpredictability and the instability of human affairs. No longer could Thierry confidently look forward to a peaceful future which would further entrench the political arrangements of the constitutional monarchy.

The fall of the July Monarchy gravely undermined liberal history's ability to function as a discourse of truth. As a consequence of the events of 1848 it became difficult if not impossible to sustain the authority of the liberal-historical text. Henceforward the deeply fractured condition of nineteenth-century France was apparent to all. Liberals had constructed and disseminated a robustly heroic narrative of national purpose which supposedly culminated in a stable, unified nation. However, the intended, the desired, reconciliation had clearly not taken place and bourgeois historiography was of little help to liberals when it came to explaining the misfortune of 1848. Liberal history, designed to stabilise French society, had singularly failed to immobilise the nation.

Notes

1 Stanley Mellon, *The Political Uses of History*, CA, Stanford, Stanford University Press, 1958.
2 Amédée Thierry, *Histoire des Gaulois depuis les temps les plus reculés jusqu'à l'entière soumission de la Gaule à la domination romaine*, Paris, Labitte 1845, p. vi.
3 Félicité de Lamennais, *Essai sur l'indifférence en matière de religion*, Paris, Pagnerre 1845, vol. 1, p. 310.
4 Stephen Holmes, *The Anatomy of Antiliberalism*, Cambridge, MA, Harvard University Press, 1993.
5 François Guizot, *Histoire des origines du gouvernement représentatif*, Paris, Didier, 2 vols, 1880, vol. 2, p. 150.
6 Guizot, *Histoire des origines du gouvernement représentatif*, vol. 1, pp. 127–8.
7 Augustin Thierry, *Essai sur l'histoire de la formation et des progrès du tiers état*, Paris, Firmin-Didot 1883, p. 1
8 Ceri Crossley, *French Historians and Romanticism*, London, Routledge, 1993, pp. 68–70.

Further reading

Ceri Crossley, *French Historians and Romanticism*, London: Routledge, 1993. Includes extensive bibliography.
François Guizot, *Histoire des origines du gouvernement représentatif*, Paris, Didier, 2 vols, 1880. Lectures delivered in 1820–22.
Stephen Holmes, *The Anatomy of Antiliberalism*, Cambridge, MA, Harvard University Press, 1993.
Félicité de Lamennais, *Essai sur l'indifférence en matière de religion*, Paris, Pagnerre, new edn, 4 vols, 1843. First published 1817–23.
Stanley Mellon, *The Political Uses of History*, Stanford, Stanford University Press, 1958.
Amédée Thierry, *Histoire des Gaulois depuis les temps les plus reculés jusqu'à l'entière soumission de la Gaule à la domination romaine*, Paris, Labitte 3rd. edn, 2 vols, 1845.
Augustin Thierry, *Essai sur l'histoire de la formation et des progrès du tiers état*, Paris, Firmin-Didot 1883. First published in 1853.

5 National unification and narrative unity

The case of Ranke's *German History*

Patrick Bahners

The state a nation builds and the story a historian tells may be seen as solutions to the same formal problem: how to create unity out of diversity? The modern nation-state incorporates older units which represent regional and confessional traditions. In telling their story, the historian has to make sense of diverging facts and opinions. Old versions of the story are superseded, but they may be given a place within a new, larger interpretation. Thus David Hume, when he wrote the history of England, took some points from the Tories and some points from the Whigs. While the nation-state is one, it is always one among many. Its unity is not only created out of an internal diversity, but must also be asserted against an external diversity. Similarly, to every story told there are other stories. Thus, both the nation-state and the historian deal with the question of inclusion and exclusion. The political problem of boundaries is analogous to the narrative problem of closure. Modern historical consciousness rests on the assumption that it cannot achieve narrative closure by simply copying the boundaries found in the external world. There is no historical reality 'out there'. Where to start and where to stop depends on the historian's point of view. Unity must indeed be created. In a very real sense, the historian makes history.

This state of affairs may be called the transcendentalist position. And ever since Kant's time critics have been asking: if this is true, does not everything then become subjective and arbitrary? An answer was provided by idealist theoreticians of hermeneutics such as Wilhelm von Humboldt and Johann Gustav Droysen. They drew a radical conclusion from the modern experience of constant change. If everything is historical, historians must understand themselves as a product of history. They will then anticipate that their point of view will be corrected by future scholars. But they will also see that it marks the end of a long line of interpretations and is thus neither arbitrary nor simply subjective. The never-ending story of historical interpretation is the image of the very process of history it interprets. Thus historical narrative is indeed mimetic without, however, falling back into what is known by the dirty word of naïve realism. This concept of history as *Mimesis des Werdens*, in Droysen's phrase, may help to explain the elective affinity between so many nineteenth-century historians and the nation-state. The nation-state is created

– but not *ex nihilo*. Its ground has been prepared in the hopes and thoughts of its future citizens or rather their ancestors. This, at least, is what the historian says about it. The successful establishment of artistic unity may give rise to a double illusion. One may believe that the nation-state is no modern creation but has been there all along. And one may imagine that the story of the nation-state is not of the historian's making but some kind of photograph of events as they really were. It is not difficult to see through these fallacies. Sophisticated practitioners of the historian's craft have felt no need to conceal the tricks of the trade. In their hands, the difficulties of narrative closure become symbolic of the problematic nature of political unity. Such is the case with Leopold Ranke.

A single theme runs through most of the fifty-four volumes of Ranke's collected works, namely the genesis of the modern world. According to Ranke, the Middle Ages were under the spell of the principle of uniformity: church and state, politics and morals were seen as identical. The modern world, by contrast, is characterised by a radical pluralism of political and religious ideas. These ideas, though often logically incompatible, do in fact coexist in a universal order of law and tolerance. This order, however, cannot be imposed from above as in medieval times; it is constantly fought over, perpetually challenged and re-established. Each of the great powers represents a distinctive, though not static principle. In a universe of instability, they seem to be the planets, islands of stability. This stability, however, is itself the product of history, that is of movement and conflict. Outward strength may be the result of internal strife. Ranke's national histories tell the story of how the individual great powers won their internal unity and their place in the world. Political conflict is shown to be about the representation of unity. Who shall speak for England, the king or the parliament? The answer is a compromise, though Ranke's rather Whiggish *Englische Geschichte* (1859–68) lets the parliament have the better of it. The king represents the kingdom only insofar as he is himself a part of its parliament. In France and also in Prussia, by contrast, the state is represented in the person of the monarch. The idea of representation connects the matter and the form of Ranke's histories. In telling the story of a nation, the historian has to choose a representative, a hero, so to speak, who holds the narrative together. Both the *Englische* and the *Französische Geschichte* (1852–61) have, in this sense, a central character, parliament in the one case, the monarch in the other. The institutional solution to the problem of unity also determines the idea carried by each great power into the outside world: the idea of tolerance and liberty on the one hand, the idea of orthodoxy and hierarchy on the other.

Neither these ideas nor their institutional forms stand in any way outside history. Ranke's theological language has been much misunderstood. When in a philosophical dialogue he called the states 'Gedanken Gottes' he did not claim a supernatural privilege for the great powers which would make them immune against historical change.[1] He was a follower of Lessing and Schleiermacher; his theology was anti-dogmatic, possibly heterodox. Revelation is progressive. The truth gradually unfolds. It is not enough to know the premises. It is not enough to know the result. The essence of truth is the very process of its unfolding. This speculative theology was the basis for Ranke's analysis of historical change. The theology of progressive revelation was transformed into a logic of institutional development. In the course of history, the English parliament emerged as the representative of the English nation. This outcome was neither predetermined nor coincidental. There was, after a time, a certain necessity to it, but this necessity was itself a product of history, of the free play of historical forces. In Ranke's view, institutions are self-stabilising. During the struggle with the king, each success for parliament made the next success not inevitable, but more likely. At the end of the day, the Stuarts were powerless against the accumulated mass of precedents, that is, against English history itself, as it had developed over hundreds of years. There is thus a pattern in English history, but it can only be seen with hindsight; this explains Ranke's Whiggism. Telling the story, the historian must be careful not to read the end into the beginning. However, he cannot help noticing hints and intimations of what was to follow. After all, this knowledge distinguishes the historian from the participant. Therefore, the narrator regularly interrupts himself, sometimes anticipating later developments, sometimes warning the reader not to overlook alternative opportunities. There is a recognisable rhythm in the narrative, a constant interplay between possibility and necessity, contingency and teleology, openness and closure.

Once the question of representation is finally decided, the story has come to an end. The unity of the nation-state has been established, and so has the unity of the historian's narrative. The analogy is perhaps even more obvious in the case of the *Französische Geschichte*. The absolute monarch may be seen as a *Doppelgänger* of the historian. Both seem all-powerful and yet are constrained by time. As in later theories of the *Sonderweg*, England and France provided Ranke with what one might call the normal model of national development. The life of the nation is represented in an institutional centre embodying a leading idea. In the case of Prussia, the model was, as it were, turned on its head. Whereas in Western Europe the nation expressed itself through its political centre, in Prussia it was the monarchical centre which created the nation. Ranke's *Preussische Geschichte* (1847–8) is therefore 'a right royal book'.[2] The *History of the Popes* (1834–6) presents us with the strange case of a nation-state *manqué*. There was, as in Prussia, a centre, the papacy and its temporal dominions. There was even a nation, the Italian. But despite the conquests of Julius II, the popes did not unite Italy. They were bound by their universalist mission, the heritage of the Middle Ages. While in the later parts of the *Französische* and *Englische Geschichte* the events focus more and more on the court and parliament respectively, in the *History of the Popes* the action moves away from Rome, one-time centre of the world. What, then, about the *Deutsche Geschichte im Zeitalter der Reformation* (1839–47), the last volume of which was published on the eve of the revolution of 1848? Do we find here the apologia for the nation-state to come? Could German bourgeois, preparing to rise against their absolutist monarchs, turn to Ranke in order to learn why the princes had defeated the towns in the sixteenth century? Or did Ranke pave the way for the nation-state which was forged through blood and iron by the exclusion of the Hapsburgs, heirs of Charles V? What nation-state would Ranke's readers create? Did he justify the *Kulturkampf,* the exclusion of all those from the nation who did not accept the Reformation? And did he perpetuate the myth of the Empire which until 1945 would tie the German nation-state to a pre-national past?

On the Western European model we should assume that Ranke would try to identify an institutional centre of German national life and build his narrative around it. Thus indeed did he set out to work – and thus indeed does he begin his narrative. As he explains in his preface, the idea to write about sixteenth-century German history came to him when he discovered, in the municipal archives of Frankfurt, a series of the records of the Imperial Diet. He hoped that this continuous documentation would supply the thread by which to connect the confusing events of an epoch which was not as well known to his contemporaries as the importance of the Reformation demanded. What has remained from this original plan is the first of the ten books, a chronicle of the meetings of the Imperial Diet between 1486 and 1517. While working on his *Englische Geschichte*, Ranke would give lectures on the parliamentary history of England, explaining that the history of the English nation was identical with the history of its parliament.[3] During his work on the records of the *Reichstag*, Ranke found out that he could not write a parliamentary history of Germany. The documents may have been continuous, but the story broke off again and again. The attempts to reform the imperial constitution were simply a number of false starts. Towards the end of the first book the author makes the extraordinary admission that during his studies he got bored by the material.[4] The message is clear: On the basis of these records narrative unity is not possible. The Imperial Diet was no real representation of the nation. It lacked unity and therefore could not represent unity. If a German history was to be told, another centre of attention had to be found.

Thus Ranke examined whether any component of the *Reichstag* might claim to be the true representative of the nation. The Pope was obviously not eligible.[5] National unity, in Ranke's eyes, meant emancipation from the universal hierarchy. The Emperor was distracted by his international interests. The knights, living in ancient castles in the midst of the woods, were too medieval.[6] The towns, unable to formulate a common policy which would override economic self-interest, were perhaps too modern.[7] This left the princes to whom indeed it was due that public order did not break down completely.[8] However, in a conflict between their territorial and their imperial duties, the territory usually won.[9] The history of the imperial constitution, as Ranke tells it, is the story of shifts, sometimes sensational, sometimes imperceptible, in the order of representation. Ranke shows how idea and appearance, concept and reality, spirit and letter came to differ. While none of the imperial estates represented the nation exclusively, each did so in a certain way. Political power had devolved upon the princes. Ultimate legal authority, however, still resided in the Emperor.[10] Even the Pope represented something, namely the responsibility of the Empire for the universal church. While this office had become anachronistic, the nation could not simply throw off its heritage. It had to transform its universal mission into something else.

Although there was no acknowledged national representation, there was a nation to be represented. The German nation was watchful, busy and articulate; we learn to know her sense, her spirit and her feeling. While the imperial institutions were losing all their credit, the unanimity of the nation was growing. Finally the whole nation was united on a point of pure negativity: Things could not stay what they were.[11] This might have been a revolutionary moment. The unity of the nation, not represented in any institution, but on the contrary forged in opposition to all positive powers, might have erupted into violent action. But what followed was not a revolution but the Reformation. Suddenly, the nation found itself represented by Martin Luther. The problem of the constitution was now combined with the problem of religion. Ranke finally had a national story to tell. It came to an end with the Augsburg Diet of 1555. Both strands of the story were joined together: the equality of the new religion was acknowledged, and the reform of the constitution was accomplished. Droysen criticised this ending for its artistic neatness, its sense of all's well that ends well.[12] The justice of this criticism may be questioned. The peace of Augsburg does not mark a high point of national development like the reign of Louis XIV in France or the wars of William of Orange for England. The Germans did not live happily ever after. Only the possibility of an autonomous development was secured in 1555; it saved the Germans from being subdued by a Catholic universal monarchy. There was still no institutional centre of national life.

When Luther and Frederick the Wise, Elector of Saxony, had formed a tacit agreement to stand together for Germany, without even setting eyes on each other,[13] it might have been expected that the Protestant princes would form the nucleus of national life. But this did not come to pass. While the support of the princes was indeed essential for the survival of the reformed religion, they did not lead the nation on a new path. Luther had criticised the dogma and hierarchy of the Roman church in the name of the Bible and of the community of all believers. In order to consolidate their position, however, the Protestants themselves founded churches, complete with dogmatic definitions and bureaucratic offices. Although Ranke justified this conservative move as the only chance to ward off the challenge from Thomas Müntzer's spiritualist anarchy, the original idea of the Reformation was thereby modified. There is no clear line of continuity linking the Protestant territories with German national aspirations in Ranke's lifetime. Has there thus been no unquestioned representative of the nation after Luther's death? But if the nation was not represented, how could it exist at all? How is the historian to represent the nation? 'Deutschland bietet kein Zentrum dar, man muss immer aufs Ganze blicken' ('Germany does not have a centre, so that one always has to take everything into account.': This methodological maxim was formulated by Ranke in 1840 and written down by Jacob Burckhardt.[14] What, however, is to be seen if the historian is forced to keep 'das Ganze' ('everything') before their eyes? In a sense, the answer is – nothing.

When discussing problems of representation, Ranke likes to play with the opposition of visibility and invisibility. It is the very meaning of representation to give visible shape to something which is invisible. In the *Deutsche Geschichte*, the contrast between what can be seen – appearances, the letter, splendour and power – and what cannot be seen – ideas, the spirit, conviction and faith – is particularly important. Cardinal Cajetanus, the Dominican apologist of papal supremacy who was asked to consider Luther's case at Augsburg in 1518, loved to exhibit himself 'in glänzenden Zeremonien' ('in dazzling ceremonies'), clothed in expensive garments;[15] the monk appeared before him 'in niedriger Gestalt' ('as a lowly person'), wearing a borrowed cowl.[16] The new church, confined within the narrow boundaries of German principalities, could not compete with the church of Rome in 'Großartigkeit und Glanz ihrer Erscheinung' ('its magnificent and radiant outer appearance'); it found its strength 'in ihrer inneren geistigen Kraft' ('its inner spiritual strength').[17] The psychological drama of Luther's life was, in the words of one of Ranke's British reviewers, the conflict between 'the inner and spiritual' and 'the outward and ritual'.[18] Luther's original idea, justification through faith as opposed to justification through good works, re-established the sovereignty of the invisible realm of God over the visible institutions of mankind. The theological argument was anticipated by popular writers such as Sebastian Brant. Ranke quotes from Brant's *Ship of Fools*: 'Glorie und Schönheit werden verachtet, weil sie vergänglich sind: "nichts ist bleiblich als die Lehre"' ('Glory and Beauty are despised, because they are transient:"nothing will endure but the doctrine"').[19]

In the colourful set-pieces of the *Deutsche Geschichte* such as the sack of Rome, the reader is 'led along like a spectator'.[20] It is important to note, however, that the detail of the description is strictly subordinate to the progress of the argument. The book does not conform to the model of a full history, giving a vivid account of a continuous series of events. The selective, even fragmentary character of Ranke's story was frequently commented upon by British readers. 'The flow of his narrative is neither continuous nor very clear', *The Times* complained. The book had value 'rather as an important compilation than as a history'.[21] Lord Morpeth, the liberal Anglican politician, found it 'a little arduous, perhaps slightly heavy'.[22] W.B. Donne remarked that the author appeared 'to aim at a sort of fragmentary conciseness, which gives his work in many places rather the air of historical notes or illustrations than of a connected narrative'.[23] By appealing to the understanding rather than to the senses, the historian proved himself to be a good Protestant. In defending Luther, the German nation emancipated itself from the medieval world of false appearances. It found its self-consciousness in understanding the superiority of the invisible but eternal truth over its visible but temporal expressions. Thus the self-recognition of the nation, as Ranke saw it, was an image of the constitution of the subject as it was conceived in the philosophy of Kant and Fichte. The truth embraced by the German nation was not Protestant dogma as opposed to Catholic dogma, but the spirit of critical examination which accepts nothing on the authority of others. 'Der gärende, gewaltsame, der bisherigen Zustände überdrüssige, nach dem neuen trachtende Geist der Nation' ('The fermenting and violent spirit of the nation, tired of the existing conditions and intent on reaching new shores') was not appeased by the removal of isolated grievances; dealing with every problem 'auf das gründlichste' ('thoroughly'), it raised fundamental questions of law and authority.[24]

Seeing through appearances, the German spirit emancipated itself not only from the spiritual tyranny of the Roman church, but also from the false idols of temporal politics. The unity of the German nation was not to be shaken by political disappointment; its foundation was something meta–political. At times, the German nation as described by Ranke comes dangerously close to a mystical community. When Luther made his way to Worms in 1521 in order to justify himself before the Imperial Diet, he did not think of politics. It is important to note Ranke's visual metaphor: 'alle Politik lag außer seinem Gesichtskreis' ('all politics lay beyond him'). But as soon as he saw the common people, 'die verwunderte, mannigfaltig bewegte, gaffende, teil-nehmende Menge' ('the gaping, interested and curious crowd, moved in manifold directions'), his mind was fortified.[25] The spectators, who were excluded from the political debates of the Diet, answered for the moral sense of the nation. Refusing to enter into political calculations likely to be thwarted by the unpredictable course of history, Luther stood by his conscience and became 'the deepest politician of his age'.[26] While the national spirit drew its strength from religious and moral resources which were beyond the reach of the powers that be, it did not deny the importance of politics; Ranke was careful to steer clear of Antinomianism. A Catholic reader might find in Ranke's frank account of diplomatic intrigue confirma-tion of the view that the introduction of Protestantism had been a political plot: 'we have all but mathematical demonstration, in this history of Ranke, that the German Reformation was the result of mere state emergency, acci-dentally concurring with a restless and wayward religious movement'.[27] In Ranke's eyes, however, the secular motives of the Protestant princes were perfectly legitimate. States were institutions for the fallen world; saints were not fit to be rulers.

In order to become effective in the world, the critical spirit had to take form. There must be something to distinguish it from the individualist inspira-tion of Thomas Müntzer. He who sought after truth had to understand that he was not alone but part of a community the members of which were engaged in the same critical project. One name for this common element which made the individual truth-seekers understand each other is 'Meinung', opinion. Opinion, sometimes called public opinion, is according to Ranke the most powerful force in the modern world.[28] It is at work in every nation-state and is thus the true heir of the universal church. In leading the opinion of mankind back to the original truth of the gospel, the German nation remained true to the universal mission it had inherited from the medieval Empire; the impartial, objective scholarship seen by Ranke as Germany's gift to the world was to preserve this universalism in his own age. In the Middle Ages, people's minds had been ruled by dogma, command and show. In the modern world, they were convinced by means of rational argument. This, at least, is the – one might say: Habermasian – idea of public opinion. In reality, opinion was constantly fluctuating, given to sudden shifts and abrupt reverses. However, it was the glory of the German nation that it fought for the modern method of rational enquiry. Opinion manifested itself in literature. The nation spoke through its writers, through poets and professors. Ranke's notion of the German nation thus acquired a sociological content: he wrote at length about the humanists who articulated the grievances of their fellow Germans and put their pens at the service of the Lutheran cause.

While nation-building was impossible without a national mind, the German case was unique in that public opinion not only called for a political representation of the nation but actually had to take its place. At the end of the tenth book, after the peace of Augsburg, the author gives indications of future dissensions within the Protestant camp, implying that national unity will not be found in a confessional state. The very last chapter deals with developments of literature. Ranke's liberal antagonist Georg Gottfried Gervinus closed his *Geschichte der poetischen Nationalliteratur der Deutschen* with the death of Goethe, calling upon the German spirit to move from the realm of ideas where no further perfection could be reached into the world of politics. Ranke told the national story exactly the other way round. The most eminent epoch of German political history made possible the future development of German literature. While literature in Ranke's sense included popular media such as ballads and flysheets, opinion as the methodical search for truth reached its highest form in scholarly literature. Enlightenment began when 'die Idee des reinen Christentums, in Folge eines neuen Studiums der heiligen Bücher in ihrer Ursprache, aus langer Verdunkelung wieder hell hervorleuchtete' ('as a result of the renewed study of the holy books in their original language, the idea of pure Christianity once again began to shine bright after a long period of darkness'.[29] By restoring the letter of the Bible and by moving beyond a literal reading to a spiritual interpretation, the Protestant humanists prepared the way for the great philologists among Ranke's contemporaries.[30] The nation is the community of those who share a common language; Charles V was an alien ruler because he did not speak German.[31]

When the 'allgemeine Bewegung der mittleren Klassen in den handel-treibenden Städten' ('general movement of the middle classes in the urban trading centres'), which had allied themselves with the Anabaptists, was put down by the princes, religion and politics were separated. The idea of the autonomous spheres of the temporal and of the spiritual may be seen as the Lutheran contribution to modern sociology.[32] One of Ranke's British reviewers praised his theory of the beneficent effects of the division of labour between church and state in Protestant Germany; relieved of political cares, the church had devoted herself to education and scholarship. 'From the Lutheran Reformation have proceeded, by very traceable descent, that high intellectual cultivation, that distinguished zeal in the investigation of truth, which distinguish the country of Luther above all others in the world'.[33] Most of Ranke's German readers did not accept the implications of a version of the national story which denied their common moral aspirations political fulfilment. In 1848 his colleagues, the descendants of the humanists, set out to realise their ideal of a common life by taking up the work of constitution-building which had been broken off in the sixteenth century.

Julian Schmidt, who in his history of German literature promoted a liberal nationalism, detected a lack of moral courage at the heart of Ranke's *Deutsche Geschichte*. Ranke's protestations of piety concealed his doubts about his own orthodoxy. The mannerisms of Ranke's style, Schmidt argued, were alien to the language of the heart which a sincere patriot would have spoken. Too fond of paradox, Ranke was a sophist masquerading as a believer.[34] According to Schmidt's view, which was echoed by conservative critics among both Catholics and Protestants, Ranke was lacking precisely that certainty about the right course of action which he praised in Luther. He admired the humanists who had brought together religion and politics, theory and practice; in his own life, 'the dispassionate Ranke'[35] separated his scholarly labours from his political commitment. It is easy nevertheless to detect a conservative bias in his writings. Significantly, however, outspoken Prussian conservatives such as Ludwig von Gerlach and Heinrich Leo never trusted him. Condemning what they called his timidity and lukewarmness, they correctly sensed that there was an indifference towards religious and political absolutes implicit in the activity of being an historian.

By isolating his version of the national past from the politics of the day, Ranke at least made sure that it could not be refuted by events. He never became an unashamed apologist for *Realpolitik*; Luther, who in his eyes embodied the German spirit, had become a national hero because he refused to be bound by the petty realism of short-sighted politicians. Carl Schurz, fleeing to Switzerland after the abortive rebellion of May 1849, found consolation in 'a good library' which contained a complete set of Ranke's works. 'I was soon again profoundly immersed in the history of the Reformation'. He hoped to establish himself as *Privatdozent* (Lecturer) of history at the University of Zürich.[36] The German nation as envisaged by Ranke did not fulfil its dream of political unity; in each age it had to confront the problem anew. But it did produce a community of scholars which in the same way did never accept any answer as final. Hanno Helbling has pointed out that each of the ten books of the *Deutsche Geschichte* has an open ending.[37] A German professor, following Melanchthon, is always on his way 'nach unbekannten Zielen' ('to unknown shores').[38] Lecturing on German history in 1863, Ranke explained that freedom of scholarship and of education was nowhere more important than in politically divided Germany. Academic debate was 'wie ein einziges grosses Gespräch' ('one large dialogue'), joining ideological foes in a common endeavour.[39] The scientific community is similar to the national community in perpetually striving for unity without ever reaching it.

Ranke proclaims in the last sentence of his Preface: 'die Wahrheit kann nur eine sein' ('There can only be one truth').[40] He invites other scholars to bring sources to his attention which he may have overlooked but he announces that he does not foresee anything which could make him change his main line of interpretation. This could be read as a confirmation of his alleged objectivism: he has found out *wie es eigentlich gewesen* (how it actually happened), and nobody can say anything against it. In fact, the idea of the unity of truth expresses precisely the opposite point of view. The historian must apply to his sources what Luther brought to the scriptures: 'die Vereinigung von Tiefsinn und gesundem Menschenverstand', the union of deep understanding and common sense.[41] Ranke at times liked to call the historian's job a priestly office. This has been understood as a claim to a special revelation, being accessible only to professional historians. It should however be obvious that from a Lutheran point of view the historian's priesthood could only be a priesthood of all believers. According to Ranke, there was not even a technical method exclusive to academic historians. The principles of historical interpretation proceed from common sense – they are implicit in what any thinking man does when reading a document. In the *Deutsche Geschichte* this common sense is identified with the virtues of the German bourgeoisie. The humanists were hard-working, decent, earnest fellows. What they achieved was highly improbable as their common sense contradicted the common prejudices of mankind. While men are fond of appearances, the humanists told them to look to the invisible idea. In their moral satires, the 'gesunde Menschenverstand' ('common sense'), despised by the powerful because it was 'prosaisch, bürgerlich, niedrig' ('prosaic, bourgeois, low'), raised itself to become 'Richter der Erscheinungen der Welt' ('judge of all phenomenons in the world').[42] The humanists brought about what we might call a *Revolution der Denkungsart* (revolution of thought). It is exemplified by Copernicus who taught men that the earth moves around the sun although the evidence of the eye tells against it: 'auf das gewaltigste durchbrach er die Welt des Scheines' ('in the most powerful way he shattered the world of make-belief').[43] Thus the Reformation changed the world and left everything in place. It was indeed a bourgeois revolution.

The historian does not only need common sense, but also deep understanding. By this is meant an individual engagement with the material. Luther found out that his salvation depended on the personal relationship between God and himself. Thus the historian must bring their whole personality, their innermost thoughts and aspirations to their task. There will always be other points of view. But one's point of view will stand if it is the expression of one's individuality. Truth can only be one because each individual must integrate what they see into a coherent view of the world. In the last analysis, as

Ranke argued in his comparison of Sarpi and Pallavicini, the rival historiographers of the council of Trent, it is the historian who gives unity to his narrative: 'der Mensch, der doch zuletzt selber die Einheit seines Werkes ist'.[44] German history in the age of the Reformation produced German historical scholarship and thus in the fullness of time the author who wrote the *German History in the Age of the Reformation*. This book may mark a *Sonderweg* among national histories as it deals with a nation-state that never was. But the lack of visible content makes the invisible form of the narrative become apparent, and it may therefore be regarded as a model of its kind. Like Proust's *Recherche*, it tells the story of its own production – of how it came to pass that there was a historian who got the idea that there was such a thing as a national history.

Notes

1 L. v. Ranke, 'Politisches Gespräch', in *Die grossen Mächte*, ed. Ulrich Muhlack, Frankfurt am Main, Insel, 1995, p. 95. This edition includes a helpful commentary.
2 'Ranke's History of Prussia', *Spectator*, 1849, vol. 22, p. 86f.
3 L. v. Ranke, *Vorlesungseinleitungen. Aus Werk und Nachlass*, vol. 4, eds V. Dotterweich and W.P. Fuchs, Munich, Oldenbourg, 1975, p. 374.
4 L. v. Ranke, *Deutsche Geschichte im Zeitalter der Reformation*, Gesamtausgabe der Deutschen Akademie, ed. P. Joachimsen, vol. 1, Munich, Drei Masken, 1925, p. 134.
5 Ibid., p. 27.
6 Ibid., pp. 145–8.
7 Ibid., vol. 3, pp. 475–7, vol. 5, pp. 18–19, 294–5.
8 Ibid., vol. 1, pp. 24, 42–5.
9 Ibid., p. 350.
10 Ibid., pp. 35–6.
11 Ibid., vol. 3, p. 3.
12 J.G. Droysen, *Historik. Vorlesungen über Enzyklopädie und Methodologie der Geschichte*, ed. R. Hübner, Darmstadt, Wissenschaftliche Buchgesellschaft, 3rd edn 1953, pp. 297–8.
13 *Deutsche Geschichte im Zeitalter der Reformation*, vol. 1, p. 227.
14 *Vorlesungseinleitungen*, p. 139. All translations in brackets are by Stefan Berger.
15 *Deutsche Geschichte im Zeitalter der Reformation*, vol. 1, p. 235.
16 Ibid., p. 291.
17 Ibid., vol. 2, p. 383.
18 'Ranke's History of the Reformation', *Eclectic Review* N.S., 1846, vol. 19, p. 350.
19 *Deutsche Geschichte im Zeitalter der Reformation*, vol. 1, p. 184.
20 'Mrs. Austin's Translation of Ranke's Reformation in Germany', *Spectator*, 1845, vol. 18, p. 63.
21 'History of the Reformation in Germany', *The Times*, 9 August 1845.
22 *Extracts from Journals kept by George Howard, Earl of Carlisle*. Selected by his sister, Lady Caroline Lascelles, London, privately printed, 1871, p. 20.
23 W.B. Donne, 'Histories of the Reformation: Ranke and D'Aubigné', *British and Foreign Review*, 1843, vol. 15, p. 101.
24 *Deutsche Geschichte im Zeitalter der Reformation*, vol. 1, pp. 157–8.
25 Ibid., p. 364.
26 Donne, 'Histories of the Reformation: Ranke and D'Aubigné', p. 127.
27 J. Ennis, 'German Reformation and its Times', *Dublin Review*, 1845, vol. 18, p. 286.

28 *Deutsche Geschichte im Zeitalter der Reformation*, vol. 1, pp. 22, 193, 199–201.
29 Ibid., vol. 3, p. 4.
30 Ibid., vol. 1, pp. 197, 316, vol. 5, p. 398.
31 Ibid., vol. 1, p. 355.
32 In a British context, it could be appropriated by dissenters protesting against 'the existing union between things sacred and secular, the incorporation of the church with the institutions and intrigues of the political world': 'Ranke's History of the Reformation', *Eclectic Review* N.S., 1847, vol. 21, p. 592.
33 Donne, 'Histories of the Reformation', pp. 150–1.
34 J. Schmidt, *Geschichte der deutschen Literatur im neunzehnten Jahrhundert*, vol. 3, Leipzig, 3rd edn 1856, pp. 396–7.
35 Donne, 'Histories of the Reformation', p. 115.
36 *The Reminiscences of Carl Schurz*, vol. 1, London, 1909, pp. 242–3.
37 H. Helbling, *Ranke und der historische Stil*, Affoltern, 1953, pp. 74–5.
38 *Deutsche Geschichte im Zeitalter der Reformation*, vol. 1, p. 298.
39 *Vorlesungseinleitungen*, p. 319.
40 *Deutsche Geschichte im Zeitalter der Reformation*, vol. 1, p. 6.
41 Ibid., pp. 333–4.
42 Ibid., p. 185.
43 Ibid., vol. 5, p. 388.
44 L. v. Ranke, *Die römischen Päpste in den letzten vier Jahrhunderten. Analekten*, Sämtliche Werke, vol. 39, Leipzig, Duncker und Humblot, 1874, p. 25.

Further reading

The problem of the unity of truth forms the unifying focus of the ingenious and elegant study by L. Krieger, *Ranke. The Meaning of History*, Chicago, University of Chicago Press, 1977. A.G. Dickens and John M. Tonkin, *The Reformation in Historical Thought*, Oxford, Blackwell, 1985, contains a good chapter on Ranke which includes an interesting comparison of his views on the Peasants' War with those of Friedrich Engels. There are several important articles in a collection edited by G.G. Iggers and J.M. Powell, *Leopold von Ranke and the Shaping of the Historical Discipline*, Syracuse, NY, Syracuse University Press, 1990. The relationship between Ranke and his most eminent pupil is explored by F. Gilbert, *History between Politics and Culture. Essays on Ranke and Burckhardt*, NJ, Princeton, Princeton University Press, 1990.

6 Unity and confederation in the Italian Risorgimento

The case of Carlo Cattaneo

Martin Thom

In the case of Italy, there have been startlingly few studies of the vicissitudes of federalist doctrine, rightly dubbed 'the forgotten solution'.[1] However, I shall not attempt a synoptic account here of the diverse forms of federalism in the Risorgimento, but will consider the life and thought of Carlo Cattaneo, a polymath from Milan, a democratic federalist and perhaps the greatest Italian historian of his day. In Italy, at least, one can no longer claim that this remarkable figure has been neglected or forgotten, yet such terms were indubitably apt in the third-quarter of the nineteenth century.[2] For the official historiography of the new state was so slanted towards the moderate and Piedmontese camp or, where it acknowledged some contribution from the left, towards the equally unitary and also somewhat mystical concept of nationality entertained by Mazzini, that the democratic federalist writings of the period were for long denied the prominence that their intrinsic merits deserved.[3] It gives us pause, for example, to discover that Cattaneo's celebrated essay on the city, first published in 1858, was not reprinted until 1931, or that there is still no satisfactory edition of the complete works.[4] The point is that Cattaneo had, from 1848–9 on, displayed a deep hostility towards the moderates who, from their stronghold in Piedmont, so dominated the struggle for national liberation in the 1850s. Even the essay on the city, though toned down at the editor's request, may be read as a critique of the Piedmontese annexationist and plebiscitary approach to nation-building.[5]

As moderate patriots in Turin worked to redefine the project of national unification, with the Piedmontese army and the Savoyard dynasty increasingly at its heart, the exiled democrats made strenuous efforts to combine in a single organisation. The story of this endeavour, being set in several different European cities, is complex, but the gist of it is that Cattaneo rebuffed all overtures, whether from the Mazzinian camp or, less predictably, from the democratic federalists.[6] Although Cattaneo's relations with Mazzini have yet to be satisfactorily described by historians, it is not difficult to see why, in the early 1850s, he should have been more hostile than ever towards unitary solutions to the national question and, especially, to tactical compromises over matters of principle. For what Cattaneo had consistently decried was any and every subordination of liberty to unity, so that federalism may in his case be construed as the expression, on the political plane, of a value that was paramount in every sphere, namely, liberty.[7] Judgement of Cattaneo's political acumen by historians has been harsh, and, if it is admitted that the hegemony of the moderates over the Action Party damaged Italian political culture in the long term, it is doubtful whether the charges against him can be entirely refuted.[8] This said, the repeated invocation of his example by serious and honourable thinkers, at moments of extreme crisis in Italy, cannot be ascribed simply to a wistful idealisation of a founding father that the nation never had. I would argue, rather, that accusations of utopianism miss the point, and that Cattaneo, despite being, as he well knew, temperamentally unsuited to politics, remains intrinsically fascinating because the tension in his thought between the federal principle and the national principle may be read as the expression of more general, but until recently obscured, fault-lines in European political thought.

To read such fault-lines accurately, it would be necessary to follow them far back into the eighteenth century, and indeed much further, but here, for Cattaneo, 1796, the year of General Buonaparte's great victories in the Italian Peninsula, will serve.[9] At any rate, to grow up in Milan in the early-nineteenth century – Cattaneo was born in 1801 and died in 1869 – was to be faced with several preliminary tasks of orientation. Simply in order to understand your exact place, and this was very much Cattaneo's preoccupation, you had to address the legacy of Jacobinism and of the First Empire; you were compelled – after 1815 – to reflect upon the nature of the Hapsburg Empire; you had to learn the lessons of London, Birmingham and Manchester, where the future, for liberals of every hue, seemed to lie; you had to wonder at the circumstance of the Swiss cantons a little to the north, for they constituted an alternative tradition to that of the unitary, national state; you had always to be mindful of the example of the Lombard Enlightenment, the revered precedent of the Verri brothers and of Cesare Beccaria, which had been honoured even in Napoleonic Milan, and which was carried forward into the 1830s by Cattaneo's teacher, Gian Domenico Romagnosi; and, finally, you had to come to terms with German idealist philosophy, with the new German historiography and with the new science of comparative linguistics. The weaving of a portrait would require all of these colours, which, like rivers, highways or railways, draw the mind across the map of nineteenth-century Europe. The adding or taking away of any one colour produces a subtle, but crucial shift of emphasis.[10] The patterns that I lay down here are therefore makeshift, loose strands to be drawn tighter in other essays.

From 1848 to 1851

Scholars are agreed that the revolutions of 1848 and, in particular, the insurrection in Milan, the *Cinque Giornate*, worked a great change in Cattaneo. Here is a self-portrait, in retrospect:

Although for many years Cattaneo had addressed all those in Milan who were promoting railways, industrial education, prison reform and other useful innovations, he would profess himself to be, and indeed was, wholly outside of any *political* associations, and would openly laugh at those who placed so much hope in Pius IX and Charles Albert.[11]

So trenchant a denial of the political as such may derive from the debacle of 1821, which condemned some of the conspirators associated with the *Conciliatore* in Milan to long years in the Austrian fortress of the Spielberg, and his teacher, Romagnosi, to the loss of a public role. The fate of the generation immediately above his own turned Cattaneo not only against secrecy and insurrection but also, it may be surmised, against a narrowly literary career and, more especially, against a literary notion of politics.[12] He became defiantly gradualist and reformist in orientation, even his philosophy of science and his insistence that description of the world, natural and civil, should be a collective endeavour, seeming to militate against the vanities of individual literary production.[13]

Those describing Cattaneo's federalist thought have generally followed Bobbio in remarking a tripartite division, with 1848 and 1859–60 as caesurae.[14] One may plausibly add further subdivisions, but I cannot see any good cause to challenge the overall framework.[15] Right up until 1848, then, Cattaneo believed that the Hapsburg Empire might revert, through a programme of Enlightened reforms, to what it had been under the Empress Maria Theresa. It was this belief that sustained him in his tireless commitment to forms of social and economic change that were 'laborious, slow and gradual',[16] for the Empire had once been federal in structure, not centralised, with Lombardy able to proceed in a different direction to, for example, Flanders or Hungary.[17] Joseph II, however, had implemented a policy of extreme centralisation, dashing the most cherished hopes of the Enlightened reformers in Milan and, more generally, subjecting the national minorities to a Germanic hegemony.[18] With the fall of Metternich, on 13 March 1848, Cattaneo expressed the hope that the Empire might once again be the heir to 'an ancient cosmopolitan authority that (had) permitted every people to live according to the customs of their ancestors'.[19] Thus, no sooner had the news of the revolution in Vienna reached Milan, on 17 March, than Cattaneo drafted a programme for a newspaper to be entitled *Il Cisalpino*, a choice that accurately reflects his persisting preoccupation, not with the Italian Peninsula as a whole, but with Lombardy-Venetia, or with the former Kingdom of Italy. In this document, 'Arms and Liberty for all the Nations of the Empire, each within its own Borders', Cattaneo celebrated the growing awareness of Poles, Italians, Czechs, Magyars and Croats that they each had their own languages, and therefore their own identities.[20]

Cattaneo's programme, vague though it may have been, rested upon a federal restructuring of the Empire, precipitated by declarations of alliance between the subject peoples. The latter would suspend financial payments to

Vienna, and withdraw their troops inside their own borders, so that 'each ...
would be master in its own house, and all ready to defend themselves against
the common enemy'.[21] Lest Cattaneo's stance in these months should strike
the reader as eccentric, or utopian, I hasten to add that it was not so markedly
dissimilar to that of the Slavic Congress whose delegates, meeting in Prague
in June, were wary of Germanic notions of primacy and regarded the
Imperial structure as a safeguard against them. Cattaneo was much concerned
with the liberties of the Southern Slavs, in fact, and his sympathy towards
them contrasts favourably with the deplorable opinions in this period of
Friedrich Engels, or with the cynical *Realpolitik* of Cesare Balbo.[22]

Notwithstanding his temperamental aversion to revolution, Cattaneo
played a leading part in the *Cinque Giornate* as a member, with Enrico
Cernuschi and other radicals, of the hurriedly constituted War Council. Taken
by surprise in March 1848, Cattaneo saw that the pacific improvement of
Lombardy-Venetia was no longer possible. Besides, he was astonished, and
much heartened, by the courage and tenacity of the Milanese insurgents, and
his political understanding was dramatically transformed by the experience.

To begin with, it must be grasped that the uprising, the sole instance of a
large-scale armed struggle in the spring of 1848, though led by middle-class
radicals and democrats, was prosecuted by a rank-and-file of urban artisans
and workers. In addition, the Lombard peasantry, contrary to the expectations
of the Austrian authorities, played a crucial role.[23] It was no doubt inevitable
that so drastic a radicalisation of the population at large should give rise to
serious differences of opinion between those who, during the withdrawal of
the occupying army, claimed to be in control of Milan and Lombardy. Thus,
the War Council could not see eye to eye with the *Congregazione municipale*,
which was dominated by moderates and which had constituted itself as the
Provisional Government on 21 March. Being much alarmed at the extent of
popular involvement in the uprising, which presaged 'anarchy' or 'Jacobinism',
the moderates sought to limit it by any means possible. The War Council spoke
of volunteer militias from various states in the Italian Peninsula and some
patriots, both in Milan and elsewhere, hoped that the armies of the French
Second Republic might also intervene. In manœuvring to pre-empt such
dangerous schemes, the Milanese nobility, who controlled the Provisional
Government, were naturally driven to make common cause with the
Piedmontese Court. For Charles Albert, being similarly alarmed, and mindful
of what might be gained by swift military action against the Austrians, invaded
Lombardy on 24 March. A week later, Cattaneo and his associates on the War
Council resigned.

In strictly military terms, Piedmontese intervention was to prove a catastrophic failure and Charles Albert, having lost the Lombard cities one by one,
surrendered to the Austrians on 5 August 1848. Cattaneo, with Cernuschi and
others, had made some desperate attempts to organise volunteer forces but,
judging it at last to be a lost cause, fled to Lugano, and to a political exile that
was to continue for the rest of his life. Notwithstanding the harsh words he

had exchanged with Mazzini in Milan three months earlier, he was now willing to collaborate with him, and therefore to sit on the Committee for National Insurrection formed in order to prosecute the war with Austria. Both men were disgusted by Charles Albert's ignominious retreat.[24] Since France was formally pledged to come to the aid of free peoples, Cattaneo now agreed to form part of a delegation, predominantly Mazzinian in composition, to Paris, in order to plead the Italian cause. With hindsight, we can judge that they would have been better advised to consider more closely the impact of the June Days upon the policies of the Second Republic, for their remonstrations came to nothing. Nonetheless, Cattaneo's mission to Paris was of great importance in the development of his own political thought, since it was there that he wrote and published his first analysis of the uprising in Lombardy. This French text, which had been intended to serve as a counter to pro-Piedmontese propaganda in Paris, was later redrafted at greater length in Italian. Subsequently, between 1850 and 1855, Cattaneo supervised the publication of the *Archivio triennale*, a compilation of documents and commentaries concerning Italy's 1848 (which Cattaneo, like many present-day historians, conceived of in terms of the three-year span running from the election of Pope Pius IX to the fall of Venice in 1849). Let me repeat, however, that although there is a scholarly consensus that Cattaneo's mature federalist doctrine was elaborated in the course of preparing these texts for the press, the later formulations can only be understood in relation to the major essays of the 1830s and 1840s.

Nation and federation in Italian historiography, 1815–48

A historian concerned with the fate of the European nations in the early nineteenth century had no choice but to refer to the legacy of the French Revolution, whether to celebrate it or to condemn it, for the Revolutionary and Imperial armies had shown how conquest re-shapes the culture of invaded peoples. After the Restoration, there was a risk in France itself that the changes effected during the previous two decades would be wholly repudiated and even reversed. In such dire circumstances, when the threat of 'White Terror' was very real, historians such as Augustin Thierry mounted a cogent defence of the Revolution. Already, in the Third Estate pamphleteering of 1788–9, there had been a strongly marked opposition between Romano-Gallic and Frankish liberties, between the settled inhabitants of the nation and the Germanic invaders, between trade and industry, on the one hand, and violence and barbarism on the other.[25] The notion of a persisting division between invaders and invaded had lost nothing of its power to fascinate in the intervening years, but had rather been enhanced by observations of the more recent impositions by force of customs, languages and law-codes. German historical scholarship, especially in the field of law, was inspired by such concerns, while in France, Augustin Thierry, adapting the thesis of the Count de Montlosier to his own purposes, admitted in 1816 that there was not one nation but two, each haunted by wholly different memories. He first applied the two-race theory, as it was sometimes known, to England, and to the centuries after the Norman conquest, later transposing his fervent identification with the defeated Anglo-Saxons to the Gallo-Romans in France. The Gallo-Roman cities then served as heroic ancestors to the insurgent Third Estate of 1789; they had been islands of trade and manufacture in a sea of barbarism and sloth, and had clawed back their independence from the feudal aristocracy and from the Capetian monarchs.[26]

Thierry deeply influenced Cattaneo, who wrote lengthy reviews of the books on the Norman conquest and on the history of the Third Estate, and whose celebrated essay on the city belongs in some respects to the same historiographical tradition. Furthermore, in March 1848, when the Milanese nobility were advocating the fusion of Lombardy with Piedmont, he protested in terms that would have been only too familiar to Thierry: 'Sires, *reigning houses are invariably foreigners*. They do not wish to belong to any nation; they follow their own interests, and are always disposed to conspire with foreigners against the people'.[27] However, in order to recover the texture and detail of the historiographical controversies of the period, and at the same time to retrace the process by which they were transmitted from Paris to Milan, I propose to follow in the footsteps of Alessandro Manzoni, a celebrated poet and novelist but, in addition, a historian of Lombard Italy. Manzoni has sometimes been said to be the founder of the neo-Guelph school of historiography, but this is not, strictly speaking, the case, for he did not subscribe to the central tenets of that school. The neo-Guelph historians set out, as their name suggests, to vaunt the role of the Papacy in medieval Italy and, in particular, to mount a defence of its temporal powers, in which Manzoni, by contrast, did not believe. The central claim of the school was that the Papacy, as an institution, had fostered, not hindered, the cause of national unity. Indeed, one of the most prominent of the neoguelph publicists, Vincenzo Gioberti, the author of *Del primato morale e civile* (1843), even proposed that the Pope might in the nineteenth century serve as president of a future Italian federation, although Cesare Balbo judged this ill-advised. For a time, from June 1846 to April 1848, Pope Pius IX appeared a plausible candidate for the role. With his recantation, the neoguelph cause was shattered, and most moderates abandoned federalism, entrusting their hopes to Piedmont and its army instead. In the Italian Peninsula, federalist ideals were, after 1851, the almost exclusive preserve of a small number of democrats, Cattaneo among them.

Manzoni had himself been resident in Paris under the First Empire, and on very close terms with the surviving idéologues, in particular Cabanis, until his death in 1808, and Claude Fauriel, a brilliant linguist and historian, an inspiration to Thierry, Guizot and many others, and the author, also, of a *History of Gaul under the Domination of the German Conquerors*. Upon his return to Paris, in 1819–20, Manzoni met Thierry and was able to read the *Letters on the History of France* as they were published in the liberal newspapers. A matter of months later, he wrote from Milan to Fauriel informing him that he was already at work on a tragedy, *Adelchi*, concerned with the fall of the Lombard Kingdom in the eighth century.[28] To the tragedy Manzoni attached a discourse on Lombard history in Italy.

In Manzoni's discourse, a closely argued work of historical scholarship, we find a reiteration of Thierry's two-race theory, applied now to Cisalpine Gaul.[29] This posed a direct challenge to authors with Ghibelline sympathies, some of whom had argued that, by the time Charlemagne invaded the Italian Peninsula, Lombards and Italians were a single people. These publicists – from Machiavelli, in the sixteenth century, to Romagnosi, in the nineteenth – had, so to speak, backed the Lombards, and had believed that Pope Hadrian I's plea to Charlemagne to invade had consolidated a fatal division in the Peninsula, ravaged in later centuries by the Guelph and Ghibelline factions. Romagnosi was less concerned, however, with the Lombards than with the fate of the cities. Endorsing Edward Gibbon's view that there had been some continuity of good government, at least at the level of the municipalities, under the Flavian and Antonine Emperors, Romagnosi stressed the survival of the spirit of Roman law despite the barbarian invasions. Furthermore, the new religion of Christianity had not invented, but had rather transmitted, the principle of equity, and its priesthood, a '*clero depositario*', deserved a historian's praise chiefly because a precious culture and language had been in its safekeeping. It was not so much that Rome had served as an unknowing instrument of the Christian faith; it was rather that ecclesiastical institutions had ensured the survival of Roman law.[30]

Romagnosi maintained that the Lombards had been 'generous' enough to permit the defeated population to live under Roman law, with some access even to their own magistrates, whereas Manzoni insisted, with Vico as his authority on nomadic mores, that generosity and mercy were not the sort of qualities to be found in a barbarian camp.[31] By the late 1830s, the neoguelph historians, Cesare Balbo and Carlo Troya, were agreed that municipal liberties had indeed not survived the Lombard invasions, and that bishops and popes had been the sole protectors of the people.[32] As regards the Papacy, I would once again draw a contrast between Manzoni, who saw the popes as merely repositories of the Word, offering the hope of 'a little more justice in the world' and, for example, Cesare Balbo, who commented again and again upon the role of Gregory the Great, Gregory II, Gregory VII, 'the greatest confederator of cities', and Alexander III, who assisted the Lombard League of the twelfth century in the wars against Frederick I, Barbarossa.[33] Yet Balbo and Gioberti only spoke of city self-government in order to subordinate it to the church, the nation and God. Their commitment to federalism was therefore instrumental, and did not long survive the setbacks of 1848–9, whereas that of Cattaneo was reinforced and enhanced.

Federation and nation in the thought of Carlo Cattaneo

Like Romagnosi, Cattaneo generally pitched his argument at once at a higher, and at a lower level, than that of the nation. At the higher level, there was a principle of equity identified in his historiography with Roman law; at the lower level, there were the cities, or even the *comuni*. Critics have expressed some scepticism about a principle that in the 1830s found its embodiment in the Hapsburg Empire, but here I simply wish to emphasise the presupposition that right is not equated with a given state or territory, but transcends them.[34] At the lower level, when defending local, communal liberties, Cattaneo excoriated the centralising tendencies of Ludovican, Jacobin and Imperial France, reserving his deepest contempt for the prefectorial system. Indeed, he favoured the forms of local governance established in Lombardy and Venetia by Maria Theresa in 1755 (and re-introduced, with some modifications, in 1816) to those derived from French tradition, imposed upon the Kingdom of Italy in 1804–5, and upon united Italy by Piedmont-Savoy in 1859–60.[35] The *comuni* were the foundation of liberty and, as such, should not be reshaped at a legislator's whim. Cattaneo was thus resolutely opposed to the legislative proposal, advanced in 1864, that all communes with populations of less than three thousand should be amalgamated with other, larger units.[36] Such a vision of local government in Lombardy may well have been idealised, and yet, as Adrian Lyttelton has noted, the defeat of those who, like Cattaneo and Minghetti, had argued for regional representation and for a greater devolution of powers was to have a deleterious effect in the long term upon Italian liberalism.[37]

Cattaneo's cardinal belief was that liberty – to run one's own affairs and to think one's own thoughts – should never be forcibly (prematurely) concentrated but should always be, so to speak, diffused, so that variety might flourish in a multiplicity of places. His writings on education, like his political texts, are thus predicated on the view that specific institutions should assume responsibility for particular kinds of scholarly or scientific enquiry, so as to address the features, geological or agricultural, of a given region. For example, hydraulic engineering ought plainly to remain a speciality of the University of Pavia, which trained those who managed the complex irrigation systems of the Po Valley:

> The principle required for the Italian faculties is thus what in political economy is known as the *division of labour*, and in chemistry as *analysis*. The synthesis will be Italy. The synthesis is not repetition, and it is not uniformity; but it is the simplest expression of the greatest possible variety.[38]

As Bobbio has noted, Cattaneo's federal politics was a direct expression of his inductive method: where distinctions were annihilated, unity was spurious.[39]

Bobbio's point is borne out by Cattaneo's historical and linguistic writings, which seem designed to reveal ever more peoples, or ever more languages (and dialects) in any given place. He in fact jettisoned much of the Romantic metaphysics of conquest, noting that Thierry, in his account of the Norman invasion of Britain, '(saw) the Anglo-Saxons solely as a conquered people, and...therefore neglected the part that they had earlier played, and cruelly, as conquerors'.[40] In conquest, nation was not pitted against nation; there were not two peoples in eleventh-century England, but three, or four, or five. The Angles, the Saxons and the Danes, being 'a military, landowning caste and therefore not very numerous', were not the sole inhabitants, and the English language did not arise simply out of a combining of Anglo–Saxon and Norman French. If, in fact, you were to remove all Latin or French elements from modern English, what remained would not be purely Anglo–Saxon but would be profoundly marked by earlier, Celtic languages.[41] Likewise, in the case of Italy, the Romans may have drawn the veil of Latin across the whole Peninsula, and the islands too, 'but even today the original nationalities are perceptible in our dialects'.[42]

It is worth reflecting upon Cattaneo's notion of the original nationalities, both because his use of classical ethnography differs so markedly from that of most German scholars of the period, and because it draws our attention to the fact that he entertains, as a historian, three different concepts of the nation. There are, first of all, the original nationalities or, in Vico's terms, first barbarism. Here, in earliest Europe, each people was a wholly separate, unconquered entity, speaking its own language. The beginnings of humanity were thus comparable to the situation in the Caucasus, geologically and geographically enclosed, with a startling number of different languages; or in the Sudan; or in pre-conquest North America.[43] Second, there are the national identities created in the aftermath of the barbarian invasions of the fifth and sixth centuries or, once again in Vico's terms, 'returned' barbarism (although Cattaneo, it should be emphasised, like Romagnosi, rejected the idea of a complete *ricorso*). These invasions, I need hardly add, loomed large in the literature of romantic nationalism. Third, there is the principle articulated by Sieyes in 1789, and transmitted to Europe in the succeeding decades by the Revolutionary and Napoleonic armies, with patriots in the conquered territories being fired at first by emulation and then by antagonism.

Where Cattaneo respected this threefold distinction, romantic nationalists tended to conflate two, or even all three of the historical moments at issue. They would, for example, run together early Germanic society (itself often a haphazard amalgamation of the world of Arminius, as described in the *Annals*, with the, in part, earlier ethnographic materials contained in the *Germania*), the barbarian invasions and the German Wars of Liberation (1813–14). The spirit of a nation was thus, being divinely guaranteed, eternal. A tiny tribe in the forests was already the nation it would be. A great nation was still the vigorous and warlike tribe it had once been. It was to capture such a state of mind that I used the term 'tribe-nation'.[44] But nations, Cattaneo protested, 'do not proceed as if they were whole, deductive, continuous systems'.[45] He was particularly caustic, therefore, about 'the great transmigration of peoples'. It was absurd to imagine, as Friedrich Schlegel had done, that the Greeks, Celts, Germans or Slavs had come out of Asia 'as already well-formed nations', and it was yet more preposterous to suppose that they might have brought a metaphysics of the infinite with them, or the spirit of Gothic architecture.[46] The nations of the nineteenth century were 'historical combinations occurring in Europe,…through the addition of successive grafts to ineradicable trunks…'.[47] Likewise, in the context of the barbarian invasions, Cattaneo's analytic dismantling of fifth- and sixth-century communities into their constituent elements – invading military aristocracies, their retinues, serfs on the land, city dwellers, each fragment in a specific relation to the overriding facts of law, the Christian religion and the Latin language – altogether wrecks the teleological claims of the advocates of national primacies.[48]

The distinction between the 'original' nationalities, known to us only through the archaic sounds of a dialect, and the principle of nationality formulated for the modern age by Sieyes, would thus seem to be absolute. Indeed, the rise of an Italian national sentiment in Austrian Lombardy-Veneto is defined by Cattaneo, in sensist terms borrowed from the idéologue, Destutt de Tracy, as an entirely contingent clash of I and not-I.[49] Interpretations of geology are a crucial index in this period of fundamental beliefs as to the destiny of nations, and in this regard the contrast between Balbo and Gioberti's famous tracts of 1843–4 and Cattaneo's study of Lombardy is very revealing. Thus, for the neo-Guelphs, even the geographical location of the Peninsula was providentially guaranteed, whereas for Cattaneo the irrigation systems of the Po Valley were, above all else, testimony to human 'acts of intelligence'. In later years he also derived some pleasure from the fact that Canton Ticino, his place of exile, was geologically and geographically – through the river system – a part of Lombardy, but politically a part of the Helvetic Federation.[50] This seems to me to be as eloquent an example as you could wish of Cattaneo's rejection of the romantic myths of the tribe-nation.

At the risk of blurring lines of interpretation advanced above, I want to conclude with a few general observations, each of which needs to be developed at length. Norberto Bobbio once remarked that Cattaneo was an 'Enlightenment thinker reborn in the age of historicism, but in certain respects a genuine Enlightenment thinker nonetheless', an elegant formula that, to my mind, does not altogether resolve the questions it raises.[51] We need, in fact, a clearer understanding of the romantic aspects of his thought, which indubitably exist, and I think that Ferruccio Focher is right to maintain that study of his work as a historian would supply the key.[52]

Second, it would be misleading to suggest that Cattaneo was wholly unmoved by his generation's fervent belief in nationality. After March 1848, he had lost much of his scorn for Mazzini's *Giovane Italia*, for example, and by 1850 he was prepared to state that 'God, who produces one thought a century, entrusted our own with seeing to it that every nation has a land of its own, and placed the sacred boundary-markers of its fatherland where the sound of its language dies…'.[53] The positing of an equation between nation, language and territory, the latter even emblazoned, in the concluding part of this same passage, with the traces of ancestral battles, seems almost to return Cattaneo to the category from which I have tried to rescue him. I think it must in fact be accepted that Cattaneo himself did not always keep his three concepts of nationality separate. Furthermore, there was, as Timpanaro acknowledges, a trace of *boria nazionale* in Cattaneo's celebration of early Etruscan civilisation and in his denigration of the Germanic and the Celtic.[54] Italy and the truly progressive, so to speak, intelligent city, the city fostering intensive agriculture in the *contado*, seem at points to be one and the same. There may, then, be no tribe-nation in the souls of Italians but the city had for millennia been their glorious inheritance. From Cattaneo's exposition, you could, for example, suppose that England's agricultural revolution in the eighteenth century was modelled wholly upon the example of Lombardy and Tuscany so much does he scale up Adam Smith's words of praise for their achievements in the *trecento* and the *quattrocento*.[55] For Cattaneo was much concerned with Italy's late industrialisation, and with the need to instil in his compatriots a spirit of emulation. Passages therefore exist in which the polycentric quality of his historiography is threatened, but they are the exception not the rule. For, in the last analysis, Cattaneo valued the federal principle more highly than he did the principle of nationality, since the former could not, in his view, effect the extinction of liberty, whereas the latter evidently could.

Notes

1 M. Tyler, *The Forgotten Solution: Some Interpretations of Federalism in Piedmont and Lombardy before 1850*, Cambridge, Ph.D., 1985.

2 N. Bobbio, 'Della sfortuna del pensiero di Carlo Cattaneo nella cultura italiana', in *Una filosofia militante; studi su Carlo Cattaneo*, Turin, Einaudi, 1971, pp. 182–209; N. Bobbio, 'Carlo Cattaneo nel primo centenario della morte', in *Paragone; letteratura*, 1973, pp. 8–9.

3 Francesco de Sanctis, for example, almost wholly neglected Cattaneo, both in his famous history of Italian literature and in his historical and political writings.

4 On the reprinting of the essay, see G. Armani, 'Un editore novecentesco di Cattaneo: G.A. Belloni', in *Notizie su Carlo Cattaneo*, Rome, Archivio Trimestrale, 1987, pp. 169–97. Luigi Ambrosoli, *Tutte le opere di Carlo Cattaneo*, Mondadori, 1967 and 1974 (henceforth *TLO*); Delia Castelnuovo Frigessi (ed.) *Opere scelte* Turin, Einaudi, 4 vols, 1972, (henceforth *OS*).

5 See C. Cattaneo, letter to Carlo Tenca, October 1858, in R. Caddeo (ed.) C. Cattaneo, *Epistolario* (henceforth *E*), Florence, Comitato Italo-Svizzero per la Pubblicazione delle Opere di Carlo Cattaneo, 1954, vol. 3, p. 82; and Tenca, letter to Cattaneo, 12 December 1858, *E*, vol. 3, pp. 548–50.

6 See F. Della Peruta, 'Discussioni e lotta di tendenze nella democrazia italiana', in F. Della Peruta (ed.) *I democratici e la rivoluzione italiana*, Milan, Feltrinelli, 1974, SC/10, pp. 179–250.

7 His unqualified belief in individual liberty stemmed from his commitment to unhindered scientific enquiry. Where Alessandro Levi, in *Il positivismo politico di Carlo Cattaneo*, Bari, Laterza, 1928, p. 1, wrote of Cattaneo as having two vocations, a love of science and a love of liberty, it is probably more accurate to treat them as one and the same, a position adopted by Levi himself in other passages from the same study.

8 For example, P. Ginsborg, *Daniele Manin and the Venetian Revolution of 1848–49*, Cambridge, Cambridge University Press, 1979.

9 For Cattaneo's own judgements on this period, see *Considerazioni (sulle cose d'Italia nel 1848)* (1850), *OS*, vol. 3, pp. 285–6.

10 Consider, for example, the light shed by Carlo Moos on the years of exile in Canton Ticino, *L' 'altro' Risorgimento; L'ultimo Cattaneo tra Italia e Svizzera*, Milan, Franco Angeli, 1992.

11 C. Cattaneo, *Archivio triennale delle cose d'Italia dall'avvenimento di Pio IX all'abbandono di Venezia*, TLO, vol. 5, t. 1, p. 296.

12 F. Focher, *Cattaneo storico e filosofo della storia*, Cremona, Annali della biblioteca statale e libreria civica di Cremona, 37, 2, 1987, p. 27.

13 C. Cattaneo, *Notizie naturali e civili su la Lombardia* (1844), *OS*, vol. 2, p. 373.

14 N. Bobbio, 'Stati uniti d' Italia' (1945), in *Una filosofia militante*, pp. 25–6.

15 C. Moos, *L' 'altro' Risorgimento*, pp. 148–52.

16 C. Cattaneo, *Interdizioni israelitiche* (1836), *OS*, vol. 1, pp. 134–5.

17 C. Cattaneo, *Considerazioni*, *OS*, vol. 3, p. 288; *Notizie*, *OS*, vol. 2, p. 454.

18 C. Cattaneo, *Dell'insurrezione di Milano nel 1848* (January 1849), *OS*, vol. 3, pp. 22–3.

19 Ibid. pp. 19–20.

20 Ibid. pp. 3–7.

21 C. Cattaneo, letter of 15 October 1848 to Giuseppe Mazzini and Francesco Restelli, *E*, vol. 1, p. 303.

22 R. Rosdolsky, *Engels and the 'Nonhistoric' Peoples: The National Question in the Revolution of 1848*, translated by J.P. Himka, Glasgow, Critique, 1987.

23 F. Della Peruta, 'I contadini nella rivoluzione lombarda del 1848', (1953), in *Democrazia e socialismo nel Risorgimento*, Rome, Universale, 1973, pp. 66, 82–106.

24 G. Mazzini, 'Agli Italiani', c.12 August 1848, in T. Grandi, A. Comba (eds) *Scritti politici di Giuseppe Mazzini*, Turin, Unione Tipografica – Editrice Torinese, 1972, pp. 576–81.

25 E. Sieyes, 'Qu'est-ce que le Tiers Etat?', in *Oeuvres de Sieyes*, Paris, EDHS, 1989, vol. 1, pp. 10–11.

26 J.N.A.Thierry, 'Sur l'affranchissement des communes' (1820), in *Dix Ans d'Etudes Historiques*, Paris, Calmann-Lévy, 1884, *Oeuvres complètes*, vol. 3, pp. 572–5.

27 C. Cattaneo, *L'Insurrection*, TLO, vol. 5, t. 1, p. 985.

28 A. Manzoni, letter of 17 October 1820 to Fauriel, in A. Chiari and F. Ghisalberti, *Tutte le opere*, Milan, Mondadori, 1963, vol. 7, p. 215.

29 C. de Sainte-Beuve, 'Claude Fauriel', *Portraits Contemporains*, Paris, Calmann-Lévy 1888–9, 5th edn, vol. 4, pp. 217–20.

30 G.D. Romagnosi, 'Dell'indole e dei fattori dell'incivilmento con'esempio del suo risorgimento' (1829–32), in E. Sestan (ed.) *Opere di Romagnosi, Cattaneo, Ferrari*, Milan and Naples, Mondadori, 1957, p. 155.

31 A. Manzoni, *Discorso storico sulla storia Longobarda* (1822), *Tutte le opere*, vol. 4, pp. 222–3.

32 For example, C. Troya, *Della condizione dei Romani vinti de' Longobardi*, Milan, 1844, 2nd edn, p. 1, pp. 35–7; C. Balbo, 'Appunti per la storia delle città italiane fino alla istituzione dei consoli' (1838), in E. Cangini (ed.) Cesare Balbo, *Scritti storici*, Rome, 1967, p. 264.

33 C. Balbo, *Delle speranze d'Italia*, (1844), Milano, Dante Alighieri, 1930, p. 35.

34 U. Puccio, Società civile, società politica e modello ideologico in Cattaneo', in C.G. Lacaità, *L'opera e l'eredità di Carlo Cattaneo*, Bologna, Il Mulino, 1975, vol. 1, pp. 112–13.

35 C. Cattaneo 'Sulla legge comunale e provinciale' (1864), *OS*, vol. 4, pp. 402–3.

36 Ibid. p. 407.

37 A. Lyttelton, 'Shifting identities: nation, region and city', in C. Levy (ed.) *Italian Regionalism*, Oxford, Berg, 1996, pp. 37–8.

38 C. Cattaneo, 'Sul riordinamento degli studi scientifici' (1862), *OS*, vol. 4, p. 339.

39 N. Bobbio, 'Stati uniti d'Italia', pp. 24–5.

40 C. Cattaneo, 'Della conquista d'Inghilterra pei Normanni' (1839), *OS*, vol. 2, p. 3.
41 Ibid. p. 4.
42 C. Cattaneo, 'Vita di Dante di Cesare Balbo' (1839), *OS*, vol. 1, pp. 319–20.
43 C. Cattaneo, 'Sul principio istorico delle lingue europee' (1841), *OS*, vol. 2, p. 182.
44 M. Thom, *Republics, Nations and Tribes*, London, Verso, 1995.
45 C. Cattaneo, 'Frammenti di storia universale. Prefazione' (1846), *OS*, vol. 2, pp. 563–4.
46 C. Cattaneo, 'Su la lingua e le leggi dei Celti' (1844), in P. Treves (ed.) C. Cattaneo, *Scritti Letterari*, Florence, Le Monnier, 1981, vol. 1, pp. 217–18.
47 Ibid. p. 218.
48 C. Cattaneo, 'Interdizioni israelitiche' (1836), *OS*, vol. 1, pp. 258–60.
49 C. Cattaneo, 'Considerazioni', *OS*, vol. 3, p. 289.
50 C. Moos, *L' 'altro' Risorgimento*, pp. 15–16.
51 N. Bobbio, *Stati uniti d'Italia*, p. 5.
52 F. Focher, *Cattaneo storico*, p. 27.
53 C. Cattaneo, Manifesto for the *Archivio Triennale* (January 1850), *TLO*, vol. 4, p. 772.
54 S. Timpanaro, 'Le idee linguistiche ed etnografiche di Carlo Cattaneo', an essay to which I am much indebted, in *Classicismo e illuminismo nel ottocento italiano*, Pisa, Nistri Lischi, 1969, 2nd edn, pp. 229–83.
55 L. Cafagna, 'Carlo Cattaneo economista militante', in C.C. Lacaità (ed.) *L'opera e l'eredità di Carlo Cattaneo*, Bologna, Il Mulino, 1978, vol. 1, pp. 207–44.

Further reading

There is not very much in English on Cattaneo but Clara M. Lovett has written a useful historical study, *Carlo Cattaneo and the Politics of the Risorgimento, 1820–60*, The Hague, Nijhoff, 1972.

The most helpful biography is now Giuseppe Armani, *Carlo Cattaneo: il padre del federalismo italiano*, Milan, Garzanti, 1997.

Mondadori in Milan launched an edition of Cattaneo's complete works, edited by Luigi Ambrosoli, under the title: *Tutte le opere di Carlo Cattaneo* (TLO) but it appears to have ground to a halt. The two volumes that have appeared are: vol. IV *Scritti dal 1848 al 1852*, 1967 and vol. V (in two parts) *Archivio triennale delle cose d'Italia dall'avvenimento di Pio IX all'abbandono di Venezia*, 1974. However, there now exists a selection of Cattaneo's writings in four volumes, ordered chronologically: Delia Castelnuovo Frigessi (ed.) *Opere scelte* (OS), Turin, Einaudi, 1972. The correspondence has been collected and annotated by Rinaldo Caddeo in four volumes: *Epistolario di Carlo Cattaneo*, Florence, Barbèra, 1949–56, but a new, more complete edition is in preparation. Ambrosoli has also edited Cattaneo's many contributions to the *Politecnico*, under the title *'Il Politecnico' 1839–1844*, 2 vols, Turin, Bollati-Borringhieri, 1989. Other editors have produced more thematic collections, for example Gaetano Salvemini and Ernesto Sestan (eds) *Scritti storici e geografici*, 4 vols, Florence, Le Monnier, 1957; Norberto Bobbio (ed.) *Scritti filosofici*, 4 vols, Florence, Le Monnier, 1960; Mario Boneschi (ed.) *Scritti politici*, 4 vols, Florence, Le Monnier, 1964–5; Piero Treves (ed.) *Scritti letterari*, 2 vols, Florence, Le Monnier, 1981.

Giuseppe Armani has also produced a bibliographical survey of secondary sources: *Gli scritti su C. Cattaneo. Saggio di una bibliografia (1836–1972)*, Pisa, Nistri Licchi, 1972. Norberto Bobbio's collection of essays *Una filosofia militante; studi su Carlo Cattaneo*, Turin, Einaudi, 1971, repays close study, as do a number of different contributions to Carlo G. Lacaità (ed.) *L'opera e l'eredità di Carlo Cattaneo*, 2 vols, Bologna, Il Mulino, 1975.

Part III

The age of the masses

In the late-nineteenth and twentieth centuries, politics ceased to be largely élite-dominated. Through the extension of the franchise (France: 1848; Britain: 1832 and 1886; Germany: 1867; Italy: 1882 and 1912), an increasing number of people participated in the electoral process. Subjects were turned into citizens and the addressees of political parties. More than ever the writing of history was used to legitimate or delegitimate particular governments or regimes.

According to Stuart Jones, the French historian Hippolyte Taine was in the forefront of those who argued that the exclusively political conception of the nation developed by revolutionaries such as Sieyes had strained the relationship between state and society. Jones emphasises three dimensions of Taine's thought: first, his typology of different routes to political modernisation, as implied in his account of the French Revolution; second, his concept of national character, and third, his contention that a reorganisation of civil society would obviate some of the dangers of the transition to a democratic regime.

The chapters on Italy and Germany clearly reveal the extraordinary extent to which the new nation-states, established in 1861 and 1871 respectively, were endorsed and perhaps even constructed by the historical profession. For both historiographies, unification became a stable point from which to view the national past. In Germany historiographical tributes to the House of Hohenzollern and the Prussian state and their role in unifying Germany abounded. Overwhelmingly, German historians accepted the authoritarian social and political order of Prussia-Germany. And yet, as Alistair Thompson argues in his chapter, a significant minority of historians became ever more critical of conservative politics within the Wilhelmine state. Whereas conservative Prussianism was increasingly identified with narrow sectional interests, a growing group of professional historians combined their wish for a more progressive reform of the Reich's constitution with a continued idealisation of the idea of the state. For these historians it was no longer the Prussian state which commanded absolute loyalty; rather it was the Imperial German state. The critique of narrow-minded Prussian conservatism by historians such as Friedrich Meinecke and Hans Delbrück connected with the self-perception of historians as 'above party' guardians of the general interest. Furthermore, they could rely on new public mood expressed in the press and in voting behaviour before 1914.

Mauro Moretti shows how in Italy important works were dedicated to the history of the Piedmontese state and to the House of Savoy. Such works also reinterpreted the period which began with the advent of the *signorie*: no longer was it regarded only as a period of decadence and oppression, but as one of political and territorial reorganisation which led ultimately to Italian unification. Given the inadequacies of these political foundations, however, Italian historians also stressed the cultural and scientific legacy of the peninsular. Nevertheless, the federal tradition, symbolised by Cattaneo, was drowned in the post-unification enthusiasm for historiographic nationalism.

7 Taine and the nation-state

Stuart Jones

In the later nineteenth century, with the advent of mass politics, all states in Western and Central Europe engaged in a process of 'nation-building'. This was as true of those which were new territorial entities as of those which were not. Unable any longer to appeal so easily to hereditary right or to religion or to the power of notables, all set about forging a sense of nationhood to provide a legitimating principle. But 'nation-building' entailed not just an 'objective' process of national integration, but also telling the nation stories about itself; persuading the nation that it had not just come into being. The Third Republic in France was notably vigorous in deploying historiography as an agent of nation-building: the work of Pierre Nora, for example, has made us fully aware of the role played by such 'official' historians as Ernest Lavisse. The version of the nation's past they promoted, notably in Lavisse's famous primary school textbook, was not a narrow or exclusive one: Lavisse's version of national history went out of its way to embrace the contribution of the *ancien régime* monarchy. But the Republic did accord a special importance to the principles of 1789. The new regime presented itself as the true realisation of those principles, which Jules Ferry declared 'the gospel of the Republic'; and jurists asserted the constitutional authority of those principles, as articulated in the Declaration of the Rights of Man and Citizen. Whilst other states typically instituted national holidays on the anniversaries of battles or other crucial moments in national unification, France chose to commemorate the Revolution by selecting 14 July as its great national holiday. The 1880s – the decade when the Republic took shape – saw the creation of the Carnavalet Museum in Paris, devoted to the history of the Revolution, and the institution by the Municipality of Paris of a lectureship (later a chair) in the same subject at the Sorbonne. The commemoration of the centenary of the Revolution in 1889 was crucial in the Republic's resistance to the Boulangist challenge which peaked in that year. Republicans might differ as to their interpretation of Jacobinism and the Terror: the moderate Ferry thought them a deviation from the true and liberal principles of 1789, while the radical Clemenceau would insist that the Revolution must be accepted *en bloc*; but all regarded 1789 at least as sacred.

If it is true that 'in nineteenth-century France historiographical discussion about the Revolution is inseparable from concrete political issues which all the actors have present in their minds',[1] it is ironic that the leading historian of the Revolution during the formative period of the Third Republic wrote from a firmly anti-revolutionary point of view. Hippolyte Taine's *Origines de la France Contemporaine* was generated by the crisis of 1871 and was published in six volumes over the period 1875–94. It thus coincided with the struggles over the legitimation of the republican regime, and it was profoundly shaped by those struggles. The publication of Taine's early volumes coincided with what Daniel Halévy was to call 'the end of the notables' and with the entrenchment of the Republic. Taine's work could hardly be thought other than subversive by a regime which regarded 1789 as sacred, for he had no sympathy for the view that the Terror was in some way a deviation from the true ideals of the French Revolution: for him, the evil had already taken root in 1789. Joseph Reinach accused Taine of questioning the 'moral unity' of the French by undermining the attachment of *les classes moyennes* to the principles of 1789; and Taine's response to Ferry's pronouncement was to confess, 'So I too am heretical, an enemy of modern France.'[2]

Disputed interpretations of the Revolution and its legacy were the stuff of ideological battles between republicans and their enemies. 'That revolution is still going on', declared Clemenceau in 1891, adding that 'always the same men are facing the same enemies'.[3] But Taine's role is interesting precisely because he was not simply reasserting an established position in the 'war of the two Frances'. He was no straightforward reactionary. In philosophical terms, he was a materialist and a determinist, and these heterodox views cost him academic preferment under the Second Empire. In religion he was a non-believer and was at least thought to be an anticlerical. In 1863 Mgr Dupanloup, the scholarly Bishop of Orleans, grouped Taine with Littré, Maury and Renan in his violent denunciation of the 'enemies of religion'; and as leader of the 'clerical party' Dupanloup was instrumental in keeping Taine out of the Académie Française until shortly after the bishop's death in October 1878. He was eventually elected, with right-wing support, the following month. This was just two years after the publication of Taine's volume on *L'Ancien Régime*, the first instalment of the *Origines de la France Contemporaine*; perhaps more significantly, it was just a few months after the appearance of his first volume on the revolutionary period, *L'Anarchie* (March 1878). It was that volume that first began to align Taine with the right in the public mind. But though he was subsequently claimed by historians close to the Action Française as one of the 'masters of counterrevolution', he never really identified himself with the counter-revolutionary right. His account of the *ancien régime* by no means supported Maurras's subsequent thesis that all had gone wrong for France when she turned her back on her past – on 'true France' – in 1789. And whilst a good number of leaders of the counter-revolutionary right were not practising Catholics, they tended at least to embrace the Catholic church as an integral component of Frenchness. They viewed Protestantism as a solvent of organic community and, indeed, as 'anti-France'; Taine, by contrast, rallied to Protestantism as the only defensible form of Christianity in the modern world. Himself brought up a Catholic, he had his own children raised as Protestants, and he received a Protestant funeral. For the counter-revolutionary right, actively to choose Protestantism was far worse than being a lapsed or agnostic Catholic. It is significant that Taine's work was reviewed unenthusiastically by the *Revue des questions historiques*, the organ of the Catholic and royalist school of historiography.

Why did Taine side so determinedly against the Revolution? There are two established explanations of his evolution, neither of which, however, seems conclusive. The first maintains that his outlook was transformed by the experience of the Paris Commune in 1871: first-hand experience of mass politics turned a progressive-minded liberal into a conservative. This would not have been an unusual experience for liberal intellectuals in the nineteenth century, and the Commune was certainly important in the reorientation of Taine's scholarly interests towards French political history; but it did not change his basic outlook on politics. Many of the distinctive undercurrents of his history of the Revolution – contempt for the application of abstract reason to politics, the belief that politics would benefit from the calm application of scientific empiricism, and so on – permeate his earlier works too, and were reinforced by his first-hand acquaintance with England in the 1860s and early 1870s. Indeed, Jacques Godechot has argued, though perhaps not conclusively, that Taine's hostility towards the Revolution was probably present in his thinking from his early days.

The second explanation has its starting-point in the idea that Taine's stance took a markedly anti-revolutionary form only in reaction to the 'Opportunist Republic' that was taking shape under Gambetta and Ferry in the late 1870s and early 1880s. This argument assumes that there is a basic tension between Taine's account of *L'Ancien Régime* in the first two volumes and his subsequent account of the revolutionary period. If the *ancien régime* was as bad as Taine painted it – so the argument goes – then surely the revolutionaries had a point after all. But this whole interpretation is misconceived. First, it was never part of Taine's intentions to argue that all of France's woes could be traced back to 1789. On the contrary, as a determinist who was influenced by Tocqueville, he wanted to stress the continuity with the *ancien régime*, which had begun the process of levelling he so deplored. As he put it in the conclusion to *L'Ancien Régime*, 'at the moment when the Estates-General opened, the course of ideas and events was not only determined, but already visible'.[4] Second, in the plan he drafted in 1871 for a single volume on 'contemporary France', the terms in which he envisaged his chapter on the Revolution were hardly positive:

> Characteristics of the French Revolution, as consequences of the preceding data and of the general character of France. Expulsion of the nobles, confiscation of national property, massacres, successive revolutions,

dictatorship, enthusiasm, abolition of small intermediate societies, levelling in the state, anarchy and ruin.[5]

Setting aside these two accounts, I propose instead to use Taine's intellectual evolution to reflect upon some important questions about the fortunes of French liberalism. What happens to liberal historiography with the advent of mass politics? It is the fact that he straddles the 'two Frances' that constitutes Taine's chief interest, for his work exhibits the demise of the so-called 'doctrinaire' tradition of French liberalism; that tradition which linked Royer-Collard, Guizot and Tocqueville. Taine was clearly influenced by this tradition. He had read the *Histoire de la Civilisation en Europe* as a schoolboy, and Guizot was to be a vigorous promoter of his literary career. He also gave weighty backing to Taine's favourite project of the early 1870s, the creation of the Ecole Libre des Sciences Politiques, which over the next seventy years was to act as an important counterpoise to the sway of democracy in the French state. One of Taine's closest friends from his schooldays was Guizot's son Guillaume; another was Guizot's son-in-law Cornélis de Witt, who served as a centre-right deputy in the 1870s. Tocqueville's influence, meanwhile, was evidently decisive for the formation of Taine's historical project: *L'Ancien Régime et la Révolution* was intended as the first volume in a multi-volume investigation of the origins of contemporary France, and this was the project that Taine brought to fruition. In doing so, he drew heavily on many of the specifics of Tocqueville's interpretation of the *ancien régime*. One example would be his use of the pivotal concepts of centralisation and atomisation, which Tocqueville himself drew from Royer-Collard and Guizot; another would be the notion that the French aristocracy had preserved its privileges at the price of sacrificing its political role.

Yet the central theme in the work of Guizot and Tocqueville had been that the Revolution was explicable in terms of fundamental social change. They were both monarchists, but neither thought that a constitutional monarchist must reject 1789: there was no sound historical reason why 1789, as opposed to 1792 or 1793, should be thought intrinsically republican. Guizot deplored the excesses of the revolutionaries, but recognised that the Revolution was the key event, and a necessary event, in the political modernisation of France. Whatever the evils produced by the Revolution, the counter-revolutionary project was chimerical, since a new kind of society had come into existence. But in Taine, by contrast, we find recurrent echoes of Bonald's view that the Revolution had involved not the replacement of one kind of society by another, but the disintegration of society. 'This was not a revolution, but a dissolution', he wrote of the events of 14–15 July 1789.[6] In Taine as in Bonald we find hierarchy and inequality written into the very definition of what constitutes society. This was the central point – not the claim that society was the product of history rather than of abstract reason, which was by no means sufficient to mark Taine as a man of the right. But how remote from Tocqueville: for him – sympathetic though he might be to the aristocratic principle – the distinctive characteristic of modern society was the growth of equality of conditions. Taine, it should be noted, envied the English model of social and political development; unlike Tocqueville, for whom England had not yet fully undergone the process of social modernisation which all societies faced. Taine admired the way in which England retained a free constitution thanks to the survival of social hierarchy; Tocqueville saw that that was the very reason why England could not serve as a model for France.

This helps to direct our attention towards one of the central issues in the regime-building of the 1870s and 1880s, namely the relationship between state and civil society. The collapse of communism in eastern Europe has revived interest in the idea that the successful functioning of democracy depends upon a strong and robust civil society, which consists of dense and intertwined networks of communication and sociability and an informed citizenry, neither deferential nor defiant, and committed to making public institutions work. But in Taine we find a very different line of argument: one which stresses the role that robust social institutions could play in blocking the excesses of democracy. And Taine was able to construct this argument because he defined civil society hierarchically. He thought that an egalitarian society was by definition an atomised society; this was contrasted with the idea of the organisation of the nation, which meant building upon natural social inequalities. He was one of those thinkers – Lamennais and Le Play were others – whose rehabilitation of 'les corps naturels' could be deployed as a weapon against the abstract republican notion of citizenship. 'True France' was not an assemblage of individuals enjoying equal citizenship rights; it was a 'community of communities', and the component communities were organic bodies with indefeasible rights against the state. The chief influence on Taine's thinking here was neither Tocqueville nor Bonald, but – much more immediately – Ernest Renan, who in a number of key works of the late 1860s and early 1870s explicitly argued that society is a hierarchy. 'A society is strong', declared Renan, 'only if it recognizes the fact of natural superiorities, which in the end are reducible to a single one, that of birth'.[7]

This theme ran right through the *Origines de la France Contemporaine* from the moment Taine first conceived the work. The original conception of the work – and it should be stressed that to embark on a major work of political history was a sharp break with Taine's previous career – was exactly contemporaneous with the composition of his *Notes sur l'Angleterre*, which he composed immediately after his third visit to England, at the time of the suppression of the Paris Commune. Implicitly, Taine's investigation of the origins of contemporary France was a comparative project, whose starting-point was the hypothesis – one might rather say the thesis – that England and France embodied the two great alternative routes to political modernity. He told the Prince Imperial in October 1877 that France had failed to accomplish in 1789 the transformation successfully accomplished, before or since, by her neighbours. 'The structure of France is an anomaly in Europe.'[8] Specifically, his chief claim was that the strength of England's political system rested on her possession of a vigorous associational culture. The chief vice of the French system, he wrote in November 1875, was its suppression or stifling at birth of all associations other than the state.[9] This was the main theme of Taine's discussion of the 'modern regime' that issued from the Napoleonic empire. In the absence of the 'voluntary subordination' that sustained natural intermediate bodies in society, the French people had been reduced to 'an arithmetical sum of disaggregated and juxtaposed units'.[10]

The recreation of a robust civil society – an associational culture not dominated by the state – was a central element in the French liberal programme in the 1860s and 1870s, not least because the liberals of that generation were formed by reaction against the Second Empire. Their programme, as expounded by such men as the Americanist Edouard Laboulaye, featured such objectives as administrative decentralisation, freedom of association, religious freedom and freedom of education – and, perhaps crucially, this last objective included the creation of autonomous provincial universities. But Laboulaye himself thought the question of the form of regime – republic or monarchy – relatively unimportant, and from the 1860s it was becoming acceptable to be both a liberal and a republican. And given the Third Republic's record in extending the powers of municipal councils (1884), in liberalising the press law (1881) and in creating the legislative framework for freedom of association (1884 and 1901), it is by no means obvious why a commitment to administrative decentralisation and a robust associational culture should have turned anyone into a man of the right.

This does raise a general problem about Taine. We know that he sought ways of preventing the oscillation between 'anarchy' and 'despotism' that had, he thought, structured the course of contemporary French history. But why did he not find the Third Republic an appealing means of achieving this end? After all, the Republic was a very moderate kind of regime – an Orleanist regime in disguise, in the eyes of one of its most incisive observers, André Siegfried – and the regime which received a (sort of) constitution from an assembly with a royalist majority in 1875 incorporated a number of institutions that broke with the republican tradition, notably a senate and an indirectly elected presidency, both of which were intended as checks on the supremacy of the popular will. In important respects it remained a most imperfectly democratic regime. So why did it not appeal to Taine?

Perhaps in the 1870s he hoped that it would. His pamphlet on indirect elections and his intimate involvement in the creation of Boutmy's Ecole Libre des Sciences Politiques both located him in the midst of debates about what sort of Republic it should be. His collaborators at the Ecole, though they were mostly conservative-minded liberals, were not on the whole anti-republican. His attitude towards the Republic undoubtedly hardened in response to Ferry's anticlerical legislation: not because he had much sympathy for the Catholic church as such, but because he saw in the legislative constraints on the *congrégations'* persecution of 'free citizens whose sole crime is wishing to live, pray and work together'.[11] It demonstrated the Republic's inability to relax the old Napoleonic stranglehold on associational life. But perhaps one point to stress about Taine is that he was a pessimist who tended to see the worst in his immediate environment. 'Whatever happens in politics, it will be for the worst', he wrote in 1877, in the aftermath of the *seize mai* crisis.[12] He was a lover of authority who found it difficult to accept any particular authority; a sceptic who was constitutionally unable to take sides in the quasi-religious 'war of the two Frances'. He was unable to swallow the cult of the Revolution. He came to depict the Third Republic as a regime that did indeed bring an end to the oscillation between anarchy and despotism, but only by combining what was worst in both. It was the role of the prefects that was central to Taine's argument here. The prefect had become an electoral streetwalker (*un racoleur de voix*):

> When the government sends a prefect from Paris to the provinces, it is in the manner of a great commercial house, to maintain and increase its clientele there, to be the resident guardian of its credit and its permanent commercial traveller, in other words its electoral agent, or still more precisely the head contractor of the next elections for the dominant party, commissioned and appointed by the ministers in office, and constantly urged, from above and from below, to retain their existing votes and win them new votes.[13]

Thus, 'between these two contradictory conceptions, both false, between the prefect of the Year VIII and the democracy of 1792, a compromise had been concluded'. The Third Republic had indeed proved able to bring about a certain political stability; but it was through a synthesis of evils, rather than by correcting France's route to modernisation.

So what, for Taine, was wrong with France's route to modernity? What did he identify as the key component of modernity? Again, a comparison with Tocqueville is appropriate. Tocqueville had defined modernity in sociological terms: the growth of equality of conditions, or 'democracy'. Taine refused this option, and instead defined it in intellectual terms, as the development of the scientific outlook. Thus:

> In this period [1789–1870] there is a general transformation of Europe, of which that of France is only a part. It can be defined by one essential characteristic, which is: the increase and establishment of science by experimental methods, science having an unlimited future, and increasingly acquiring the authority of religion by dethroning it, and expanding into new territories, notably into the whole moral world (history, philology…)[14]

Taine's thesis was that in France the development of science had been deformed by the power of the 'classical spirit' – which we might, perhaps, equate with the Cartesian mind-set. This caused 'science' to be confused with the application of abstract reason to a small number of basic postulates which were taken to be true a priori, so that science in pre-Revolutionary France took the form of 'hasty, ill-formed, aprioristic science'.[15] This had dangerous consequences because, whereas few are scientists, all are endowed with reason: hence, for example, the notion of framing constitutions in accordance with a set of 'rights of man' of supposedly universal validity. Jacobinism could thus be treated as a consequence, even the apotheosis, of the classical spirit: Robespierre developed that spirit 'to its highest point and to an extreme of intellectual sterility which has not been surpassed'.[16] Revolutionary ideas had a special appeal, Taine thought, to men whose classical education equipped them to make logical deductions from abstract propositions, but whose lack of experience of affairs rendered them incapable of grasping the reality of complex social organisms. It was the classical spirit, with its potentially democratic implications, which frustrated the emergence in France of a modern and scientific 'clerisy'. 'From the first to the last sentence of my book', he told Monod, 'that spirit is my only and principal subject.'[17] 'The new France', he was to conclude, 'is the masterpiece of the classical spirit'.[18]

Taine has often been described (though sometimes uncritically) as a positivist; and here he seems to be close to the classic Comtean thesis: that 'modernity' is to be defined by the supersession of theology by science, that all societies need a 'spiritual power' distinct from the temporal power, and that in modern society that spiritual power can only be supplied by scientists. But Comte would have said – and by his lights rightly – that in Taine this 'positivist' thesis is contaminated by 'feudal' residues. That is, Taine was interested in using the spiritual power of science to shore up the social importance of inherited wealth, now that it had been driven out of politics. His chief hope lay not in a counter-revolutionary political project – he was too much of a pessimist for that, which is why it is misleading to claim him as one of the 'masters of counter-revolution', unless that term is understood in a strictly intellectual sense – but in an alliance of brains and birth. As he told Emile Boutmy in July 1877:

> As a general rule, with us as in Switzerland, I see only one function for the upper class in modern democracy: excluded from political command, it can become a secular clergy, a scientific adviser of a higher and independent kind; I see no other future, for a man of good family and wealth, than the cultivation of a science, especially a moral science, the career of our friends the Leroy-Beaulieu brothers.[19]

As founder and director of the Ecole Libre des Sciences Politiques, we may add, Boutmy fully endorsed this point of view; indeed, it underpinned the creation of the Ecole back in 1872. At the time Boutmy told his co-founder, Ernest Vinet, that the abolition of an hereditary upper house and of the property qualification for the franchise threatened to destroy 'the two vital conditions for any progressive society, the empire of the mind and government by the best'. Privilege had been destroyed for good. 'Forced to submit to the right of the most numerous, the classes which call themselves the upper classes can preserve their political hegemony only by invoking the right of the most capable.' The formation of the Ecole – which was aimed at 'the classes which have an established position and the leisure to cultivate their mind' – was thus conceived as part of a project of saving 'the cult of knowledge and the empire of the mind'.[20]

Taine's ambiguity with respect to the Comtean thesis has its origins, I want to argue, in an ambiguous attitude towards modernity. Taine *says* that the rise of science is the defining characteristic of modernity; but in that case why is he so pessimistic about the possibility of checking the advance of democracy? Is he saying that democracy will triumph over science *everywhere* – in which case, what is left of his definition of modernity? Or is he saying that this will occur only in France, where 'science' had taken a perverted form which reinforced (rather than tempering) the rise of democracy?

It was not Taine's belief in intellectual authority that separated him from liberalism. In fact there was an important strand in nineteenth-century European liberalism which insisted on the necessity of 'cultural authority' to social order. It can be found, for instance, in Mme de Staël, in John Stuart Mill, and in Matthew Arnold; and I would argue that it did not undermine their liberalism. What made them liberals was, in a sense, their insistence that in the modern world cultural authority must have new foundations. It must rest with intellect, with science, and not with ecclesiastical or social hierarchy. Taine deserted the liberal cause on precisely these points: he admired the Church of England because it had proved capable of synthesising ecclesiastical authority with modern learning; and he sought, as we have seen, to deploy the power of science to shore up the social authority of notables.

In other words, Taine saw the remedy for the excesses of democracy and state power in an alliance between traditional social institutions and the scientific intellect. This was credible only because he deployed a theory of civil society that was evidently not a liberal theory. The unravelling of Taine's liberalism comes out most clearly if we contrast his understanding of civil society with the account advanced by Ernest Gellner in his book *Conditions of Liberty: Civil Society and its Rivals*. Gellner begins with a provisional definition of civil society as 'that set of diverse non-governmental institutions which is strong enough to counterbalance the state and, while not preventing the state from fulfilling its role of keeper of the peace and arbitrator between major interests, can nevertheless prevent it from dominating and atomizing the rest of society'.[21] But he then goes on to insist on the importance of distinguishing civil society from 'the segmentary community which avoids central tyranny by firmly turning the individual into an integral part of the social sub-unit'.[22] He also draws out the intimate connection between nation–state formation and the development of civil society: 'the rhetoric of nationalism is inversely related to its social reality: it speaks of *Gemeinschaft*, and is rooted in a semantically and often phonetically standardized *Gesellschaft*'.[23] Nation-state formation, entailing as it did the creation of a broad cultural homogeneity, 'the marriage of state and culture', necessarily crushed the organic social sub-units characteristic of segmentary communities. Yet these were precisely the kinds of social organisms that nurtured the 'natural' social authorities that Taine invoked. Having begun by trying to chart two alternative routes to modernity, Taine ended up looking rather like an obscurantist opponent of the modern nation-state itself. He praised the Prusso-German route to modernity under Stein, as an alternative to the French model; but he deplored the introduction into France of two of the defining institutions associated with nineteenth-century Prussia, namely universal primary education and universal military service. He was dismissive of the idea that true authority could be exercised by 'alien officials, removable and transitory': people might accord them 'external obedience', but not 'personal deference'.[24] Like Renan and Le Play, Taine held that authority, to be effective, must feed on the social influence of 'natural leaders'. Their absence in France, due to a historically ingrained suspicion of aristocracies, was the chief cause of the social disaggregation that made centralisation unavoidable.[25]

The real problem with Taine *as a social theorist* is this. As a pessimistic and on the whole rather acute social observer, he was convinced that the sway of numbers was inevitable. But he was not *intellectually* or *theoretically* convinced – by which I mean that he remained attached to a theory of historical change which was essentially intellectualist. He defined modernity in terms of the rise of science; he explained French exceptionalism in terms of the consequences of the classical spirit. Again, the contrast with Tocqueville is pertinent. Tocqueville was deeply attached, as we know, to the aristocratic principle; he was also, like Taine, deeply pessimistic about its prospects in the modern world. But he also had – as Taine did not – an account of long-term historical change which explained this: the central, defining feature of modernity was the growth of social equality. What he saw, therefore, was that the defence of liberty in the modern world must take the form of an egalitarian associational culture on the American model; must take the form of *civil society*. This is precisely what Taine did not see: he continued to look to segmentary community as the only barrier against democratic despotism; and he became increasingly attracted to Le Playist social theory. Hence the paradox that the aristocratic Tocqueville has an honoured place in the lineage of theorists of bourgeois civil society; whilst the bourgeois Taine has been lionised by conservatives and reactionaries from Barrès and Maurras to Robert Nisbet.

Notes

1 François Furet, *La Gauche et la Révolution au milieu du XIXᵉ siècle*, Paris, Hachette, 1986, p. 8.
2 Taine to Gaston Paris, 28 June 1879, in H. Taine, *Sa Vie et Sa Correspondance* (henceforth *Corresp*), 4 vols, Paris, Hachette, 1902–7, vol. iv, pp. 92–3.
3 Pieter Geyl, *Encounters in History*, London, Collins, 1963, pp. 170–1.

4 H. Taine, *Origines de la France Contemporaine* (henceforth *Origines*), 6 vols, Paris, Hachette, 1876–94, vol. ii, p. 315.
5 *Corresp*, vol. iii, p. 298.
6 *Origines*, vol. iii, p. 4.
7 Ernest Renan, *La Réforme intellectuelle et morale* (ed. P.E. Charvet), Cambridge, Cambridge University Press, 1950, p. 36.
8 *Corresp*, vol. iv, p. 39.
9 Taine to Joseph Harnung, 19 November 1875: *Corresp*, vol. iii, pp. 287–8.
10 *Origines*, vol. ix, p. 189.
11 *Origines*, vol. xi, p. 171.
12 Taine to Boutmy, 10 August 1877: *Corresp*, vol. iv, p. 36.
13 *Origines*, vol. x, p. 291.
14 *Corresp*, vol. iii, pp. 313–14.
15 *Corresp*, vol. iii, appendix, p. 306 (early notes for *Origines de la France Contemporaine*).
16 *Origines*, vol. v, p. 26.
17 *Corresp*, vol. iv, 124.
18 *Origines*, vol. ix, p. 220.
19 *Corresp*, vol. iv, p. 32.
20 Boutmy to Vinet, 25 February 1871: in E. Boutmy and E. Vinet, *Quelques idées sur la création d'une faculté libre d'enseignement supérieur*, Paris, Laîné 1871, pp. 14–15.
21 Ernest Gellner, *Conditions of Liberty: civil society and its rivals*, Harmondsworth, Penguin, 1996, p. 5.
22 Gellner, *Conditions of Liberty*, p. 8.
23 Gellner, *Conditions of Liberty*, p. 107.
24 H. Taine, *Notes sur l'Angleterre*, Paris, Hachette, 1872, vol. ii, p. 27.
25 *Origines*, vol. x, p. 290.

Further reading

Hippolyte Taine, *Origines de la France contemporaine*, 6 vols, Paris, Hachette 1876–94. Citations here are from the 23rd edition in 11 volumes.
Hippolyte Taine, *Notes sur l'Angleterre*, Paris, Hachette 1872.
Hippolyte Taine, *Sa Vie et sa Correspondance*, 4 vols, Paris, Hachette, 1902–7.
Charles-Olivier Carbonnel, 'L'histoire dite positiviste en France', *Romantisme*, 1978, nos 21–2, pp. 173–85.
François Furet, *La Gauche et la Révolution au milieu du XIXᵉ siècle*, Paris, Hachette, 1986.
Eric Gasparini, *La Pensée politique d'Hippolyte Taine: entre traditionalisme et libéralisme*, Aix-en-Provence, Presses Universitaires d'Aix-Marseille, 1993.
Ernest Gellner, *Conditions of Liberty: Civil Society and its Rivals*, Harmondsworth, Penguin, 1996.
Pieter Geyl, *Encounters in History*, London, Collins, 1963.
Robert Gildea, *The Past in French History*, New Haven, Conn., and London, Yale University Press, 1994.
Jacques Godechot, 'Taine historien de la Révolution française', *Romantisme*, 1981, no. 32, pp. 31–40.
François Leger, *Monsieur Taine*, Paris, Critérion, 1993.
François Leger, 'Taine historien: "Les Origines de la France Contemporaine"', *Revue philosophique*, 1987, vol. 177, pp. 463–76.
Mona Ozouf, 'Taine', in F. Furet and M. Ozouf, *Critical Dictionary of the French Revolution*, Cambridge, MA and London, Harvard University Press, 1989, pp. 1,011–20.

Regina Pozzi, *Hippolyte Taine. Scienze umane e politica nell'Ottocento*, Venice, Marsilio, 1993.

Ernest Renan, *La Réforme intellectuelle et morale* (ed. P.E. Charvet), Cambridge, Cambridge University Press, 1950.

Edward Shils, 'Nation, Nationality, Nationalism and Civil Society', *Nations and Nationalism*, 1995, vol. 1, pp. 93–118.

8 'Prussians in a good sense'

German historians as critics of Prussian conservatism, 1890–1920

Alastair Thompson

German historians were expected to be apologists for Imperial Germany from its inception in 1871 to its demise in 1918. A university professor was a direct official of the state obliged to show public loyalty and, in Prussia particularly, subject to a strict disciplinary code governing officials' conduct both outside and inside the workplace. Yet for most German historians support for a Prussian-led Germany was less a matter of careerism and conformity than of inner conviction. Their belief in a Prussian model for a German national state started well before German unification and continued after the Empire's collapse. Friedrich Dahlmann (1785–1860) likened the Prussian state to 'the magic spear which heals as well as wounds', whilst his fellow historian and liberal parliamentarian Johann Gustav Droysen (1808–84) looked upon the Prussian bureaucracy as 'the most noble spiritual force in the fatherland'.[1]

The next generation of this predominant Prussian school of historians, spearheaded by Heinrich von Treitschke (1834–96) and Heinrich von Sybel (1817–95), were equally insistent champions of a Prussian-led German state. This was no less the case for the mainstream of the German profession in the period 1890 to 1920. There were, admittedly, shifts in tone and intellectual climate. Only Dietrich Schäfer (1845–1929) became a Treitschke on a smaller canvas. Neo-Rankean historians such as Max Lenz (1850–1932) and Erich Marcks (1861–1938) were certainly less colourfully strident. Yet they diverged little in their interpretation of Prussia's historical mission. Bismarck and the Prussian monarchy, army and bureaucracy remained the unmistakable heroes, the forgers of German unification after the defeat of Jena, and the continuing pillars of the Reich after 1871. Max Lenz's biography of Bismarck, for example, readily concurred with Treitschke's glorification of Prussian leaders and institutions after the Napoleonic era. And readers were clearly invited to identify with Bismarck 'our hero' and to condemn those features of the Reich which contradicted Prussian virtues: 'never-ending quarrelling, the chaos of competing interests', particularism, and confessional sentiment.[2]

Whilst the political activism of the Prussian school was condoned, the failed academic career of the medieval historian Ludwig Quidde (1858–1941) indicated that a fundamental rejection of Imperial Germany was hardly possible within the profession. As a republican, democrat, and pacifist who had originally preferred a 'greater-German' (*großdeutsch*) German unity to the Prussian-led state created in 1871, the Bavarian Quidde directly contradicted the aspects of the German Empire lionised by the Prussian School. His *Caligula*, purportedly a historical sketch of the mad Roman emperor, was easily recognised as a scathing critique of Kaiser Wilhelm II. Its publication in 1894 removed any prospect of an academic career and was condemned as grossly improper across the profession. Although Quidde continued to believe in 'another true Germany' his election to the National Assembly after the 1918 German Revolution proved a false dawn. By the end of 1919 he had again been marginalised, and he was to die impoverished in exile in Switzerland during the Second World War.[3]

If political radicals were excluded from the mainstream of the German historical profession so too were those who sought to challenge the established focus on the political history of the state. Karl Lamprecht, who was no opponent but a keen defender of the German state, was vehemently attacked by German academic historians for putting forward a materialist interpretation of German history. In a similar vein, Werner Sombart's *Modern Capitalism* (1902) was roundly and complacently condemned as an inevitably erroneous product of someone without formal historical academic training. Whilst some historians acknowledged the growing importance and influence of the social sciences – the Freiburg historian Alfred Dove described the period as 'the age of political economy' – new disciplines and insights were generally shunned by the established profession. Otto Hintze, whose work has proved more lasting and influential, was an exception in engaging seriously and productively with sociology and political economy.[4]

Thus the intellectual and political views of historians were constrained both from within and without. Marcks's comment that his favourite student Veit Valentin was too 'multifaceted' (*vielseitig*) to become an established Wilhelmine academic provides a telling, if unintended, insight into the narrowness of this university world, from which Valentin was indeed excluded in 1917.[5] Thomas Nipperdey's conclusion that the German professoriate 'remained a critical body with sufficient – and socially recognised – independence' is excessively generous.[6] It would be erroneous, for example, to see Hans Delbrück, as editor of the *Preußische Jahrbücher* from 1890 to 1919 the most directly political history professor of the time, primarily, as Anneliese Thimme implies, as a 'critic of the Wilhelmine epoch'. The popular Berlin newspaper *Die Welt am Montag* was surely more accurate in regarding Delbrück as essentially a 'conservative or rather governmental man'. In November 1918 Delbrück shunned much of the effusive seventieth birthday celebrations customary in the established middle class not only on account of military defeat, but because with the collapse of Imperial Germany he felt the object of his beliefs had passed away.[7]

Yet if belief in Prussia's historical role, and in the position of university professors as part of a trained and qualified governing elite, retained a powerful purchase, it is important to recognise a growing sense of the need for reform and an erosion of support for a traditional conservative or right-wing National Liberal belief in Prussian domination in the two decades before 1914. I intend first to emphasise competing ideas about Prussia's contribution, and second to present a more nuanced and differentiated view of German historians' attitudes towards the state and popular politics.

Prussia and the Reich

The period of the German Empire undoubtedly saw a growth of belief in the Reich at the expense of a primary attachment to Prussia. It is important to note that this shift can be seen on the right as well as the left. For Baltic-born radical nationalist historians like Johannes Haller and Theodor Schiemann desire for territorial expansion incorporating German populations in the East far outweighed any concern about a dilution of Prussia's position. Even the Conservative historian and public defender of the restrictive three-class Prussian franchise, Georg von Below, was insulted at being called 'below the Prussian' or 'just a Prussian', insisting that he was German first, second and third.[8] And amongst those more open to progressive reform the primacy of the Reich was absolutely central. The liberal imperialism voiced by the left-liberal publicist Friedrich Naumann, and supported and influenced by reformist academics including historians like Friedrich Meinecke, Delbrück, Hermann Oncken and Walter Goetz, was dominated by adherence to the 'idea of the Reich' rather than the primacy of Prussia.

The evolution of Meinecke's politics and writing since 1890 underlines this shift in attitude. From a classic Protestant, Prussian, Conservative background, the small-town son of a government official, he had followed Naumann in rejecting the Conservative Party by the mid-1890s and supporting domestic reform and Liberal-Social Democrat cooperation in the pre-war decade. Although determined not to be considered 'a liberal party historian' his historical work became increasingly critical of Prussian conservatism. In the second volume of his life of Field Marshall Hermann von Boyen, which covered the key years 1815–19, he had discovered 'an eye for the sins of Prussian Junkerdom', prompted in part by left-liberal press reviews of the first volume published three years earlier in 1896. Meinecke's address on the theme of 'Prussia and Germany' to the 1906 Conference of German Historians in Stuttgart and his widely-read *Weltbürgertum und Machtstaat* (1908) both emphasised 'the inner necessity of a development in a unitary direction, of the victory of the idea of the Reich over that of Prussia'.[9]

Whilst there were those, including some Prussian ministers and parliamentarians, who would even have contemplated the downfall of the Reich rather than concede far-reaching reform within Prussia,[10] particularism held little appeal to historians. Academics generally shunned the *Preußenbund*, a small and much derided association founded in June 1913 as rallying point against incipient pressure for reform within Prussia. Whilst identification with the idea and perceived needs of the Reich was the most important source of disquiet about Prussian Conservatism, Prussian-born academics were also influenced by their own experience of living outside Prussia. Meinecke found his Prussianism had been modified and had become more German whilst working in Strassburg and Freiburg universities from 1901 to 1914. The lawyer Gerhard Anschütz, though never the sort of narrow conservative particularist who would think of hoisting the black and white flag of Prussia rather than the black-white-red banner of the Reich, shared the perceptions of Prussian superiority typical of those with a Prussian civil service background. However the social harmony and political cooperation he experienced at Tübingen and Heidelberg rapidly converted him to the belief that it was Prussia that should learn from Southern Germany: 'I saw in this world of south-west Germany foundations, pre-conditions and possibilities of a democratic state form which in Prussia then was not or not yet present, but whose growth increasingly seemed to me to be desirable'.[11] The celebrated sociologist Max Weber was another Prussian believer in the liberal values of south-west Germany. He likened his move to Heidelberg university to 'arrival in clean air' compared to the web of patronage spun by Friedrich Althoff at Prussian universities. Admittedly, the more liberal atmosphere of south-west Germany did not provide a uniform effect. Whilst the religious historian Ernst Troeltsch and Eberhard Gothein, one of the few Wilhelmine historians interested in social, economic and cultural history, like Meinecke, became more progressive, Haller at Tübingen and Below in Freiburg used the greater latitude customary in south-west Germany for a vigorous expression of right-wing politics. The overall pattern, however, was clear. Whilst the late 1870s and 1880s had seen intellectual current flowing away from Liberalism and towards Conservatism the tide had turned by the pre-war decade. Archaic Prussian institutions and particularist interests were not to hinder the development of the Reich. Ironically, whilst Karl Lamprecht's historical methods remained despised, his political attitudes towards Prussia and the Reich were increasingly typical of Wilhelmine historians. He was an ardent patriot who visited the western front shortly before his death in 1915, but he was a patriot of the Reich rather than Prussia.[12]

Historians and the state

Increasing criticism of Prussian conservatism was no reflection of a lack of confidence and attachment towards the Wilhelmine state. On the contrary, reform-minded academics tended to be far more optimistic about the capacity and prospects of the Wilhelmine state than non-political or right-wing colleagues. Take, for example, the vital issue of the challenge posed by burgeoning socialism. Far from feeling threatened by the world's largest labour movement with 34.7 per cent of the vote, 110 of 397 Reichstag seats and 2.5 million members of the free trade unions by 1912, observers like Hans Delbrück and Max Weber had a certainty bordering on the complacent that the Social Democratic leadership and rank-and-file were in practice far less radical than their formal party programme and would easily be incorporated into the state by measured domestic reform. Walter Goetz, probably the most unambiguous and politically active liberal history professor over the Wilhelmine and Weimar period, put forward a prognosis for a more liberal Imperial state in early 1914 remarkable in its optimistic ardour:

> We do not, to be sure, have an ideal liberal state. But today's legally-based and civilised state (*Rechtsstaat und Kulturstaat*) is indeed on the way towards that highest form of which we dream....It is our state whatever its government happens to be. It will grow with us and sink with us. We serve it for our own sakes. A pure anti-liberal party state is no longer possible in Germany today, even where a conservative or clerical majority rules amongst ministers....Thus the task of today's liberalism lies clearly before us: we must regard the modern state as our state; the goal of all our efforts, with whose life we bound up with to the last.[13]

Research on Imperial Germany has continued to differ sharply on the extent and capacity of political reform at the time of the outbreak of the First World War. Verdicts range from a continual process of silent parliamentarisation, to a cul-de-sac of enmeshed institutions incapable of reform. Certainly Goetz's optimism was overstated, just as right-wing perceptions that the Reich was being threatened by alien forces, betrayed by weak leadership and that the Reich office of the interior had become a nest of reds, were inaccurate and unduly apocalyptic.[14] What is germane here, however, is less the accuracy of such sentiments but that they reflected progressive academics' very high expectations of the state and strong identification with it. Such expectations were mutual. Academics in general and historians in particular were called on to participate in public commemoration of the Emperor's birthday, Sedan Day and what seemed an increasingly rapid succession of anniversaries. Celebrations reached a height in 1913, with the centenary of liberation from the French at the battle of Leipzig and the twenty-fifth anniversary of Wilhelm II's accession. Doubtless, 1915, with the 500th anniversary of the Hohenzollerns and Bismarck's centenary, would have led to celebrations at least as extensive had it not been for the war. Hundreds of monuments littered the Imperial German countryside by 1914, and historians could frequently be found on committees for their construction and delivering addresses at their unveiling.[15]

All this emphasised that history professors had a significant and respected public role. Moreover, history was considered important in influencing national identity and attitudes towards state institutions in an Empire established for fewer than fifty years. Hintze's *The Hohenzollerns and their Work*, for example, was commissioned by the authorities to mark the dynasty's 500th anniversary and was distributed across Prussia's secondary schools. Although measured in tone – Hintze rejected Wilhelm II's attempted intervention in its writing – it was unmistakably an act of homage to:

the special political make-up of our people, the strict military and monarchical discipline, which alone had enabled Prussia and Germany, in the middle of the continent, surrounded by strong and often hostile neighbours, to establish an independent existence and achieve respect for Germany's name in the world.[16]

Yet no matter how close the ties between historians and the state, their relations were also problematic. Reverence towards individual representatives of the state could betoken dissonance rather than abject loyalty. Open support for Bismarck in the 1890s was frequently also a criticism of unworthy successors and the Kaiser who had dismissed him. The label Bismarck-Fronde clearly indicated this was far from being an example of German obedience towards authority. Wilhelm II declared, with characteristic poor judgement, that Bernhard von Bülow, appointed State Secretary for Foreign Affairs in 1897 and Chancellor in 1900, would be his Bismarck. Bülow did prove to be another Bismarck, not in statesmanlike achievement, but in proving a thorough nuisance after leaving office. Valentini, the head of the Kaiser's privy civil cabinet, regarded Bülow's historical dabblings with justifiable suspicion. He considered the work *Germany under Wilhelm II* (1913), with which the ex-Chancellor was involved, read more like 'Germany under Bülow'. However, Bülow's attempted rehabilitation found few champions. Haller, supplied with material by Philipp Eulenburg, who had helped Bülow into office only to be abandoned when faced by sexual scandal, vigorously attacked Bülow's record. The slippery chancellor was regarded with no more favour by reformist historians. Part of the contempt that Oncken showed for the 'Bassermann corps' at the head of National Liberal politics reflected disagreement with the blind faith in Bülow and hostility towards his successor Bethmann Hollweg shown by Bassermann. Delbrück, who had resolutely defended Caprivi's policies against the attack of Bismarck's supporters, was equally clear that Bülow's plotting against Bethmann should not succeed.[17]

In the end Bülow's intrigues after leaving office in 1909 did not prove divisive amongst German historians for the ex-chancellor had too few supporters. However the chancellorship of Bethmann Hollweg (1909–17) produced sharp contrasts. Even before 1914 right-wing nationalists and Prussian conservatives were accusing the chancellor of weak and dithering leadership. By the second-half of the war annexationist pressure groups, which had attracted the support of most German academics, were demanding that the Chancellor be replaced by a much-needed strong man. However, Bethmann continued to be defended. Karl Lamprecht, a class-mate, was drawn into public political intervention, albeit largely ineffectual, on Bethmann's behalf. Delbrück's more effective backing was based less on personal attachment, although he did dine with the Chancellor and responded to Bethmann's request for his 1913 work *Regierung und Volkswille*. Moderate reformers like Delbrück and Oncken were not particularly convinced by Bethmann's leadership qualities, but believed in the measured change which

Bethmann's slogans 'politics of the diagonal' and 'new orientation' seemed to promise. The articles Oncken and Delbrück published in the *Quarterly Review* (1910 and 1913) and *Everyman* in 1912 were written in support of Bethmann's aim of an Anglo-German rapprochement which retained scope for German imperialism. Such efforts, like Theodor Mommsen's and Lamprecht's correspondence with James Bryce contemplating how to improve Anglo-German relations after the Boer War, or Marcks's and Oncken's contacts with the USA,[18] showed historians' attempts to act as informal ambassadors, but also their ineffectiveness in this role. For Eyre Crowe, the germanophobe British Foreign Office official, Delbrück remained 'a slim fellow' who was attempting to gloss over the Prussian militarism of the German Empire.[19]

In domestic politics reformist historians' desire to see the labour movement incorporated within the Wilhelmine state generated a very different attitude than the right towards Bethmann's policies. For reformists the acceptance of an assembly for Alsace-Lorraine elected on a broadly based franchise was the opposite of a betrayal of the nation by the Chancellor. They considered the assembly would both increase identification with Imperial Germany inside Alsace-Lorraine and improve relations between the state and the Social Democrats who had been part of the large Reichstag majority for the assembly. Similarly, after 1914, promises of reform to the Prussian three-class franchise, consultation with union leaders and avoiding express support for widespread annexations formed a platform designed to maintain the labour movement's support for the war effort which was shared by Bethmann and historians like Delbrück, Oncken, Goetz and Meinecke, supporters of domestic reform before 1914, together with wartime converts like Friedrich Thimme.[20]

Thus, whilst there was nearly universal support for the Reich idea this did not transpose itself into unquestioning governmentalism. The educated middle class held high expectations of the state as well as strong obligations towards it. Even memorials and monuments should not be interpreted as symbols of Byzantine loyalty towards authority. Some of the support for Bismarck monuments continued to reflect dissatisfaction with weak leadership or the growth of the Social Democrats. Some liberal subscribers to memorials for Friedrich III were mourning the rapid passing of a man who might have led the nation in a more enlightened and constant direction. These were not, it should be stressed, the sole motive behind contributions to monuments. Some subscribers doubtless sought prestige and recognition from state or community. Some Friedrich III memorial donations came from Prussian army officers, not out of sympathy for liberal reform, but from admiration of the crown prince's military role in the wars of unification. Nevertheless, the social momentum behind such memorials, or indeed commemorations by traditional oppositional groups like left-liberals, Catholics and Social Democrats of their own leaders like Richter, Windhorst and Singer, do contrast with the orchestrated attempts by Wilhelm II to have his grandfather venerated as 'Wilhelm the Great'. The Kaiser's campaign may have appealed to the sycophantic and honours-seeking, and led to a series of unimaginative statues of Wilhelm I on horseback, but it failed to generate lasting enthusiasm, or to displace Bismarck in the public mind as the Reich's founder. Indeed, historians' attitudes towards Wilhelm II personally were perhaps final testimony that their attachment was towards a state ideal rather than to the unquestioning obedience presented in Heinrich Mann's novel *Der Untertan*. True, only an outsider like Quidde would risk direct public criticism, declaring that the only value of the description 'Wilhelm the Great' was to distinguish the first Kaiser from a subsequent 'Wilhelm the Small', but after the 1908 *Daily Telegraph* Affair historians' private correspondence, including even an equable conservative like Erich Marcks, increasingly despaired of the Kaiser's fitness to rule. And in 1913, when, tellingly, commemorations of the 1813 uprising generated greater interest than the twenty-fifth anniversary of Wilhelm II's accession, addresses celebrating the latter often highlighted economic and technological advances of the period and the avoidance of war, rather than the personal role of the Kaiser.[21]

Whilst the attachment to the state was undoubted, the period before 1914 only really became a golden age in retrospect, when seen from the perspective of those who had endured the privation and turmoil of the subsequent decade. The Wilhelmine state was still one which could wound as well as heal. The experience of Hans Delbrück exemplified the Janus-faced uncertainty of the Wilhelmine state. No historian had closer ties to the state. Delbrück came from a family steeped in the Prussian civil service. His uncle Rudolf had been a leading minister in the 1870s and his cousin Clemens was Reich state secretary for the interior on the eve of the First World War. Delbrück himself had fought as a reserve officer in the Franco-Prussian war and been the personal tutor to Prince Waldemar, Wilhelm II's brother, from 1874 to 1879. Yet Delbrück twice, in 1895 and 1898–9, found himself facing charges of insulting the Prussian authorities following articles in the *Preußische Jahrbücher*.

Both cases are open to interpretation. It might be argued that in neither was Delbrück punished in the end. In 1895 the charges were withdrawn, and the Kaiser was persuaded to rescind the 500 mark fine imposed on Delbrück by the disciplinary court for officials in 1899. Moreover, on both occasions ministers and officials interceded on his behalf. However, in both cases there was a clear intent to enforce limits on free expression. And whilst some in government felt such disciplinary moves ill-advised and inflammatory, others, including the Kaiser, the Prussian interior and education ministers and the Prussian police, were eager to have Delbrück punished. The 1898–9 case, in particular, must be regarded as a very serious attack on Delbrück, for the state prosecutor demanded his forced transfer from Berlin to another Prussian university. Not only did Berlin far outweigh the other university in terms of prestige and fee income, but a base in the capital was vital to Delbrück's political and publicistic life. Indeed the court itself recognised the particular significance accorded someone 'who holds a history chair at Prussia's greatest university and whose words as a result have a great weight at home and abroad and are capable of substantially damaging the reputation of the Prussian state'.[22]

Ironically, the disciplinary case affected Prussia's reputation much more than Delbrück's original remarks criticising anti-Danish policies in North Schleswig. The case, and the notion that a university might function as a place of internal exile, was widely criticised by the German press, apart from maverick right-wing papers like the *Hamburger Nachrichten* and the anti-Semitic *Staatsbürger Zeitung* which regarded Delbrück as a supporter of socialists and non-Germans deserving of all he got. The foreign press was no more sympathetic towards the Prussian authorities. *The Times* conjured up the image of the 'stigma [resting] upon the seat of learning selected as a kind of penal settlement'.[23]

Did the authorities' actions against Delbrück achieve anything? They certainly did not prevent Delbrück reiterating the points objected to in 1895 and 1898 – that the state was wrong-headed in seeking to suppress socialists and national minorities by police action, discriminatory laws and bureaucratic chicanery. And not only was Delbrück ultimately pardoned, but subsequent disciplinary action was not taken against other Prussian professors for their political comments. Yet the 1899 judgement did emphasise that, although history professors like Delbrück could consider they had a right and even a duty to express opinions in public, and should have more leeway than political officials, their position imposed limits to what they could say and write. Whether the point was of much value, however, is debatable. For Delbrück and other politically active history professors did not dispute that their position brought responsibilities, and that there was a boundary somewhere which should not be crossed. The problem was not one of principle, but practice; of where and how the boundary should be drawn. There was not even agreement between ministers on this, and Delbrück and others continued to assert that the scope should be much wider than the impulsive Kaiser and the more reactionary elements of the Prussian cabinet believed. Delbrück and Lenz, for example, insisted that the state was wrong in removing Leo Arons, a socialist and physics *Privatdozent* from the Berlin university faculty. They argued forcefully that *Privatdozenten*, unsalaried lecturers who relied on fee income, were entitled to pursue any political activity they wished outside the lecture hall and laboratory providing it did not involve direct agitation against the state. The fate of Arons, who was only rehabilitated after 1918 and then essentially symbolically as he was already mortally ill, indicated that the state had the power to prevail in direct conflict with academics and the universities.[24] The same applied to the appointment of Martin Spahn (1875–1945) to a chair in Catholic history at the University of Strassburg in 1901. This action produced a more widespread and condemnatory response from Wilhelmine academics than any before the war. The notion of a confessional history chair was as abhorrent as the imposition against the faculty's will of an insufficiently qualified 25-year-old son of Peter Spahn, a leading Centre Party politician. Conservatives and liberals, activists and the usually non-political united in protest. Yet Spahn's appointment was forced through.[25]

Such incidents undoubtedly raised real passions. Nevertheless they risk projecting a rather distorted image of relations between academics and the state. First, criticism and differences over individual episodes did not over-shadow the ties and mutual expectation between academics and the state outlined above. Second, it would be incorrect to generalise the image of an almighty authoritarian Prussian state imposing itself on powerless academics. On several occasions academics were involved in the successful mobilisation of parliamentary and public opinion against proposed government measures. Zedlitz's 1892 Prussian school bill was warded off, as were attempted repressive measures in the second half of the 1890s, the Anti-Revolution bill, the Penitentiary Bill, and the Lex Heinze. Academic and wider public reaction made the government reluctant to risk repeating episodes like those of Arons and Spahn. The conservative-dominated Protestant church leadership in the supreme church council (*Oberkirchenrat*) may have enraged liberal Protestant opinion by removing pastors Carl Jatho and Gottfried Traub from office in 1911–12, but the Reich political leadership became increasingly concerned to avoid such provocation, urging more traditional conservative colleagues in the Prussian cabinet and field administration not to engage in high-handed and repressive conduct which could only lead to scathing comment in the press and Reichstag. Reformist academics, as Goetz's optimism exemplified, no longer feared repressive measures by the pre-war decade. Though still foolish and impetuous, Wilhelm II's attempted interventions became less frequent after the turn of the century, and he withdrew further after the *Daily Telegraph* Affair. With ever fewer Conservatives, Free Conservatives and right-wing National Liberals – less than a fifth of deputies taken together by 1912 – the Reichstag offered an insuperable barrier to repressive legislation. Even for the Prussian parliament to pass significant restrictive legislation, as had happened with the 'lex Arons' in 1899, was no longer practical, for, as Bülow and his successors recognised, it would wreck relations between the Reichstag and Reich leadership and exacerbate tensions between the Reich and Prussia.

Historians and mass politics

The second-half of the nineteenth century is generally regarded as one in which academics increasingly withdrew from direct political activity. Certainly no academic matched the political importance of *Vormärz* predecessors like Karl Rotteck and Carl Theodor Welcker. And while the Arons and Spahn cases undoubtedly stirred opinion they did not match the political symbolism and resonance of the 'Göttingen Seven', including the historians Dahlmann and Gervinus, who in 1837 refused to obey the King of Hanover's command. The numbers of academics in parliament also declined from a size-able presence in the 1848 Frankfurt parliament to barely a handful of Reichstag deputies by the pre-war decade. Academics and other notables (*Honoratioren*), it has been argued, were largely swept aside by mass mobilisation and populist campaigning which clearly dominated Reichstag electioneering by the 1890s. Not only was the academic world of German history professors becoming increasingly professionalised and time-consuming, so also were the activities of Reichstag politicians making the two roles increasingly difficult to combine. Those in full-time academic posts increasingly considered themselves to be, to use Max Weber's phrase, 'unabkömmlich' (unavailable) for elected office in the national or even state parliaments. Delbrück willingly withdrew from parliament after serving two terms in the Reichstag and one term in the Prussian Chamber of Deputies. He had not, in any event, intended a long parliamentary party career, but rather to make contacts and observe the workings of politics from close quarters. Similarly, Hermann Oncken deliberately spurned the rare opportunity to make an effortless entry into the Reichstag as chairman of the National Liberal constituency party required to select a candidate for the uncontested Heidelberg by-election in 1916.[26]

Even politically engaged academics had, as Eberhard Demm's study of Alfred Weber put it, fractured relations with party politics.[27] Many academics were absolutely determined to remain 'above party'. Max Lenz, sounded out as a prospective chairman by the founders of what was to become the Fatherland Party in 1917, responded in a typical fashion: he was interested only if it refrained from direct opposition to the government and remained a loose-limbed 'Bismarck League' rather than an organised party.[28] Even Delbrück, with extensive political knowledge and a suitably sharp temperament, chose in the first place to join the Free Conservatives, a grouping barely bound by programme and organisation, and later proclaimed that he had become even less a party man with the passing of time. Lamprecht was not only politically inconsistent, engaging with radical nationalists at one stage and pacifists at another, but naive. Bethmann's 1910 bill putting forward limited changes to the Prussian three-class franchise, which termed ministers, professors and others 'bearers of culture', thus saving many of them from the ignominy of voting in lowest class, was hardly likely to be salvaged by Lamprecht's article claiming such moves represented the realisation of 'new ideals'. The great majority was outraged at measures which still viewed 80 per cent of the Prussian electorate as third class, and now intended to label them as uncivilised to boot. Such 'new ideals' were derided, and Lamprecht told to get back to his study, whilst the bill, caught between overwhelming public hostility and conservative intransigence, had to be withdrawn.

There was undoubtedly a sense of detachment, of differing methods and priorities between academics and politicians. Wilhelm Ohr, who interrupted his career as a history *Privatdozent* to become a full-time politician as general secretary of the 'National Association for a Liberal Germany' and left-liberal Reichstag candidate, experienced not only the contrasts between academic and political life, but the difficulties of becoming fully established in either. Reichstag seats and university chairs were hard to obtain regardless of aptitude. And the few that achieved both found the roles difficult to combine. The venerable Roman historian and left-liberal parliamentarian Theodor Mommsen closed his life and career despairing of the German middle classes, whilst the two most prominent academics in the Reichstag on the eve of war, the Berlin criminal law expert Franz von Liszt and Freiburg political economist Gerhart von Schulze-Gävernitz, though maintaining an optimism typical of Naumannites, were largely marginalised within parliament. Yet academic detachment from party politics is easily exaggerated. Parties and party leaders were an increasing area of study. Oncken published biographies of Ferdinand Lassalle and Rudolf Bennigsen. Felix Rachfahl wrote a substantial account of Eugen Richter, and Erich Brandenburg agreed to commemorate the fiftieth anniversary of the National Liberal party in 1917 with a brief party history.[29] More significantly, the press provided an important conduit between academics and politics. Delbrück's commentaries in the *Preußische Jahrbücher* were not just aimed at the journal's 1,600 subscribers. Its articles were discussed extensively in the dailies, as were contributions to Naumann's *Die Hilfe*. When Meinecke wrote political articles for the *Strassburger Post* or the *Breisgauer Zeitung* again these were reprinted and commented on in major papers across Germany.

The press offered academics the opportunity to comment on the major political issues of the day. Their influence cannot be gauged exactly. Nevertheless, direct attacks on Conservative politics, especially over the 1909 finance reform and the Prussian three-class franchise issue, undoubtedly weakened and further isolated Conservative leaders. Historians' criticism of Conservative particularism resonated both because it chimed in with the public mood and because it was being voiced by prestigious figures, often with previous Conservative associations. Like reformist historians, the great majority of public opinion no longer recognised Conservatism as the guardian of good Prussian tradition, but as the proponent of sectional interest. Conservative agrarianism, narrow Protestantism and blocking of reform had threatened to turn Prussia, as Below had discovered, into a label of abuse. Indeed, it is important to recall that Prussia always had had a negative connotation for substantial numbers of Catholics and workers. And for the majority of those who remained positively attached to Prussian virtues, these were the reverse of what Prussian conservatism was now held to represent. The Prussianism believed in by left-liberals like Mommsen and Richter, or by Social Democratic Prussian ministers like Otto Braun and Carl Severing in the 1920s, concerned the achievements of honesty, hard work and frugality, and the contributions these made to the general, not sectional, interest.

Notes

1 Cited in James J. Sheehan, *German Liberalism in the Nineteenth Century*, Chicago, University of Chicago Press, 1978, pp. 39–40.
2 Max Lenz, *Geschichte Bismarcks*, 3rd edn, Leipzig, Duncker and Humblot, 1911, pp. 3–4, 497.
3 Bundesarchiv (hereafter BA) Koblenz, Nachlaß Ludwig Quidde 82; L. Quidde, *Der deutsche Pazifismus während des Weltkrieges 1914–1918* ed. by K. Holl and H. Donat, Boppard, Boldt, 1979.

4 Roger Chickering, *Karl Lamprecht: A German Academic Life (1856–1915)*, New Jersey, Humanities Press, 1993; Friedrich Lenger, *Werner Sombart 1863–1941: eine Biographie*, Munich, C.H. Beck, 1994; Deutsche Staatsbibliothek Berlin, Nachlaß Hans Delbrück (hereafter DSB Delbrück), Below correspondence, Below to Delbrück, 30.7.1903; Alfred Dove, *Ausgewählte Aufsätze und Briefe*, ed. F. Meinecke, 2 vols, Munich, F. Bruckmann, 1925; Otto Büsch *et al.* (eds) *Otto Hintze und die moderne Geschichtswissenschaft*, Berlin, Colloquium Verlag, 1983.

5 Geheimes Staatsarchiv Berlin-Dahlem, Nachlaß Friedrich Meinecke 25, Marcks to Meinecke, 16.1.1910; Hans Schleier, *Die bürgerliche deutsche Geschichtsschreibung der Weimarer Republik*, Berlin, Akademie Verlag, 1975, pp. 346–98.

6 Thomas Nipperdey, *Deutsche Geschichte 1866–1918* 2 vols, Munich, C.H. Beck, 1991–1993, vol. 1, p. 578.

7 *Die Welt am Montag*, 27.3.1899; DSB Delbrück 3 and 4; Anneliese Thimme, *Hans Delbrück als Kritiker der Wilhelminischen Epoche*, Düsseldorf, 1955.

8 M. von Below, *Georg von Below: ein Lebensbild*, Stuttgart, W. Kohlhammer, 1930, p. 123.

9 Friedrich Meinecke, *Erlebtes, 1862–1901*, Leipzig, Koehler and Amelang, 1941, pp. 207–9; Dirk Blasius (ed.) *Preußen in der deutschen Geschichte*, Königstein, Athenäum-Hain-Scriptor-Hanstein, 1980, pp. 49–56; Friedrich Meinecke, *Strassburg, Freiburg, Berlin, 1901–1919; Erinnerungen*, Stuttgart, K.F. Koehler, 1949, p. 42; *Frankfurter Zeitung* 92, 2.4.1915.

10 BA Koblenz, Nachlaß Bülow 105, Mirbach to Loebell, Prussian Interior Minister, 10.2.1915 (copy).

11 Gerhard Anschütz, *Aus meinem Leben*, Frankfurt am Main, V. Klostermann, 1993, pp. 67–70.

12 See the references to Lamprecht in the inaugural lecture of Walter Goetz, his successor at Leipzig, in *Vossische Zeitung* 553, 29.10.1915.

13 Walter Goetz, 'Der Liberalismus und der Staat', *Die Hilfe*, 1914, p. 40.

14 For a discussion of Meinecke's dismissal of these Conservative fears see *Berliner Tageblatt* 61, 3.2.1917.

15 See, for example, DSB Delbrück 28, nos 2–3.

16 Meinecke, *Strassburg*, p. 158; Otto Hintze, *Die Hohenzollern und ihr Werk; fünfhundert Jahre vaterländischer Geschichte*, Berlin, P. Parey, 1915, p. vi.

17 BA Berlin, Reichslandbund R 8034 III, 175, fos. 113–30; Johannes Haller, *Die Aera Bülow. Eine historisch-politische Studie*, Stuttgart, Cotta, 1922; Geheimes Staatsarchiv Berlin-Dahlem, Nachlaß Valentini 13A, fos. 25–26, Loebell to Valentini, 19.11.1913; and Valentini 4, correspondence with Hans Delbrück passim.

18 Rüdiger vom Bruch, *Wissenschaft und öffentliche Meinung. Gelehrtenpolitik im wilhelminischen Deutschland (1890–1914)*, Husum, Matthiesen, 1980, p. 218; DSB Delbrück, Oncken correspondence, passim.

19 University of Edinburgh Library, Sarolea Collection 13; Bodleian Library Oxford, James Bryce papers.

20 Friedrich Thimme (ed.) *Vom inneren Frieden des deutschen Volkes*, Leipzig, S. Hitzel, 1916; Anneliese Thimme (ed.) *Friedrich Thimme, 1868–1938: ein politischer Historiker, Publizist und Schriftsteller in seinen Briefen*, Boppard, Boldt, 1994.

21 D. Sarason (ed.) *Das Jahr 1913: ein Gesamtbild der Kulturentwicklung*, Leipzig, B.G. Teubner, 1913.

22 DSB Delbrück 15.

23 *The Times* 27.3.1899.

24 DSB Delbrück 19; and Arons correspondence.

25 C. Weber, *Der 'Fall Spahn' (1901): Ein Beitrag zur Wissenschafts- und Kulturdiskussion im ausgehenden 19. Jahrhundert*, Rome, Herder, 1980.

26 DSB Delbrück, Oncken correspondence, Oncken to Delbrück, 14.4.1916 and 19.4.1916.

27 Eberhard Demm, *Ein Liberaler in Kaiserreich und Republik. Der politische Weg Alfred Webers bis 1920*, Boppard, Boldt, 1990, p. 310.
28 H. Hagenlücke, *Deutsche Vaterlandspartei: die nationale Rechte am Ende des Kaiserreiches*, Düsseldorf, Droste, 1997, pp. 150–1.
29 Hermann Oncken, *Rudolf von Bennigsen: ein deutscher liberaler Politiker*, Stuttgart, DVA, 1910; *idem, Lassalle: eine politische Biographie*, Stuttgart, F. Frommanns, 1904; F. Rachfahl, 'Eugen Richter und der Linksliberalismus', *Zeitschrift für Politik* 5 (1912); E. Brandenburg, *50 Jahre Nationalliberale Partei, 1867–1917*, Berlin, Kalkhoff, 1917.

Further reading

Chickering, Roger (ed.) *Imperial Germany: A Historiographical Companion*, Westport, Conn., Greenwood Press, 1996.
Fulbrook, Mary (ed.) *German History since 1800*, London, Edward Arnold, 1997.
Hübinger, Gangolf, *Kulturprotestantismus und Politik: zum Verhältnis von Liberalismus und Protestantismus im wilhelminischen Deutschland*, Tübingen, Mohr, 1994.
Iggers, Georg G., *The German Conception of History: the National Tradition of Historical Thought from Herder to the Present*, 2nd edn, Middletown, Conn., Wesleyan University Press, 1983.
Meineke, Stefan, *Friedrich Meinecke: Persönlichkeit und politisches Denken bis zum Ende des Ersten Weltkrieges*, Berlin, de Gruyter, 1995.
Mommsen, Wolfgang J., *Imperial Germany 1867–1918: Politics, Culture, and Society in an Authoritarian State*, London, Edward Arnold, 1995.
Nipperdey, Thomas, *Deutsche Geschichte 1866–1918*, 2 vols, Munich, C.H. Beck, 1991–3.
Ringer, Fritz K. *The Decline of the German Mandarins: The German Academic Community, 1890–1933*, Cambridge, MA, Harvard University Press, 1969.
Schwabe, Klaus, *Wissenschaft und Kriegsmoral: die deutschen Hochschullehrer und die politischen Grundfragen des Ersten Weltkrieges*, Göttingen, Musterschmidt, 1969.
vom Brocke, Bernhard (ed.) *Wissenschaftsgeschichte und Wissenschaftspolitik im Industriezeitalter: das 'System Althoff' in historischer Perspektive*, Hildesheim, August Lax, 1991.
vom Bruch, Rüdiger, *Wissenschaft, Politik und öffentliche Meinung: Gelehrtenpolitik im wilhelminischen Deutschland (1890–1914)*, Husum, Matthiesen, 1980.

9 The search for a 'national' history

Italian historiographical trends following unification

Mauro Moretti

History assumed an important role in the political culture of the Risorgimento. Political forces and figures with different ideals and outlooks were all looking for legitimation and a reference point in the Italian past. As Gioacchino Volpe observed in 1927, 'Everybody used to refer to history. But which history?'.[1]

The problem of singling out the unifying elements of medieval and modern Italian history had been discussed in the Risorgimento.[2] The unification of Italy and the setting up of a monarchy resulting from national emancipation seemed to offer historians a stable point from which to view the national past. Soon after unification, Alessandro D'Ancona, a historian of literature and one of the most representative scholars of the second-half of the nineteenth century, made very precise observations regarding this. In a letter to Giuseppe De Blasiis, who taught modern history at Naples university, D'Ancona observed that it was finally possible to write the whole history of Italy because the goal the Italian people had aspired to for centuries, consciously or unconsciously, had been reached. The march was finally over, a significant and enduring result had been achieved and it was possible to better understand the deviations, withdrawals and mistaken routes that had for a long time impeded it.[3] D'Ancona himself worked on a truly exemplary study informed by this view, dedicated to the idea of political unity in Italian poetry.[4]

In presenting, in broad outline, the contribution of Italian historians to nation-building during the first decades after unification, some clarification is necessary. The observations that follow are limited to the work of professional scholars whereas historical material was far more widely used in attempts to construct and consolidate a national identity: in the journalistic-literary, celebratory, monumental, iconographic and scholastic fields; in the last with a real effort towards national pedagogy.[5] Nevertheless, the professionalisation of historical studies, together with the fixation of methodological canons centred on the supremacy of learned work and a 'historical method' grounded on a positivistic basis, conditioned research orientation and content.

At unification, the teaching of history played only a marginal role in the universities of the Italian states. There were history chairs in the Hapsburg universities in Pavia and Padua, and one had been set up in Pisa under the reforms of 1839–41. The most important history chair was that founded at

Turin university in 1846, occupied by Ercole Ricotti, where the organisation of historical studies had been accorded a degree of importance at a political level since 1833.[6] In the months before the declaration of the Kingdom of Italy, the provisional governments of some states had already nominated university history teachers. Later, with the university regulations of September 1862, which formed part of the centralised order imposed on the university system of the new kingdom, courses in modern and ancient history became obligatory in literature and philosophy faculties. Albeit the teaching of history in universities differed from the dictates of the regulations, within approximately fifteen years the academic establishment of historical studies was visibly consolidated. Not all the twenty-three universities and institutes for higher education in the kingdom had literature faculties. In 1874–5, twelve universities held twenty-six courses in general history and auxiliary subjects, and the trend was for further increases in the number of history chairs and studies.

The first 'generation' of Italian university historians was made up of figures who, whilst very different from one another, shared two characteristics. First, they were largely self-taught, or had a non-specialist training. Possibly only Giuseppe De Leva, at Padua, could boast an academic curriculum gained at the Hapsburg university. Second, they were appointed to university teaching posts directly by the Minister of Public Education. In the new context of the unified state and constitutional monarchy, these appointments were politically motivated. Among the professors of historical subjects in the first decades after unification, there were poets and men of letters alongside scholars and specialists in particular subjects, above all in auxiliary disciplines, as well as a number of scholars with relatively wide historiographical horizons (Ricotti, Villari, De Blasiis, De Leva) who played an important role in the birth of the modern 'craft' of the historian in Italy.[7]

The organisation of history teaching was not easy to reduce to a unitary plan. On the one hand there was a desire to lay the foundations for a new scientific community. On the other hand, it was important, through the universities, to train a new teaching body for the secondary schools and particularly the lycées. Giving university teaching this double aim created both organisational and managerial problems which have still not been studied in depth. Nevertheless, academic historiography, with its methodological backbone and the themes it encompassed, had a clear impact on the culture of the country, or rather of the restricted cultured groups existing in Italy at that time, thanks to the middle school teachers. This impact was much greater than would have been possible through books and scientific journals.

According to some contemporary sources, the predominantly critical-philological training received at university had a negative effect on the culture of history teachers. In a famous work of 1908 dealing with the middle school reform, Gaetano Salvemini deplored the 'laboured and muddled studies in the cellars of erudition' carried out during university study, which produced 'the pedantic ranks [...] of the *landesknechts* [war-mongering mercenaries] of erudition', unsuited to the educational task they would have to perform as teachers.[8] These were harsh words, yet they were grounded in some element of truth. On the other hand, that type of critical discipline had been set up against a more traditional culture of rhetorical formulation. Indeed, the new 'science' now taught at the universities had been looked to also to correct the political distortions of the historiography of the preceding decades.

In 1878 Francesco Lanzani — a scholar, and later a senior official in the Ministry for Public Education — published a stimulating essay emphasising the role of historians in the first half of the nineteenth century in preparing the Risorgimento. Lanzani underlined the importance of political passions in determining the themes and content of their works which had been 'generous anachronisms of Italian patriotism' typical of 'militant' historiography. Now, however, was the time for scientific historiography. This, Lanzani held, should provide a comprehensive view of the past and relate to the new economic and social sciences by abandoning polemical excesses without, however, renouncing its role as a moral educator. Lanzani was certainly animated by a strong patriotic spirit: he specified that the proceeds of the sale of this work be donated to a fund for the building of a monument to the recently deceased king.[9] The vision of a historiography that was not instrumentally political yet able to contribute to the civil education of Italians and to the country's prestige enjoyed a certain vogue at this time, at least as a normative ideal. This vision was inspired by methodological positivism, as championed by Pasquale Villari — arguably the greatest Italian historian of the second-half of the century.[10]

Another important Italian historian of the period, Carlo Cipolla, singled out 'research of the facts' as the main task of Italian contemporary historiography in his 1882 inaugural lecture 'Aims and Methods in the Exposition of Italian History'. The coordination of studies would ensure the creation of wider frameworks, almost a mosaic, that in the end would reveal the face of national history.[11] In 1929, Benedetto Croce noted that in united Italy, unlike Germany, there had been little room for 'passionately tendentious historiography'. 'History however modestly or mediocrely it was practiced', Croce opined, 'was not conceived of as militant, but as objective, and militant only with this objectivity'.[12] Thus it was thought that a new history of Italy would spring from the concentrated study of sources, learned research and the scholarly piecing together of these initiatives. This programme was often mentioned in discussions between contemporary historians, and it was further repeated in the six history conferences which were held in Italy between 1879 and 1895.[13] Two general observations must be made on this subject.

First, a significant proportion of publishing and research at that time was conducted outside the universities in the history societies founded as a result of private and public (the Deputations for 'Homeland' history [*Storia patria*]) initiative. The Turin Deputation, founded in 1833, was taken as a model, and in other capitals of the old states, such as Florence, the Deputations gained a degree of importance. The scholars who worked in these Deputations were not, in the main, linked to university teaching. They were aristocrats, archivists or officials of the pre-unification governments. In Turin, the link to court circles was particularly clear. The new men emerging from the university system sometimes had different social, and usually different geographic origins so that their participation in the Deputations often proved difficult. Over several decades the number of history societies increased. The Tuscan Deputation, which originally covered also the Marches and Umbria, lost control over these areas when they set up their own research centres. The proliferation of Deputations and societies (which among other things organised the above-mentioned history conferences) made the oft-invoked coordination between the work of the various local groups more problematic. In many cases, institutional fragmentation translated into localism.

Second, and furthermore, in this situation, historiographical reference to the new unified political scene often remained an extrinsic reminder. During the fourth Italian history conference, held in Florence in September 1889, Pasquale Villari underlined the delays and difficulties encountered in historical research, especially in identifying the unifying elements of national history, and he attempted to point out a preferential research field. Villari felt that it would be possible to find in the history of public and private law traces of the life common to all Italy which had existed despite the numerous internal conflicts and the convulsive succession of events. Such research was not 'merely a scientific need, but also a patriotic duty'; there was a pressing need to show that national unification had not been 'a sudden, artificial creation', but the fruit of a long and slow process. It was, furthermore, necessary to go beyond merely underlining the ancient origins of the recent unification: historical research conducted in this way would make it possible to better understand the true identity of the new state, 'what its real needs are', and to visualise its future role in an international sphere.[14] The most self-evident aspect of Villari's thought was the desire to delineate a national horizon which could be used as a reference point in the work of scholars, and be given political connotations. Analysis of the proceedings of these history meetings and other writings of the time, however, reveals that, besides these political interests, the more sensitive exponents of national historical culture were concerned with other equally strongly-felt questions of a technical nature. It is also possible to discern an effort to organise a modern scientific backbone for the study of history – though the objective of raising the scientific level to that of more advanced countries was not without politico–national implications in terms of the kingdom's reputation and prestige.

The persistence of strong particularistic tendencies mentioned above was accompanied by other clear reflections of the tensions in the political life of the unified country. Thus, at least in the field of professional historiography, cultural and historiographical currents of a federalist–republican nature weakened following unification. Only in the last years of the century were they strengthened by the writings of the young Salvemini. Similarly, the capture of Rome in 1870 marked the high-point of tension between the new state and the church and some of the most noteworthy historiography of the period was dedicated to the relationship between state and church in the Middle Ages, including Crivellucci's strongly anticlerical work.[15] The clash with the papacy even inspired specific political-historiographic projects: in 1876–7 the Ministry of Justice sought to promote a great documentary publication on the relationship between the Italian states and the church from the thirteenth to the nineteenth century in order to reconstruct the 'noble struggle of the Italian states' against papal usurpation.[16] This did not prevent there being a number of Catholic historians of note in the Italian universities, such as Giuseppe De Leva, formerly a teacher, at the university of Padua under Austrian rule, and later Rector, and Carlo Cipolla in Turin. Politically loyal patriots such as De Leva devoted their studies principally to sixteenth-century religious history from a perspective that was hostile to the Reformation, and set store by the reforming currents within Catholicism.[17]

The neo-Guelph, Catholic historiographic trend which had been strong in the 1830s and 1840s had,[18] nevertheless, weakened before 1861. The theme of the relationship between papal Rome and the history of Italy was certainly present in post-unification historiography, but Rome was not considered the unifying centre of Italian history. Classical studies remained important in various ways, [19] but in discussing the character of Italian national history during the First World War years, Benedetto Croce emphasised how right historians in the romantic age were in 'cutting out [...] the history of ancient Rome' from national history.[20] Yet the question remained open, and was very complex. For example, one of the most characteristic publications of Italian historical culture after unification, edited, at least in name, by Pasquale Villari, also addressed the ancient history of Italy.[21] The national or universalistic traits of Roman history, and its specific relationship with the Peninsula, had been, was still, and continued to be discussed, both in Italy itself and elsewhere. And the problem of dating the beginning of a specifically Italian history remained unresolved.[22]

In political history particularly, it was not easy to single out a continuous unifying thread unless the role of the House of Savoy and Piedmont was exaggerated anachronistically. After some initial excesses a more cautious line was adopted even in the school history syllabuses. The history of culture and national spirit, in spite of its complexity, was better suited to the reconstruction of a less tortuous route. Particular anniversaries in the decade following unification (the centenary celebrations for Galileo, 1864; Dante, 1865; and Machiavelli, 1869) contributed to creating an image of Italy defined more as an intellectual and spiritual nation than as a political one. Such figures conjured up a great national, cultural and scientific tradition the clear anticlerical implications of which gave new weight to old and widely-held historiographic theses, for example Machiavelli's belief that the papal states were the principal obstacle to Italian unification was taken up again. In 1875 Antonio Cosci described the papacy as the 'bitter enemy of national unity and not infrequently also of Italian independence'.[23] Similar ideas, linked as they were to a seemingly ineluctable problem, were widely discussed in the following decades and were still to be found in the twentieth century in Gioacchino Volpe's historical writings.[24]

Some of the most important historical works of the period were dedicated to Machiavelli, such as the biographies by Villari and Tommasini.[25] Dante, Machiavelli and Galileo were among the most prominent figures in Francesco De Sanctis's *History of Italian Literature*. This is certainly the most important of the histories of Italy published at that time, although it was not well received when it appeared. De Sanctis looked to literature for evidence of spiritual and civic life, the history of 'national consciousness'; this was one of the issues that gave his work historical unity. But intellectual and moral history, like Italian political history, displayed fractures. Inevitably, the sixteenth-century Italian crisis and the theme of post-Renaissance decadence raised awkward questions for any history of developing national identity. De Sanctis dwelt on the role of late-Renaissance philosophers and scientists, the first heroes of the 'modern world who carried a new Italy and a new literature in their breasts'; he opposed them to the spirit of the Counter-Reformation and 'Jesuit education'.[26] The new national life was born from the thinking of a heroic minority, men who had made their mark on European culture and left a heritage that the new national state could claim almost as the legitimation, and proof, of Italy's participation in European history.

Historians and scholars often discussed the link between Italian and European history. In the history of culture, the ideas of philosophers such as Bertrando Spaventa concerning the diffusion of Italian Renaissance thought should not be overlooked.[27] In political and social history, Villari's observations on the international dimensions of many fundamental episodes in Italian history, from the dispute between the communes and the Hohenstaufen Empire to the origins of the Risorgimento, are notable.[28] Historiographic production itself, however, remained concentrated on Italian history, although there was an increasing broadening of interests towards the modern era and changes in the analytical approach.

For a long period the history of the age of the communes was a favourite field for research, especially in some centres of study such as Florence. Neo-Guelph historiography, with its defence of the national role of the papacy as protector of Italian towns, was no longer tenable; and the significance of the theme of the history of medieval liberties, associated especially with the work of Sismondi, was waning. For a while, there were still interpretative ideas that had clear national political implications. The case of Villari is a good example. In 1861, when the memory of the alliance between Piedmont and the France of Napoleon III against Austria was still very much alive, Villari glorified the victory of the Latin principle over the Teutonic in his study of the struggles of the people against the Grandi of Florence, thus revamping an important motif in romantic historiography: that of the contrast between 'conquerors' and the 'vanquished'. However, within a few years, Villari shifted his analysis from national to social antagonism. The history of the age of the communes had to be studied not only to trace the origins and the first signs of liberty and Italian nationality, but also to reconstruct the institutional, juridical and economic genesis of 'modern society', its characteristics and conflicts. The society of the communes, concluded Villari, had not known how to found the modern state; state organisation had been headed by sovereigns and tyrants with the consequent sacrifice of ancient civic liberties.[29]

Cesare Balbo had already drawn attention, during the Risorgimento, to the process of the formation of Italian states.[30] Emphasising the importance of the passage from the communes to the state, as Villari was to do, opened up different perspectives in the interpretation of Italian history from the four-teenth century, shedding new light on the problem of decadence. Certainly these centuries had been marked by wars among Italians, the loss of indepen-dence and enormous corruption in the ruling classes which was also due to the weakening of faith. And thus, Carlo Cipolla described these centuries, refusing to attribute a positive connotation to the term 'Renaissance'.[31] Other Italian historians, however, comparing themselves with Burckhardt and Symonds, ascribed the complex profile of the period to the end of political universalism and the birth of a 'clear concept of society and the modern state',[32] which was an important aspect of the rich contribution that Italian civilisation had given to the birth of the modern world.

Italian history had been more important in the theoretical and intellectual field than in terms of concrete political achievements. At the time of the birth of the great European monarchies (which, according to the widely-held historiographic thought of the time, were a necessary condition for 'civic equality' – the basis for 'all liberties'),[33] Italy was, and remained, divided. However, even in the negative context of foreign domination, at least a part of Italian society had been subject to political and territorial reorganisation anal-ogous to that which had occurred elsewhere. This was, in essence, the point of view behind one of the few general works dedicated at that time to Italian history between the sixteenth and eighteenth centuries: Antonio Cosci's *Italy Under Foreign Domination, 1530 to 1789*. Italian decadence and the loss of a central position in international politics and in the history of civilisation were not minimised or denied by Cosci who expressed strong anticlerical feelings and brought clear, antiFrench political attitudes onto a historiograph-ical level. He emphasised the pettiness of the lives of the small Italian states, the jealousies which divided them, and the inability to follow any policy that did not merely aim for servile survival. On the other hand Cosci noted the importance of the transformation that began in Italy in the sixteenth century to 'create present conditions' which clearly derived more from the modest history of the Italian states than from the great age of the communes. He emphasised the importance of the common servitude which had taken the place of 'fratricidal wars' in determining the slow and unconscious maturing of a united attitude. However, particularly in the decadent centuries, a new protagonist in Italian history had evolved thanks to its military prowess and importance in international politics: the House of Savoy and the Piedmontese state. Cosci did not hold a purely apologetic attitude in this regard. Piedmontese politics, he wrote, had been determined by particularistic interests, and the development of national consciousness and ideals had been slow and controversial. Nevertheless, from the second half of the sixteenth century, 'the strength, credit and political importance of Italy' had been concentrated in the state of Savoy; the politics of the House of Savoy would become the corner-stone of Italian unification.[34]

The role played by Piedmont and the House of Savoy among Italian states was naturally confirmed at a historiographic level, and not only as dynastic national glorification. Among the great number of works produced, often of a strongly political nature and marked by the polemics associated with court circles and old-style Piedmont, two are particularly worthy of note. The first, by Ercole Ricotti, contained an extensive apologia of the main figures in the dynasty, but also addressed the problem of the passage from a feudal to an absolute monarchy in its various political and administrative aspects.[35] The second, the unfinished work by Nicomede Bianchi, attempted to analyse the brief period when Piedmont had 'gradually' become 'the centre of the formative process for independence and the political unity of the nation'. Bianchi's research contributed to the work of 'minute analyses in regional histories' from which it would then be possible to pass on to national history. Central, here, is the appraisal of the revolutionary and Napoleonic periods and of the impact of these events on Italian history.[36]

Interest in the history of Italian states was not limited to Piedmont. Later other Italian states, such as Tuscany, were examined, with particular attention paid to the birth period of the state and the eighteenth-century reforms. The latter period was considered to be closely linked to the question of the origins of the Risorgimento, with the accent varyingly placed on the importance of the experience of autonomy or on the decisive influence of the French Revolution.[37] By the beginning of the twentieth century, historians such as Antonio Anzilotti saw single states as the places where, from the middle of the eighteenth century, those social and moral forces that started the national movement, had gradually formed and grown.[38] The 'centre' of Italian history was perhaps to be looked for in its polycentricity, in the slow development of numerous specific social realities.

From this perspective, the outline of a specifically national history, which had always remained somewhat undefined, could be understood in the context of a shorter length of time. Benedetto Croce was certainly not thinking only about the distortions of war propaganda, but about the fact that what was complex and incomplete was the conceptual elaboration of the history of Italy, when he wrote in 1916, 'the history of Italy is not ancient or centuries old but *recent*, not outstanding but *modest*, not radiant but *laboured*'. Croce felt that not only Roman history, but also the history of the communes and the Renaissance, should be left out of the picture of a real history of Italy. The 'present Italian physiognomy', now far from that of ancient times, showed the signs of recent events that went no further back than the eighteenth-century reforms and the French Revolution.[39]

From the point of view of the characterisation of 'national' history, the periodisation set out by Croce implied scientific concentration upon contemporary history. Indeed, at the beginning of the twentieth century, and particularly in the years after the First World War, professional historians changed their field of interest to contemporary history.[40] However for a certain time research in this area remained fluid and uncertain. Towards the end of the century a historiography of the Risorgimento, which had some importance from the perspective of strengthening national identity, was being outlined. It is not easy, however, to isolate works with scientific connotations. Political polemics, memoirs and historiography were contiguous for a long time; and professional historians (such as the ageing Villari, but also the young Volpe) did not look with favour on the teaching of Risorgimento history in Italian universities. Both in celebratory as well as in more serious works, such as Carlo Tivaroni's,[41] however, there emerged a view of national emancipation which reconciled the conflicts among the different main players of these events, casting them collectively as the founders of the fatherland.

The promoters of the new directions of study in contemporary Italy were two scholars trained in the medievalist tradition, Gaetano Salvemini and Gioacchino Volpe, who hailed from different intellectual and political poles. Salvemini believed in a democratic-radical interpretation of recent Italian history which he had developed as a result of his direct political experiences. At first bitterly critical of the policies of the moderates, Salvemini later reached more balanced evaluations of the work of the ruling groups in liberal Italy and was among the first and most consistent opponents of fascism.[42] Volpe's vision, on the other hand, embraced a long period in the history of the people and the Italian nation: from its ethnic and social origins, consolidated around 1000 AD, to its full development and the fusion of various elements which had matured in the course of Italian history thanks to the fevered atmosphere of the First World War. Volpe's history, with its final identification of the people, the ruling class and the state, presented fascism as its climactic moment.[43]

Notes

1 G. Volpe, *L'Italia in cammino* (1927), Rome and Bari, Laterza, 1991, pp. 24–5. B. Croce, *Storia della storiografia italiana nel secolo decimonono*, Bari, Laterza, 2nd edn, 1930.

2 E. Sestan, 'Per la storia di un'idea storiografica: l'idea di una unità della storia italiana' (1950), in E. Sestan, *Storiografia dell'Otto e Novecento*, G. Pinto (ed.) Florence, Le Lettere, 1991, pp. 163–81; G. Galasso, *L'Italia come problema storiografico*, Turin, UTET, 1979.

3 D'Ancona's undated letter, in M. Schipa, 'Giuseppe De Blasiis e l'Università di Napoli', *Archivio storico per le province napoletane*, 1915, N.S., vol. 1, p. 79.

4 A. D'Ancona, 'Il concetto dell'unità politica nei poeti italiani' (1875), in A. D'Ancona, *Studi di critica e storia letteraria*, Bologna, Zanichelli, 1912, vol. 1, pp. 3–100.

5 S. Soldani and G. Turi (eds) *Fare gli italiani. Scuola e cultura nell'Italia contemporanea*. I. *La nascita dello Stato nazionale*, Bologna, Il Mulino, 1993; G. Di Pietro, *Da strumento ideologico a disciplina formativa. I programme di storia nell' Italia contemporanea*, Milan, Mondadori, 1991; B. Tobia, *Una patria per gli italiani. Spazi, itinerari, monumenti nell'Italia unita (1870–1900)*, Rome and Bari, Laterza, 1991; I. Porciani, *La festa della nazione. Rappresentazioni dello Stato e spazi sociali nell'Italia unita*, Bologna, Il Mulino, 1997.

6 G. P. Romagnani, *Storiografia e politica culturale nel Piemonte di Carlo Alberto*, Turin, Deputazione subalpina di storia patria, 1985; E. Breccia, 'Ippolito Rosellini e la cattedra di Storia nell'Università di Pisa', *Bollettino storico pisano*, 1942–4, vol. xi–xiii, pp. 139–58.

7 M. Moretti, 'Note su storia e storici in Italia nel primo venticinquennio postunitario', in P. Schiera and F. Tenbruck (eds) *Gustav Schmoller e il suo tempo: la nascita delle scienze sociali in Germania e in Italia*, Bologna-Berlin, Il Mulino-Duncker and Humblot, 1989, pp. 55–94; M. Moretti, 'Storici accademici e insegnamento superiore della storia nell'Italia unita. Dati e questioni preliminari', *Quaderni storici*, 1993, vol. 82, pp. 61–98. I. Porciani (ed.) *L'Università tra Otto e Novecento: i modelli europei e il caso italiano*, Naples, Jovene, 1994; S. Polenghi, *La politica universitaria italiana nell'età della Destra storica (1848–1876)*, Brescia, La Scuola, 1993.

8 G. Salvemini and A. Galletti, *La riforma della scuola media* (1908), reprinted in G. Salvemini, *Scritti sulla scuola*, ed. L. Borghi and B. Finocchiaro, Milan, Feltrinelli 1966, pp. 566–7.

9 F. Lanzani, *Del carattere e degli intendimenti della istoriografia italiana nel secolo XIX*, Padua, Sacchetto, 1878, pp. 26, 33.

10 For Villari's philosophical and methodological attitudes, see E. Garin, 'Il positivismo come metodo e come concezione del mondo', in E. Garin, *Tra due secoli. Socialismo e filosofia in Italia dopo l'Unità*, Bari, De Donato, 1983, pp. 65–89; F. Tessitore, *Introduzione allo storicismo*, Rome-Bari, Laterza, 1991, pp. 111–53; G. Cacciatore, 'Cultura positivistica e metodo storico in Italia', in G. Cacciatore, *La lancia di Odino. Teorie e metodi della storia in Italia e Germania tra '800 e '900*, Milan, Guerini e Associati, 1994, pp. 87–155. Villari was John Stuart Mill's most significant Italian correspondent.

11 C. Cipolla, 'I metodi e i fini nella esposizione della storia italiana' (1882), in C. Cipolla, *Per la storia d'Italia e de'suoi conquistatori nel Medio Evo più antico. Ricerche varie*, Bologna, Zanichelli, 1895, pp. 9–56.

12 B. Croce, 'Intorno alle condizioni presenti della storiografia in Italia', *La Critica*, 1929, vol. 27, pp. 4–5.

13 I. Cervelli, 'Cultura e politica nella storiografia italiana ed europea fra Otto e Novecento (A proposito della nuova edizione di 'Storici e maestri' di Gioacchino Volpe)', *Belfagor*, 1968, vol. 23, pp. 596–616.

14 P. Villari, 'Di un possibile coordinamento dei lavori e delle pubblicazioni delle singole Deputazioni e Società storiche; e della relazione di queste tra loro e coll'Istituto storico italiano', *Archivio storico italiano*, 1890, serie V, vol. 6 (Atti del quarto Congresso storico italiano), pp. 65–78 (quotations from pp. 69–70).

15 B. Malfatti, *Imperatori e papi ai tempi della Signoria dei Franchi in Italia*, Milan, Hoepli, 1876; A. Crivellucci, *Storia delle relazioni tra lo Stato e la Chiesa*, Bologna, Zanichelli, 1885–1907.

16 U. Levra, *Fare gli italiani: Memoria e celebrazione del Risorgimento*, Turin, Istituto per la storia del Risorgimento italiano, 1992, pp. 265–6. Publication did not, in the event, take place.

17 G. De Leva, *Storia documentata di Carlo V in correlazione all'Italia*, Venice-Padua-Bologna, Naratovich-Sacchetto-Zanichelli, 1863–94.

18 Croce, *Storia della storiografia italiana*, pp. 97–160; P. Herde, *Guelfen und Neoguelfen. Zur Geschichte einer nationalen Ideologie vom Mittelalter zum Risorgimento*, Stuttgart, Steiner, 1986; W. Krogel, 'Freiheit und Bürgerlichkeit. Das Verfassungsleben der italienischen Stadtrepubliken im historisch-politischen Denken Deutschlands und Italiens (1807–1848)', in R. Koselleck and K. Schreiner (eds) *Bürgerschaft. Rezeption und Innovation der Begrifflichkeit vom Hohen Mittelalter bis ins 19. Jahrhundert*, Stuttgart, Klett-Cotta, 1994, pp. 455–502.

19 P. Treves, *L'idea di Roma e la cultura italiana del secolo XIX*, Milan-Naples, Ricciardi, 1962; P. Treves, *Tradizione classica e rinnovamento della storiografia*, Milan-Naples, Ricciardi, 1992; L. Polverini (ed.) *Lo studio storico del mondo antico nella cultura italiana dell'Ottocento*, Naples, ESI, 1993.

20 B. Croce, 'Epopea e storia' (1916), in B. Croce, *L'Italia dal 1914 al 1918. Pagine sulla guerra*, Bari, Laterza, 1950, p. 135.

21 M. Moretti, 'Carlo Cipolla, Pasquale Villari e l'Istituto di Studi superiori di Firenze', in G.M. Varanini (ed.) *Carlo Cipolla e la storiografia italiana fra Otto e Novecento*, Verona, Accademia di agricoltura scienze e lettere, 1994, pp. 41–4. The volume on Italy's ancient history was entrusted to Francesco Bertolini; K. Christ and A. Momigliano (eds) *L'Antichità nell'Ottocento in Italia e Germania*, Bologna, Il Mulino and Berlin, Duncker and Humblot, 1988.

22 See Galasso, *L'Italia*, pp. 167–70.

23 A. Cosci, *L'Italia durante le preponderanze straniere dal 1530 al 1789*, Milan, Vallardi, 1875, p. 153.

24 See, for example, G. Volpe, *Il Medioevo*, Florence, Vallecchi, 1927, pp. 103–4.

25 P. Villari, *Niccolò Machiavelli e i suoi tempi*, Florence, Le Monnier, 1877–82; O. Tommasini, *La vita e gli scritti di Niccolò Machiavelli*, Rome, Loescher, 1883–1911.

26 F. De Sanctis, *Storia della letteratura italiana* (1870–71), ed. N. Gallo, Turin, Einaudi, 1975, pp. 742–3 for the quotations. The most significant general study on De Sanctis is still S. Landucci's, *Cultura e ideologia in Francesco De Sanctis*, Milan, Feltrinelli, 2nd edn, 1977; however there is an enormous amount of critical literature on De Sanctis. See the collective works, C. Muscetta (ed.) *Francesco De Sanctis nella storia della cultura*, Rome-Bari, Laterza, 1984, and A. Marinari (ed.) *Francesco De Sanctis un secolo dopo*, Rome-Bari, Laterza, 1985. For the points mentioned in the text, see the works in F. Wolfzettel and P. Ihring (eds) *Literarische Tradition und nationale Identität. Literaturgeschichtsschreibung im italienischen Risorgimento*, Tübingen, Niemeyer, 1991.

27 B. Spaventa, 'Carattere e sviluppo della filosofia italiana dal secolo XVI sino al nostro tempo, prolusione alle lezioni di storia della filosofia nell'Università di Bologna' (1860), in B. Spaventa, *Scritti filosofici*, collected and published by G. Gentile, Naples, Morano, 1900, pp. 115–52.

28 P. Villari, 'Prefazione alla prima edizione' (1901), in P. Villari, *Le invasioni barbariche in Italia*, Milan, Hoepli, 1920, pp. x–xii.

29 For these aspects of Villari's historiographic work, see M. Moretti, ' "L'Italia, la civiltà latina e la civiltà germanica" (1861). Sulle origini degli studi medievistici di Pasquale Villari', in R. Elze and P. Schiera (eds) *Italia e Germania: Immagini, modelli, mitifra due popoli nell'Ottocento-il Medioevo*, Bologna, Il Mulino and Berlin, Drucker and Humblot, 1988, pp. 299–371.

30 C. Balbo, *Sommario della storia d'Italia* (1846), republished in C. Balbo, *Storia d'Italia e altri scritti editi e inediti*, ed. M. Fubini Leuzzi, Turin, UTET, 1984.

31 C. Cipolla, *Storia delle Signorie italiane dal 1313 al 1530*, Milan, Vallardi, 1881; Moretti, 'Carlo Cipolla, Pasquale Villari', pp. 48–9. On the issue of state history, see G. Galasso, 'La storia regionale e la formazione dello Stato moderno', in B. Vigezzi

(ed.) *Federico Chabod e la 'nuova storiografia' italiana 1919–1950*, Milan, Jaca Book, 1984, pp. 163–210.

32 Moretti, 'Carlo Cipolla, Pasquale Villari', pp. 48–50; F. Tessitore, 'L'idea di Rinascimento nella cultura idealistica italiana tra '800 e '900', in F. Tessitore, *Storiografia e storia della cultura*, Bologna, Il Mulino, 1990, pp. 89–123.

33 Cosci, *L'Italia durante le preponderanze straniere*, p. 1.

34 Cosci, *L'Italia durante le preponderanze straniere*, pp. 1, 29, 112–13.

35 E. Ricotti, *Storia della monarchia piemontese*, Florence, Barbèra, 1861–9. G. Ricuperati, 'Lo stato sabaudo e la storia da Emanuele Filiberto a Vittorio Amedeo II. Bilancio di studi e prospettive di ricerca', *Studi Piemontesi*, 1980, vol. ix, special edition, pp. 20–41; Moretti, 'Note su storia e storici in Italia', pp. 75–8.

36 N. Bianchi, *Storia della monarchia piemontese dal 1773 sino al 1861*, Rome-Turin-Florence, Bocca, 1877–85; for the quotation, vol. 1, p. ix; Levra, *Fare gli italiani*, pp. 247–56; W. Maturi, *Interpretazioni del Risorgimento. Lezioni di storia della storiografia*, Turin, Einaudi, 1962, pp. 299–302.

37 For the origins of Risorgimento historiography, see, besides the works by Maturi and Levra above, R. Romeo, *Il giudizio storico sul Risorgimento*, Acireale, Bonanno, 1987; and the polemical arguments in F. Diaz, *L'incomprensione italiana della Rivoluzione francese*, Turin, Bollati Boringhieri, 1989.

38 For Anzilotti's historical works, see G. Sofri, 'Ritratto di uno storico: Antonio Anzilotti', *Rivista storica italiana*, 1961, vol. 73, pp. 699–738.

39 Croce, 'Epopea e storia', pp. 135–7.

40 F. Barbagallo, 'Le origini della storia contemporanea in Italia tra metodo e politica', in G. Di Costanzo (ed.) *La cultura storica italiana tra Otto e Novecento*, I, Naples, Morano, 1990, pp. 133–59.

41 C. Tivaroni, *Storia critica del Risorgimento italiano*, Turin, Roux e Frassati, 1888–97; A. Galante Garrone, 'Carlo Tivaroni: come divenne storico del Risorgimento', *Rivista storica italiana*, 1967, vol. 79, pp. 313–54.

42 H. Bütler, *Gaetano Salvemini und die italienische Politik vor dem Ersten Weltkrieg*, Tübingen, Niemeyer, 1978; E. Artifoni, *Salvemini e il Medioevo. Storici italiani fra Otto e Novecento*, Naples, Liguori, 1990; R. Vivarelli, 'Salvemini e Mazzini', *Rivista storica italiana*, 1985, vol. 97, pp. 42–85; M. Moretti, 'Il giovane Salvemini fra storiografia e "scienza sociale"', *Rivista storica italiana*, 1992, vol. 104, pp. 203–45; M. Moretti, 'Salvemini e Villari. Frammenti', in D. Antiseri (ed.) *Gaetano Salvemini metodologo delle scienze sociali*, Soveria Mannelli, Rubbettino, 1996, pp. 19–68.

43 I. Cervelli, *Gioacchino Volpe*, Naples, Guida, 1977; G. Belardelli, *Il mito della 'nuova Italia'. Gioacchino Volpe tra guerra e fascismo*, Rome, Edizioni Lavoro, 1988. See also G. Belardelli's Introduction to Volpe, *L'Italia in cammino*, pp. v–xxxv, and C. Violante's Introduction to G. Volpe, *Medio Evo italiano*, Rome-Bari, Laterza, 1992, pp. v–xli.

Further reading

B. Croce's *Storia della storiografia italiana nel secolo decimonono*, Bari, Laterza, 2nd edn, 1930, is still the fundamental work on Italian historiography between the nineteenth and twentieth centuries.

For the history of the Italian university system after unification, see I. Porciani (ed.) *L'Università tra Otto e Novecento: i modelli europei e il caso italiano*, Naples, Jovene, 1994.

Part IV

Liberal democracy and antifascism (1918–45)

This section moves the story of the interplay between historiography and nationalism into the twentieth century. The idea of liberal nationalism had been strengthened by the victory of the Western democracies in the Great War and by the destruction of the multinational Ottoman, Russian and Hapsburg Empires. Nevertheless, in this 'age of ideologies' (Karl Dietrich Bracher) liberal–democratic historiography found itself beleaguered by fascist claims on the nation on the one hand and communist denunciations of it on the other.

An alternative to the hegemonic nationalism of the right can be found in Marc Bloch's writings. His enthusiastic support for French war efforts in both world wars demonstrates his commitment to the national principle. Nevertheless one would be hard pressed to name another French (or, for that matter, European) historian in the interwar period who was so systematically critical of any kind of historiographic nationalism. Peter Schöttler's chapter examines Bloch's position by looking at his reviews of books by German historians. The chapter casts light upon the targets of Bloch's criticisms, the manner in which it was expressed, his alternatives to nationalism and the intellectual and emotional sources of his campaign against the national narrow-mindedness of his colleagues.

As Peter Lambert shows for Germany, there were few supporters of the democratic Weimar Republic amongst historians. Fritz Rörig, a historian of medieval towns and merchants, was amongst that tiny minority. His politics in the 1920s were decidedly left-liberal. From 1930, he recognised nazism as the chief danger to bourgeois life. He defended Social Democrats from the allegation that in 1918 they had 'stabbed Germany in the back', disputed attempts to construct political action around anti-Semitism and denounced the Nazi cult of violence. Yet, as Lambert goes on to show, after 1933 Rörig came close to joining the Nazi Party, redefined his notion of *Volk* so as to fit the Nazi-sponsored racist *Volksgeschichte* and propagandised in favour of the war effort. Lambert concludes that it was Rörig's lack of conceptual clarity which was at the heart of his political *volte face*.

Philip Morgan investigates the writings of historians organised in the antifascist movement *Giustizia e Libertà*, founded in exile in 1929. Based on a survey of the group's literature in the 1930s and the war years, and of the published historical writings of GL's protagonists, the chapter uncovers the extent to which *Giustizia e Libertà*'s treatment of Italy's national history from the Risorgimento onwards was used not only to explain the rise of fascism and refute its claim to represent the nation, but also to develop a view of Italy's recent past which would validate their hoped-for 'liberal-socialist', republican reconstruction of Italy after the defeat of fascism.

10 Marc Bloch as a critic of historiographical nationalism in the interwar years

Peter Schöttler

Translation by Laura Deiulio and Stefan Berger

La coopération intellectuelle est à l'ordre du jour, mais qui donnera aux historiens une âme de coopérateurs?[1]

The French historian Marc Bloch (1886–1944) is without a doubt one of the great scholars and emblematic figures of our century. He has become a symbol of the union of scholarly and democratic engagement not only through his writings, but also through his participation in the Resistance and his heroic death from the bullets of the Gestapo. His books, especially *The Historian's Craft*, have been translated into all major languages and have been reprinted many times. Research centres and professorships have been founded in Bloch's name, including even a class of the French military academy and the *Ecole Nationale d'Administration*.[2]

In the scholarly world, the name Bloch is inseparable from the project of the journal he founded in 1929 together with Lucien Febvre, the *Annales d'histoire économique et sociale*, the *Annales* for short. This journal is known today to every historian and student of history and stands for an innovative, comparative and interdisciplinary understanding of history; that is, for a turning away from traditional political and intellectual history and an embracing of the history of societies and mentalities. Whether one calls it 'history from below', or 'Alltagsgeschichte' or 'microhistory' – none of these new developments of the last decades would have been possible without the example set by the *Annales*.[3]

Yet, the *Annales* and Marc Bloch have become, over the years, a myth, a projection screen, which all too often serves the purpose of legitimising the particular viewpoints of historians, or even journalists, in different countries. Thus it is the more interesting, as well as crucial, to uncover and objectify the history of the *Annales* and their protagonists.

For some time now this has been the concern of my own research which focuses in particular on the specific mode of production of both founders of the *Annales*: how did they write, how did they collect their material, how did they constitute their 'paradigm', and how did they define it *vis-à-vis* other 'paradigms'? Here I am especially interested in the relationship of the *Annales* to Germany and to the German historians who, from the very start, occupied the role of counterparts and rivals. Following Henri Pirenne's post-1918 slogan 'Unlearning from the Germans' ('Désapprendre de l'Allemagne'), the *Annales* developed a historiographical discourse which permanently oscillated between enthusiastic reception and decisive rejection of German historiography.[4] Lucien Febvre dealt directly with 'German questions', for example in his books about Luther (1928) and about the Rhine (1931).[5] Yet it was, above all, Marc Bloch who emerged as a critical observer of the German historical production and who shaped the *Annales*' perception of Germany. How he did will be the topic of this chapter.

Marc Bloch had an intimate relationship to Germany. In 1908 and 1909, after graduation from the *École Normale Supérieure*, he followed the example of many French students by studying for two semesters in Germany – first in Berlin and then in Leipzig.[6] He became acquainted with German university life from the inside; he knew the practices of German 'seminars' (of which there was no equivalent in France at that time) and also the student rituals. In later years he would sometimes return to the experiences he had made whilst studying in Germany, for example in his obituary for his Leipzig teacher Karl Bücher:

> Those amongst us who embarked on their tour of Germany twenty or twenty-five years ago and who came to Leipzig, will never be able to forget the seminars of Karl Bücher. The image is still before us of this tall man whose energetic mind criticised in turn the speaker and his opponents, and turned the discussion of papers into the most instructive high drama.[7]

However, the most important result of Bloch's stay in Germany was that he mastered the German language – not only in a vague and passive way, like many of his French colleagues – rather, he could interpret every nuance and often read 'between the lines'. In later years he was therefore in a position to exchange letters with his German colleagues and to conduct meaningful discussions. When the project of the *Annales* was to be explained to German historians or when the latter were to be won as authors or collaborators in the 1920s and 1930s, it was almost always Bloch who initiated contacts and facilitated correspondences.[8]

In the years following the Great War the forging of such contacts was, of course, difficult. Like most academics of his generation Bloch had donned the uniform in August 1914. Having seen action in several battles he was promoted to the rank of captain.[9] Quite apart from the fact that his Jewishness contributed to his identification with the secular republic, his republican patriotism was not merely 'theoretical'. During those traumatic years patriotism became second nature to Bloch. In the 1920s he confronted his Strasbourg students, who nicknamed him 'Captain Bloch' (*le capitaine Bloch*), with the strictness of a former officer who had seen active service.[10] As a rationalist, however, this did not prevent him from seeking international solutions to conflicts on the basis of an improved mutual understanding to which, he believed, the historians could make a significant contribution.

That is why Bloch tirelessly concerned himself with the history of other countries and in particular with Germany. He made good use of his experiences at Berlin and Leipzig. He developed the habit of studying recent German scholarly literature, and of using it on a daily basis – handbooks and reference material, journals and editions of historical sources – just as he had done in German departmental libraries. He even paged regularly through the *Deutscher Literaturanzeiger*, so that no single new publication escaped his attention, and so that he could order review copies from the publishing houses.[11]

Bloch was indeed a great reviewer of books.[12] With enormous diligence, with never-flagging attention and with pencil sharpened, he read his way almost through the entire international scholarly literature in his field. German publications – after the French literature, of course! – were given top priority in his reading. After Bloch's pioneering books on medieval Europe,[13] and participation in the collective project of the *Annales*, this enormous body of book reviews can be seen as Bloch's 'third great work'. It represents a wide-ranging and disparate 'work in progress' which branches off in many directions but which is rigorously critical of the historiography of the interwar years. One can only hope that someday this giant work will be collected and published as a whole.

From this massive body of book reviews we have, as a first step, selected those which focus on German history, or on German authors.[14] The total number of books and articles discussed by Bloch either in individual reviews, or in longer review essays, comes to around 500. Distributed among six journals – above all the *Annales*, the *Revue de Synthèse*, the *Revue historique* and the *Revue critique d'histoire et de littérature*, this body of work is a kind of *glossa continua* to the German historiography of the interwar years. And this huge, and formally seen relatively unified material, offers privileged access to Bloch's view of Germany and to his critical examination of a nationalistic means of writing history. True, Bloch never actually wrote a book *about* Germany, yet in his reviews we have the near equivalent of such a book, but only in a most disparate form.[15]

How can we best approach such material? And how can this body of texts most appropriately be 'read'? Various methods are to be considered: analysis of content and critique of ideology, analysis of language, discourse analysis, and so forth. In the remarks that follow I can only sketch out several aspects and select several concrete examples. Therefore, what I am offering is only a preliminary analysis.

The first step is of course to read all the book reviews from the first to the last and to describe the spectrum constituted therein, including, for example, the selection of topics, titles and authors. Naturally this reveals that Bloch's focus is on medievalist literature, even though he often reviews works which bridge epochs, or on contemporary history. Further, one will see that some books on the German Middle Ages which are viewed today as especially controversial or important are not discussed. This is true above all for the years after 1933, when visibly fewer review copies of German books were released by publishers to foreign journals. I am thinking, for example, of Franz Petri's *Germanisches Volkserbe in Nordfrankreich und Wallonien* (*German Bloodlines in Northern France and Wallonia*) (1937), a huge book about one of Bloch's research areas by an outstanding Nazi historian which, if he had known it, he would certainly have criticised,[16] or of Otto Brunner's *Land und Herrschaft* (*Land and Lordship*) (1939), which was obviously not reviewed in France until after the War.[17] Yet despite these gaps it is possible to distil the content of Bloch's reviews into an overall impression, which one could sketch out as follows.

Marc Bloch applies extremely strict scholarly standards: his highest criteria are innovative thought and diligent research; but almost as important are clearly structured thinking and the avoidance of unnecessary digressions. Bloch criticises again and again the confusion and prolixity of the authors he reviews – especially writers of '*Inauguraldissertationen*' (Ph.D.s) – the length of which was often to be found inversely proportionate to profitable content. He sees in this situation a typical product of the German university system, which in comparison with the French system was, to be sure, much more research-orientated, but which also encouraged every 'beginner' to present himself as a 'little master'. He saw the time wasted by bad and thick books as scandalous in a profession so pressured by lack of time. Writing to Pirenne at the time that he was writing a review article for the *Revue historique* he complained:

> German production is suffering from galloping inflation; they write too quickly and they never take any care to give the appropriate form to an idea. Their thinking is often distorted. 'Geopolitics' is nothing but a thinly veiled 'world politics' [*Weltpolitik*], and 'stylistic analysis' [*Stilkritik*] is a sick joke which takes itself seriously. Yet it is to their credit that they problematise a whole range of areas which my fellow countrymen would never discover in their academic routine.[18]

Bloch reacts especially sensitively to national, nationalistic and even racist prejudice. Although he wants to judge each book as objectively as possible and therefore almost always tries to begin by summing up its content in a manner 'not governed by subjective values' (*wertfrei*), as a reviewer he cannot escape a standpoint grounded in value judgements. This individual standpoint emerges stylistically through irony and epistemologically through the demarcation of boundaries. This process can be illustrated by two concrete examples, which must stand here for many others.

In 1934, the economic historian Friedrich Lütge published a study of the agrarian order in Thuringia.[19] Bloch devoted a lengthy discussion in the *Annales* to this work.[20] In this review, he praised the clearly structured and precise presentation, but found fault with the fact that the author had hardly worked with archival sources and therefore, according to Bloch, over-emphasised the legal aspects of the problem at the cost of the social reality. Only at the end does Bloch turn his attention to the hidden bias of the book: if the author didn't sufficiently stress the disadvantages of the '*Gesindezwang*', i.e. the compulsory work and control over servants, it was because he sympa-thised with an archaic agrarian order. His 'preferences for an authoritarian regime' and an 'economy run by an iron hand', Bloch argued, had most likely 'damaged' his 'objective judgement of the facts'. Altogether Bloch saw the book not only as a 'useful source of information', but also as 'significant testi-mony on the present state of events'.

Another example: in 1935–6 Adolf Helbok, one of the most important representatives of the so-called 'people's history' (*Volksgeschichte*), published a two-volume work on the *Volksgeschichte Deutschlands und Frankreichs* (*People's History of Germany and France*), which bore the programmatic subtitle *Vergleichende Studien zur deutschen Rassen-, Kultur- und Staatsgeschichte* (*Comparative Studies on German Racial, Cultural and State History*).[21] Bloch, who was, as is well known, a decided proponent of comparative historiography,[22] knew of course where the German–French comparison was heading in this case; it would not have been difficult for him to show that the author had racist prejudices and to condemn his shoddy effort as dubious from the beginning. Instead of this, he nonetheless made an effort even here to achieve objectivity, and began by emphasising the rich source material and the scholarly character of the book: 'The intention is fascinating', he writes.[23] 'The information is in general very solid, above all, of course, in aspects that concern Germany'. Nonetheless, Bloch found Helbok's interpretation somewhat one-sided. He concluded that 'It would really be too bad if such a patiently constructed documentation in the end served only to legitimise the shallowest banalities of a social philos-ophy entirely orientated at the extreme end of present-day thinking'. This, too, is a way to denounce Nazi ideology.

As this second example shows, Bloch adhered to the rule of objectivity even when the book lying open before him used racist argumentation, and therefore would hardly be taken seriously today. As a historian – although not as a *citoyen*! – he wanted to take a stand *sine ira et studio* even when confronting national socialism. Right up to France's military defeat of 1940 he almost lived the illusion that a diplomatic division of 'science' (*Wissenschaft*) and politics was possible and that one was only allowed a kind of indirect 'policing of science' (*Wissenschaftspolizei*), for example by means of ironic reviews. Only after the Phoney War did he change this attitude, when writing his book *L'Étrange défaite* (*The Strange Defeat*).[24] Soon after he joined the Resistance.[25]

Under both democracy and dictatorship Bloch developed a characteristic

curiosity for the ideological confusions and complexities of German historiography. This problem is worthy of a detailed analysis at some point. I am
thinking here especially of the possibility of a systematic 'discourse analysis' in
which one could consider all of these reviews as a kind of unified 'block' and
deconstruct them 'from within'.[26] Which vocabulary, which metaphors,
which types of arguments, does Marc Bloch use in order to sum up the
contents of books, or to praise, criticise or to relativise books, and how does
he himself enter the discussion in specific instances? How does he at the same
time set boundaries through language? As a first step the use of concepts like
'state', 'people' (*Volk*) or 'race', and then the opposing concepts of 'nation',
'society' and so forth could serve as an indicator. But such an extensive examination – which would be important as a means of 'objectifying' Bloch's own
approach – is not possible here. Instead of this I would simply like to offer
some further perspectives, from which one can consider Bloch's critique of
historiographical nationalism, in order to grasp his uniqueness.

First, one would have to examine Bloch's reviews not only 'synchronically',
but also in terms of changes in the position of the critic himself. This is interesting in cases where the same author appears at different times, with different
books – or perhaps with the same one. I am thinking for example of the
Viennese historian Alphons Dopsch, upon whose work Bloch commented no
fewer than thirteen times between 1923 and 1938 and whom he frequently
criticised on matters of detail but with whom he remained on friendly
terms.[27] Or of Ernst Kantorowicz: Bloch gave his opinion of Kantorowicz's
biography of Friedrich II in 1928, 1932 and 1937 – with an increasingly positive slant.[28] Or to take another example, Bloch's statements on Georg von
Below, whose work he reviewed many times from 1918, form a chapter in
and of themselves. Indeed, I feel that it was not Karl Lamprecht – as is often
erroneously claimed[29] – but rather Below who was the German medievalist
with whom Bloch concerned himself most intensely and whom he considered the archetypal German historian whose example should not be followed.
As is well known, Below was one of the two founders and editors of the
Vierteljahrschrift für Sozial- und Wirtschaftsgeschichte (*Quarterly for Social and
Economic History*) – that is, the German counterpart to the *Annales*, which was
regarded highly by Bloch, who wrote in 1931 that 'we are all indebted to
it'.[30] And like Bloch, Below had written extensively on methodological and
historiographical questions.[31] Yet even while showing all due respect to the
broad knowledge and the scholarly rigour of the German historian, Bloch
criticised his methodological and national bigotry over and over again. Below,
he writes in 1918, sees the 'state' everywhere and shows too little interest in
the formation of the German 'nation'.[32] And in 1931 Bloch adds that Below
unfortunately was acquainted only with Germany, knew too little about
Europe and mistrusted comparative analyses. By contrast, Bloch claimed:
'A historian, like the kind that Below wanted to be, may belong politically to
the party of his choice, but as a scholar he must be a good European'.[33] When
the above-cited Friedrich Lütge posthumously published some fragments of

Below on agrarian history in 1938 Bloch once again returned to this topic. As always, he conceded, Below's writings were solid and worthwhile. But, he went on, they lacked an overall perspective:

> The whole book is characterised by a complete contempt for compara-
> tive historiography. It is as if Germany exists in a vacuum. Most
> provocatively, the problems of the different agrarian systems are treated
> and sometimes even solved as if no one had ever analysed or written
> about an open or closed field outside the borders of the Reich.[34]

One could object both to 'synchronic' and 'diachronic' readings on the grounds that they are immanent interpretations which – even when they are 'linguistically' objectified – are distorted by Bloch's specific view of Germany. Therefore, it is necessary to find standards of comparison.

One possible procedure would be to compare Bloch's reviews with other discussions of the same books. One could then establish whether Bloch's judgements are actually harsher or more mild – or whether (and this is my impression) his criteria were not to some extent simply different. As an example I would like to mention his comments on Friedrich Meinecke's 1936 book on historicism.[35] There are many other reviews besides that of Bloch, among them a very critical one by the philosopher Herbert Marcuse in the *Zeitschrift für Sozialforschung*.[36] Marcuse, as a German emigré, takes to task the conservative worldview of the book – its resigned fatalism. Bloch, meanwhile, as a Frenchman, looks beyond the political implications of the book. It is as if it was too simple to attack the elderly editor of the *Historische Zeitschrift* on this profane level, who had, after all, been removed from his position by the Nazis.[37] On the contrary, he emphasised the 'courageous independent opinion' of the author and the subtlety of his analysis. Yet at the same time he had to concede with a sigh how alien this book remained to him: 'For an historian with a different training [i.e. like Bloch] such a book is immensely disappointing! Even when the historian is, as I believe this one is, as far removed as possible from nationalist prejudice – at least conscious preju-dice'.[38] A non-German – read Marc Bloch – has to remain unconvinced, for example, by the personification, yes even worship, of the state and by the refusal of any attempt to extend historiography to an all-encompassing human science (*Humanwissenschaft*). Above all, however, the book lacks any considera-tion of the specific *practice* of writing history. Anyone, he argues, who writes about the history of physics must take into account the practical possibilities of the laboratory. Bloch did not hesitate to use the provocative comparison with the natural sciences to underline the deep gulf between German intel-lectual history (*Geistesgeschichte*) and French social science (*science sociale*): *l'idée contre le Begriff*.[39]

A last standard of comparison is presented by Bloch's treatment of German and French authors. How does he treat them? How does he react to their weaknesses and how does he speak about their national prejudices? Does he criticise their exaggerations as well, or does he let them go as 'good' patriotism? Again, one could introduce many examples, not only of reviews of French books, but also of authors from 'allied' countries, such as Poland. Bloch consistently differentiates the latter from German historians; by no means does he hide his 'national' sympathies. But surprisingly there is also differential treatment of German authors with whom he himself or the *Annales* are in direct contact: Carl Brinkmann, Walther Vogel, Fritz Rörig, Richard Koebner for example – the latter are always treated favourably. Their greater proximity to the *Annales* causes at most a difference in mood – as if in the background a kind of dialogue was taking place. Nevertheless, there is not a complete reversal of the standards applied to German historiography.

The most striking comparison, however, is with Bloch's reviews of books by his fellow countrymen. An excellent example is provided by Bloch's review of Ferdinand Lot's *Les invasions barbares*.[40] Lot was at the time a professor emeritus at the Sorbonne and was much admired by Bloch. The general discussion is therefore positive.[41] But at the end of the review Bloch does raise some grave reservations, concerning the merit of the book as a whole. For Bloch, Lot wishes more than anything to 'understand', and has 'no particular sympathy for the extreme nationalism', which since the war had been prevalent in many countries. But, writes Bloch, Lot holds that 'understanding' does not exclude 'judgement'; and that 'The most important task of the historian consists […] not only in differentiating the "true from the false", but also 'the good from the evil'. Here, Bloch draws a sharp line:

> Unfortunately, we cannot agree with this formulation. For us, truly scholarly findings are incompatible with value judgements. In this principle, as well as probably in the stronger emphasis on the material substratum of cultures and their class structure, lies the difference between the conception of history which we are here [that is, in the *Annales*] attempting to defend, and that which Ferdinand Lot represents.

More amicable words follow, in which Bloch emphasises how much he respects Lot, even if unwilling to follow his lead in every respect.

This text from 1938 is especially interesting, because in it two different types of French historiographical patriotism confront each other in a virtually paradigmatic way: on the one side is the older patriotism which Lot represents – one can also call it nationalism – and which characterised, for example, the position of most of the French historians in the First World War, inducing many of them to set aside their scholarly standards, at least temporarily, for the benefit of political objectives.[42] The Third Republic was for them the logical consequence of a two thousand year history; the German past had inevitably produced the militarism of Bismarck and Wilhelm II, not to speak of Hitler. In contrast to this 'twisted patriotism',[43] Bloch stood for a historiography which admitted its patriotism as a 'value judgement', just as an author could disclose his religious affiliation, but in which value judgement

would have the least possible influence on scholarly investigation. 'I am terri-
fied of every scientific nationalism', Bloch wrote in a letter of 1934.[44] Thus,
the symmetry of the Franco-German 'hereditary enmity' (*Erbfeindschaft*) and
the traditional understanding of a 'national' historiography is destroyed.
Instead of responding to the nationalism of the other side with its own
nationalism, Bloch held that one should respond with methodological criticism and constructive dialogue. It is in keeping with this philosophy that,
following the Great War, Bloch, together with Lucien Febvre, Henri Hauser,
Maurice Halbwachs and others like-minded, should have endeavoured to lay
the foundations of another kind of historiography. One means to this end was
the new journal *Annales*, which should have been baptised as early as 1923 at
the international congress of historians in Brussels. Indeed, the *Annales* formed
part of a broader project that included collaborative participation in international conferences, trips abroad, international correspondence and last but not
least a comparative history of European society.

It is one of the tragic paradoxes of our century that Marc Bloch, of all
French historians the one who most consistently argued for international
dialogue and the most knowledgeable about 'German science' (*Wissenschaft*),
should have died in the Second World War as a combatant in the struggle
against the German occupation. He symbolised a characteristic attempt to
reconcile an emphatic patriotism – that is identification with one's own
country – with scientific 'internationalism'.

Notes

1 Marc Bloch, 'L'histoire locale en Allemagne', *Annales d'histoire économique et sociale*,
   1929, Vol.1, p. 306. 'Co-operation is at the head of the agenda. But who will give
   historians the souls of co-operators?'
2 See Carole Fink, *Marc Bloch, A Life in History*, Cambridge, Cambridge University
   Press, 1989, and more recently, Etienne Bloch, *Marc Bloch 1886–1944: Une biographie impossible. An Impossible Biography*, foreword by Jacques Le Goff, Limoges,
   Culture & Patrimoine en Limousin, 1997 (bilingual book). Since 1994 the
   secondary literature about Bloch is systematically recorded in the annual *Cahiers
   Marc Bloch*.
3 Whole libraries could be filled with publications on the *Annales* project. Brief
   sketches are provided by Peter Burke, *The French Historical Revolution: The Annales
   School 1929–89*, Cambridge, Polity Press, 1990; François Dosse, *L'histoire en miettes:
   des Annales à la 'nouvelle histoire'*, Paris, La Découverte, 1987.
4 Cf. Peter Schöttler, ' "Désapprendre de l'Allemagne": Les *Annales* et l'histoire alle-
   mande dans les années trente', in Hans-Manfred Bock, Reinhart Meyer-Kalkus,
   Michel Trebitsch (ed.) *Entre Locarno et Vichy: Les relations culturelles franco-allemandes
   dans les années 1930*, Paris, CNRS-éditions, 1993, pp. 439–61.
5 See Lucien Febvre, *Martin Luther: A Destiny*, New York, Dutton, 1929 (first
   published in France in 1928); *Le Rhin, Histoire, mythes et réalités*, ed. Peter Schöttler,
   Paris, Librairie Académique Perrin, 1997 (first French edition 1931). See also my
   article 'The Rhine as an Object of Historical Controversy in the Inter-war Years:
   Towards a History of Frontier Mentalities', *History Workshop Journal*, 1995, no. 39,
   Spring, pp. 1–21.
6 Cf. Hélène Barbey-Say, *Le voyage en Allemagne de 1871 à 1914*, Nancy, Presses

universitaires de Nancy, 1994; Christophe Charle, *La République des universitaires 1870–1940*, Paris, Seuil, 1994, pp. 21ff.

7 Marc Bloch, 'Karl Bücher', *Annales d'histoire économique et sociale*, 1932, vol. 4, pp. 65–6.

8 Peter Schöttler (ed.) 'Marc Bloch – Fritz Rörig, Correspondance (1928–1932)', in *Cahiers Marc Bloch*, 1994, vol. 1, pp. 17–52; Marc Bloch, 'Lettres à Richard Koebner (1931–1934)', in P. Schöttler (ed.) *Cahiers Marc Bloch*, 1997, vol. 5, pp. 73–82.

9 See Marc Bloch, *Écrits de guerre 1914–1918*, ed. Etienne Bloch, Paris, Armand Colin, 1997; *Marc Bloch, Memoirs of War, 1914–1915*, Carole Fink (ed.) Ithaca, NY, Cornell University Press, 1980.

10 Interview of the author with Henri Brunschwig, 24 November 1987.

11 This becomes clear when looking through Marc Bloch's papers in the National Archives in Paris. See especially AB XIX 3,796–851. An exact catalogue which has recently been completed by Matthias Grässlin will be published soon.

12 The same is true for his colleague Lucien Febvre. See Bertrand Müller, 'Lucien Febvre et la politique du compte rendu', in *Le Goût de l'histoire, des idées et des hommes: Mélanges en hommage au professeur Jean-Pierre Aguet*, Vevey, L'Air, 1996, pp. 437–59.

13 Marc Bloch, *Feudal Society*, 2 vols, London, Routledge and Kegan Paul, 1961. First published in French in 1939–40.

14 An edition of all reviews of Marc Bloch concerning German history and historiography is currently being prepared by Bertrand Müller and the author. It will be published within the book series of the Max Planck Institute for History in Göttingen in 1999. An (almost) complete bibliography of all of Marc Bloch's publications, including his reviews, can be found in the Appendix to the edition of his articles entitled *Mélanges historiques*, Paris, Ecole des Hautes Etudes, 1962, vol. II, pp. 1,031–104. The *Cahiers Marc Bloch* keeps its readers up to date with new editions of Bloch's texts.

15 Even whilst the war was still raging, he planned to write a history of 'the first German Reich'. See his letter to Febvre of 8 May 1942.

16 On Petri see my article 'Die historische Westforschung zwischen "Abwehrkampf" und territorialer Offensive', in Peter Schöttler (ed.) *Geschichtsschreibung als Legitimationswissenschaft 1918–1945*, Frankfurt am Main, Suhrkamp, 1997, pp. 204–61.

17 On Brunner, whose book has now also been translated into English as *Land and Lordship. Structures of Governance in Medieval Austria*, ed. by Howard Kaminsky and James Van Horn Melton, Philadelphia, 1992, see the article by Gadi Algazi, 'Otto Brunner – 'konkrete Ordnung' und Sprache der Zeit', in P. Schöttler (ed.) *Geschichtsschreibung*, pp. 166–203.

18 Letter to Henri Pirenne, 6 November 1932, in *The Birth of Annales History: The Letters of Lucien Febvre and Marc Bloch to Henri Pirenne (1921–1935)*, Bryce and Mary Lyon (eds) Brussels, Commission Royale d'Histoire, 1991, p. 149.

19 Friedrich Lütge, *Die mittelalterliche Gutsherrschaft. Untersuchungen über die bäuerlichen Verhältnisse (Agrarverfassung) Mitteldeutschlands im 16.–18. Jahrhundert*, Jena, Fischer, 1934.

20 Marc Bloch, 'Problèmes seigneuriaux dans l'Allemagne moderne', *Annales d'histoire économique et sociale*, 1936, vol. 8, pp. 491–4.

21 Adolf Helbok, *Grundlagen der Volksgeschichte Deutschlands und Frankreichs. Vergleichende Studien zur deutschen Rassen-, Kultur- und Staatsgeschichte*, Berlin, de Gruyter, 1935–6.

22 See his famous article of 1928 'Pour une histoire comparative des sociétés européennes' which is now easily accessible in Marc Bloch, *Histoire et Historiens*, ed. Etienne Bloch, Paris, Armand Colin, 1995, pp. 94–123.

23 Marc Bloch, 'Histoire d'Allemagne: Moyen Age', *Revue historique*, 1937, vol. 181, pp. 405–9.

24 Marc Bloch, *Strange Defeat*, New York, 1953.

25 On Bloch's relationship to national socialism and his entry into the Resistance see Fink, *Marc Bloch*, pp. 205ff; Bertrand Müller, 'Marc Bloch, historien, citoyen, résistant', in André Gueslin (ed.) *Les Facs sous Vichy*, Clermont-Ferrand, Institut d'études du Massif central, 1994, pp. 39–50; and Peter Schöttler, 'Marc Bloch et Lucien Febvre face à l'Allemagne nazie', *Genèses*, 1995, no. 21, pp. 75–95

26 In the 1920s Bloch and Febvre themselves sketched out some of the opportunities offered by historical discourse analysis. See Peter Schöttler, 'Historians and Discourse Analysis', *History Workshop Journal*, 1989, no. 27, Spring, pp. 37–65.

27 See the detailed account of and commentary on these controversies in Peter Schöttler, 'Die *Annales* und Österreich in den zwanziger und dreißiger Jahren', *Österreichische Zeitschrift für Geschichtswissenschaften*, 1993, vol. 4, pp. 74–99.

28 For more details see Peter Schöttler, 'Ernst Kantorowicz und Frankreich', in Robert L. Benson and Johannes Fried (eds) *Ernst Kantorowicz*, Stuttgart, Franz Steiner, 1997, pp. 144–61.

29 So, for example Bryce Lyon, 'Marc Bloch: did he repudiate *Annales* History?', *Journal of Medieval History*, 1985, vol. 11, p. 183; Burke, *The French Historical Revolution*, p. 183; Catherine Devulder, *L'histoire en Allemagne au XIXe siècle*, Paris, Méridiens-Klincksieck, 1993, pp. 157ff.

30 Marc Bloch, 'Un tempérament: Georg von Below', *Annales d'histoire économique et sociale*, vol. 3, 1931, pp. 554.

31 On the work of Below see Otto Gerhard Oexle, 'Ein politischer Historiker: Georg von Below', in Notker Hammerstein (ed.) *Deutsche Geschichtswissenschaft um 1900*, Stuttgart, Steiner, 1988, pp. 283–312.

32 Marc Bloch, review of Georg von Below, 'Der deutsche Staat des Mittelalters', 1914, *Revue historique*, 1918, vol. 128, pp. 343–7. As becomes clear from a letter, Bloch apparently wrote this review at the beginning of 1918 whilst still serving in the front line. See his *Ecrits de guerre 1914–1918*, Paris, Armand Colin, 1997, pp. 157ff.

33 Marc Bloch, 'Un tempérament: Georg von Below', *Annales d'histoire économique et sociale*, 3, 1931, pp. 553–9; this text is now reprinted in *Histoire et Historiens*, pp. 240–7.

34 Marc Bloch, 'Une histoire rurale de l'Allemagne au moyen âge', *Annales d'histoire économique et sociale*, 1938, vol. 10, pp. 461–2.

35 Friedrich Meinecke, *Die Entstehung des Historismus*, München, Oldenbourg, 1965 (first published 1936).

36 Herbert Marcuse, *Zeitschrift für Sozialforschung*, 1937, vol. 6, pp. 182–3.

37 Bloch and Febvre knew that Meinecke, under pressure from the Nazi administration, had had to quit the editorship of the *Historische Zeitschrift* (see Bloch's letter to Febvre from 7 May 1941).

38 Marc Bloch, ' "Historisme" ou "travail d'historien" ', *Annales d'histoire sociale*, 1939, vol. 1, pp. 429–30; now also in *Histoire et historiens*, pp. 82–3, where the following citations can be found.

39 Ibid. Bloch, however, concedes that not all 'ideas' could be found on 'one side of the linguistic barrier' and not all 'terms' (Begriffe) on the other (p. 83).

40 Ferdinand Lot, *Les invasions barbares*, Paris, 1938.

41 *Annales d'histoire économique et sociale*, 1938, vol. 10, pp. 62–3. On Lot, whose two sons-in-law fought in the Resistance and were murdered, see Charles-Edmond Perrin, *Un historien français: Ferdinand Lot 1866–1952*, Geneva, Droz, 1968.

42 See Sergio Luzzato, *L'impôt du sang. La gauche française à l'épreuve de la guerre mondiale (1900–1945)*, Lyon, Presses universitaires de Lyon, 1996, pp. 17ff; Martha Hanna, *The Mobilization of Intellect. French Scholars and Writers during the Great War*, Cambridge, MA, Harvard University Press, 1996.

43 Such is Bloch's criticism of Fritz Kern's book, 'Gottesgnadentum und Widerstandsrecht im frühen Mittelalter', *Revue historique*, 1921, vol. 138, p. 253.
44 To Georges Espinas, 21 July 1934 (Espinas papers in the possession of Professor Pierre Toubert whom I would like to thank for his permission to consult them).

Further reading

Many important works of the *Annales*, including the voluminous exchange of letters between Marc Bloch and Lucien Febvre, unfortunately, have not yet been translated into English.

Works of Marc Bloch

Marc Bloch, *Memoirs of War 1914–15*, Ithaca, NY, Cornell University Press, 1988.
Marc Bloch, *Feudal Society*, 2 vols, London, Routledge and Kegan Paul, 1961.
Marc Bloch, *The Historian's Craft*, Manchester, Manchester University Press, 1953.

Works about Marc Bloch

Carole Fink, *Marc Bloch, A Life in History*, Cambridge, Cambridge University Press, 1989. A good biography, marred only by the fact that Bloch's intellectual work, including the project of the *Annales* is discussed only briefly.
Susan W. Friedman, *Marc Bloch, Sociology and Geography. Encountering Changing Disciplines*, Cambridge, Cambridge University Press, 1996. Situates Bloch's work in the context of the social science of his time.
Etienne Bloch, *Marc Bloch 1886–1944. Une biographie impossible. An Impossible Biography*. Foreword by Jacques Le Goff, Limoges, Culture & Patrimoine en Limousin, 1997 (distribution: La Boutique de l'Histoire, Paris). A bilingual biography with many good documents and illustrations.

On the Annales

Traian Stoianovich, *French Historical Method: The* Annales *Paradigm*, Foreword by Fernand Braudel, Ithaca, NY, Cornell University Press, 1976. A critical analysis of the *Annales* movement since 1946.
Peter Burke, *The French Historical Revolution. The* Annales *School 1929–89*, Cambridge, Polity Press, 1990. An excellent survey, including a bibliography which emphasises the postwar period.

On the relationship of the Annales to Germany

Peter Schöttler, 'Lucie Varga: A Central European Refugee in the Circle of the French *Annales*, 1934–1941', *History Workshop Journal*, 1992, vol. 33, Spring, pp. 100–20.
Peter Schöttler, 'The Rhine as an Object of Historical Controversy in the Inter-war Years. Towards a History of Frontier Mentalities', *History Workshop Journal*, 1995, no. 39, Spring, pp. 1–21.

11 From antifascist to *Volkshistoriker*

Demos and *ethnos* in the political thought of Fritz Rörig, 1921–45

Peter Lambert

The route that took the bulk of German historicists, adherents of a statist and nationalist conception of history, into a collaboration with Nazism which often predated the establishment of the Third Reich has been well documented in the history of German historiography. A shared hostility to parliamentary democracy, yearning for a *Führer*, affronted nationalism, and anti-Marxism meant that there was plenty of common ground between the conventional right-wing majority within the historical profession and the Nazis. The minority of *Vernunftrepublikaner* (the term coined by Friedrich Meinecke to denote those who remained monarchists at heart, yet accepted the republic by virtue of reason) were on the whole won over by Nazism, but only in the Third Reich, and then incompletely and only over the years of Nazi foreign policy successes. More recently, historians of German historiography have turned their attention to a number of historians who challenged aspects of the historicist paradigm and whose peculiar brand of social history – *Volksgeschichte* – was riddled with racist rhetoric and assumptions which made their journey into the Third Reich smoother still. This essay concerns one historian, Fritz Rörig,[1] whose path into the Nazi dictatorship was *sui generis*. How did this man, with an established reputation not only as a methodologically, but as a politically progressive scholar, whose pacifist credentials had cost him one promotion in the Weimar Republic and whose distaste for the company of 'reactionary' colleagues had led him to turn down another prestigious appointment, become one of the most persistent and stridently racist academic contributors to Nazi propaganda before and during the Second World War?

On the face of it, neither the record of Rörig's political affiliations in general, nor of his thoughts on Nazism before 1933, nor yet of his scholarship during the Weimar Republic afford evidence of an emergent enthusiasm for Hitler. Rörig was a liberal. He stood out among liberals for the vehemence with which he denounced vestiges of 'feudal' rule in the Bismarckian Reich. Indeed, he counted himself a 'pronounced anti-East Elbian'[2] and trenchant critic of the Wilhelmine system.

He condemned both the limitations the Wilhelmine system had imposed on the potential development of active citizenship within the bourgeoisie and its treatment of the social democracy and the working class. The latter were turned into 'vagrants without a Fatherland' by government policies and through no fault of their own.[3] Much of Rörig's political thought before 1933 would not have been out of place in the formative phases of the Christian Democratic Union in occupied Germany after the Second World War. He supported 'a socially restrained capitalism', capitalism 'bound by social legislation and a social mentality'.[4] These pronounced 'modern' traits in his thought were perhaps especially rare among medieval historians: Rörig seems at least to have displayed little sign of inclination to prefer a mythical, organic and rurally based *Gemeinschaft* to a socially mobile and urban *Gesellschaft*. His first objection to 'the lamentable declaration of the Hitler–Hugenberg Government' was to 'that passage…which 'writes off' trade and industry as already finished and which wishes only to prevent the downfall of the farmer (for which read the great estate owner)'.[5]

However, his political and academic contacts were not with the isolated handful of genuinely left-wing liberals within the historical profession, but with *Vernunftrepublikaner*. A certain aloofness from party politics, characteristically bound up with estatist sensibilities, circumscribed his engagement as a citizen of the Republic just as it did that of the *Vernunftrepublikaner*. 'I have', as he put it in April 1933, 'maintained a distance from actual everyday politics for reasons arising out of my deep commitment to my professional task, and indeed see this as my professional duty as an historian'.[6] Although he never joined a political party in the Weimar Republic, he was politically active at a local level and periodically sought to influence the realignment of bourgeois party politics at a national level.

In 1930, Rörig held the Deutsche Volkspartei (DVP) responsible for the break-up of the Great Coalition and argued that government without the SPD was impossible in the longer term. And from that point until February 1933, he argued tenaciously for a regrouping of the bourgeois centre, indeed for its reconstitution as 'a new party of united anti-fascist resistance'.[7] Certainly, then, he took the Nazi challenge very seriously, and interpreted it principally as a threat. And he was nothing less than clear-sighted respecting the Nazis' violence.

On 5 November 1930 he added the following postscript to a letter in which he had denounced the Nazis in general and that 'rotten egg', the 'raw *radikalinski* [sic] Goebbels' in particular: 'Given the uncertainty of our times, I do ask that you consign this letter to the fire. Otherwise it may perhaps at some point result in my enjoying the famous Goebbels recipe: 1 litre of castor oil!'[8]

The surviving carbon copies of his outgoing correspondence supply ample evidence of a longstanding and earnest endeavour on Rörig's part to resist Nazi influence wherever he could. 'Over long years of very intimate knowledge of the influence of the National Socialists above all on students', he wrote in February 1931, 'I have been able to establish some very worrying facts. Politics on the basis of a peremptorily disciplined fanaticism can and will lead only to ruin. I am sceptical about the current "successes" of the

Movement but fear the very worst should it come to power even for just a fort-night'. And in the same letter his penchant for prophecy was given full rein:

> My dear fellow: in 1912 I said that 'We will be able to survive the rule of Wilhelm II so long as we do not get a war under him. Should we get a war under him, we are lost without hope of rescue.' You see that I have some aptitude where Cassandra is concerned. But, from a Hugenberg–Hitler regime, I prophesy that there will come a catastrophe of proportions so terrible that the blood of even the most fanatical of the supporters of the Movement would run cold could they even imagine a fraction of it.[9]

Clearly, then, Rörig was alarmed at the Nazi menace to law and order within Germany. 'Consider', he demanded of one correspondent, 'what Goebbels said about the sabotage of bourgeois justice!'[10] But, as the passage cited above already implies, he was still more worried by the logic of Deutschnationale Volkspartei (DNVP) and Nazi foreign policy, that is, by the prospect of another world war.[11] In focusing on this danger above all, he was surely exceptional among German anti-Nazis. Even on the left of the labour movement one would be hard pressed to find such fears articulated with such clarity. And it was rarer still to find them expressed by the 'moderate' German bourgeois nationalists among whose ranks Rörig might in some other respects be counted. His sympathies with peace movements may have been constrained by his nationalism, and certainly he was not disposed to accept Germany's being at a disadvantage in any arms build-up. The prospect of an arms race filled him with dread nonetheless:

> Can post-1918 Europe really still afford to arm in the style of the 18th and 19th Centuries? To be sure, we will have to *insist* on our share, and do what the others do. Quite right. But can you imagine the *consequences* of a future European war? I can't. It would only be waged to America's advan-tage and lead to Europe's inevitable abdication.[12]

Indeed, the ubiquitous presence of extreme nationalism, and its hegemonic hold on contemporary definitions of German national consciousness, far from tempting Rörig to give way to the prevailing current seem only to have stiff-ened his oppositional resolve. Contesting the claim of the DNVP and Nazis to 'present themselves as guardians of the national idea' or as ' "the" national unity front', he insisted on a clear distinction between their conception of Germanness and his own. 'Because I am "national", I cannot be a "nationalist" '. 'Nationalists', he argued, did severe damage to Germany's real national interests, but also to the improvements in international relations which he had welcomed during the Stresemann era. 'I feel that so much mischief has been made with the holy word "national" over the last decade that I like to emphasise the necessity of supra-national openmindedness and intellectual connections'. And his definition of German nationhood itself was, on the face of it, commensurately inclusive and unthreatening:

> May the German house only be built broadly enough to have space for all those who are of good will, and let it not lose its old architectonic advantages: of openness to the world and of development of the world. Else a stifling atmosphere could all too easily permeate its rooms.[13]

How were these concerns refracted through Rörig's scholarship and wider historical imagination? Rörig was primarily a historian of the medieval Hansa. Until the end of the First World War, Hanseatic historiography had been dominated by a circle of historians around the pan-German Dietrich Schäfer, under whose academic leadership it had remained locked within the paradigmatic parameters of diplomatic and high political history. Virtually single-handedly, Rörig enlivened a field pronounced exhausted by Schäfer in 1908 through a sequence of highly influential essays which propelled a new generation of researchers in the directions of social and economic historical research. The principal focus of his own work was on the development of long-distance trade and its connection with processes of medieval urbanisation. His proposition that the foundation of Hanseatic towns was not a product of princely patronage but the work of an 'entrepreneurial consortium' provoked controversy bordering on consternation among statist colleagues. This thesis, which emerged from his detailed investigation of Lübeck, exploited sources ranging from the physical evidence of street plans to the trading ledgers of merchants to show high levels of organisation within the mercantile class. Although he encountered the pioneering work of Henri Pirenne only when his research was well under way, he saw parallels in and drew inspiration from the Belgian scholar's approach. The comparisons were sufficiently evident to interest the *Annales* in Rörig's work. Marc Bloch, who was otherwise highly critical of the output of *Volkshistoriker*, himself undertook the translation of a Rörig article for the *Annales*, making Rörig the first (and until after the War, only) German historian to be published in the journal.[14]

In 1932, Rörig published a forceful synthetic statement of his work in the *Propyläenweltgeschichte* edited by his longstanding political associate Walter Goetz.[15] It was a hymn of praise to the medieval urban German bourgeoisie. Rörig's purpose was as much political as academic. As his correspondence made clear, he intended the essay to be read in the context of current attempts to re-establish a strong bourgeois centre in the face of the Nazi-DNVP advance. More specifically, he sought to counter a bourgeois propensity to acknowledge and internalise a Nazi propaganda message which denigrated it: 'to give this bourgeoisie, which no longer possesses any self-respect, a bit of backbone again'.[16] This political mobilisation of Hanseatic history did not end with the stabilisation of Nazi rule. October 1933 found him 'speaking in the Club zu Bremen about "The German Hansa and Present-Day Germany". Here, I will gently but clearly remind people that there is still a bourgeoisie of quality'.[17] By then, however, his criticism of the state of the nation was no longer that of an 'antifascist', but of a loyal friend to the Nazi regime.

As I have already suggested, careerism will not suffice to account for Rörig's apparently abrupt and ill-prepared accommodation with the new regime. Certainly, a survivor's instinct may have played its part in shaping his responses. His subsequent readiness – on finding himself employed within the Soviet-occupied zone of Berlin in 1945 – to build bridges with Marxism, might suggest so relatively easy (and intellectually unrewarding) a conclusion. On 17 March 1933, he stated simply: 'We are standing before a fact: the fact of the NSDAP's take-over of power within the state'. On the other hand, even under these first strong impressions of Nazi victory in 1933, he did not deny the validity of the political projects he had underwritten in the later 1920s and early 1930s, least of all his support for Stresemann and for stable coalitions which included the SPD. He was disposed rather to consider them a closed chapter of irredeemably lost opportunities ('Well, all of that has ceased to be.') So I would prefer to take at face value the evidence of soul-searching, agonising and uneasy yet clear decision-making recorded in his correspondence. 'For me', he announced to one old friend and colleague, 'to whom the words "*Bürger*" and "Liberal" are, after all, something other than throwaway terms of abuse, the transition into this "new era" is not easy. But I seek to understand it and then, in accordance with my duty, to adjust to it'.[18] Nor do I lightly dismiss even his claims to political and historiographical integrity and consistency, claims which he interwove in his letters.

Clearly, he had grave misgivings about the first policy initiatives of the Nazi regime. Racial and political anti-Semitism had long alarmed him. He had 'known' himself to be 'free of anti-Semitism as a militant mentality' even while protesting at the much vaunted over-representation of Jews in the faculties of some German universities before 1933.[19] Although worries for German national interests did intrude in his commentary on the aftermath of the boycott of Jewish concerns, it also betrayed genuine moral outrage and a real sympathy with German Jewish targets of the first attempts at 'Aryanisation':

> I was in a dreadful state of mind when, on 1 April [1933] I bought a brochure from an SA man on the street. It declared: the Jews want to murder Hitler! (the business was an official party campaign) and the man explained to his customers: 'they (the Jews) will all have to be put to the sword'. There are bound to be consequences for cultural policy and politics in general. (E.g. Einstein and the English House of Commons.) Foreign (e.g. Polish) Jews will have to be protected because of their nationality, and honourable branches of old Jewish German houses will be deprived of their honour and their professions. – Not that I am surprised by what is happening. Had it not been announced to us over and over again for years that *this* was how things were going to be?[20]

And there were other causes for complaint. Although he thought it an 'achievement' that the 'upheaval' had occurred without giving rise to a general strike, it had 'involved measures which, *in particular cases*, brought the severest personal suffering to those affected and, seen from a legal point of view, brought injustice and indeed lawlessness'.[21]

From around March 1933 onward, however, Rörig appears to have been bombarded with appeals to join the NSDAP, all of which shared the premise that such a step should come naturally to him – that 'if my publications were anything to go by, I belonged entirely within the National Socialist front. And my National Socialist students have just told me something of the sort in respect of my lectures. And I fully understand that'.[22]

Rörig persuaded himself that Nazism in power would be more responsible than it had been in opposition. Certainly, there are no echoes even in the confidential record of his correspondence from March 1933 onward of the fear that the Nazis might indulge in dangerous 'socialist experiments', indeed that they were 'extreme socialists', an anxiety which had preoccupied him before that date.[23] Two further factors combined to reassure him that he had real grounds for optimism where Nazi rule was concerned. First, he drew comfort from what he perceived as the regime's drive towards the goal of a unitary state. Second, and in some respects precisely because of the peculiar nature of his hitherto democratic convictions, he found himself very much at home in *völkisch* discourse. Throughout, he backed up his political decisions with the weight of historical judgements.

> For me it is not something that happened at some time or other in the past that has value. On the contrary, I measure all that has happened in German history according to the value it had for the nation....Hence the bitterness of my long years of struggle against the fundamental constitutional evil besetting Germany, namely statist particularism.

Rörig experienced 'genuine delight' as he observed particularism 'currently being dealt blows from which it will never again recover'.[24] From May 1933, he could preen himself on hearing an essay discussing particularism which he had published in 1921 described as 'the programme of our Führer and Chancellor'.[25] These threatened to be his overwhelming first impressions of Nazi rule. Thus, as early as mid-March 1933, he could

> openly affirm that certain deeds of the new power impress me, and that I welcome them. Above all, I would name the damper put on South German particularist tendencies, especially within Bavaria. Of course...I see in *statist* particularism the source of endless misfortunes. There was no prospect of advancing by a single step along a path of negotiation here.[26]

This thought brought Rörig immediately to his second, *völkisch*, theme. For, he reasoned, these Nazi triumphs over particularism should be seen as the work of a 'movement of the *Volk* coming from below'.[27] Rörig's *Volk* was not the putty of politics, an inorganic mass to be moulded by elites and princes, portrayed by the statist historians. It was instead a well-spring of energy, and Rörig judged political systems and leadership according to whether they promoted or constrained the outflow of that energy.

From as early as 1921 onward, *völkisch* terms and concepts had periodically surfaced in Rörig's work. They underpinned his understanding of nationhood, sovereignty and active citizenship. And he was to be almost as tenacious in his adherence to the word *völkisch* after 1945 as he had been to the word 'liberal' in 1933. I do not of course suggest, as was done in the Federal Republic of Germany in the 1950s, that Rörig's employment of *völkisch* concepts was benign nor that these were sullied only retrospectively by Nazi abuses. Rather, they were fundamentally ambiguous, conveying both democratic *and* racialist meanings. There is verisimilitude, to put it no more strongly, in his claim of September 1933, to be as comfortable with the label 'Germanic democrat' – which he recalled an 'authoritative' source having recently used to describe Nazism – as he had been with the label 'democrat' in the Weimar Republic.[28] The ambiguity ran into Rörig's application of *völkisch* principles to questions of foreign policy: they could lead him as readily into justifying territorial expansionism as into warning against untrammelled acquisitive aggression. In an addendum to a rehearsal of forebodings of a future world war penned in 1930, he had stressed that he thought differently concerning the advisability of a local war with Poland, and even pondered the possibility that 'the Nazi Movement improves our international position'.[29] In 1933, the cautionary tone prevailed:

> In my view, expansionist undertakings on a *völkisch* basis can enjoy prospects of success only if they do not proceed from the Reich. On the contrary, they must serve as proof of the Reich's gravitational pull....Because we used to talk too much of the wish that those limbs of the German *Volk* which had been separated from the main body might find their way back to us, it was easy to represent and falsify this as a desire for conquest on our part. Imbecilic braggarts in the Reich itself provided the advance guard for this [falsification]. Now I do believe that the Reich has not gained in its powers of attraction just lately. Although certain pretty poor propaganda agencies have been created, they cannot be really effective if only because they call themselves propaganda agencies.[30]

Völkisch nationalism and militarism had in fact long been integral to Rörig's critiques of the DNVP and the conservative tradition, of the Bismarckian and Wilhelmine polity, and of the decisions for war in 1914.

Resentment of the DNVP's appropriation of nationalism spilled over in Rörig's correspondence with one conservative in February, 1932. He quoted at length from an article published in the Prussian conservative *Kreuzzeitung* on 11 June 1864 denouncing 'the principle of nationality' as 'a mighty weapon against the legitimate order', neither 'holy' nor even 'justified' but 'lawless, criminal and anti-Christian' and engaged in an 'of course heathen' endeavour to remould polities and peoples on 'the basis of blood and descent....We have no right to tear a province from any state whatsoever on the grounds that its inhabitants happen to speak our language and to share our ancestry'. This 'profession of a party which may be found in the immediate family tree of the DNVP' had, as Rörig pointedly remarked, been penned 'at a time when Bismarck already had his inspired solution to the Schleswig-Hollstein question under way'.[31]

Under the immediate impact of defeat in 1945, Rörig was to refer to Nazism as 'a dreadful, exaggerated Wilhelmism'.[32] So lest it appear paradoxical or arbitrary to seek in Rörig's critique of Imperial Germany a key to understanding his positive reception of aspects of Nazi thought, be it said that that is precisely where he began his own explanation, explicitly recognising the close resemblance of Hitler's views on the Second Reich as they were expressed in *Mein Kampf* to his own.[33] Prussian conservatism and 'feudalism' had, Rörig argued, left the Bismarckian Reich fatally flawed from the outset. A history of disempowerment and denigration of the bourgeoisie deprived Germany of the 'best and strongest elements of the *Volk*' which, 'again and again' had 'bled to death as they came up against this nonsensical principle of legitimacy'. The agrarian elites' continued influence, allied to the inhibitions of dynastic prejudice, had, after 1871, militated against the *völkisch* expansion of the Reich at Austria's expense.[34] Above all, he persistently maintained that German unpreparedness for war in 1914 was a direct consequence of the power of 'feudal' elites. German policy-makers 'did not see, or did not wish to see' the necessity of the 'ruthless introduction of general conscription to the army'.[35] Their 'irresponsible neglect of the army' was, he reasoned, a direct consequence of their refusal to see the aristocratic officer corps 'diluted' through recruitment of a strong bourgeois cohort – which expansion of the army would of course have entailed.[36] Narrow class interest had thus been placed before 'the general interest'.[37]

If Rörig's conception of the *Bürger* bore little resemblance to the staid and complacent stereotype of Imperial Germany, it was bound up not only with his democratic emphasis on notions of active citizenship but also with a commitment to seeing that citizenry in arms and at the service of the nation. Here was another theme consistently pursued within his historical writing. His 1932 essay on the European town had, as he reminded colleagues during the Third Reich, dwelt on urban German contributions to the technical development of warfare, and on the dire consequences of the subsequent 'demilitarisation' of the 'true *Bürgertum*'.[38] Rörig saw social and economic history not as an alternative, but as a contribution to political history. His historiographical battles in the Third Reich were necessarily fought on two fronts. On one, he continued to battle against statist orthodoxies to insist that the urban bourgeoisie, and not nobles and monarchs alone, had contributed decisively to nation-building within Germany and to the extension of German power.[39] On the other, he sought to wrest the concept of the *Volk* from those who cast it as an exclusively rural category. Both struggles were bound up with the core of his intellectual agenda, which explored the foundations, and celebrated the practice, of power politics through an interdisciplinary approach. 'You are going down Schäfer's road,' he wrote to one of his former doctoral supervisees,

> which takes you into…the modern period. But it must not be forgotten that, in spite of quantitative significance, these are centuries of decline for us. For what do all our achievements in the 17th and 18th centuries amount to when measured against England and Holland, and how utterly different had the comparison been earlier on! That is why I consciously took the other road, into the period of the Hansa's greatest power, but working on *all* its facets and with all the disciplines….My 'continuity' is not directed at the course of events so much as at demonstrating the best forces at work in our periods of strength and at the beacons lit up in people's minds at these times.[40]

Even when faced with what he termed an 'acutely unhistorical mood of the moment' in late 1933 – a point at which he was keen that professional historians should defend their terrain against Rosenberg and Darré, he could still 'see…that a synthesis of the new with historical thinking is possible. Nay, more: that it can even be very fruitful'.[41] To another (non-Nazi) acquaintance he went so far as to assert that, although professional inhibitions had prevented him from becoming one of the 'fallen of March' (i.e. from joining the Nazi Party in the wake of its take-over of power), 'by the standards of professional historians, I am surely unusually close to the conception of history expressed by Hitler in *Mein Kampf* – and above all, have been close to it *for long years*'.[42]

The advent of the Nazi regime no doubt added a fresh impulse to the development of *Volksgeschichte*, and Rörig could have little difficulty in attaching himself to it given 'the attempts which have run through my work for long years, for once to act upon the demand that history be seen from the perspective of the *Volk* [*vom Volke her*]'. But, he added in implied criticism of at least some *Volkshistoriker*, this must be done 'in a way which satisfies scholarly criteria'.[43] For Rörig, 'the primacy of the political' was absolute.[44] These were convictions which brought him into 'a fundamental debate' with advocates of 'an isolated "geopolitics"' which can conflict dreadfully with a genuine *Volksgeschichte*'.[45] They brought sharp exchanges, too, with advocates of 'cultic' and tribal Germanic continuities. He had to exert himself to fend off an allegation that he was in fact peddling a 'materialist' conception of history.[46] But there was a price to be paid if such lines of defence were to be made effective. *Völkisch* language had, until 1933, played a striking part in his general observations about the course of German history. Thereafter, it began to infest his analysis of the core enterprises of his research. He 'coordinated' his work (i.e. brought it into line with regime expectations) by sleight of hand.

Painstaking reconstructions of the strengthening of a medieval Hanseatic mercantile identity through marriage alliances were now neatly turned into evidence of a racial identity, and cited as evidence that he had always thought in terms of blood. In 1940, he retreated even from using the concept of an 'entrepreneurial consortium', substituting the term 'entrepreneurial guild' as being less susceptible to 'misunderstanding'. These concessions once made, he could remain comfortably ensconced in the chair to which he had been appointed in Berlin in 1935 and bask in the 'influence' he enjoyed as a medieval historian ready and able to put his expertise at the disposal of the foreign policy of the Third Reich.[47] During the War, he was even to hold up the Hansa as the model for the 'new order in Europe'.[48]

Increasingly, and once he had come to acknowledge that the regime had brought about congruence between the state and nation 'carried by a political *Volk*',[49] his inhibitions and pessimism regarding Nazi foreign policy were overcome. By the end of September 1939, the prospect of another world war was one which Rörig could contemplate, if not with equanimity, then with confidence:

> If it does come, then it can be fought out under no better circumstances than these. I consider it entirely possible that the governing powers in England and in France will stick to their watchword of war in spite of everything, but that they will have no practical possibility of executing it themselves and that this will result in a rupture between the government and the people. In other words, those who set out to overthrow our regime will one day see before them, as terrible reality, the discrepancy between their regime and their people. This means in turn: the collapse of the democratic form of government in the face of the authoritarian states. And one more thing: I remember with some satisfaction that, since the beginning of the summer semester of 1938, I have been pointing out that the political supremacy of the European West must necessarily be an episode.[50]

Did this mark the end of Rörig's commitment to democracy? Perhaps not altogether. Even in the middle of the Second World War, while Rörig's propagandist activities on behalf of Nazi expansionism were at their height, he never entirely lost sight of the democratic values with which his version of *völkisch* thought had been imbued. In March 1938, he hinted at present concerns and postwar political ambitions in correspondence with the Strasbourg-based political scientist Ernst Huber. A challenge to Nazism, or at the very least to the current practice of the regime, was heavily implied:

> You wrote one terse sentence: 'Nothing great in history is without danger'. With that, you are – consciously – expressing a conviction about the present day. For this much is just as true today: the threat 'That something will be lost in the concept of the *Volk*' comes from the totality of the state. And the threat is not only to the concept of the *Volk*, but also

to its ethos. In many respects, the *Volk* has become an 'object'....Certainly, we have to put up with all that in order first to create the new world-view in this hard struggle. But after the struggle, we cannot mobilise the 'original' energies of the *Volk* enough.[51]

The fundamental tension between *ethnos* and *demos*, between racialist and democratic approaches to understanding the *Volk* and its history, remained unresolved in Rörig's political thought to the bitter end. It was a tension which repeatedly prompted Rörig to criticise Nazism, but it simultaneously provided him with the ideological equipment to rationalise his support for Nazism. Perhaps it even inspired that support. Certainly, it helps account for what would otherwise appear an abrupt turning point in Rörig's political trajectory in March, 1933. And the tension was, after all, peculiar neither to Rörig himself, nor to the period discussed in this essay. In German law and current political discourse, democratic and ethnic delineations of citizenship still variously compete, coexist and even collapse into each other.

Unquestionably, Rörig was in some respects a trimmer. Yet his claim that his work required no substantive adjustment to meet the Third Reich's understandings of history and the function of the historian was not without foundation. Rörig had only to be eclectic in the pursuit of themes already well-established in his own writing. Already adept in the use of *völkisch* terminology, he now employed it more comprehensively in his scholarship. Of course, from March 1933 onward, he ceased to describe his intentions as 'antifascist'. Shorn of this connotation, his continued celebration of the bourgeoisie did involve an implied critique of certain regime attitudes, but propagated others. Thus, in both his public and his confidential statements during the Third Reich, he simultaneously exhibited characteristics of 'structural resistance' to the totalising claims of the regime and of 'volunteerism' in the freely made offer of his professional services on the regime's behalf.

Notes

1 1882–1952, *Ordinarius* Professor of History at Kiel (1923–35) and Berlin (1935–50). Except where otherwise stated, all subsequent references are to carbon copies of outgoing correspondence in the Rörig Papers, *Archiv der Hansestadt Lübeck*. Emphasis within direct quotations is as in the original.
2 No. 44, to Joseph Hansen, 5.11.1930.
3 No. 48, to Walther Kassel, 27.2.1932.
4 No. 44, to Hansen, 30.10.1930.
5 No. 34, to *Oberverwaltungsrat a. D.* von Eynern, 4.2.1933.
6 No. 33, to Dr Dullien, 9.4.1933.
7 No. 43, to Goetz, 22.5.1932; cf. also no. 34, to von Eynern, 4.2.1933.
8 No. 44, to Hansen, 5.11.1930.
9 No. 33, to 'Hans' (no surname recorded), 18.2.1931.
10 No. 44, to Hansen, 5.11.1930.
11 A full discussion of the twists and turns in Rörig's own conception of the practicalities and principles appropriate to German foreign policy would exceed the

148 *Historians and liberal democracy*

scope of this essay. I intend to return to this subject in a future article.

12 Ibid.

13 No. 48, to Kassel, 27.2.1932.

14 Rörig, 'Les raisons intellectuelles d'une suprématie commerciale: la Hanse', *Annales d'histoire économique et sociale*, 1930, vol. 2, pp. 481–98; cf. Peter Schöttler 'Marc Bloch – Fritz Rörig, Correspondance (1928–1932)', in Peter Schöttler (ed.) *Cahiers Marc Bloch*, 1994, vol. 1, pp. 17–52.

15 Rörig, 'Die europäische Stadt', in Walter Goetz (ed.) *Propyläenweltgeschichte* vol. IV, Berlin, 1932, pp. 277–392.

16 No. 34, to von Eynern, 4.2.1933. For Nazi views on the historical and contemporary shortcomings of the bourgeoisie and the coming 'end of the bourgeois era', see Frank-Lothar Kroll, 'Geschichte und Politik im Weltbild Hitlers', *Vierteljahrshefte für Zeitgeschichte*, 1996, vol. 44, issue 3, pp. 327–54, 349 especially note 47.

17 No. 53, to Hermann Oncken, 6.10.1933.

18 No. 62, to Walter Vogel, 17.3.1933.

19 No. 44, to Fritz Hartung, 9.11.1930.

20 No. 62, to Vogel, 15.4.1933.

21 No. 62, to Vogel, 17.3.1933.

22 No. 33, to Dullien, 9.4.1933.

23 No. 44, to Hansen, 5.11.1930.

24 No. 33, to Dullien, 9.4.1933.

25 No. 39, to Friedrich Carl vom Bruck, 3.9.1933.

26 No. 62, to Vogel, 17.3.1933.

27 Ibid.

28 No. 39, to vom Bruck, 27.9.1933.

29 No. 44, to Hansen, 5.11.1930.

30 No. 39, to vom Bruck, 25.9.1933.

31 No. 33, to Kassel, 27.2.1932.

32 No. 64, to Fritz Wüssing, 6.7.1945. This was not an entirely illegitimate reading of Hitler's highly critical observations on Imperial Germany: cf. Kroll, *op. cit.*, p. 350.

33 No. 39, to vom Bruck, 27.9.1933.

34 No. 52, to Meyer, 25.11.1925.

35 No. 47, to Ernst Huber, 5.8.1938.

36 No. 52, to Oncken, 6.10.1933.

37 No. 47, to Huber, 5.8.1938.

38 Rörig, 'Die europäische Stadt', pp. 377ff and 388ff; No. 47, to Huber, 5.8.1938.

39 No. 44, to Johannes Haller, 10.2.1943; and Haller to Rörig, 7.2.1943.

40 No. 66, to Ahasver von Brandt, 22.2.1942.

41 No. 52, to Oncken, 6.10.1933.

42 No. 39, to vom Bruck, 27.9.1933.

43 No. 46, to Huber, 2.1.1938.

44 No. 45, to Hermann Heimpel, 9.2.1934.

45 No. 45, to Willi Hoppe, 26.2.1935. The reference is to Rörig's debate with the geopolitician O. Weber-Krohse. Cf. Rörig, 'Volkstum und Imperialismus', *Völkische Kultur*, 1935, pp. 43–6, and 'Raum und Volk', ibid., pp. 124–9.

46 Otto Höfler 'Volkskunde und politische Geschichte', *Historische Zeitschrift*, 1940, vol. 162, pp. 1–18; Rörig, 'Volkskunde, Hanse und materialistische Geschichtsschreibung', ibid., 1941, vol. 163, pp. 490–502.

47 No. 66, to von Brandt, 22.2.1942.

48 Staatsbibliothek Berlin, Hartung Papers no. 59/26, Rörig to 'Cari amici armati', 16.11.1939.

49 No. 45, to Heimpel, 9.2.1934.

50 No. 40, to Karl August Eckardt, 30.9.1939.

51 No. 46, to Huber, 8.3.1942.

Further reading

Relationships between nationalism, nazism and German historical scholarship are addressed in Bernd Faulenbach, *Ideologie des deutschen Weges. Die deutsche Geschichte in der Historiographie zwischen Kaiserreich und Nationalsozialismus*, Munich, C.H. Beck, 1980; Karen Schönwälder, *Historiker und Politik. Geschichtswissenschaft im National-sozialismus*, Frankfurt am Main, Campus, 1992; Peter Lambert, 'Paving Germany's 'Peculiar Path': German Nationalism and Historiography since Ranke', in Geoffrey Cubitt (ed.) *Imagining Nations*, Manchester, Manchester University Press, 1998. Several essays on ruralist *Volkshistoriker*, and some debate on the claim of *Volksgeschichte* to be seen as methodologically progressive and a genuine attempt at creating social history in interwar Germany, are included in Hartmut Lehmann and James van Horn Melton (eds) *Paths of Continuity. Central European Historiography from the 1930s to the 1950s*, Cambridge, Cambridge University Press, 1994.

A comprehensive bibliography of Rörig's works (together with a list of forty disserta-tions which emerged from his 'school') compiled by Paul Kaegbein is in Ahasver von Brandt and Willi Koppe (eds) *Städtewesen und Bürgertum als geschichtliche Kräfte. Gedächtnisschrift für Fritz Rörig*, Lübeck, 1953, pp. 535–60. There is a biographical essay, Wilhelm Koppe 'Fritz Rörig und sein Werk', *ibid.*, pp. 9–24. Equally apologetic in tone, an essay by a GDR historian, Peter Neumeister 'Fritz Rörig', in Heinz Heitzer *et al.* (eds) *Wegbereiter der DDR-Geschichtswissenschaft. Biographien*, Berlin, 1989, pp. 216–30. More critically on his scholarship and its significance for Hanseatic studies, see Philippe Dollinger, *The German Hansa*, London, 1970, pp. 20–1 and 159; and (from a GDR perspective) Walter Stark, *Lübeck und Danzig in der zweiten Hälfte des 15. Jahrhunderts*, Weimar, 1973, pp. 9–15.

An expanded version of Rörig's contribution to the *Propyläenweltgeschichte*, prepared from the original manuscript now in the Rörig Papers, appeared posthumously as *Die europäische Stadt und die Kultur des Bürgertums im Mittelalter. Hrsg. von Luise Rörig*, Göttingen, 1955 (4th edn 1964), and (badly) translated into English as *The Medieval Town*, London, 1967.

Some of the most important of his Hanseatic essays and other studies of medieval towns and trade were collected in three volumes: *Hansische Beiträge zur deutschen Wirtschaftsgeschichte*, Breslau, 1928; *Vom Werden und Wesen der Hanse*, Leipzig, 1940; *Wirtschaftskräfte im Mittelalter. Abhandlungen zur Stadt- und Hansegeschichte* ed. Paul Kaegbein, Köln, 1959. In the last of these, the language employed in essays first published between 1933 and 1945 was lightly and inconsistently deracinated, presum-ably by the editor. More explicitly political essays, which already made use of *völkisch* terminology, included the pamphlet *Geschichtsbetrachtung und deutsche Bildung*, Leipzig, 1921, and 'Staatenbildung auf deutschem Boden' in Bernhard Harms (ed.) *Volk und Reich der Deutschen* vol. I, Berlin, 1929, pp. 45–83. Another pamphlet, *Ursachen und Auswirkungen des deutschen Partikularismus*, Tübingen, 1937, amounted to a plea that the Third Reich reconstitute itself as a unitary state.

12 Reclaiming Italy?

Antifascist historians and history in Justice and Liberty

Philip Morgan

Leone Ginzburg lost his lecturing post in literature at the university of Turin after refusing to take the required oath of loyalty to the Italian fascist regime, and was a longtime organiser of the antifascist movement *Giustizia e Libertà* (Justice and Liberty) and, later, of the *Partito d'Azione* (Action Party). He wrote from prison in 1943 about the Risorgimento, the early- to mid-nineteenth century national political and cultural revival, which had as its outcome the political and territorial unification of Italy between 1859 and 1871.

> For the Italians of today [he asserted], the Risorgimento is not simply the name of an historical period;...it is, rather, a still vital and jealously guarded tradition to which we refer continuously in order to derive from it standards of judgement and incentives to action....For Italians, the attitude to take to the Risorgimento still implies...an unequivocal choice which precedes any historiographical evaluation.[1]

It is important to recognise from the start that the historiography of the Risorgimento and the process of national unification in Italy has always been ahistorical. Taken, naturally enough, as the most important defining event of Italy's national history, the Risorgimento has been constantly re-enacted and re-evaluated to match the political conflicts of the time. The study of the Risorgimento is a standing example of the uses, or abuses, of history, occupying as it does the ground between politics and history.

This chapter looks at the uses to which national history was put by the Italian antifascist movement, *Giustizia e Libertà*. It was founded by and largely composed of middle-class intellectuals on the democratic left, drawing heavily on the democratic interventionism of the First World War, which looked to Italy achieving its 'natural' political frontiers at the expense of the Austro-Hungarian Empire and taking its place in a Wilsonian postwar international order. Fascism changed all that; emerging in French exile in 1929, *Giustizia e Libertà* was, with the Italian Communist Party, the only antifascist movement which tried to sustain a presence and activity within Italy itself in the 1930s. Its units in Italy were successively and effectively infiltrated and dismantled by the Italian police, and by the late 1930s, as an organisation it only really survived in exile. Most of its former and current activists, whether in Italy or in exile, joined the Action Party, which, in its brief existence between 1943 and 1947, saw itself as the political heir of *Giustizia e Libertà*. It remained a movement of intellectuals, and some of them were professional historians who held down university posts before and after 1945. Both *Giustizia e Libertà* and the *Partito d'Azione* were the only antifascist political formations in Italy which derived their very existence and rationale from the struggle against fascism. They were the quintessential resistance movements.

There will be some emphasis on the positions of the founder and leader of *Giustizia and Libertà*, Carlo Rosselli, a student of Gaetano Salvemini and for a short time a university lecturer in political economy, before being imprisoned for antifascist activities in the late 1920s; and of his brother, Nello Rosselli, to whom he was personally and politically close. Nello Rosselli was also a student of Salvemini, and a professional historian who held, for a while, a research position at the School of Modern and Contemporary History, the official institute of historical research, whose director was Gioacchino Volpe. Even after two periods of *confino* (internal exile) imposed for antifascist contacts and activities in 1927 and 1929, he was allowed to retain his working contacts with the School. Both brothers were murdered in France in 1937 by French fascists acting on the orders and in the pay of the Italian fascist government.

Both men joined short-lived antifascist organisations before and after early 1925, the decisive point at which Mussolini embarked on the transformation of the liberal parliamentary system into the first 'totalitarian' state, and contributed to antifascist or independent reviews and journals, prior to the formation of *Giustizia e Libertà*. From the start, they identified the need to articulate an antifascist national historiography, because the success of fascism at all seemed to demand some *historical* analysis and explanation. How had it come about? What were the connections, if any, to Italy's recent past? Was fascism in some way the culmination of an imperfect or deformed process of nation-formation which had its roots in the Risorgimento? A proper understanding of fascism, the better to combat it, could only apparently emerge once fascism was set in the context of national history, exploring the linkages between the Risorgimento and postunification Italy, and between liberal Italy and fascism. Ultimately, this historical contextualisation of fascism would be used to justify *Giustizia e Libertà*'s 'break with the past'. The movement's vision of a postfascist society was premised on its rejection both of fascism and of the pre-fascist political system which had made fascism feasible; no 'restoration' was possible. In a very overt and direct way, *Giustizia e Libertà* sought to legitimise antifascism by locating itself and its enemy in Italian history.

If fascism's consolidation in power seemed self-evidently to point to a revision of Italy's recent history, so did the appearance of alternative histories and historiographies, which similarly attempted to situate fascism in national history. Benedetto Croce, perhaps the most important Italian intellectual and historian of his age, had published his *Storia d'Italia dal 1871 al 1915* (*History of Italy from 1871 to 1915*) in 1928. A paean to the idea of liberty and of the civil-ising force of nineteenth-century liberalism, Croce's book practically denied fascism any legitimate space in Italian history, viewing it as a brutal interruption of the country's linear path towards the realisation of a regime of liberty.

The crude fascist appropriation of the Risorgimento appeared in the philosophical and allegedly historical essays of the idealist philosopher and pedagogue, Giovanni Gentile, who became the regime's official ideologue in the 1920s. In *Risorgimento e Fascismo*, published in 1931, Gentile worked back-wards from his own conception of fascism as the realisation of the 'totalitarian' 'ethical state', a state which both embodied the moral values of the nation and educated the nation in those values, to claim a lineage with the ethical and religious concept of life which Giuseppe Mazzini, Vincenzo Gioberti and others imparted to the Risorgimento. The 'liberty' aspired to by the great men of the Risorgimento was the 'liberty' of the state, through and in which the people realised their own 'true' freedom.

There are echoes of this statist interpretation of the Risorgimento in the far more subtle, nuanced and properly historical works of Volpe himself. His Whiggish perspective on the national past was conveyed by the title of his history of Italy, *L'Italia in cammino* (*Italy on its Way*), published in 1927. In this book and in his history of fascism, *Storia del movimento fascista*, published in 1933, Volpe described fascism as a new Risorgimento or as a completion of the Risorgimento and the postunification liberal state, in the sense that fascism has finally inserted the people into state and nation. This was hardly perfect fascist history, since it indicated that the pre-fascist liberal state had national virtues and had started on the process of nation and state formation, when fascists themselves wanted to emphasise that the Italy they were building was everything that the despised liberal 'little Italy' was not. Volpe was too good an historian to allow his work to become an apologia for the fascist regime. But as the head of a major historical research institute, which gathered in the best young professional historians, and as effectively the editor of a major history journal, the *Rivista Storica Italiana*, Volpe certainly influenced the direction and orientation of contemporary historical studies. A tendency to favour studies in foreign policy and diplomacy suggested that the real gain and point of the Risorgimento were to achieve unity and independence, understood as the basis of state power in the international arena rather than as the basis of popular liberty at home. Nello Rosselli was himself a 'victim' of this process: the research task assigned to him by Volpe in the School of Modern and Contemporary History in 1927 was a study of the relations between Britain and the Italian states between 1815 and 1847, a commission which Nello reluctantly and laboriously worked on until 1937.

In the end, Volpe's concern with the history of Italy's *realpolitik* matched the reorganisation of historical studies, and of Risorgimento studies in particular, undertaken from 1933 by the later Minister of National Education, Cesare Maria De Vecchi, who as President of the National Society for the History of the Risorgimento, wanted to put the history profession at the service of the fascist regime. In line with his own clericalist and monarchist version of fascism, De Vecchi encouraged and published studies which pushed the 'origins' of the Risorgimento back to the 'national' groundwork of the early eighteenth century absolutist Piedmontese kings. This slant again put the emphasis on the development of state power before the achievement of unity under liberty, and as a corollary, on the intrinsic and native Italian roots of the national revival, isolating and immunising the country's history from that of the rest of Western Europe. It was this nationalistic closing down of options for historical study and the official historiography's implicit and explicit rejection of a European dimension to Italy's historical development, which the Rossellis were concerned to challenge.

So, in this light, the Rosselli brothers' historical reflections and studies were meant to meet *both* historiographical and political imperatives. In a rather anguished correspondence with his mentor, Salvemini, in late 1930, Nello Rosselli was trying to reconcile his duty as an historian with his duty as an antifascist. He had already rejected the deal offered to him during his first spell in *confino*, after Volpe and Paolo Boselli, the then President of the National Society for the History of the Risorgimento, had interceded with Mussolini on his behalf, that he should devote himself to nothing but historical research and writing. Feeling that the ivory tower of professional detachment was unacceptable, Nello now urged Salvemini to help him find ways of writing 'objective' history which would also contribute 'in not too indirect a fashion to the development of the political struggle'.[2] His brother, Carlo, had fewer doubts about what Nello should do. In Carlo's view, writing 'objective' history in the fascist regime was itself a tendentious and 'political' activity; and, anyway, 'objectivity' was an illusion, since all great historians were 'interpreters of the concrete historical needs of their country'.[3] If there was a tension between historical scholarship and political commitment, then it could not be allowed to inhibit either the writing of history or the activity of politics, as both men were self-consciously occupying and contesting the same historical ground as the fascist regime; part of the point of being an antifascist was to redefine the meaning of Italy's recent national history.

Carlo Rosselli's interpretation of Italy's past was based substantially on the insights and intuitions of a young and influential antifascist intellectual, Piero Gobetti, who famously described fascism as the autobiography of the nation. Gobetti, in turn, was indebted to Giustino Fortunato, the antifascist liberal writer and politician with a special interest in Southern Italy, who so famously defined fascism as revelation rather than revolution. Gobetti's *Risorgimento senza eroi* (Risorgimento without Heroes; again, the title said it all), published in 1926, was not really a systematic history at all, more a series of polemical historical judgements which were used to support his antifascist stance.

For Carlo Rosselli, then, fascism was not *just* a bourgeois class reaction against the post-First World War gains and advances of the organised industrial and agricultural proletariat. It was also the outcome and accentuation of congenital, historical defects of the Italian nation, which were as much moral and temperamental as political and social weaknesses, and amounted to a political immaturity and lack of civic responsibility among Italians: 'Fascism…is Italy, the product of all our history, all our traditions, the current expression of the economic and moral situation of the country, the logical conclusion of a long process slowly maturing from before the First World War'.[4] In this kind of historical perspective, the Risorgimento and political-territorial unification were a 'failure', or at least an incomplete and imperfect achievement, one of the many occasions (the Reformation was another) when Italy had missed its appointment with history. So unity was the work of an aristocratic and bourgeois liberal minority, who as the new nation's political class, had failed to create a really democratic nation-state. The way unification occurred, through diplomacy and war and the enlargement of Piedmont, had deliberately served to exclude and inhibit popular participation and involvement, and in fear of it. As a result, postunification Italy had not seen the integration of the people into the nation-state, which was the unresolved issue of national formation. This diagnosis, if nothing else, indicated the ambiguous historical legacy of the Risorgimento: 'making the nation', unmade during the Risorgimento, was precisely what fascism claimed to be doing through the 'totalitarian' state.

Carlo Rosselli wanted to recover a popular and socialist Risorgimento, neglected or obscured in the 'official' historiography, the Risorgimento of those men and movements who had been 'defeated' in the Piedmontese, monarchical-liberal and socially conservative outcome of the process of national unification: the democratic and republican nationalists, Mazzini and Giuseppe Garibaldi; the socialists and federalists, Carlo Pisacane, Giuseppe Ferrari, Giuseppe Montanelli and Carlo Cattaneo. All this served Rosselli's critique of Marxist socialism and his articulation of an alternative 'liberal socialism'. Finding socialism in the Risorgimento, finding a Risorgimento socialism, allowed him to disengage socialism from Marxism and recouple it to a national tradition which informed his own political stance: a democratic and republican socialism, a socialism achieved through democracy and the exercise of liberty.

What Carlo Rosselli did politically, his brother Nello did historically. The 'forgotten' Risorgimento was essentially Nello's concern, too, as he kicked against the actual research programme which he had been allocated by Volpe in the School of Modern and Contemporary History. A reworking of his graduation thesis, *Mazzini e Bakunin*, appeared in 1927; his *Carlo Pisacane nel Risorgimento Italiano*, which he had been working on since 1925, came out in 1932. The subject matter was itself part of a revision of Risorgimento history. His Mazzini was not the romantic and romanticised visionary in exile, the Mazzini of *Young Italy*, but the 'social' Mazzini, with Rosselli locating the start of a socialist workers' movement in Italy in the 1850s and showing how Mazzinian and Garibaldian workers' associations found their way into an anarchist-dominated First International in the early 1860s.

What had apparently started out as a slim, straightforward narrative biography of the Risorgimento socialist, Pisacane, became the peg for a more general historical re-evaluation of the Risorgimento. Nello Rosselli regarded Pisacane's aborted vision of national self-liberation through a popular peasant revolution, inspired by the Mazzinian socialism of 'liberty and association', as anachronistic, out of its time; national unification was impossible to achieve on these terms in the 1850s. Nevertheless, Pisacane's inevitable 'failure' was set in a general overview of the Risorgimento which emphasised the absence of popular involvement and choice in the actual outcome of unification, vitiating the workings and development of the postunification political system. It scarcely needs emphasising that this was a political as much as an historical judgement, or an historical judgement which was transformed into a political one.

It can perhaps now be understood why Nello Rosselli's biography of Pisacane was regarded at the time by the protagonists of *Giustizia e Libertà* as a major contribution to the struggle against fascism. The movement incorporated the analysis of the 'failed' Risorgimento into its projections of a postfascist Italy. It came most strikingly in Carlo Rosselli's idea of the antifascist resistance as an act of national self-liberation, like a 'second Risorgimento' which 'must shatter the compromises of the first and open the way to social emancipation'.[5] So, *Giustizia e Libertà* was the vanguard of a 'second Risorgimento': 'second' because it would not repeat the mistakes of the first and would, in fact, make good the defects and limitations of the first; 'second', because of the 'two' Risorgimentos, the 'official' and the defeated 'popular' one, it was the latter which *Giustizia e Libertà* looked to for that combination of liberty and social justice which inspired its own antifascist political programme.

Carlo Rosselli's view of the 'second Risorgimento' was not uncontested within *Giustizia e Libertà* itself. There was a vigorous debate in the movement's weekly newspaper in May 1935, over the significance of the 'first' Risorgimento for the antifascist struggle.[6] Some contributors, who significantly soon left the movement for the Socialist Party, argued that the Risorgimento was a bad teacher because nationalism was demonstrably destructive of individual liberty and social emancipation, then as now; and that the Risorgimento should be left well alone as a model for present and future political action, since it provided more lessons and myths for fascism than for revolutionaries like themselves who wanted to remake Italy altogether on the ruins of fascism.

Carlo Rosselli's intervention in the debate made it clear that he saw legitimate parallels between the past and the present. He seemed to regard *Giustizia e Libertà* as the *analogue* of the popular version of the Risorgimento. This ran consciously through the activities and aims of the movement in the 1930s. With explicit reference to the expatriation of Mazzini, Garibaldi, Pisacane and others, *Giustizia e Libertà* took what comfort it could from the fact of political exile. Extrapolating from the 'first' Risorgimento, the movement could say that sometimes it was necessary to live outside one's country when it no longer embodied one's ideals, that one could fight for the liberty of another country and since liberty was indivisible, be also fighting for the liberty of one's own country, drawing the parallel here between *Giustizia e Libertà*'s raising of a unit to join the republican side in the Spanish Civil War and the Italian patriots who participated in the Spanish liberal revolutions against the absolute monarchy in the first half of the nineteenth century. The provocative, high-profile gestures of resistance to the fascist regime in the early 1930s emulated the heroic, conspiratorial acts of *Young Italy*. The leaflets dropped over Milan from a light aircraft in 1930 reminded the Milanese of the glorious 'five days' of the 1848 Revolution in the city, when the citizens' militia had expelled the Austrian garrison; fascism was now the 'internal' 'Austrian' despotism.

Again, *Giustizia e Libertà*'s political programme was in its name, 'Justice and Liberty', a synthesis of 'liberal-socialism' which explicitly revised and rejected the Marxist reformist and maximalist wings of pre-fascist Italian socialism. Carlo Rosselli's 'humanistic' socialism, rather more a well-meaning expression of human solidarity and fraternity across the classes than the product of class struggle, with social justice arriving as a result of individuals and groups exercising democratic rights and freedoms in a democratic republic, was as near to Mazzinian socialism as one could get. The Action Party of 1943 took the name of the Mazzinian formation it meant to emulate, and aspired to be the core of an intended broad, non-Marxist antifascist democratic and republican front.

We have seen that the Rosselli brothers' treatment of national history was used to try to explain the rise of fascism and refute what they saw as the distorted claims of fascism's place in the nation's history. They also attempted to develop a view of Italy's recent past which would validate both their repudiation of fascism and pre-fascism and their claim to shape the new, postfascist Italy. On the basis of what Carlo Rosselli saw as a continuity of ideals linking antifascism and the 'popular' Risorgimento, *Giustizia e Libertà* looked to a 'liberal-socialist' reconstruction of Italy after the defeat of fascism.

Whether it achieved this is, of course, another story. But there is a final Mazzinian flourish or twist to the historiographical and political tale of *Giustizia e Libertà*. Between 1932 and 1934, Nello Rosselli tried to found a journal of nineteenth-century European history, with the declared aim of the 'de-toxification of the nationalistic germ of modern historiography'.[7] He wanted historians from other European countries to contribute, as well as the bright young men whom Volpe had recruited to his research institute. The project never materialised. Volpe endorsed it, and induced Mussolini to give his consent, though at the very point Nello was deciding to abandon the initiative. Official approval probably reinforced Nello's decision not to pursue the matter any further; he seemed to think that it would prejudice the independence of the proposed journal. Most of his fellow young historians in the School were cautious and non-committal, and effectively making themselves unavailable, if only for fear of being associated professionally with a person who had been imprisoned for his antifascism. But the project was significant precisely because it ran counter to the current nationalistic reorganisation of historical studies under De Vecchi. Against an approach which focused exclusively on Italian history and on an autarchic reconstruction of that history, Nello Rosselli wanted to expose Italian historians to the work and methods of historians from other countries, and re-connect Italian history to European history, bringing out what was common or supranational to national histories in terms of interests, culture and ideals. So the Risorgimento, in a European historical perspective, could be studied as the realisation in Italy of Europe-wide ideals of liberty and nationhood, which was the force of Franco Venturi's intervention in the 1935 *Giustizia e Libertà* debate on the legacy of the Risorgimento.

This abortive attempt to make Italy part of Europe historically, matched the political Europeanism of both the Rosselli brothers, which once again was supported by reference to Risorgimento models. In the debate on the Risorgimento in 1935, Carlo had conceded the point that nationalism was inimical to liberty but recognised that national sentiments were real and strong in Italy, as elsewhere. The challenge, to him, was to transcend nationalism by disassociating the idea of the nation from the statolatry, the imperialism and the xenophobia which was epitomised in fascism. This was what lay behind *Giustizia e Libertà*'s opposition to the Italian conquest of Ethiopia in 1935–6, and Carlo Rosselli's extraordinary 'Reply to Mussolini': 'To you, Fascists, the empire; to us the nation'.[8] Antifascists were quite consciously 'traitors of the Fascist *patria*', and 'the loyal followers (*fedeli*) of another *patria*'.[9] The alternative *patria* was both a 'free' Italy, a nation whose citizens enjoyed and exercised their liberties internally and respected other similarly constituted nations, and also therefore by extension, humanity. One could only be properly patriotic about one's country if it was free, if it was a nation of free and equal citizens. The human and humane values of liberty and social justice which *Giustizia e Libertà* espoused were by their nature indivisible and universal, oblivious to nationality. The references back to the Risorgimento were self-evident. In opposition to the exclusive, statist, nationalistic and imperialist stance of fascism, Carlo Rosselli wanted to resurrect the Risorgimento meaning of nation, the republican and libertarian patriotism of Mazzini, who in the manifesto of *Young Europe* envisaged Italy and other European countries becoming free nation-states and then associating in a European republican confederation. The political programmes of both *Giustizia e Libertà* and the Action Party contained a commitment to forms of federalism at home and abroad, in common with practically all non-communist antifascist resistance groups in Western Europe. It would perhaps be too much to say that *Giustizia e Libertà* repudiated the nation-state as the most appropriate area for people's social and political activity. But one could only expect that their experience of and opposition to interwar fascism, buttressed by a selective reading of Italy's own recent history, would weaken their sentimental and political attachment to the nation-state.

Notes

1 'La tradizione del Risorgimento', *Il Ponte*, 17, 1, 1961, p. 43.
2 Letter of 4 November 1930, in Z. Ciuffoletti (ed.) *Nello Rosselli. Uno storico sotto il fascismo. Lettere e scritti vari (1924–1937)*, Florence, La Nuova Italia, 1979, p. 74.
3 Letter from Carlo Rosselli to his mother, 16 December 1927, quoted in Ciuffoletti, *Nello Rosselli*, p. xxxvii.
4 This characteristic judgement is taken from his article, 'Contro il pessimismo', in the anti-Fascist journal *Il Quarto Stato*, 26 June 1926, quoted in P. Bagnoli, 'La battaglia socialista de *Il Quarto Stato*', in Istituto Storico della Resistenza in Toscana, *'Giustizia e Libertà' nella lotta antifascista e nella storia d'Italia*, Florence, La Nuova Italia, 1978, p.137.
5 Carlo Rosselli, 'Per l'unificazione politica del proletariato italiano', *Giustizia e Libertà* (the movement's weekly newspaper, published in Paris, 1934–40), 14 May 1937.
6 See Andrea Caffi ('Andrea'), 'Appunti su Mazzini', *Giustizia e Libertà*, 29 March 1935; Franco Venturi ('Gianfranchi'), 'Sul Risorgimento Italiano', *Giustizia e Libertà*, 5 April 1935; Nicola Chiaromonte ('Luciano'), 'Sul Risorgimento', *Giustizia e Libertà*, 19 April 1935; Carlo Rosselli ('Curzio'), 'Discussione sul Risorgimento', *Giustizia e Libertà*, 26 April 1935; Franco Venturi, 'Discussione sul Risorgimento. Replica de Gianfranchi', *Giustizia e Libertà*, 3 May 1935; Andrea Caffi, 'Discussione sul Risorgimento', *Giustizia e Libertà*, 10 May 1935.
7 Quoted in G. Belardelli, *Nello Rosselli. Uno storico antifascista*, Florence, Passigli Editori, 1982, p. 151.
8 'Risposta a Mussolini', *Giustizia e Libertà*, 21 May 1936.
9 'Realismo', *Giustizia e Libertà*, 10 April 1936.

Further reading

A. Casali, *Storici Italiani fra le due guerre. La 'Nuova Rivista Storica' (1917–1943)*, Naples, Guida Editore, 1980. A study of the 'schools' of Italian historiography in the interwar period, focusing on the historical journal *Nuova Rivista Storica*, which maintained its independence in the 1930s and kept alive the 'economic-juridical' historiographical line.

C. Casucci (ed.) *Carlo Rosselli. Scritti dell'esilio*, vol. 1, *Giustizia e Libertà e la Concentrazione Antifascista (1929–1934)*, Turin, Einaudi, 1988; vol. 2, *Dallo scioglimento della Concentrazione Antifascista alla guerra di Spagna (1934–1937)*, Turin, Einaudi, 1992. An anthology, with introduction, of Carlo Rosselli's writings, mainly taken from *Giustizia e Libertà*.

A. Garosci, *La vita di Carlo Rosselli*, 2 vols, Rome, Edizioni U, 1945. The earliest biography of Carlo Rosselli, written by a historian who was a member of *Giustizia e Libertà*.

C. Rosselli, *Socialismo Liberale*, Turin, Einaudi, 1979. Rosselli's political testament, first published in 1930, and including a Gobettian analysis of Italian history.

N. Rosselli, *Carlo Pisacane nel Risorgimento Italiano*, Turin, Einaudi, 1977. A re-publication of Rosselli's biography of the Risorgimento socialist.

N. Rosselli, *Mazzini e Bakunin. Dodici anni di movimento operaio in Italia (1860–1872)*, Turin, Einaudi, 1972. A re-publication of Rosselli's study of the origins of the Italian working-class movement.

N. Rosselli, *Saggi sul Risorgimento e altri scritti*, Turin, Einaudi, 1980. A posthumous collection of Rosselli's historical writings, first published in 1946.

S.J. Woolf, *The Italian Risorgimento*, London, Longmans, 1969. A short anthology of texts, with commentary, on interpretations of the Risorgimento.

K.R. Greenfield, 'The Historiography of the Risorgimento since 1920', *Journal of Modern History*, 1935, vol. 7, 1. A contemporary view of Italian historiographical trends.

C. Pavone, 'Le idee della Resistenza. Antifascisti e fascisti di fronte alla tradizione del Risorgimento', *Passato e Presente*, 1959, vol. 7. An analysis of the various attempts of both the fascist regime and the antifascist resistance movements to identity themselves with Risorgimento traditions.

N. Tranfaglia, 'Carlo Rosselli dal processo di Savona alla fondazione di *GL* (1927–1929)', *Il Movimento di Liberazione in Italia*, 1972, vol. 24, pp. 106ff. A study of Carlo Rosselli's political evolution and of the writing of *Socialismo Liberale*.

Part V

Fascist historiography and the nation-state

After the First World War, Europe descended into economic chaos and political instability. Fascist movements emerged in most European states. Benito Mussolini came to power in Italy in 1922 and established a fascist dictatorship from 1925; in Germany Adolf Hitler was appointed Chancellor in January 1933 and within a few months had set up a dictatorship. In France, the fascist leagues which prospered in the 1930s failed to topple the republican regime, but an extreme right-wing government, possessed of a minority fascist current, was installed as a result of the defeat of France at the hands of the Nazis in 1940. All three regimes endeavoured to use history to bolster their policies. However, rather surprisingly, there was a distinct lack of a specifically fascist historiography in all three countries.

Whereas historians in Italy and Germany had to come to terms in the interwar period with fascist governments or choose political exile, French historians were confronted with an authoritarian regime only after defeat in the Second World War. Bertram Gordon shows that most university historians kept their distance from nationalist and racist historical interpretations, and the attempts of the Vichy government to direct research into particular areas were largely unsuccessful. The Vichy government could rely only upon an amateur right-wing historiography, the basis of which had been laid in the period 1885 to 1914. Some such historians launched frankly into racist nationalism.

In the German case, as Hans Schleier shows, many of the traditional paradigms of dominant Protestant-Prussian and, a little more surprisingly, minority Catholic historiography, fitted well with aspects of Nazi ideology. Schleier demonstrates that *Volksgeschichte* (people's history) was especially closely allied to propagating and justifying Nazi race policies. Some historians were even involved in the planning of measures that led to the Holocaust. Many professional historians, even those sympathetic to the regime, were suspicious of Nazi attempts to write a racially based history, not least because racism was often connected to a disdain for conventional historiographical methods. Mainstream historians nevertheless modified their subject matter and thereby endorsed many of the aims of the regime, including military conquest in the east at the expense of the Slavs.

The Italian historical profession was even more divided on the question of fascism. Martin Clark assesses the work of the most eminent Italian historian of the period, Gioacchino Volpe. Volpe presented the Risorgimento as an essentially nationalist movement and thus as a kind of precursor to fascism. Volpe was, however, no mere propagandist. He wrote history designed to foster specific political aims of Italian fascism, founding, for example, the *Archivio Storico della Corsica*, a journal devoted to the '*italianità*' of Corsica – to support Italian expansionism in the Mediterranean. Yet he also used his influence to protect antifascist historians.

13 Right-wing historiographical models in France, 1918–45

Bertram M. Gordon

As in the case of French politics, there was no one unified right-wing historiography between the end of the First World War and the Second in France. Indeed, most striking in this period is the relative lack of a right-wing historiography among the professional university-affiliated historians. Rather, right-wing approaches to French history were more prominent among non-professionals writing history in France, many of whom were partisans of Charles Maurras's antidemocratic, antirepublican, anti-Semitic, and royalist *Action Française*. Others, more extreme in a taxonomy of nationalist and racialist thought, held more marginal views and, after 1940, were often propagandists for the Axis new order.

Virtually all of these writers focused on the nation, which, on occasion, was associated with ethnicity and race. Although their views were invariably exclusionary, aimed at Jews and freemasons, among others, they did not always converge regarding specific events in French history. The 1789 Revolution, for example, usually condemned by *Action Française* sympathisers, such as Jacques Bainville and Pierre Gaxotte, was praised by Georges Soulès, André Mahé and Louis Thomas, who promoted varieties of racial populism after the 1940 defeat. None of these writers were university historians. Interestingly as well, the post-1940 writers said little about the significance of the 1940 armistice, signed at Compiègne, the site of the 1918 armistice imposed by the Allies on defeated Germany. Their focus instead was on the deficiencies of the Third Republic and the anticipated opportunities offered by the new government of Marshal Philippe Pétain.

Action Française cast a lengthy shadow across French literary life during the first-half of the twentieth century and the writing of history was no exception, as the work of Bainville and Gaxotte was to show. The publication in 1924 of Bainville's *Histoire de France*, although criticised by professional historians, had an undoubted sales success for the next thirty years among the generally educated French public. Beyond *Action Française*, French history was given a racial interpretation by George Montandon, who held university posts in anthropology rather than history. His views were given greater opportunities by the pro-Axis perspectives opened with the defeat of 1940.

In contrast to *Action Française*, the community of university historians was not a fertile field for the right. Trained as positivists in the late-nineteenth century, most university historians paid at least lip service to the ideal of an objective history divorced from partisan politics. By the interwar years, the primacy of the nation in French history had come to transcend left–right distinctions in the writings of the university historians. The teaching and writing of secondary school historians and geographers – the two were taught together in France – were informed by a republican and national belief system that, in Ernest Lavisse's words of 1885, portrayed the 'unfolding of the French genius'.[1] Emerging from the Dreyfus Affair, followed by the First World War, the writing of history, not surprisingly, was put to the service of the 'nation' not only on the right but also by historians such as Albert Mathiez in his work on the French Revolution. A Carnegie Foundation study in 1923 found French history textbooks replete with unverifiable accounts extolling national feeling, with most of the books expressing deep reservations regarding the League of Nations. While the importance of the nation was accepted across the political spectrum in the teaching of history in France, by the 1930s the cutting edge of university research had shifted to the '*Annales*' approach, which meant privileging the accounts of large socioeconomic forces in history, often leaving the consideration of the individual and the nation to the non-professionals of *Action Française*. Defence of the nation was associated with the right, as the left assumed a more internationalist stance, and professional historians sought to remain above the fray. The divorce between the nation and historical science left the partisan right-wing interpretations of French history mainly to non-university amateurs.[2]

The February riots of 1934 politicised a bit more the world of the university historians, a few of whom joined the *Cercles Fustel de Coulanges*, which, although an autonomous organisation, had been organised by *Action Française* in 1928. The *Cercles Fustel* promoted historians such as Pierre Heinrich, who taught at Lyon, and Antoinette de Beaucorp, whose *Histoire de France* was published in 1933. De Beaucorp's book suggested that the Third Republic, by focusing on colonial expansion, had distracted France from her patriotic duty to seek the return of Alsace-Lorraine, taken by the Germans in 1871, thereby contributing to the perpetuation of tension and the coming of war.[3] A petition circulated on 4 October 1935 for the 'defence of the West', following the Italian invasion of Ethiopia, was drafted by Henri Massis and signed by several prominent *Action Française* personalities, including Maurras and Gaxotte. The 150th anniversary celebrations of the French Revolution in 1939 were criticised by Gaxotte and other *Action Française* sympathisers but the university historians maintained relative silence in the name of objectivity.

The terrain abandoned by the university historians was claimed in large measure by *Action Française* through the work of Bainville and Gaxotte. Bainville's 1924 *Histoire de France* treated late-nineteenth- and twentieth-century French history in a neutral tone but the book reflected an *Action Française* view of history. Portraying the history of France as a national epic with the French nation a composite of races, Bainville depicted a France in continual conflict with Germans, English or Spanish, and sometimes a coalition of two or more of these powers. By the early twentieth century, Germany, 'driven to invade her neighbours', was determined for war with France.[4] The 1918 victory had not freed France from danger. 'France [he wrote] was to find again the permanent laws of her history; between England and Germany, she was still compelled to make her way'.[5] Bainville saw in history a constant struggle between the 'revolutionary spirit' and the 'conservative spirit' and between 'anarchy' and 'order'. The Catholic party represented order and national unity. Enemies were Jacobins, demagogues, rioters and Protestants, the last by their very nature incorporating revolution. The revolutionary lower classes were described as 'rabble' in Bainville's account of the French Revolution.[6]

The publication of Gaxotte's first book, *La Révolution Française*, in 1928, complemented Bainville's in its construction of an *Action Française* historiography. A consistent critic of the 1789 Revolution, Gaxotte extolled the venerability of old regime inequalities, which, he contended, had preserved the liberties of the French, in contrast to the eighteenth-century abstract rationalism he saw in the post-revolutionary settlement. He praised a regionalism that was integrally tied to national sentiment, a connection that would also be made by Vichy. As Bainville, Gaxotte favoured hierarchy and order, all of which, he wrote, characterised the France of Louis XIV, Colbert, Vauban, Racine, Poussin and Bossuet. To Gaxotte, the Reformation 'was a preliminary explosion of destructive individualism and republican sentimentality'.[7] The baleful influence of the eighteenth-century *philosophes* combined with a lack of leadership on the part of the government of Louis XVI, and a stirring up of the mob by the 'liberals', produced the 'anarchy' of the Revolution. Gaxotte's account of the Revolution focused on the role of personalities and his sympathies were clearly with the king and the church. Proceedings of the Legislative Assembly were described as 'a debauch of words'.[8]

Ironically, in view of the importance he usually placed on personalities in explaining historical events, Gaxotte downplayed that of Robespierre. Condemning Robespierre, Gaxotte, however, aimed harsher criticism at historians who had tried to exculpate the Revolution itself by emphasising the excesses of the Jacobin leader. To Gaxotte, the issue was less the personality and role of Robespierre than the Terror itself as the 'essence of the Revolution'. The *sans-culottes*' movement during the Terror represented to Gaxotte, who might also have had the 1871 Commune and the 1917 Bolshevik Revolution in mind, a proletarian revolution under the guise of the 'despotism of Liberty, the dogmatism of Reason', all of which was the regime of 'oppression, tyranny, and hell' in which the 'dregs' governed France.[9]

In their relatively dispassionate-sounding histories, Bainville and Gaxotte said little of race. In contrast, the work of George Montandon, whose book, *L'Ethnie Française*, was published in 1935, argued for a French *ethnie* (ethnic group identity) as a physical (*somatique*) construction built on elements of several races. Born and educated as a medical doctor in Switzerland, Montandon had emigrated to France, where he turned to anthropology. In 1928 he was named member of the *Institut français d'anthropologie*, in 1933 professor at the *École d'anthropologie*, and in 1936 was naturalised as a French citizen. He also occupied the chair of anthropology at the *Musée d'histoire naturelle*.

In *L'Ethnie Française*, Montandon argued for the adoption of a new term, '*ethnie*' (ethnic group), to correspond to 'nationality'. Nation and nationality might be coterminous in France, he argued, but in Switzerland a person might be of the Swiss nation but of Swiss-German nationality. 'Ethnic group', or nationality was to be understood as 'a natural group established by its members and its neighbours'. The French ethnic group, he wrote, embraced the three main races of the 'grand Europoid or white race', whereas the 'nation' was a political grouping, created by history and contained in the fabric of the state. Race, he concluded, was a scholarly or learned concept, ethnic group a natural one, and nation a political one.[10] In *L'Ethnie Française*, Montandon argued that the correspondence between race and ethnic group was rare and France was a country with no one race of its own. If one wanted to design a racial type for the French nation, it would be the Alpine type. In other words, the French were not a race but possessed a 'racial type'.[11]

Montandon's view of history was framed largely in terms of his racial typologies, for which he offered examples of photographs of prominent French political, literary, and anthropological personalities. The French Revolution and the era of democratisation that followed he saw as a revenge of a brachycephalous autocthonous race against the dominant caste of 'sub-Nordics', comprised of German and Gallic stock. After cautioning that contemporary nations drew their population from all kinds of racial groups in their territory, Montandon nevertheless noted a large proportion of 'Alpine types' among the Paris police services – fewer among the uniformed than among the plainclothes services, the latter recruited among the 'sturdy fellows'.[12] He argued that there was no Jewish 'race' but, as with the French, went on to discuss what he called a Jewish 'type', in this case characterised most commonly by a convex nose.[13] He proposed the creation of an independent Palestine to which those Jews who wished to maintain their identity could go, whereas the remaining ones would be forced to assimilate. In the end, Montandon argued for the persistence of racial types, personified by psychic qualities. Racial differences, he concluded, were reflected in politics as well, as in the distinction between the more 'democratic' Alpine and the more 'feudal' sub-Nordic types.

The defeat of 1940 did little to alter the relationship of professional university historians to their *confrères* outside the history faculties, except to offer greater opportunities to the latter to promote right-wing views. Vichy wanted historians to defend the 'national revolution' by exhorting the love of the fatherland and extolling symbols, such as Joan of Arc, whose sites and images were used to generate anti-English feeling and evoke France's peasant traditions. To better promote the study of the '*enracinement*' (rootedness) of the nation, the Vichy government reformed the administration of local archaeological study in France. In February 1941, Pétain appointed as Minister of Education Jérôme Carcopino, a professor of ancient Roman history at the Sorbonne, who was especially involved in the promotion of archaeology. Vichy favoured the professionalisation of archaeology by creating a consultative division of the *CNRS* (*Centre National des Recherches Scientifiques*), which named directors of antiquities, often university people, who were given powers over local sites, collections and museums. Although Carcopino's aims were technical, his reforms fit in with Vichy's goals of promoting national and regional history. The fact that these reforms were maintained after the Liberation, was recalled by Carcopino with satisfaction in his memoirs in 1953.

The national revolution emphasised a 'return to the soil', that promoted regional folklore and the role of the peasant, extolled by Gustav Thibon. Promoting a folklore of regional antiquities, Vichy's reforms cut across disciplines such as history, sociology and anthropology, orientated in large measure around the *Musée National des Arts et Traditions Populaires*. The study of folklore had been promoted by the Popular Front government, whose introduction of paid vacations had been accompanied with programmes for the new vacationers to learn more about the regions of France. Under the Popular Front, however, the focus of folklore had embraced the totality of popular culture, whereas Vichy restricted it to the study of the peasantry.

An *Action Française* mentality informed much of the work to promote folklore and regional studies during the first two years of the Vichy government but in April 1942, the return to power of Pierre Laval, uninterested in traditionalist folklore, the increasing demands of the German Occupation, and the changing fortunes of the War slowed the process. Historic architecture was privileged with the publications of books such as Maurice Wanecq's *Défense et illustration de la Maison Française*, whose title proclaims its agenda, in 1942 and directives given to museums to focus on houses and buildings constructed before 1870. The regional studies promoted by Vichy through conferences and study groups, and Pétain's argument that love of the nation was expressed in the love of its regions, echoed the *Action Française* emphasis on the historic provinces of France. Both Pétain and Maurras had Mediterranean orientations to the South of France, in part because the South was unoccupied before November 1942, but also because of *Action Française*'s partiality for ancient Greece and its culture. Maurras, Thibon and Pétain also shared a partiality for the Provençal poet Frédéric Mistral.

Vichy's promotion of peasant and artisanal life, however, denied their historicity and gave them an artificial non-temporal quality. In addition, the regionalism favoured by Vichy was lost in a uniformity of images orchestrated by the government to portray a traditional France, with Pétain at the helm. A language of religion was used by people with little or no religious faith, a characteristic of many of the *Action Française* leaders, who were seeking to promote the image of an 'authentic France', in reality the evocation of a traditional, provincial, and religious France by urban, centralising social and intellectual elites.[14] The university historians' community, as represented in the academic *Revue Historique*, called for caution in assessing the new emphasis on tradition and folklore. A review of Albert Dauzat's *Le Village et le Paysan de France* noted that folklore, regionalism, and return to the soil were in vogue, but still called for better documentation. It criticised the book for the 'banal praise' with which it treated the return to the soil campaign and for being too casual in its use of sources.[15]

An example of the tension that could develop between the non-university right-wing historians and the professional historical establishment was manifested in 1941 with the appearance of Louis Thomas's book, *Alphonse Toussenel, socialiste national anti-sémite*, part of a series called *Precursors*, designed to show historical precedents for the Nazi new order. The book sought to revive from obscurity and extol the memory of Toussenel (1803–85), described by Thomas as an anti-Semitic socialist. Seeing Toussenel as a spiritual precursor to *Mein Kampf*, Thomas complained that the nineteenth-century writer had been ignored by historians in France and that he been the subject of no university studies. Edouard Drumont's anti-Semitism, Thomas argued, had been an 'elegant' anti-Semitism of the fashionable Saint-Germain district of Paris, occasioned by the Dreyfus Affair of the 1890s, whereas Toussenel's had been a more visceral socialist anti-Semitism, rooted in the peasantry.[16] To both Toussenel and Thomas, the Jews were the eternal Shylock, the most acquisitive 'nation' in the world with the possible exception of the Chinese.[17]

Key for Thomas was Toussenel's message: '*La France aux Français*' (France for the French).[18] A review of Thomas's book in the *Revue Historique* described it as a 'mediocre' contribution to the history of anti-Semitism, with a 'polemical accent' that made it difficult to be considered as a work of history.[19] On 6 November 1942, following Laval's return to power and the replacement of Carcopino as Minister of Education with the veteran of the *Cercles Fustel* and collaborationist Abel Bonnard, a new Chair of the History of Judaism was created, held by Henri Labroué, to promote anti-Semitism. Labroué's courses were boycotted by most of the students. When Labroué proposed in 1943 to add 'the Jewish question in the world' to the examination for the *histoire en licence* (certificate in history), to the baccalaureate, and the *agrégation*, the Sorbonne History Committee stalled it by making no official response. By a vote of 33 to 1 the historians then backed the recommendation of the History Committee. In February 1943, Bonnard convened a meeting on the teaching of history and geography, accompanied by an attack of the collaborationist press against the 'fallacious scientific objectivity' of the professional historians. At the meeting, Bonnard called for the historians to fight against 'unhealthy egalitarianism'. His ideological initiatives, however, foundered as discussion focused on professional and technical issues. Censorship restraints and growing paper shortages also helped inhibit educational change under Vichy.

The lack of interest among professional historians in bending to the political winds of Vichy was reflected in the recommendations regarding library acquisitions, made by the members of the *Section Contemporaine* of the *Comité des travaux historiques et scientifiques*. They rejected the self-flagellation literature born of the defeat, such as René Benjamin's *Le printemps tragique*, and Bertrand de Jouvenel's *Après la défaite*. In addition, they passed negative judgements on Pétain's *Appels* of 1940, Daniel Halévy's *Nos épreuves 1814, 1871, 1940*, René Benjamin's *Le Maréchal et son peuple*, and a book by *Action Française* sympathiser Robert Vallery-Radot on the freemasons. The *Revue Historique* criticised Vallery-Radot's work as 'mediocre' and Halévy's as a 'curious disconcerting mélange of history and polemic'. Although the Halévy notice appeared after the Liberation, it was undoubtedly written during the Occupation.[20] The *Ecole des Chartes* was the only right-wing pole of the historical profession but its work was limited largely to the elucidation and publication of medieval texts.

Again, as before 1940, right-wing histories came mainly from outside the universities. An example, representing *Action Française* thought, was the work of Vallery-Radot, whose antimasonic work had already been criticised by the *Revue Historique*. Like Maurras, who welcomed the advent of the Pétain government, if not the defeat of France, as a 'divine surprise', Vallery-Radot saw a 'bad dream dissipating' with the arrival of Pétain. In *Sources d'une Doctrine Nationale*, a book published in 1942, Vallery-Radot traced the problems of France back to what he called the false doctrines of 1789, based on freemasonry and the 'dictatorship of the so-called Sovereign People [his capitals] imagined by Jean-Jacques [Rousseau]'.[21] Seeing French precursors for German nazism and Italian fascism in the French theorists Arthur de Gobineau and Maurras, respectively, Vallery-Radot contended that the French, themselves, had needed the defeat to wake up to the 'chimeras of 1789'.

Even more racially focused than *Action Française* during the Occupation years were collaborationist publications such as Thomas's book on Toussenel. Such literature was often produced with German support in occupied Paris. Representing this viewpoint with respect to history were the scathing and denunciatory *Les Décombres* (*The Ruins*) by Lucien Rebatet, published in July 1942, and *La Fin du Nihilisme* (*The End of Nihilism*), a book intended to provide what would be called today a sociobiological doctrine for the national revolution, by Georges Soulès and André Mahé, published in 1943. The appearance of *Les Décombres*, which even Vichy tried to suppress, made Rebatet a celebrity *de scandale* in occupied Paris. A dissident from *Action Française* who specialised in cinema and the arts, and an avowedly fascist and anti-Semitic journalist even before the War, Rebatet presented the recent history of France as one of a decadence, caused largely by the Jews, that had continued unchanged even into the Vichy years. *Les Décombres* was more autobiographical than historical in the sense of Bainville and Gaxotte, but its story was set against the history of France during the late 1930s and early 1940s.

In a sequence similar to *Mein Kampf*, Rebatet describes how the onset of his anti-Semitism had been awakened in him by *Action Française*, whose hostility to the Jews, however, had aged and lost its fervour since 1918.[22] Key to the history of modern France, Rebatet wrote, in a passage that bore similarities to the arguments of Bainville and Gaxotte, had been the development of the 'insane dogma of the equality of men', the cover under which the Jews had infiltrated virtually all aspects of French life during the previous century and a half. At a time when round-ups for concentration camps were already occurring in occupied France, Rebatet wrote that there was no longer a 'Jewish question' but a 'Christian question'. Beyond ethics, the issue of Jews to him was a matter for the police.[23]

In words that echoed Maurras's 'divine surprise' following the 10 July 1940 replacement of the parliamentary government by what would become known as the Vichy government, Rebatet rejoiced that 'the operation dreamt of and desired for so many years had lasted five hours'. The defeat was better than a military victory as it had destroyed parliamentary government.[24] A national socialist renewal awaited a France, wounded but still intact and no longer '*enjuivé*' [literally: en-Jewed]. What France had not been able to achieve herself, the defeat would bring about.[25]

La Fin du Nihilisme was the effort of Soulès and Mahé to replace the 'myths' of 1789: liberty, equality, fraternity and progress, with a new set: race, soil and the mission of France. Written in 1942 and published the following year, *La Fin du Nihilisme* was based on the ideas of Maurice Barrès, Georges Sorel, Friedrich Nietzsche and Alfred Rosenberg. The book called for a new elite to rejuvenate France by giving her a corporate society built upon 'natural' communities, and integrating her into the new Europe. Citing Montandon's definition of races, the authors called for a new racial myth that would liberate the energies of the French as Hitlerism had done for the Germans. There was, however, a greater emphasis placed upon the role of elites, more specific to French fascism, and social Darwinist violence in history was downplayed.[26]

More a history of ideas and less autobiographical than *Les Décombres*, *La Fin du Nihilisme* shared the anti-Semitism of Rebatet, whose perspective on the interwar years was mentioned with approval, even if the language was less blatant. Attracted by what they perceived as the revolutionary activity of Eugène Deloncle, the former leader of the interwar right-wing *Cagoule*, who had established the collaborationist *Mouvement Social Révolutionnaire* in 1940, Soulès, who was to become better known as Raymond Abellio after the War, and Mahé had been socialists prior to the War. After 1940, race seemed to acquire a newly important role in history for them.

The West as a whole, according to Soulès and Mahé, had seen a spirit of hierarchical Aryan virility come into conflict in the nineteenth century with a Christianity which had fallen into a myth of progress, opening the way to the 'decomposition' characteristic of the 'Hebrews'. The Jews, meanwhile, had shifted their ideal from the coming of the Messiah to one of world domination. As so many of their colleagues on the right, Soulès and Mahé saw

Rousseau as having opened the door to an individualism that dissolved the 'natural communities' of family, town, province, profession, parish and corporation. The spreading 'myth' of progress based on individualism in the nineteenth century had deprived the French of their natural communities, according to Soulès and Mahé. By the beginning of the twentieth century, acceptance of the idea that 'France is a nation of 100 million inhabitants', including the colonial populations, 'had placed France at the level of Negroes....The capitalist and Masonic democracy celebrated the colonial conquests of France with a negrophilia...[that] brought into disrepute the purity of the race which had justly made them possible'.[27]

Unlike the *Action Française* sympathisers, Soulès and Mahé did not condemn the 1789 Revolution, which, they argued, as a popular protest against privileges, had actually expressed the vitality of the race. Unable to replace a dead hierarchy with a living one, however, the Revolution introduced universalism, egalitarianism, liberalism, freemasonry and an anarchic reign of gold under which only the Jews could prosper. Marxism, which cut the working class off from the nation, was a Jewish, rather than a Western product. It concealed the Jew, dissimulating the notion of race, under the category of social class.[28]

Critiquing Maurras for basing French culture solely on *Latinité*, Soulès and Mahé found a Celtic spiritualism that gave rise to chivalry, along with Germanic and Greco-Roman legacies, in Clovis and his entourage, the warriors of the Albigensian struggles, and in successive kings, notably Louis XI, all of whom had helped forge the French nation. The centralisation of Louis XIV had produced the divorce between the state and the people that led to the 1789 Revolution. Napoleon and his young marshals were yet again an emanation of what Soulès and Mahé called a popular elite. After each surge of this chivalric popular elite, however, the leadership had lost touch with the people. In an unusual argument for the time, the authors granted good intentions to liberalism and Marxism, adding, however, that the road to hell was paved with good intentions.[29] The Romans, Charlemagne, Otto the Great, and Napoleon had been precursors to a united Europe, which was being built, Soulès and Mahé contended, by the 'revolutionary' war of 1940.

The racial perspectives of the right were put into practice by the *Institut d'études des questions juives (IEQJ)*, an anti-Semitic propaganda group created in May 1941 in Paris and funded by the Germans. Although the *IEQJ* published *La Question Juive en France*, with scientific pretensions, there were no university professors serving in it. At German demand, Montandon was attached to Vichy's *Commissariat général aux questions juives (CGQJ)*. He conducted racial examinations and, for a price, declared people non-Jewish. In 1941 he helped prepare a German-financed exposition, '*La France et le Juif*'. From March 1941 to February 1943 he was editor-in-chief of an anti-Semitic magazine with the same title as his 1935 book, *L'Ethnie Française*. In February 1943 Montandon was named head of the *Institut d'étude des questions juives et ethnoraciales*, successor to the *IEQJ*, reorganised and incorporated into the

CGQ J. He taught courses on 'Jewish ethno-raciology' and 'racial hygiene'. Montandon was executed by the Resistance in 1944.[30]

The post-1940 right-wing histories shared with their interwar counterparts a critique of the Republican parliamentary democracy that they amalgamated in visions of corrosive cosmopolitan and occult forces, notably finance, Marxist revolution, freemasons and Jews. After the 1940 defeat, the right-wing writers offered a dual message of disaster combined with the redemptive character of a new order rising from the ruins, to use Rebatet's term. In presenting the defeat as a disaster necessitating a moral renewal, as early as 20 June 1940 – even before the beginning of the negotiations that led to Compiègne armistice – Pétain led the way. His argument that France had played when she should have worked, that she had shown a moral decay and had strayed from her Christian, corporate, peasant 'mission' had been foreshadowed in the historical works of Bainville and Gaxotte. Vichy's criticism of Third Republican parliamentary democracy was also shared by many among the early *Résistants*, among whom General de Gaulle was not especially kind to the late Republic in his war memoirs. As most of the histories written during the Occupation focused on the magnitude of the disaster, less attention was paid, at least in print, because of restricted information and the fear of censorship, to analysing the consequences of the 1940 armistice for the continuing course of the war.

After the war, in his *Sixty Days That Shook the West* (1956), Jacques Benoist-Méchin, who in the mid-1930's had joined Jacques Doriot's *Parti Populaire Française*, had written *Eclaircissements sur Mein Kampf d'Adolf Hitler* (Paris, 1939) with pro-Nazi sympathies, and had served as Secretary of State for the Council of Ministers under Vichy, argued that the 1940 armistice had been a major mistake by the Germans. According to Benoist-Méchin, Hitler would have had a better chance of winning the War with either a consistent Mediterranean forward strategy, a quick arrangement with General Francisco Franco taking the German forces into Spain, Gibraltar and North Africa and severing the British from their empire, or generous peace accords with Norway, Holland, Belgium and France that would have allowed the Germans to focus entirely on the East. Had Hitler concluded an arrangement with Spain immediately after the defeat of France instead of waiting and being rebuffed three months later, the outcome of the War might have been quite different.

Benoist-Méchin and other Vichy supporters had reason to claim after the War that the Pétain government had pursued a clever double game ruse against the Germans, when, in fact the evidence points to their sincerity in collaboration, but the possibility remains that the existence of Vichy worked against German interests in the War. The wartime historians were unable to assess the German decision-making process that led to the Compiègne armistice, with its symbolism designed to humiliate the very French with whom the Germans wished to negotiate. De Gaulle later stated that the French had not needed someone with the prestige of a Marshal of France to conclude an agreement such as the Compiègne armistice and Laval complained bitterly after 1942 that rapacious German policies toward occupied France were discrediting their would-be French allies.

The decision, however, to grant the French the armistice at Compiègne settled nothing militarily, and, if the German military leaders' accounts are to be believed, reflected more Nazi spite than calculated long-term political and military planning. With little information about the Compiègne armistice and the military situation available to them, the French right-wing authors crafted their histories to offer context for the events of 1940 that looked so full of promise to them: the 'revolution' (their term) that had brought Pétain and an authoritarian state to power, the opportunity to purge their enemies, and the chance to create the New Europe. The professional university historians generally accepted the new regime, busied themselves with administrative matters, and remained aloof in their scientific pretensions from the partisans on the right who welcomed the political changes. What changed in 1940 for those writing history on the Right was the 'divine surprise', which destroyed the system they opposed and, even at the cost of the French defeat and subsequent mistreatment by the Germans, opened the possibility to the new order that they sought. The 1944 Liberation swept away *Action Française* and the collaborationists. French right-wing historiography, however, continued, as before more the product of amateur than professional historians. During the late 1940s and 1950s, the '*Hussars*' carried the torch of '*La France aux Français*', the *Nouvelle Droite* followed in the 1970s, and the *Front National* thereafter.

Notes

1 Quoted in Suzanne Citron, 'Positivisme, corporatisme et pouvoir dans la société des professeurs d'histoire de 1910 à 1917', *Revue française de science politique*, 1977, vol. 27, p. 696.

2 Olivier Dumoulin, 'Histoire et Historiens de droite', in Jean-François Sirinelli (ed.) *Histoire des Droites en France*, 3 vols, Paris, Gallimard, 1992, vol. 2, p. 358.

3 Eugen Weber, *Action Française: Royalism and Reaction in Twentieth-Century France*, Stanford, CA, Stanford University Press, 1962, p. 264, footnote d.

4 Jacques Bainville, *History of France*, translated by Alice Gauss and Christian Gauss, New York, D. Appleton, 1926, p. 453.

5 Ibid., p. 468.

6 Ibid., p. 301.

7 Pierre Gaxotte, *The French Revolution*, translated by Walter Alison Phillips, London, Charles Scribner's Sons, 1932, pp. 39–40.

8 Ibid., p. 177.

9 Ibid., pp. 306–8.

10 George Montandon, *L'Ethnie Française*, Paris, Payot, 1935, pp. 27–9.

11 Ibid., p. 103.

12 Ibid., pp. 112–13.

13 Ibid., p. 139.

14 Christian Faure, *Le Projet Culturel de Vichy: Folklore et révolution nationale 1940–1944*, Lyon, Presses Universitaires de Lyon, 1989, pp. 272–4.

15 E. Py, 'L'histoire agraire…', in 'Notes Bibliographiques', *Revue Historique*, 1942–3, vol. 67, p. 166.

16 Louis Thomas, *Alphonse Toussenel, socialiste national anti-sémite 1803–1885*, Paris, Mercure de France, 1941, pp. 14–16.
17 Ibid., p. 99.
18 Ibid., p. 152.
19 G. Bn., 'Dans la collection…', in 'Notes Bibliographiques', *Revue Historique*, vol. 67, 1942–3, p. 84.
20 G. Bn., 'Le petit livre…' and 'Il y a dans le dernier livre…', in 'Notes Bibliographiques', *Revue Historique*, vol. 67, 1942–3, p. 175 and vol. 68, 1944, p. 282, respectively.
21 Robert Vallery-Radot, *Sources d'une Doctrine Nationale: de Joseph de Maistre à Charles Péguy*, Paris, Sequana, 1942, pp. 14–15.
22 Lucien Rebatet, *Les Décombres*, Paris, Denoël, 1942, p. 32.
23 Ibid., pp. 107–8.
24 Ibid., p. 467.
25 Ibid., p. 476.
26 Georges Soulès and André Mahé, *La Fin du Nihilisme*, Paris, Fernand Sorlot, 1943, pp. 61–2 and 221; also author's interview with Soulès, 20 July 1973.
27 Soulès and Mahé, *La Fin du Nihilisme*, p. 39.
28 Ibid., pp. 42–3 and 51–3.
29 Ibid., p. 124.
30 Donna Evleth, 'Montandon, George', in Bertram M. Gordon (ed.) *Historical Dictionary of World War II France: The Occupation, Vichy and the Resistance, 1938–1946*, Westport, Conn, Greenwood Press, 199, p. 247.

Further reading

Jacques Bainville, *History of France*, translated by Alice Gauss and Christian Gauss, New York, D. Appleton, 1926.
Jacques Benoist-Méchin, *Sixty Days That Shook the West*, translated by Peter Wiles, New York, G.P. Putnam's Sons, 1963. Original French edition, *Soixante Jours qui Ebranlèrent l'Occident*, Paris, Albin Michel, 1956.
Pierre Birnbaum, *'La France aux Français': Histoire des haines nationalistes*, Paris, Seuil, 1993.
Jérôme Carcopino, *Souvenirs de sept ans, 1937–1944*, Paris, Flammarion, 1953.
Suzanne Citron, 'Positivisme, corporatisme et pouvoir dans la société des professeurs d'histoire de 1910 à 1917', *Revue française de science politique*, 1977, vol. 27, pp. 691–716.
Pierre-Marie Dioudonnat, *Je Suis Partout 1930–1944, Les Maurrassiens devant la tentation fasciste*, Paris, La Table Ronde, 1973.
Olivier Dumoulin, 'Histoire et Historiens de droite', in Jean-François Sirinelli (ed.) *Histoire des Droites en France*, 3 vols, Paris, Gallimard, 1992, vol. 2, pp. 327–98.
Olivier Dumoulin, 'L'histoire et les historiens 1937–1947', in Jean-Pierre Rioux (ed.) *La Vie culturelle sous Vichy*, Brussels, Complexe, 1990, pp. 241–68.
Donna Evleth, 'Montandon, George', W. Scott Haine, 'Education under Vichy', and Michael Kelly, 'Universities', in Bertram M. Gordon (ed.) *Historical Dictionary of World War II France: The Occupation, Vichy and the Resistance, 1938–1946*, Westport, Conn., Greenwood Press, 1998, pp. 46–7, 117–19, 356–7.
Christian Faure, *Le Projet Culturel de Vichy: Folklore et révolution nationale (1940–1944)*, Lyon, Presses Universitaires de Lyon, 1989.
Bertram M. Gordon, *Collaborationism in France during the Second World War*, Ithaca, NY, Cornell University Press, 1980.
Gerd Krumeich, 'The Cult of Joan of Arc under the Vichy Régime', in Gerhard Hirschfeld and Patrick Marsh (eds) *Collaboration in France: Politics and Culture during the Nazi Occupation, 1940–1944*, Oxford, Berg, 1989, pp. 92–102.

George Montandon, *L'Ethnie Française*, Paris, Payot, 1935.

Philippe Pétain, *La France Nouvelle: Principes de la Communauté suivis des Appels et Messages 17 Juin 1940–17 Juin 1941*, Paris, Fasquelle, 1941.

Lucien Rebatet, *Les Décombres*, Paris, Denoël, 1942.

Georges Soulès and André Mahé, *La Fin du Nihilisme*, Paris, Fernand Sorlot, 1943.

Gustave Thibon, *Retour au Réel, Nouveaux Diagnostiques*, Lyon, H. Lardanchet, 1943.

Louis Thomas, *Alphonse Toussenel, socialiste national anti-sémite (1803–1885)*, Paris, Mercure de France, 1941.

Robert Vallery-Radot, *Sources d'une Doctrine Nationale: de Joseph de Maistre à Charles Péguy*, Paris, Sequana, 1942.

Maurice Wanecq, *Défense et illustration de la Maison Française*, Paris, Bernard Grasset, 1942.

14 German historiography under National Socialism

Dreams of a powerful nation–state and German *Volkstum* come true

Hans Schleier

Translated by Stefan Berger

After the national socialist dictatorship had been established many German historians supported the Nazis politically and ideologically – some only for the first couple of years, others until German military reverses in the Second World War and not a few remained faithful to the very last hour of the Third Reich. Yet until 1933 history professors and lecturers had rarely joined the NSDAP. It was only in the spring of 1933 that numerous well-known scholars and younger historians swelled the ranks of the party and other national socialist organisations, realising that membership might well help their university careers. Political opportunism went hand in hand with ideological conviction to facilitate the 'streamlining' of history departments (*Gleichschaltung*) which the Nazi administration began to organise systematically from 1933.

The years 1933 to 1935, when the Nazis routed the much-hated Weimar Republic, and from 1938 to 1941, when German armies marched from victory to victory, marked the highpoints of the historical profession's acclamation of the Nazi regime. During these periods historians were particularly willing to volunteer their support for the *Führer*, the Third Reich, the national socialist revolution and its declared ambition to regain German power and fulfil the age-old dream of a 'great-German Reich' by redrawing the map of Europe.

Such widespread political acceptance of Nazism cannot be explained only by reference to short-term tactical motivations. It was rooted in the political and ideological conditions and historiographic ideas which had shaped the historical profession in Germany since the nineteenth century. For mainstream German historians the collapse of the Kaiserreich in 1918, the Versailles peace treaty and the loss of large German territories were an unprecedented disaster. The world they had loved had gone and the much-hated parliamentary republic was a reality. Faced with this situation, the vast majority of historians actively supported a revision of postwar borders and favoured a return either to monarchy or to an authoritarian state which would be 'above parties'. By contrast there was no revision of the dominant paradigms and leading ideas that structured the writing of German history. The genuinely liberal and democratic historians were vehemently attacked. Because the majority of conservative nationalist historians, including some right-wing liberals, agreed to, or at least tolerated, the abolition of the hated 'Weimar system', i.e. the end of parliamentary rule, the dissolution of the political parties, and the destruction of democratic organisations and trade unions, they found it relatively easy to praise the 'national socialist revolution'. Furthermore, most found themselves in basic agreement with national socialist attempts to overcome regional particularisms by strengthening the central state. The expectation that the 'Third Reich' would mark a funda-mental turning point in German politics received further nourishment from the so-called 'Potsdam Day' on 21 March 1933. The Nazis used the official opening of the new Reichstag to lay claim symbolically and in demagogic fashion to the conservative and militaristic traditions of Prussia. On 30 June 1934, when the whole of the SA leadership was murdered on Hitler's orders, middle-class fears of the proletarian and rough side of the Nazi movement and its pseudo-revolutionary rhetoric, were laid to rest. The traditional anti-Marxism of the German historical profession developed after 1918 into a virulent anticommunism, providing yet another affinity with the Nazis. Historians had even fewer reservations as far as Nazi foreign policy was concerned: they had long favoured the revision of the Versailles Treaty and they had few qualms about the open rearmament of Germany under Hitler. They celebrated when German troops marched into the demilitarised Rhineland in 1935; they cheered when Austria became part of the Reich in 1938, and fully endorsed all other moves designed to bring about the rise of the German Reich to a new era of national glory and power.

After 1933 there was a revival of certain nineteenth-century historiograph-ical ideas: for example the stress upon the historical significance of the powerful nation-state, connected to the idea of the Reich (*Reichsidee*), the notion of Prussia's 'German vocation' and the celebration of heroism and war as vital elements in the eternal struggle between peoples. It was now espe-cially emphasised that the German people had time and again proven themselves in war. All of these ideas were also part and parcel of Nazi ideology. And one should also not forget that anti-Semitism had been a respectable part of German academic life since Treitschke.

Some National Socialist, *völkisch* and conservative-nationalist historians began to develop theories and methodologies which were to prepare a common spiritual defence against the perceived internal and external enemies of the German people. They declared the principles of the twentieth century to be 'struggle' for struggle's sake, 'revolutionary' action, 'right-wing revolu-tion' (Hans Freyer), and '*Volksgemeinschaft*'. The forces allegedly moving the process of history forwards were those of *Volkstum*, blood and race. These forces were frequently connected to equally mystical and blurred ideas of *Heimat*, of the land and special attachment to specific landscapes. These pseudo-theories were frequently contradictory. Those who adhered to them

despised empiricism and facts. Instead they turned to radical forms of irrationalism and claimed that new categories and hypotheses could be developed
by way of intuition. In other words they did not believe in the laborious task
of research to test and falsify particular hypotheses. In their view theories
could only be validated by means of 'experience' (*Erleben*) and 'belief'.
According to them, the most important categories which were to guide
research in the new Germany were 'faith', 'experience', 'the language of
blood' and 'decisiveness'. The 'bloodless objectivism' of historiography was
attacked well before 1933. One can trace the views of such 'thinkers of
struggle' (*Kampfdenker*, Moeller van den Bruck) not only amongst the writers
committed to *völkisch* and Nazi ideology but also, and prominently, amongst
internationally renowned scholars who gave much serious attention to these
ideas. Thus an intellectual climate receptive to Nazi ideology had arisen
during the Weimar Republic undermining the maintenance of firm boundaries to professional history writing.

As a general rule, most historians aligned themselves quickly after 1933.
But the extent and forms of political opportunism varied greatly. Often one
comes across conflicting reactions on the part of a single historian. Some were
superficially influenced by Nazi ideology, taking care to cite Hitler and to
endorse the Third Reich where it was necessary. Others, however, actively
cooperated with Nazi purges of the profession. Some scholars hoped that they
might be able to prevent excesses by collaborating with the Nazis. The many
endorsements of the regime did not rule out the existence of worries, reservations and anger about Nazi policies and historical pseudo-theories. The
actions and beliefs of German historians under Nazism were determined to a
large extent by terror, censorship, force, the *Führer* principle and career
considerations. Those writers closest to Nazi ideology railed endlessly against
the reluctant reception of specifically Nazi pseudo-theories amongst professional historians, and even well-established professors were attacked in reviews
and journals for such diffidence.

Although the Nazis tried hard to project their own ideology onto professional history-writing, professional historians found it far more difficult to
accept unconditionally Nazi theories and methodologies than to endorse the
regime politically. This was partly due to the fact that Nazi idology was not
homogeneous but consisted of an eclectic and often self-contradictory
mixture of ideas. Frequently, the protégés of competing Nazi bigwigs struggled over the true meaning of Nazism as an ideology. Nevertheless, the main
ideas of Nazism's historical ideology can be summarised in five points:

1   a belief in racial theory and *völkisch* theories,
2   commitment to 'leadership' (*Führertum*) and holistic principles,
3   social demagogy and pseudo-revolutionary ideas (the notion of national
    socialism as a 'national revolution') which served as means of ideological
    mobilisation,

4   the notion of 'struggle', *'Lebensraum'* (living space) and the idea of the
     'Reich',
5   a rejection of empirical methods of research which were replaced by the
     categories of 'experience' (*Erleben*), 'belief' and 'blood feelings' (*blutmäßiges
     Empfinden*)

Many Nazi authors and historians failed to adhere to all of those principles,
and professional historians were even less likely to do so. On the contrary,
there was a degree of resistance, overt or covert, to Nazi ideals – especially the
race theories which even pro-*völkisch* historians tended to find problematic.
Yet it would be totally wrong to assess the degree of Nazification of the
German historical profession only in terms of racism. However, until the end
of the 1960s this was exactly what was done in the Federal Republic in order
to whitewash German historiography. If, instead, we make the above five
principles the measure of judgement then we can recognise immediately how
much professional historians and Nazi ideologists had in common.

There had been attempts after 1918 and especially after 1933 to rethink
the role of nation and *Volkstum* in history in connection with the race theories,
the *völkisch* ideas and the theories about struggle and Lebensraum. To put it in
a nutshell, an increasing number of historians had become interested in
German *Volksgeschichte* rather than in the traditional history of nation-states.
From the early nineteenth century onwards national sentiment, spurred on by
the so-called wars of liberation against the Napoleonic occupation of
Germany, had been directed towards the much-desired creation of a united
German nation-state. The founders of the *Historische Zeitschrift* (founded in
1859), professional historians such as von Sybel, Giesebrecht and Waitz, who
perceived themselves as representing 'modern' German historical writing,
argued that historiography was irrevocably bound up with the ideas of nation
and nation-state. In their thinking the nation became almost an a priori historical category. The 'small-German' (*kleindeutsche*) unification of Germany
achieved by Bismarck in 1871 appeared to many contemporaries as little less
than a political miracle. However it left dissatisfied those who would have
liked to incorporate vast swathes of Austria-Hungary and Central Europe into
the new Germany. In the Imperialist era that followed the unification of
Germany, the nation-state was increasingly judged according to its international power and prestige. Social Darwinist and geopolitical arguments now
came to the fore to define the essence of nation-states. Nationalism increasingly became one-dimensional. Its earlier revolutionary-democratic variant
was championed only by relatively marginal groups on the left whilst an integral and expansionist nationalism propagating national prejudices came to
dominate the picture. However, expansionism was not the preserve of right-
wing nationalisms. The democratic nationalists of 1848, debating their ideas of
the future German nation-state in the Frankfurt Parliament, had little difficulty in justifying the annexation of Prussian or Austrian territories mainly
occupied by non-German nationalities.

After 1918 national revanchism dominated German historiography. German historians cultivated the hatred of the so-called 'hereditary enemy' (*Erbfeind*), France, by demanding the return of Alsace and Lorraine and by portraying French demands for the Rhine frontier as an age-old principle governing French politics. So-called border (*Grenzland*) research was aimed in particular against Poland and France. German and Austrian historians also held that the incorporation of Austria into Germany would complete the formation of the German nation-state. In this intellectual climate Hitler's 'national–German revolution' was widely endorsed after 1933 both as a means of overcoming class divisions and the much-hated party-political system in domestic politics and as a first step towards regaining national sovereignty and power in foreign policy. Many historians hailed Nazism as a political regime which would give Germans a new pride in their nation after years of national humiliation. Yet such political-historical perceptions which neatly divided the world into friends and enemies of the German nation still owed much to traditional state-centred ideas of the nation-state. However there was already a distinct group of historians such as Willy Andreas, Karl Alexander von Müller, Otto Hoetzsch, Martin Spahn and Wilhelm Weber who, in fairly mystical terms, linked the old nationalism with a new 'fighting nationalism' or with 'National-Socialism' and the idea of the *Volksgemeinschaft*.

Already before 1933 aspects of a so-called *Volks-* or *Volkstumsgeschichte* had coexisted with the more traditional ideal of a powerful nation-state. In the nineteenth century the term '*Volk*' had been almost synonymous with the 'nation'. However, from early on there were also attempts to differentiate the two. So, for example, both terms were used in juxtaposition: a 'nation' was a people (*Volkskörper*) the members of which consciously but subjectively identified which each other. By contrast, '*Volk*' was seen as an objective ethnic, linguistic and cultural community. Others attempted to extend Herder's idea of the 'people's spirit' (*Volksgeist*) to provide the basis for holistic notions of a 'people's character' (*Volkscharakter*) or *Volkstum*. Yet the criteria which distinguished different 'people's characters' from each other were often ill-defined, so there was a temptation to resort to a 'feeling' for *Volkstum* and the 'people's soul' (*Volksseele*), ideas which were frequently connected to traditions and culture. Yet another attempt to define the '*Volk*' was characterised by the increasing endeavours of natural scientists on establishing biological criteria for definitions of the *Volk*. From the last third of the nineteenth century onwards highly popular authors such as Eugen Dühring, Ludwig Schemann and Otto Ammon argued that an ethnic 'purification' of the 'people's body' (*Volkskörper*) was necessary to overcome the alleged 'cultural crisis' (*Kulturkrise*) of contemporary society.

Historical thinking after 1918 was increasingly influenced by these ideas. Since the nation-state had been defeated in 1918 many looked to the refreshing powers of *Volkstum*. Friedrich Georg Jünger wrote in 1928: 'Nationalism is born out of a new consciousness of a community rooted in the blood; such nationalism will ensure that the blood will rule supreme…'.[1]

Occasionally historians such as Alexander Cartellieri, Fritz Kern, Adalbert Wahl and Wilhelm Weber attempted to merge race theories with ideas of *Volkstum*, not by postulating unchangeable and inherited characteristics of whole 'bodies of the *Volk*' (*Volkskörper*), but by incorporating the historical development of races and of the mixing of races into the mainstream of historical research. They tended to understand *Volk* as a holistic 'organism', a 'unity' (*Ganzheit*), characterised by irrational ties of blood, language, territory ('*Volksboden*') and the unanimity ('*Einmütigkeit*') of the '*Volkstum*'. Methodological mysticism and political confessions were important ingredients of the new *Volkstumsgeschichte*. One of its representatives, Max Hildebert Boehm, proclaimed: 'The theory of the *Volk* is political knowledge and as such it stands between mere observation and deed. Its terms are not only descriptive but at the same time calls to action'.[2]

For Erich Keyser, 'German *Volksgeschichte*' was a summary of all the diverse aspects of political, economic and cultural history. It fully explained the development and the character of the German *Volkstum*.[3] Adolf Helbok suggested subdividing '*Volkstumsgeschichte*' into the history of settlement, the history of the 'body of the *Volk*' (*Volkskörper*), racial history and *völkisch* history of culture which was to provide the basis for the *völkisch* racial policies of the Nazi regime.[4] The connection of *Volksgeschichte* with traditional state history was not solved satisfactorily as many historians remained very aware of the fact that the 'struggle of the Volkstum' (*Volkstumskampf*) depended on the power of nation-states. In other words, peoples (*Völker*) had to be constituted as states in order to be successful. Nevertheless Keyser thought that the house of German historical sciences needed to be rebuilt; German historiography stood at a 'turning point'.[5] The university curricula in Germany and Austria reflected the remarkable popularity of the new *Volksgeschichte*. Several Nazi ideologists turned the new ideas into a dogma of historical research and tried to instrumentalise the *völkisch* ideology even more directly for the political tasks of the present.

Yet *Volksgeschichte* research was by no means a homogeneous body of knowledge. Already after 1918, and increasingly after 1933, historians, under the explicit sponsorship of the state, allowed political interests to guide their research. At the same time they began to cooperate closely with other human and social sciences. Such cooperation was often based on new research institutions and united professional attitudes with an explicitly ideological orientation. Three examples demonstrate this: first, there were the publications about the so-called 'Germans in the borderlands and abroad' (*Grenz- und Auslandsdeutschtum*) coordinated by the German Academy in Munich employing, amongst others, Hermann Oncken, Arnold Oscar Meyer and Karl Alexander von Müller. This work aimed to legitimate both a revision of the borders of 1918 and the aggressive acquisition of *Lebensraum* in Eastern Europe (Hermann Aubin, Albert Brackmann, Erich Maschke, Rudolf Craemer). The history of settlements and the history of individual German states (*Landes- und Siedlungsgeschichte*) included the development of new specialisms to do with 'landscape' (*Landschaft*), '*Heimat*', '*Volk*' and 'traditions' (*Brauchtum*). These specialisms were simply extended to other territories after 1933.

The second example is provided by activities focusing on the so-called 'German people's and cultural soil' (*Volks- und Kulturboden*). Their ambition was to deflect from the current preoccupation with state forms and instead attempt to reorder the European territory from the point of view of an allegedly unitary *Volkstum*. *Volksboden* meant the territories where German settlers lived (even as a minority), whereas *Kulturboden* meant in an even more evasive manner the territory and peoples which had previously been touched by German influence.

The third example concerns research on individual German states (*Landesgeschichte*) and the sociology of 'the development of peoples' (*Volkswerdung*). Both used new empirical and interdisciplinary methods to establish a history of peoples living in specific border regions and 'landscapes' which emphasised in particular their social structures and cultural traditions ('*völkisch* social development'). Much of this research was carried out with the explicit aim of demonstrating via '*Volksforschung*' the superiority of 'German culture' (*deutsche Kulturträger*). Functional and calculated rationality combined with *völkisch* mysticism. Several of these historical projects were closely connected to Nazi plans for a new territorial order in Europe which included the enforced resettlement of millions of people and genocide.

The *Deutsche Archiv für Landes- und Volksforschung*, founded in 1937, became the most important journal reflecting these new approaches to historical writing. The 'national revolution' of 1933 and the increased turn towards *Volkstum* history brought with it changes in the most popular themes of historical writing. 'Race research' became increasingly popular not only amongst Nazi ideologists but also amongst university historians. The most macabre research programmes were undertaken in the area of the 'Jewish question'. Historians such as Walter Frank, Richard Fester, Johann von Leers and Peter-Heinz Seraphim were particularly prominent here. The *Historische Zeitschrift* under its new editor Karl Alexander von Müller published a new rubric after 1936 entitled 'Concerning the History of the Jewish Question'. Apart from 'race history', *völkisch* interests were strongest, first, in the areas of pre- and early history as well as the history of the Germanic and Indo-Germanic tribes and 'Nordic' history. Historians could link their own research projects to a long, often nationalist tradition ranging back to the nineteenth century. Many lectures and publications demonstrated how the Germanic and the German *Volkstum* had been preserved throughout the centuries.[6] Furthermore, historians attempted to provide historical evidence for the idea that the Germanic tribes possessed superior characteristics compared to other peoples. They were also held to be endowed with a mission ('*sendungsbewußtes Deutschtum*') that time and again led them to expand across existing borders.

Second, *völkisch* interests were much in evidence in numerous publications on the idea and history of the Reich, beginning with the Reich of the Carolingians and stretching to the medieval Reich and beyond to the 'Third Reich' in a conscious attempt to link the medieval idea of the Reich to modern times.[7] The national idea provided the ahistorical basis of such constructions. 'All-German' historical views, as represented by Heinrich von Srbik, attempted to bridge the differences between 'small-German' and 'greater German' historiography. Yet around 1936, some historians, such as Erich Brandenburg, Wilhelm Mommsen and Fritz Hartung, refused to go along with the more critical reassessment of Bismarck's 'small-German' foundation of the Reich in 1871 provided by the 'all-German' historians. However, political events were soon to change the preoccupations of historians. From 1938/9 onwards debates surrounding the so-called 'restructuring of Europe' (*Neuordnung Europas*), especially concerned with Central Europe, took pride of place. University historians were much more prominent here than in the debates on race history.

The third example of historical research being influenced by *völkisch* ideas is provided by the numerous publications which concerned themselves with providing hate-filled histories of 'enemy' nation-states. Distorted histories of the major enemy countries, Poland, France, the Soviet Union and Britain, were published and the polemics against the alleged international Jewish conspiracy and the evils of usurious capitalism reached fever pitch. Whole tracts were directed against allegedly inferior enemy peoples and their political and social ideologies, in particular, bolshevism, pacifism, democracy and individualism. Theories of the eternal struggles of peoples in which only the fittest could survive, the attribution of different value to different peoples and races and the notion that the German *Volkstum* had to be protected from 'pollution' by other races, all prepared the practice of resettling millions of people during the War ('*Umvolkung*') and they also paved the way for the Nazis' euthanasia programmes and the Holocaust.

Fourth, *völkisch* interests were fundamental in the glorification of the peasantry as the traditional basis of the nation. This research often took up older notions of the alleged unity of the peasantry as an estate (*Stand*). Historians such as Günther Franz published histories of the peasantry, and there were numerous interdisciplinary population studies. *Volksforschung* was boosted by an ethnology that concentrated on rural traditions and a whole new sociology of 'rural peoples' (*Landvolk*). All of these studies strongly emphasised their relevance for contemporary politics. The close ties of the peasantry with the soil and the idea of '*Heimat*' was instrumentalised in a *völkisch* and also partly antimodernist way. Furthermore, research tended to concentrate on national-*völkisch* symbols and festivities such as the swastika, runes or summer solstices which were widely used in mystical Nazi rituals and events.

Fifth, vigorous *völkisch* interests also led to a renaissance of war and military history as well as to a renewed interest in the military spirit (*soldatischer Geist*) of the Prussian-German tradition. Traditional subjects such as 'military politics' (*Wehrpolitik*), 'military studies' (*Wehrwissenschaften*) and 'war studies' (*Kriegswissenschaft*) were systematically reorganised at the universities and research institutes and redefined in the specialist journals. The *völkisch* virtue of struggle and war as a means of reinvigoration of the people became the leading principles. Old nationalist and *völkisch* ideas were adapted and given a new Nazi coating.[8] The same was true for the '*Führer* principle' and the idea of fealty in German history.[9] The concept of the *Führer*, the cult of the hero and the emphasis on loyalty and obedience already had a long tradition in German historiography. But in the national socialist state these ideas were linked to the principles of unconditional loyalty and total subservience within the '*Volksgemeinschaft*'.

There were many areas of controversy, especially as historians often represented feuding Nazi bureaucracies. Additionally, some individual opponents of nazism dared, in spite of the obvious dangers, to contradict publicly the Nazi view of history. Sometimes, even historians loyal to the regime rejected all too obvious manipulations of history by the Nazis. For example, Heinrich Dannenbauer spoke out against the crass race doctrines propagated by the regime. And, quite apart from Nazi attempts to instrumentalise history writing, traditional methods were still used to write valuable historical monographs and edit editions of texts and documents. These no doubt reflected the strengths and weaknesses of traditional historiography but retained their worth well after the collapse of the national socialist regime. Of all the modern topics it was the history of Prussia which was written in the most conventional style and with fewest concessions to the racist and *völkisch* ideas. Nevertheless, the nationalist apologetics of Prussianism and Prussian militarism served the politics of the 'Third Reich' well in any case, whether this was intended by the historians or not.

The few years until the beginning of the War in 1939 witnessed a substantial reorganisation of the historical profession: the '*Gleichschaltung*' of academic institutions, historians' organisations and journals, together with dismissals, new appointments and the adoption of the '*Führer* principle'. The new *völkisch* theories and topics demanded the foundation or restructuring of professorships, university departments and research institutes. Prominent new subjects included 'race science', 'Indo-Germanic intellectual history', '*Volk* theory', '*Volkstum* sociology', 'borderland science', 'history of Germandom overseas', 'military science' and the infamous 'Jewish question'. A so-called 'Faculty for International Sciences' (*Auslandswissenschaftliche Fakultät*) was founded at the University of Berlin. The already-mentioned '*Volks* German Research Communities' coordinated not only university departments but also research and publication. The 'Reich Institute for the History of the New Germany' (*Reichsinstitut für Geschichte des neuen Deutschlands*) was founded in 1935 with considerable pomp and opulence. It gained some influence on recruitment policy within the historical profession. Its president Walter Frank and several well-known professors who served as 'honorary members' and 'experts', financed more than fifty research assignments on race and *völkisch* topics. Largely due to its lack of personnel and financial power it could never really fulfil its planned role as the leading institution of a revamped German history. However, it did not really need to do so, as the university departments fulfilled their task of legitimating the regime anyway, and, from a professional viewpoint, they often did a better job of it than specific Nazi institutes. This did not prevent the Nazis from setting up another so-called 'Reich Institute' – the 'Reich Institute for Older German History' (*Reichsinstitut für ältere deutsche Geschichte*), i.e. for the Middle Ages, in 1935. A planned 'Reich Institute for Pre- and Early History' (*Reichsinstitut für Vor- und Frühgeschichte*) never materialised because rival Nazi bureaucracies, often in alliance with rival historians, struggled over areas of responsibility and competence. Further centralisation of the historical profession, referred to as 'leadership in science' (*Wissenschaftsführung*), was discussed and planned. The Ministry of Sciences, founded in 1934, was intrigued by the idea of a 'planned economy of all questions to do with historical research'. Yet such drastic measures had to be abandoned because competing Nazi bureaucracies could not agree on any plans. Yet the Nazi 'leadership in science' principle had direct influence on the organisation of the German Historians' Congress (*Historikertag*) of 1937 in Erfurt and the international conferences of historians of 1933 in Warsaw and of 1938 in Zurich. In all three cases there was tight control of the topics which could be discussed and of the historians who were allowed to attend.

Well-established journals such as *Historische Zeitschrift*, *Vergangenheit und Gegenwart* and *Osteuropa* decided to recast their editorial boards and, in some cases, appoint new editors who took up the *völkisch* themes. New journals were also founded, such as *Volk im Werden* (1933), *Wille und Macht* (1933), *Monatsschrift für den nordischen Gedanken* (1934), *Zeitschrift für Rassenkunde* (1935), *Germanen-Erbe* (1936), *Gegenwärtiges Altertum* (1936), *Wehrwissenschaftliche Rundschau* (1936), *Jomsburg. Völker und Staaten im Osten und Norden Europas* (1937), all of which systematically propagated the *völkisch* teachings and leading theories of Nazi ideology.

When, after 1938, the Nazi regime began to expand German territory and when it could celebrate its first victories in the War, many German historians felt called upon once again to defend its policies. They hailed the alleged completion of nation-state building and the beginning of the 'restructuring' (*Neuordnung*) of Europe – including the occupation and conquest of foreign territories. Such enthusiasm also goes some way towards explaining the extraordinary willingness of historians to participate in the so-called 'Humanities' military campaign' (*Kriegseinsatz der Geisteswissenschaften*) initiated by the Nazi authorities. Historians queued up to attend the conferences organised by the study group carrying the same name. It is almost impossible to keep count of all the conferences, lectures, and seminars, all the newspapers, articles and pamphlets which justified the German war effort.

Many Austrian historians such as Ludwig Bittner, Adolf Helbok, Hellmuth Roesler, Harold Steinacker, Heinrich von Srbik and Hans Uebersberger as well as many historians from the former German University of Prague such as Josef Pfitzner and Heinz Zatschek also put themselves at the disposal of the Nazis and propagated the idea of the 'reordering' of Europe. Historians such as von Srbik and Wilhelm Schüßler now combined the 'all-German' view of history with ideas of a Central Europe (*Mitteleuropa*) to legitimate Nazi expansionism. Attempts to rewrite history so as to fit the new 'great German Reich' (*Großdeutsches Reich*) could even be found amongst medievalists. Otto Brunner's much hailed break-through to structural social history in his seminal *Land und Herrschaft* of 1939 was, in its original version, motivated by geopolitical and *völkisch* views directed against liberal theories of the state – a fact that is often passed over.

During the War, historians published several volumes which explicitly stressed the historical importance of Germans living outside the boundaries of the Reich for the character of Germany. Hence, as these publications argued, it was justifiable to incorporate into the 'Great German Reich' much of the territories where German settlers had once lived.[10] Racialist, *völkisch* and militarist ideologies now also became the guiding principles for new syntheses of German and world history.[11] The flood of publications included all genres ranging from comprehensive monographs to war brochures some of which were especially printed on behalf of the Wehrmacht or other Nazi institutions and enjoyed very wide circulation. These books and pamphlets conjured up memories of a Prussia characterised by its soldierly spirit, of the Hohenzollerns and their generals, of the bravery and loyalty of the German tribes and of the strength of character of the German *Volkstum*. The aim was to encourage the population to hold out and retain their faith in Germany's 'final victory' (*Endsieg*). Despite the increased *völkisch* emphasis of historical writing, the nationalist and 'statist' aspects of historiography remained intact and, if anything, increased in importance once the War had started.

Amongst the numerous organisational changes of the historical profession and the many new foundations of historical institutions, I have the space only to refer to the example of the new 'Reich Universities' of Straßburg (Strasbourg), founded in 1940, and of Posen (Poznàn), founded in 1941. Of the historians employed here, many of the best known such as Ernst Anrich, Günther Franz and Hermann Heimpel in Straßburg (Strasbourg) and Gerhard Krüger, Hermann Ludat and Reinhart Wittram in Posen (Poznàn), explicitly supported the Nazi regime. These Reich Universities were meant to be 'spiritual bastions of Germandom' communicating the values of the German *Volk* both westwards and eastwards. The so-called 'Institute for the German Colonisation of the East in Cracow' (*Institut für Deutsche Ostarbeit in Krakau*) had more practical tasks. Several of its employees, together with many others employed by different institutions of 'research on the East' (*Ostforschung*) became hopelessly entangled in the occupation and extermination policies of the Nazi regime, especially in Poland and the Soviet Union. Famous historians such as Hermann Aubin, Bolko von Richthofen, Hans Koch, Erich Keyser, Walter Kuhn, Manfred Laubert, Theodor Oberländer, Peter Heinz Seraphim and Hans Uebersberger were actively involved in planning and implementing the so-called 'repopulation' (*Umvolkung*) of German, Polish, Jewish and other ethnic groups living in occupied territories. They advised and informed state bureaucracies as well as military and Nazi institutions and organisations and they willingly trained their personnel. In some cases, such activities on the part of historians have emerged only from recently made available archival material. The expulsion and imprisonment of Polish historians did not generate any significant protests by their German colleagues. There was widespread silence on the criminal war and occupation policies of the Nazi regime including the Holocaust. One should also not forget that foreign archives, e.g. in France, were systematically searched and raided. Tons of archival material was transported to Germany.

The early military successes of the fascist states were not only welcomed by *völkisch* and nationalist historians but also contributed to a process where those who had initially kept at a distance from the regime now 'rethought' their position and moved closer to the Third Reich. Gerhard Ritter and Friedrich Meinecke provide just two examples of such a 'rethinking'. Only when the defeat of the German Wehrmacht and its allies finally became apparent with the capitulation of the German armies at Stalingrad in February 1943 did some historians tentatively begin to reorientate themselves. Few made contact with the resistance of 20 July 1944. Gerhard Ritter, Hans Freyer and Fritz Kern were amongst those who began to argue for cooperating with the Western allies so as to limit the consequences of the defeat and to prevent the advance of communism. The first works of a pro-Western European history were therefore written before the end of the War. The nationalist tirades were already removed from the writing of German history and the *völkisch* ideas of *Volkstum* were deleted.

On the whole, however, nationalism and the idea of the nation-state, of *Volkstum* and '*Volkswissenschaft*' were important ingredients of an historical profession which overwhelmingly legitimated the national socialist regime.

Notes

1 Cited in Otto Brunner, Werner Conze and Reinhart Koselleck (eds) *Geschichtliche Grundbegriffe*, vol. 7, Stuttgart, Klett-Cotta, 1992, p. 400.
2 Cited in Karl C. v. Loesch, 'Der Durchbruch der Volksforschung an den Universitäten', *Volk und Reich* 1932, vol. 9, p. 946f.
3 Erich Keyser, *Die Geschichtswissenschaft. Aufbau und Aufgaben*, Munich, R. Oldenbourg, 1931, p. 115f.
4 Cited in Heinrich von Srbik, *Geist und Geschichte vom deutschen Humanismus bis zur Gegenwart*, Munich, F. Bruckmann/Otto Müller, 1951, vol. 2, p. 342
5 Keyser, *Die Geschichtswissenschaft*, p. III.
6 One example amongst many is provided by Heinrich Dannenbauer, *Vom Werden des deutschen Volkes. Indogermanen-Germanen-Deutsche*, Tübingen, Mohr, 1935.
7 For examples see Hermann Heimpel, 'Reich und Staat im deutschen Mittelalter', *Archiv des öffentlichen Rechts*, 1936–7, N.F. vol. 27, pp. 257ff.; Karl Alexander von Müller, *Probleme des Zweiten Reiches im Lichte des Dritten*, Munich, Bruckmann, 1935; Erich Marcks, *Der Aufstieg des Reiches*, 2 vols, Stuttgart, Deutsche Verlagsanstalt, 1936; Wilhelm Weber, *Vom neuen Reich der Deutschen*, Berlin, Preußische Druckerei- und Verlags AG, 1935; Wilhelm Schüssler, *Vom Reich und der Reichsidee in der deutschen Geschichte*, Leipzig, Teubner, 1942.
8 See Wilhelm Bauer, *Der Krieg in der deutschen Geschichtsschreibung von Leopold von Ranke bis Karl Lamprecht*, Stuttgart, Kohlhammer, 1941.
9 Willy Hoppe, *Die Führerpersönlichkeiten in der deutschen Geschichte*, Berlin, Juncker and Dünnhaupt, 1934.

10 Some examples are provided by Reinhold Lorenz, *Drei Jahrhunderte Volk, Staat und Reich*, Vienna, Wiener Verlagsgesellschaft, 1942; Reinhard Wittram, *Rückkehr ins Reich. Vorträge und Aufsätze*, Posen, Universitätsbuchhandlung Kluge und Ströhm, 1942; Erich Keyser, *Geschichte des deutschen Weichsellandes*, 2nd edn, Leipzig, Hirzel, 1940; Hermann Aubin, Otto Brunner, Wolfgang Kohte and Johannes Papritz (eds) *Deutsche Ostforschung*, 2 vols, Leipzig, Hirzel, 1942–3.

11 Prominent examples include Adolf Helbok, *Deutsche Geschichte auf rassischer Grundlage*, Halle, Niemeyer, 1939; Otto Westphal, *Das Reich. Aufgang und Vollendung*, vol. 1, Stuttgart, Kohlhammer, 1941, and the coffee-table book *Gestalt und Wandel des Reiches. Ein Bilderatlas zur deutschen Geschichte*, edited in cooperation with Karl Alexander von Müller and Eberhard Lutze by Hans Hagemeyer, Berlin, Propyläen, 1944. It was published following a lavish exhibition on the topic organised by Alfred Rosenberg in 1940–1. See also Karl F. Chudoba (ed.) *Der Kampf um den Rhein (Kriegsvorträge)*, vol. 1, Bonn, Bonner Universitätsbuchdruck, 1943, which carried contributions by, amongst others, Fritz Kern and Erich Rothacker. Furthermore compare Willy Andreas (ed.) *Neue Propyläen Weltgeschichte*, 4 vols, Berlin, Propyläen, 1940–3 which was rewritten from a *völkisch* perspective.

Further reading

The best and most detailed publication on the attitude of German historians to power, German nation-state, Reich, *Volkstum*, and especially on the ideology and practice of Nazi foreign policy is Karen Schönwälder, *Historiker und Politik. Geschichtswissenschaft im Nationalsozialismus*, Frankfurt am Main, Campus, 1992. Some of her key findings and arguments are also available in English. See *idem*, ' "Taking Their Place in the Front-line"(?): German Historians During Nazism and War', *Tel Aviver Jahrbuch für deutsche Geschichte*, 1996, vol. 25, pp. 205–17, and *idem*, 'The Fascination of Power: Historical Scholarship in Nazi Germany', *History Workshop Journal*, 1996, no. 42, pp. 19–40. A very knowledgeable and carefully differentiated survey of the different *Volkstum* ideas in German historical writing is provided by Willi Oberkrome, *Volksgeschichte. Methodische Innovation und völkische Ideologisierung in der deutschen Geschichtswissenschaft 1918–1945*, Göttingen, Vandenhoeck & Ruprecht, 1993. For articles on individual historians, disciplines and themes see also Peter Lundgreen (ed.) *Wissenschaft im Dritten Reich*, Frankfurt am Main, Suhrkamp, 1985; O.D. Kulka, 'Major Trends and Tendencies in German Historiography on National Socialism and the "Jewish Question" (1924–1984)', *Year Book of the Leo Baeck Institute*, 1985, vol. 30, pp. 215–42. The positioning of ten of the most famous German and Austrian historians before and after 1945 is detailed in case studies by Hartmut Lehmann and James van Horn Melton (eds) *Paths of Continuity: Central European Historiography from the 1930s to the 1950s*, Cambridge, Cambridge University Press, 1994. The best monograph on German '*Ostforschung*' which relies on detailed archival research in particular on the 'North East German Research Community' and its close involvement with the criminal occupation policies has been written by Michael Burleigh, *Germany Turns Eastwards. A Study of Ostforschung in the Third Reich*, Cambridge, Cambridge University Press, 1988. The close alliance of the historical profession with both revisionist and Nazi politics before and after 1933 is the topic of Peter Schöttler (ed.) *Geschichtsschreibung als Legitimationswissenschaft*, Frankfurt am Main, Suhrkamp, 1997. The critical perception of nationalist historiography by those German historians who had been forced into exile is analysed by Hartmut Lehmann and James J. Sheehan (eds) *An Interrupted Past. German-Speaking Refugee Historians in the United States after 1933*, Cambridge, Cambridge University Press, 1991.

15 Gioacchino Volpe and fascist historiography in Italy

Martin Clark

However we define the 'nation-state', it certainly did not exist in Italy before the early twentieth century, if then. Nor did most political forces want it to. The left (socialists and communists) had other preoccupations and focuses for their loyalty, often regarded the 'nation' as a bourgeois con, and thought little about the state. The radicals/republicans liked Mazzini and assumed the reality of the nation, but strongly disliked the militarism of real existing states, colonialism, etc. and after the First World War many became Europhiles and Eurofederalists. The Catholics had no time for the usurping Italian state; they were keen on 'society' but did not equate it with the nation, and their perspective was international. The liberals also tended to be 'European' in outlook, keen on free trade, liberty and 'universal' Enlightenment values. The conservatives were monarchists, devoted to the interests of the House of Savoy and suspicious of any popular involvement in politics.

This meant that the only groups to take the 'nation-state' seriously were the national liberals, nationalists and fascists. The latter two groups, at least, defined the 'nation-state' as a recent creation, derived essentially from the First World War; and as the basic unit of foreign policy and war, seen as the major activity of the 'nation-state'. Their views may be summarised under the following five propositions:

1   the Italian 'nation' had existed for a long time, probably since the late Middle Ages;
2   the Risorgimento had been heroic but only very partially successful, creating a 'state' but not a 'nation-state' (because too monarchical, elitist, etc.);
3   post-Risorgimento history had been contemptible – decadent parliamentarism, '*Italietta*' etc. – the wrong sort of state;
4   it was Italy's 'intervention' in the First World War, the war itself, and post-war *squadrismo* that created a new elite, a new national consciousness and, after 1922, a new state, the fascist 'nation-state'. As Mussolini proclaimed just before the March on Rome: 'the clash is between nation and state. Italy is a nation. Italy is not a state'.[1] The fascist state – not liberal, not parliamentary – was the fascists' real achievement;

5   future wars would be needed, to maintain this modern, disciplined nation-state. It was the state's permanent task to mould and mobilise the nation. Virtue did not reside in the nation (all too unheroic) but in the new state – cf. German views of the *Volk*.

Ideally, historians were needed to demonstrate these five points.

But no historian met all these requirements. The most widely read one, Benedetto Croce, was actively hostile, especially on point 3; his *Storia d'Italia dal 1870 al 1914* (1928) was a deliberate praise of liberal, pre-fascist Italy. Antifascist and/or Catholic historians were obviously unsuitable. The most characteristically 'fascist' historian was Alfredo Oriani, whom hardly anybody read and who had died in 1909! The most influential was Gioacchino Volpe (who lived on to 1971), but he was too subtle and professional a historian to serve all the fascists' needs.

Gioacchino Volpe, historian and academic baron

In the 1920s, the most eminent historians were Benedetto Croce, Gaetano Salvemini and Gioacchino Volpe. The latter two were both medieval historians who later turned to contemporary themes (in Volpe's case because of the war); they were both, as young men, members of the '*economico-giuridico*' school, strongly influenced by historical materialism and very anxious to write social history, the history of the people rather than simply of the rulers. But in 1925 came the 'war of manifestos', and intellectuals had to choose. Salvemini went into exile, but Volpe remained – that rarity, a right-wing social historian. And a very good one: he wrote clearly and with great vigour, he was interested in everything (except perhaps religion and the church, for which despite his early works he clearly had little sympathy), he had lots of down-to-earth common sense and a passionate commitment to his subject, above all he knew that every subject has multiple aspects and can be approached from multiple angles.

Volpe was an enthusiastic supporter of the fascist movement, although as a national–liberal '*fiancheggiatore*' (sympathiser) rather than a true fascist. As early as November 1920 he had written an open letter to Mussolini's paper the *Popolo d'Italia* (21 November 1920) congratulating it and him for its campaigns on foreign policy, for backing D'Annunzio in Fiume, for helping to reintegrate returned soldiers into civilian life, and for its work of civil restoration at home. Mussolini splashed this letter on the front page – it was the first recognition his movement had ever received from an eminent intellectual figure of the establishment (Volpe was professor of history at Milan). Several other open letters followed, and in 1924 Volpe was even elected deputy on Mussolini's '*listone*'.

However, his political usefulness was over by 1925, like that of the other *fiancheggiatori*. In any case, he was not politically reliable. In 1923, researching on the 'economic and social history of the war' for the Carnegie–Yale series, he was excluded from the archives of the Committee of Industrial Mobilisation when the archive supervisor noticed that

> he restricted himself by choice solely to the study of workers' agitations, of revolutionary and Communist movements i.e. the workers' state of mind during that period, and hence a subject of extreme delicacy...the conclusions to which such a study might lead are of an enormous gravity, worst of all if published abroad.[2]

Volpe appealed to Mussolini personally, but to no avail, and had to give the project up. Similarly, when Volpe in 1928 gave a favourable review to Croce's book on Italian history from 1870 to 1914, the fascist party secretary was horrified – 'if I had to decide on your admission to the Party from such an article, I will not conceal from you that I would have to give a distinctly negative opinion'.[3] Volpe was, in fact, and remained, a national liberal, committed to national 'renewal' and to an effective foreign policy, but he disliked talk of a 'fascist revolution', strongly disliked the 'corporate state', and was very opposed to any attacks on the crown. Perhaps for these reasons he was not re-elected deputy in 1929 and never held any ministerial position. After December 1934 he was under police surveillance, and in 1936 Mussolini exclaimed 'I never liked him. I put up with him for the sake of his seven children. Cold, grey, antifascist'.[4]

To portray Volpe, then, as the regime's tame historian, or as a party hack, as Gabriele Turi has done,[5] is to misinterpret both his role and the nature of the regime. Yet he was given high academic posts: in 1925 he moved from Milan to the chair of modern history at Rome and became director of the new 'School (later Institute) of Modern and Contemporary History' where he assembled a number of brilliant research students. Here, perhaps, lay his real importance. Volpe was an admirable academic 'baron' – highly intelligent, *simpatico*, helpful, fair and open-minded. Furthermore, he had time for the young, required no political orthodoxy from them, and several times intervened with Mussolini to help those suspected of antifascism. In Nello Rosselli's case, Volpe twice helped to get him out of *confino* and twice secured him passports to study in London, in addition to screwing 20,000 lire out of the Academy to publish Rosselli's work. This was not without some risk – when Rosselli was late returning from London, Mussolini himself wrote to Volpe in wonderfully mordant tones:

> As you will certainly recall, Professor Sabatino Enrico Rosselli was issued a passport to visit Britain, where he was to study and collect documents concerning our Risorgimento, purely as a result of your repeated and insistent requests – requests which had already secured his liberation from the penalty of *confino* rightly inflicted on him. And permission to go abroad temporarily was granted solely because Your Excellency held the

view that it was not possible to complete our History without the exceptional expertise of Rosselli, of whom you – despite the contrary view of the Ministry of the Interior – made yourself absolute guarantor. But Rosselli, for whom History and the Risorgimento are merely pretexts to obtain your passionate intervention on his behalf, once in London has shown no inclination to return to Italy, so much so that he has invited his wife to join him there. With the result that the Ministry of the Interior has no choice but to issue a passport immediately to his wife as well, so as to prevent you being bothered with tiresome pressure from the Rosselli family, and having to make further requests for another permission to go abroad.

Yours sincerely, Mussolini.[6]

I should stress that Volpe's group at the 'School' was extremely talented – it included not only Rosselli but Walter Maturi, Rodolfo Morandi, Delio Cantimori and Federico Chabod. In many ways the 1930s were a golden age of Italian historiography, a period in which far more exciting work was done than at any time before or since.

But the question is, what influence did Volpe have on the young? Certainly he helped them, and certainly he suggested foreign policy themes to them (item '5' of my list), but young research students after 1918 were bound to be interested in foreign policy and war anyway, as Croce remarked –

generations who had not known wars, defeats, insurrections, victories, economic crises, revolutions and reaction, struggles between freedom and authority, coups d'etat, the rise of new ruling classes and so forth, except in a theoretical, superficial way or by reading historical accounts of them in the past, now know all about such matters because they have lived through them and suffered them themselves.[7]

Volpe was always read by fewer people than Croce (alas), and his influence among the historians was perhaps less than that of some foreign scholars like Meinecke; many of the School's students spent time in Berlin, listening to Meinecke's lectures. Still, Volpe got his *protégés* access to the archives, access to research funds and publications, and gave them some political protection – not bad in an avowedly totalitarian state. And Volpe's 'School' did not merely stress foreign policy. It produced and published the documentary base for it, and it insisted on studying it in a 'European' context. Above all, foreign policy was *not* 'what one clerk said to another'. It was seen as '*economico-giuridico*' too, a subject open to values, passions, and sentiments, and much affected by internal political struggles and the fears and hopes of the ruling class. Italian historians would undoubtedly have turned to foreign policy in any case; but without Volpe they might not have done it so well.

Volpe also was a member of the new Italian Academy, and became its secretary in 1929. This gave him free first class rail travel and the right to be addressed as 'Excellency'. More importantly, it gave him the chance to direct research programmes, distribute scholarships, find funding for publications etc. The Academy was a ludicrous body – its members carried swords and wore fezes – but it was not particularly 'fascist'. It was, like similar bodies elsewhere, a means for top university barons to further their research projects. Moreover, Volpe also ran the *Rivista Storica Italiana* in the 1930s (although Ernesto Sestan did most of the work), and so could get his *protégés* published in a prestigious journal; and he was on the board of the Institute for Studies of International Politics in Milan, financed by Alberto Pirelli – another wonderful outlet and one which planned the 'History of Italian Foreign Policy 1861–1914', of which Federico Chabod's magnificent work on Italian Foreign Policy after 1870 (published 1951, English translation 1996) was the ultimate outcome. Not only that, but Volpe represented Italy at international historical congresses, consistently arguing against the 'pacifists', i.e. earnest Scandinavian or Indian historians who thought all history-writing on war, diplomacy and states should be banned for creating hatred among the nations. History, in their view, should stress the 'common heritage' of mankind, and international committees should go through text books and weed out opprobrious references to other countries. Volpe, needless to say, thought all this was rubbish: history-writing should not be propaganda, even propaganda for peace, and war could hardly be left out, since it was the major agent of social change.[8]

Perhaps Volpe's most widespread influence came from the *Encyclopedia Italiana*, a project thought up and edited by Giovanni Gentile, long a close associate. Volpe was in charge of the medieval and modern history section, selected the entries, chose the contributors (10 per cent of them from abroad) and issued their instructions, much ignored in practice by the academics. Very few refused to contribute, apart from Croce; indeed, the whole *Encyclopedia* was partly a Gentilian cultural enterprise directed against Croce, and inspired by the rival cultural manifestos of 1925. At any rate, it was a real, prestigious occasion, the first true encyclopaedia in Italian history (except for the nineteenth century *Popular Encyclopedia*, largely taken from the version of the same name published by Collins in Glasgow). The model was the *Britannica*, but Italianised and concentrating on Italian specialisms like art history and architecture. Of course, encyclopaedias are prestigious but usually little read; articles in them tend to be scholarly but rather generalised and bland; they are not places for controversy. The Italian encyclopaedia was no exception. The real importance for the theme of this chapter is that it gave Volpe the opportunity to write his best-known history of the fascist movement (item '4' in my scheme). This long article (1932) became the virtually unchallenged official history, much used in schools and colleges, and was reissued in 1934 as a basic text bound together with Mussolini's (or rather, Gentile's) 'The Doctrine of Fascism'. It was this work that made Volpe synonymous with 'fascism' in the popular mind – and which, in 1945, led to his being purged, dismissed from his chair and losing all his civil rights, including the vote.

Volpe and the Risorgimento

Volpe had much less influence on Risorgimento history (point '2' of my original list) than in other areas. Indeed, the Risorgimento was the one area of Italian history where Volpe's writ did not run. This was due mainly to the fact that one of the Quadrumvirs of the March on Rome, Cesare Maria De Vecchi, was a self-styled Piedmontese aristocrat, a devotee of the Risorgimento and influential enough to corner the market. De Vecchi ran the Institute for Risorgimento Studies and after 1933 edited the *Rassegna Storica del Risorgimento*. De Vecchi, reactionary and ultra-Savoyard, had little time for foreign policy or the diplomacy of the period, rejected the idea that other countries might have had some influence during the Risorgimento, and detested Mazzini and Garibaldi or any whiff of popular initiative. As a result, Risorgimento studies stagnated. Indeed, arguably the fascist period saw quite the opposite of an apologia for the nation-state; there was an amazing lack of attention to a period normally regarded as the time of its origins.

De Vecchi's view was, of course, quite incompatible with the general fascist stress on the 'nation' and the inadequacies of pre-fascist Italy, but Volpe could hardly challenge De Vecchi: he was less politically influential. In any case, Volpe was a monarchist too – not so fervent as De Vecchi, it was true, but Volpe had lived through the 1890s as a young man and through the war later on, and he knew the Italian state was weak and needed all the sources of legitimacy it could find. Besides, Risorgimento history had never had much appeal to Volpe: it was too narrow, too celebratory, too patriotic and not 'social' enough. In 1907 he had even opposed founding new chairs in it, to general dismay. Volpe therefore took a more nuanced line on the period than De Vecchi and avoided any direct challenge to him. However, he did insist on encouraging studies of foreign policy during and before the Risorgimento period – De Vecchi had no interest in this, and the work could be done in Volpe's institutes without much interference.

Regarding the nature of the state, i.e. the monarchy's role in the Risorgimento, Volpe argued that the Italian state had been created by the House of Savoy in 1861 – but *also* by the nation, or at least the most active and energetic part of the nation. Indeed, the crown had been forced to act by the people; and at the end it was popular plebiscites that had legitimised the Italian monarchy. Furthermore, international diplomacy and other states had played a major part. For Volpe, Italian history did not begin in 1861, but centuries earlier; the Italian 'nation' had been forged over centuries, in struggle against foreign invaders, but only the monarchy had managed to mobilise it and maintain it united; the Italian state had not been founded anew after the First World War, but had essentially been the same since 1861, although becoming more 'popular' as time went on; what mattered most, at all times, were the links between state and nation, i.e. between crown and people. In short, a 'nation-state' was not something created once and for all, but a continuous dialogue between 'nation' and 'state', in which each influenced the other. But, to repeat, he knew that the 'Risorgimento' had been partial, the work of tiny elites – elites who were often wildly out of touch with ordinary people and totally ignorant of the 'real Italy' of malaria, deforestation and poverty; and he knew too that it was northern and often much resented and opposed further south. Indeed, Volpe was particularly good on the unification's impact on southern society – on how values, institutions, hierarchies and economies were all shattered.[9] He could recognise popular discontent when he saw it, and he saw plenty during and after the Risorgimento. Even so, he could not reject the Risorgimento (and the monarchy): unity was vital, and could not have been achieved any other way.

Italietta and the post-Risorgimento

Volpe's writings on the post-Risorgimento (1870–1914), particularly his *L'Italia in Cammino* (1927) and *L'Italia Moderna* (1943), are arguably his least 'fascist' works. The title of the first sums up Volpe's view: Italy progressed, indeed it was transformed, and Volpe aimed to show how and why. He paid much attention to economic and social history, particularly emigration, labour disputes, the growth of steel and shipbuilding, the impact of railways and so forth; he stressed also conflicts, strikes and rioting. Above all, Volpe depicted the gradual formation of a modern nation – by urbanisation, by migration, conscription, education, journalism, trade unions, parties (for example, he *welcomed* the rise of the Socialist Party, because it was a national organisation that absorbed (his word) the proletariat into the political life of the country). His tone was positive, even Whiggish, rather than denunciatory; he left very little out, and he was subtle in depicting the relations between state and people. Above all, he was merciless in denouncing those (like Pelloux) who relied on mere repression to maintain class privileges, and succeeded thereby only in 'increasing the number of real subversives, turning moderate men into quasi-subversives or allies of subversives, making the police forces as detested as in the worst times of the old Governments, discrediting the army and making people disaffected even with the Monarchy'.[10]

All this was, it seems to me, rather good social history, even though Volpe certainly exaggerated the speed of change. Despite all the efforts of village schoolteachers and army sergeants, Italy was not a 'nation' in 1914 (or even in 1939). She remained as diverse as ever, with a host of regional issues to prove it – the 'Roman question', the 'Southern problem', the 'State of Milan', the 'Sicilian problem' (Mafia), the 'Sardinian problem' (banditry) and so forth. Still, at least in these works Volpe provided an 'apology for the nation' that he thought had been formed. But was it what the fascists wanted to hear about pre-fascist times? In some ways it was, as regards Volpe's essential message: on the one hand, the birth of a nation; on the other, the state's slowness to adapt to this newly-formed nation. Parliament was corrupt, the parties intrigued constantly and had no legitimacy, the bureaucracy was too centralised and too subject to political interference. Furthermore, the state failed in its major task, that of being effective in Europe and acquiring colonies in Africa. The nation, said Volpe, was 'better than its government, and worthy of a better government'.[11]

But even here Volpe's message was ambiguous, and even barbed. For, of course, the 'nation' had not made itself against the 'state', or despite the 'state': *Italietta* (little Italy), yes, but not cowardly, not unaware of problems that were later tackled with greater energy; not so dominated by lawyers and parliamentary wrangles as to prevent any great debates and contrasts of high ideas. It founded a network of industries, not all of them beneficiaries of tariff protection or state procurements. It revived its old, exhausted agriculture. It undertook the task of raising its people, who were little more than a plebs, to the status of a nation'.[12] Thus pre-fascist Italy could appear a reasonably effective state after all. Moreover, it was the corrupt, parliamentary regime of the arch-neutralist Giolitti that had occupied Libya (and the Dodecanese) in 1911–12. Nor was Giolitti the first, or the only, coloniser of African territory: Italy already possessed Somalia and Eritrea. Volpe probably exaggerated the success of pre-1914 'Italians' in forming a nation; but he rather downplayed the Italian state's reluctance to act as he – and the fascists – thought states should.

Fortunately, few fascists minded, or even noticed. Croce came to Volpe's rescue, producing in 1928, a few months after *L'Italia in Cammino*, a *Storia dell'Italia 1871–1914* that was a ludicrously optimistic hymn of praise to the pre-fascist (especially Giolittian) state: all peace, progress and harmony, with economic and social conflict largely left out. The resultant fuss, and the somewhat contrived *Historikerstreit* (Historians' dispute) that followed, made Volpe seem far more plausible as a historian, and also more orthodox as a fascist. The fact that Volpe too had praised pre-fascist Italy – admittedly usually for its social and economic progress, rather than its politics – was soon forgotten, even though Volpe repeated his views over the years, often very explicitly.[13] Volpe was essentially a 'continuationist': fascist Italy was the continuation – or development, elevation – of the pre-fascist regime, but fascism was not superimposed on a recalcitrant 'Italy', it was Italy herself.

Making the fascist state

As for the history of fascism itself, Volpe was not only the 'official' historian of the movement (thanks to the *Encyclopedia Italiana* article), but virtually the only one, apart from some party hacks and the exiles, to tackle the subject. But his *Storia del Movimento Fascista* was more a study of a dramatic period of Italian history than one of the fascist movement itself, which clearly did not interest him greatly. Indeed, Volpe wrote it from his usual 'national liberal' viewpoint – monarchical, Salandrian, but with a marked social and economic awareness. Early 'fascism' was seen as simply one of a number of competing interventionist groups, all equally admirable and equally personifying the ardour and creative zeal of the Italian people. In 1914–15 the 'nation' (i.e. the interventionists) had become a direct actor in Italian politics, had imposed a 'national-popular' solution, had then gone on to win the war and to overturn the old political order. The old regime was discredited by its neutralism in 1914–15, by its wartime incapacity and, above all, by its failure to 'win the peace' at Versailles. Volpe presented fascism as a synthesis of nationalism, activism, antiparliamentarism, and socialism(!) – above all as an 'elevation' of the people to a greater role in the state. The fascists had carried out a revolution, indeed, theirs was the first popular revolution in Italian history, but it was inspired by the foreign policy failures of the old elite, and by ideas not interests – although Volpe could not help himself from discussing the role of new landowners and leaseholders in the Po valley, and he noted the predominantly urban nature of the fascist movement even though it was the peasants who had fought in the war. Mussolini's early governments after 1922 were praised as 'normalising' – internal order was restored, national reconciliation pursued, and an effective foreign policy implemented. As for the Matteotti crisis and the events of 1925–6, here Volpe showed some embarrassment, typical of *fiancheggiatori* like himself: 'in 1925–6 many irreconcilable opponents went into exile voluntarily, or were forced to do so, and it was not all an advantage for fascism and its international reputation'.[14] But essentially the message was clear. Fascism was not the work of small groups, as the Risorgimento had been, nor was it imposed from above; it was the result of a complex of 'new' social forces, of a new generation toned by war, impatient, resolute and successful.

This interpretation, although obviously acceptable and adopted in schools, did not please everyone: even the *Popolo d'Italia* pointed out it was a 'book not written by a fascist'. It was too 'national', not 'fascist' enough, underplaying the role of fascist heroes in 1914–15 and 1919–22; it was also remarkably soft on liberalism, free trade and the monarchy; it was even soft on socialism and class conflict, welcomed by Volpe as a sign of dynamism. Above all, Volpe was obviously soft on pre-fascist Italy. He was, as I have argued, a 'continuationist'; and to many fascists this implied that fascism had not been a 'revolution' after all. This was not quite Volpe's view, but Volpe did think that 'fascism' – in the sense of initiative, impatient creativity, a certain contempt for bureaucratic rules – was not new, indeed was a normal feature of Italian life.

Above all, Volpe saw little reason to change the structure of the state in 1925–6. Hence Volpe was very lukewarm in his account of the institutions of the new fascist state, particularly the corporations, and underplayed their importance. He clearly disliked the loss of individual liberties and the abolition of free trade unionism, which he regarded as destructive of economic liberty; he also disliked the architect of the new corporate state, Alfredo Rocco. Above all, he defended the role of the king. In short, he did *not* meet all the requirements of point '4' in my list: in his view the fascists had not set up a new state, different from that founded by the Risorgimento, or if they had he did his best to ignore it.

There are other historiographical ironies here. Like some later historians, Volpe clearly exaggerated fascist 'consensus' (though one should remember he wrote in 1932) and he also exaggerated the 'nationalisation of the masses', not that evident even in the 1930s. More importantly, Volpe's view of history from 1914 to 1925 was very different from that of Croce (who idealised Giolittian Italy, and saw both Crispi and, later, fascism as 'parentheses') and of the liberals who denounced the 'fascist revolution'. On the other hand, his 'national continuity' theme was rather similar to that of Piero Gobetti and the radical school (fascism as 'revelation not revolution'), and a version of this 'continuity' theme became popular even on the Marxist left in the 1970s, referring partic- ularly to state institutions. Above all, I would stress that Volpe was not interested in party history, but in 'global' social history, and in the relations between state and society. Hence after 1945 he continued to defend the fascist regime, not merely for its achievements (strong foreign policy, national consensus, etc.) but because one could not ignore twenty years of Italian social history, or pretend that the whole nation had not been involved.[15]

War and the primacy of foreign policy

On this issue Volpe again met the 'fascist requirements', but again ambiguously and incompletely. He agreed that foreign policy, war and (especially) colonial expansion was the purpose of the modern state. As mentor of young histo- rians, he encouraged and stimulated a huge attention to foreign policy issues. As I have argued, this was more or less inevitable – if the *Kriegsschuldfrage* (war guilt question) died down in Italy after 1919 because of victory, the *Kriegszielfrage* (war aim question) remained a live issue for years to come. In any case, foreign policy had always been a contentious issue in Italy, long before 1914, as the debates over the Roman question, Tunisia, the Triple Alliance, Crispi, irredentism, Adua and Libya amply prove.

On the other hand, Volpe always took a peculiarly generous view of what 'foreign policy' meant. He regarded it as an area to which the whole nation contributed, and which was much affected by both popular and elite ideas and sentiments. So diplomatic history became broader, and more interesting, than normally supposed. Second, he was always well aware that foreign policy was a game with many other actors. In Europe, it was a sophisticated game, played for centuries by people who knew each other, were often inter-related, and who knew the rules. In short, Italy was one state among many, and it was much affected by the others – and by their values, ideas, sentiments, etc. too. Third, Mussolini's foreign policy, although commendably resolute and deter- mined, was in Volpe's view no way different from that of many of his predecessors, either in Africa or the Adriatic. True, Italy had been 'left behind' in the 1880s, but thereafter even Rudini and Giolitti had not been able to avoid colonial expansion. In some ways, therefore, Volpe's argument was exactly the opposite of what fascist propaganda required. It was the 'nation' that had often forced the 'state' into colonies and war, not the other way round. So some virtue resided in the 'nation' after all, and now there was a 'nation–state' the state might be expected to be much more responsive to national demands.

Irredentism: Corsica

Strangely, the only real effort by Italian historians in the fascist period to justify further expansion – a new irredentism – referred not to Africa or to the Adriatic, but to Corsica. From the early 1920s Volpe and a few colleagues set out to show that Corsica always had been 'Italian', that it had been wrongly appropriated by France in 1769 after Paoli's revolt against Genoa, that it had remained strongly 'Italian' in sentiment and commerce until at least 1870, and that in sentiment and culture it still was 'Italian'. Volpe wrote prolifically about the island for twenty years in a host of articles, chapters and prefaces, and in 1939 produced a *Storia della Corsica Italiana*. As a true academic baron, he founded and organised a number of other enterprises, including the *Archivio Storico della Corsica* (f. 1925), a Centre of Corsican Studies (f. 1940), and a massive *Bibliografia della Corsica* by Carmine Starace, published in 1943 with the inevitable preface by Volpe, and still a major source of historical research. All this was part of a long campaign, as Volpe wrote, to remind Italians of the existence of 'a proud people speaking our language and belonging to our race'.

But, as usual, he did it too well. His *Storia della Corsica Italiana* was not propaganda at all. It was an excellent overall history of the island, with a strong social-economic content and always inserted into a European context. Moreover, Volpe was even willing to admit that Corsica by the twentieth century was no longer 'Italian', rather it was torn between two nations – 'this small people, which is no longer Italian but has never managed to become altogether French; the drama of its decline as a Corsican or Italian nation'.[16] This kind of frank admission is fatal to nationalist propaganda.

But perhaps one has to be careful about attributing a political motive to Volpe's histories of Corsica. His very real enthusiasm for the island may have been just a personal foible, like Boswell's, Rousseau's or Gregorovius' (and Volpe was always well aware of his illustrious predecessors, despite regarding Boswell as English). Indeed, Volpe himself denied a political motive, or at least an exclusively political motive:

> did we – and I speak here of our Review – intend to found a new irredentism, now that the old one had been resolved successfully? We can say, categorically, no. But this does not mean we had no political motive. How could a historian fail to want to clarify the claims to nobility of his own land and his own people, defending their ideal boundaries in the past as in the present? Only God could write a purely rational history.[17]

I would conclude that Volpe's rather odd 'Corsican' enthusiasm certainly fitted in well with the needs of fascist historiography, but it was virtually the only example of 'irredentist' history in the fascist period, it may have been a personal foible, and it certainly produced good history rather than propaganda. Indeed, as propaganda it was a dismal failure. Few Italians, even fascist

Italians, were interested in Corsica at all until the late 1930s, and not much then. As for the Corsicans, they showed little desire to be annexed to Italy, least of all fascist Italy.[18] What many of them did want was some form of regional 'autonomy', not conceded by the French government but even less likely to be granted by the Italian. And when the Italians did occupy Corsica in 1942, Volpe's efforts to go there as propagandist were rebuffed by the High Command.

Conclusion

In the fascist period, the 'ideal fascist' historiographical line was toed by very few historians, even 'fascist' ones. The major innovation was a greater stress on diplomatic history, but this was seen firmly in a 'European' context. Risorgimento history was noticeably neglected. However, the 'nation-state' became an ideal, allegedly realised by fascism, and Volpe lent some very quali-fied support to this view. In reality, the 'nation' was more diverse and faction-ridden than he supposed; the 'state' less legitimate, especially about foreign policy; the relationship between the two less close. It is the perennial Italian problem.

But arguably we are looking at this question from the wrong end. Volpe aspired to write 'global' history: 'we are coming back to political history after passing through a period of writing history rich in so-called social elements, and we aspire to a kind of synthesis of the two types of history, which will truly be History'.[19] He was a social historian of national-liberal views, reared in the materialist 'economic-juridical' school but convinced also of the social, historical importance of the state, of foreign policy and of war. He wanted to write 'total' history, leaving nothing out, and he needed a framework. The 'nation-state' provided the best available unit of analysis. What else would have served? Even Corsica could only be understood in the light of the activities of surrounding 'metropolitan' states. Volpe's 'nation-state' focus may not always have been good history, but it was – at Volpe's best – marvellous History. And even at Volpe's worst – when ranting on, say, about the strong state and mani-fest destiny, or writing medieval history with the church left out – he was always better than his major competitor, Croce. He was down to earth, and he wrote about the people.

Notes

1 Speech of 4 October 1922; B. Mussolini, *Opera Omnia*, ed. D. Susmel, Florence, La Fenice, 1951–73, xviii, p. 434.
2 R. De Felice, 'Gli storici italiani nel periodo fascista', in B. Vigezzi (ed.) *Federico Chabod e la Nuova Storiografia Italiana*, Milan, Jaca Book, 1984, pp. 559–618, at pp. 563–4.
3 G. Belardelli, 'L'adesione di Gioacchino Volpe al Fascismo', *Storia Contemporanea*, 1983, xiv, pp. 649–94, at p. 670.

4 De Felice, 'Gli storici italiani', p. 565; also *Mussolini il Duce*, Turin, Einaudi, 1974, i, p. 800. In fact, Volpe had only six children. The original document is in *Archivio Centrale dello Stato, Rome, Segretaria Particolare del Duce*, cart. ris., b. 93.

5 G. Turi, 'Il problema Volpe', *Studi Storici* 1978, xix, pp. 175–86; *Il Fascismo e il Consenso degli intellettuali*, Bologna, Il Mulino, 1980, pp. 110–30.

6 Letter of 10 December 1930, in G. Volpe, *Storici e Maestri*, 2nd edn, Florence, Sansoni, 1967, p. 494.

7 B. Croce, *Storia della Storiografia italiana nel secolo decimonono*, Bari, Laterza, 1947, ii, p. 168.

8 Volpe, *Storici*, especially pp. 370–81.

9 G. Volpe, *L'Italia in Cammino*, Milan, Treves, 1927, p. 34.

10 G. Volpe, *L'Italia Moderna*, 2nd edn, Florence, Sansoni, 1958, vol. i, p. 357.

11 Ibid., vol. iii, p. 645.

12 Ibid., vol. i, x; *idem, Storici*, p. 282.

13 For example, in an open letter to the fascist journal *Il Tevere* 27 November 1931; now in P. Meldini (ed.) *Reazionaria*, Rimini, Guaraldi, 1973, pp. 70–3.

14 G. Volpe, *Storia del Movimento Fascista*, Rome, Istituto della enciclopedia italiana, 1934, p. 125.

15 G. Volpe, *L'Italia Che Fu*, Milan, Borghese, 1961, p. 245.

16 G. Volpe, *Storia della Corsica Italiana*, Milan, Istituto per gli studi di politica internazionale, 1939, p. 283.

17 Ibid., p. 288.

18 'Gardez pour vous le manganello', P. Andreani, *Le Fascisme et la Corse*, Marseille, 1939, p. 32.

19 Volpe, *Storici*, p. 244; from Preface to lst edn of *Momenti di Storia Italiana*, Florence, Vallecchi, 1925.

Further reading

The following texts discuss Italian national identity generally, and more specifically the relationship between foreign policy and public opinion:

A. Agnelli *et al.*, in G. Spadolini (ed.) *Nazione e Nazionalità in Italia dall'alba del secolo ai giorni nostri*, Bari, Laterza, 1994.

G. Are *et al.*, *Studi e Ricerche in onore di G. Volpe nel Centenario della Nascita*, Rome, 1978.

F. Chabod, *Italian Foreign Policy. The Statecraft of the Founders*, Princeton, NJ, Princeton University Press, 1996 (originally Bari, Laterza, 1951).

L. Del Piano, *Gioacchino Volpe e la Corsica*, Cagliari, 1987.

E. Gentile, 'La nazione del Fascismo', *Storia Contemporanea*, 1993, xxiv, pp. 833–87.

A. Montenegro, 'Politica estera e organizzazione del consenso', *Studi Storici*, 1978, xix, pp. 777–818.

B. Vigezzi (ed.) *Federico Chabod e la Nuova Storiografia Italiana*, Milan, Jaca Book, 1984.

B. Vigezzi, *Politica Estera e Opinione Pubblica in Italia, dall' Unità ai Giorni Nostri*, Milan, Jaca Book, 1991.

Part VI

The Cold War years

With fascism buried in the burned-out ruins of 1945, the task of rebuilding the present by defining and reconstructing the past once again gave prominence to historical writing.

Hugo Frey examines a number of histories of the Second World War which were marked with a Gaullist bias. He pays special attention to the narrative structures found in two representative examples – Louis-Henri Paria, *Trente ans d'histoire* (1949) and Georges Cattaui, *Charles de Gaulle* (1956) – both of which contributed to a new vision of French identity and redrew the cognitive maps by means of which the national past was surveyed. Frey emphasises that these accounts divided the national past into periods of decline and of resurgence. This cyclical narrative supported the Gaullist conception of French identity, with its discourse of national remaking through a popular movement led by an *homme providentiel*.

After 1949, as Mary Fulbrook points out, the historical professions in the two Germanies elaborated very different stories of a national past in their attempts to legitimate their respective regimes. Both historiographies, she contends, were intimately related to political programmes and sympathies. The major difference between eastern and western historical writing, she argues, lay less in the fact that one was more biased than the other than in the much greater ability in West Germany of dissenting historians to gain access to a wide readership.

In contrast to their German and French counterparts, Italian historians, according to Roberto Vivarelli, refused to recognise the new republican state as a continuity of the pre-fascist liberal regime. Instead, antifascist historians replaced the national with diverse points of reference. Historians were either Catholic or Marxist, and only occasionally liberal. Especially within the Marxist camp, the student revolt of 1968 brought further attacks on the nation-state and its role in Italian history.

16 Rebuilding France

Gaullist historiography, the rise–fall myth and French identity (1945–58)

Hugo Frey[1]

The Fourth Republic was a critical moment for historians, intellectuals, journalists and politicians to assert their interpretation of what it meant to be French. After the ambiguities and compromises of the Occupation, the Liberation brought with it the opportunity to redraw the cognitive maps with which the past was to be surveyed. Notably, representations of the history of the previous War facilitated new understandings of the national heritage and by implication France's role in the postwar world. In this chapter I will examine ideologically marked histories of the conflict which were produced by Gaullist writers and which supported a Gaullian notion of French identity. First, I detail the contextual background to two examples of Gaullist War historiography. The body of argument which follows emphasises how the writings of Jacques Madaule and Georges Cattaui categorised the Occupation into periods of national decline and subsequent renaissance and revival. This consistent framing of the national past (and future) between eras of rise and fall is understood as a political myth similar to those discussed by Raoul Girardet in his work on French political discourse.[2] I will illustrate that many of the functions of the rise–fall myth of the War were centred on the reconstruction of a post-1945 French identity. The myth I delineate is compared with Henry Rousso's study of historical memory, *The Vichy Syndrome*.[3]

Readers are probably familiar with at least one example of Fourth Republic Gaullist War historiography, Charles de Gaulle's *Mémoires de guerre*.[4] French specialists will know of his assistant Jacques Soustelle's two-volume account of the Free French movement, *Envers et contre tout*.[5] However, I will study two lesser known examples: a volume edited by Louis-Henri Parias, entitled, *Trente ans d'histoire – de Clemenceau à de Gaulle*, 1949, and Georges Cattaui's *Charles de Gaulle*, 1956 (henceforth abbreviated to *Trente ans* and *CDG*).[6] Ignored or neglected by the secondary literature on Gaullism, the two books are both typical and exceptional of the type. The Parias collection was one of the rare examples of Gaullist representation which was neither based on a personal reminiscence nor the biographical style. On the other hand, Cattaui's *CDG* was one of many hagiographic portraits of de Gaulle's life to be sold during the Fourth Republic. To an extent the two books are important precisely because they were written by neo-Gaullists, influenced by the life and thinking of de Gaulle, but are not a part of his *oeuvre*. Since neither of the titles are 'well known' members of the canon readers will need more details.

Trente ans was a grand folio-size collection of history writing produced by the *Nouvelle Librairie de France* in a luxury edition. It combined historical narration with numerous montages of photographic journalism and reproductions of contemporary political cartoons, such as those drawn by Sennep and Ralph Soupault. As the title and subtitle indicate, it covered French history from 1918 to 1948. Its editor, Parias, was a publisher and journalist. He founded the popular history magazine, *Miroir de l'histoire*, and by the 1960s was director of historical publications at the Arthème Fayard house. Narration, description and political analysis was divided into separate *Livres* and written by the three principal historians Jacques Boudet, Jacques Madaule and Michel Habib. These core sections are framed by three introductory essays on Georges Clemenceau and mirrored at the end of the text with a further three biographical presentations of de Gaulle. The collection was completed with eye-witness reportage and thematic essays on recent political and cultural history. *Trente ans* is a weighty but elegant 426 pages long.

The political profiles of Parias's contributors are of central importance. In addition to the three main authors, the collection included essays and accounts from: Winston Churchill, General de Monsabert, Colonel l'Hopital, Pasteur Vallery-Radot, Geneviève de Gaulle, André le Troquer, René Cassin, Jacques Soustelle, Adrien Dansette, General Ingold, Raymond Aron, Jean de Fabrègues, Pierre Alleray, Albert Ollivier, Edmond Michelet, Louis Vallon, J.A. Godin, Henri Rollet, Pierre-Olivier Lapie, René Pinon, Edouard Dudon, Georges Cattaui, Stanislas Fumet and Rémy. These politicians and cultural figures are an almost perfect reflection of the range of intellectuals who were drawn to de Gaulle at this time. Thus, on the socialist left of Gaullism we have the *Combat* journalist, and member of the SFIO, Pierre-Olivier Lapie. He was joined on the left by a number of social Christian democrats, the Resistance press impresario Stanislas Fumet, and the one time *Mouvement républicain populaire* (MRP) members, Jacques Madaule and Edmond Michelet. In addition, Catholic thought was also present in the form of the editor, Parias (between 1945 and 1948 he had also edited the newspaper *La France Catholique*), the intellectual Jean de Fabrègues, our second author Georges Cattaui and General Leclerc's brother-in-law, the professional historian Adrien Dansette. To the centre right Godin was on the radical wing of the group. Furthermore, *Trente ans* included writing from high-ranking Gaullists who were active in the politics of the *Rassemblement du peuple français* (de Gaulle's political movement/party of the late 1940s which ultimately collapsed in 1953): Pasteur Vallery-Radot, General de Monsabert, Jacques Soustelle, Louis Vallon, Albert Ollivier (from André Malraux's personal coterie), and the maverick RPF head of propaganda, Rémy. The RPF's 'non-aligned' think-tank, the *Comité national d'études*, was represented by the sociologist Raymond

Aron. As if to demonstrate that *Trente ans* was a Gaullist team publication it was favourably reviewed by two of its own contributors, Edmond Michelet and Adrien Dansette. Writing in the sympathetic weeklies *Carrefour* and *La France Catholique* they immodestly considered the collection to be a rewarding example of contemporary historiographic writing.[7] Michelet promoted the volume in the following terms, reporting, 'this book has a place in all French libraries'.

The second selected text, *CDG*, was published seven years after the *Trente ans* collection. By 1956, politically, much had changed: the RPF group had broken apart, de Gaulle had retired for a second time and the *Plon* publishing house had printed the first two volumes of the general's own account of the War years. *CDG* was a short paperback biography of the life of de Gaulle, from his childhood to the contemporary period. Published by the academically named *Editions Universitaires* it was a monograph in a series of studies of major figures who had influenced the twentieth century. Appropriately enough the biographies were presented under the rubric 'Witnesses of the Twentieth Century', which when completed, the publisher's claimed, would offer the French public, 'in words and images, a biographical encyclopedia'.[8] Before Cattaui's *CDG* the series had included works on Kondrad Adenauer, Simone Weil and Jean Rostand.

Despite the pedagogical marketing of *CDG*, the sympathy which Cattaui showed for his subject was marked. This is evidenced by his previous commitments on behalf of Gaullism. For instance, during the Liberation, he had produced a glorification of de Gaulle, whilst when the RPF project was under way he contributed, on more than one occasion, to the movement's cultural review *Liberté de l'esprit*. Cattaui was a journeyman intellectual who was able to comment on literature as well as pen a hagiography of his preferred political figurehead. In fact, by 1960, he had published three different biographies of the general.[9]

Although the production of *Trente ans* and *CDG* provide a fascinating glimpse into what Jean Charlot has described as the 'inner circle' of Fourth Republic Gaullism, I am interested in the two books as examples of contemporary historiographic interpretation of the War.[10] Here, one feature of the writings appears to be of particular importance to the general understanding of Gaullism and its contribution to postwar French identity formation: the texts articulated their representation of the national past around the interrelated concepts of France's propensity to be in either acute national decline or spiralling renewal. These themes have already been noted by others who work on Gaullist discourse but perhaps has not been sufficiently foregrounded. For instance, in two chapters of the impressive *Les Lieux de mémoire*, written by Philipe Burrin and Pierre Nora, this aspect is referred to as part of Charles de Gaulle's writing and speeches. More recently, Christopher Flood's theoretical treatment of political myth-making, *Political Myth*, presents de Gaulle's famous postwar Bayeux speech, 16 June 1946, as an evocation of French history which relied on themes such as national decline and suffering, sacrifice and rebirth.[11] My research on Gaullist historiographic sources suggests that, while not precisely replicating de Gaulle's personal vision of history, the fellow-traveller historians were equally preoccupied with these notions. So much so, that it is possible to see the construction of French history through periods of national rise and fall as a new category of mythopeic story-type. Fashioning the past around themes of either extraordinary failure or triumph appears to mark the Gaullist accounts of the Second World War to the core. Let us begin by illustrating how this kind of construction worked in the *Trente ans* collection's treatment of the Vichy government and second in its portrayal of de Gaulle's resistance.

Jacques Madaule repeatedly associates the Vichy regime with an inevitable course of decline. The theme is evoked in two ways: in the structure of the general charting of the years 1940 to 1944; and through numerous direct allusions to the debasement of the Vichy government. Taken together these devices give the reader the impression that Pétain's reign was illegitimate and predestined to fail. The writing restructures the course of the Vichy regime through a number of staging posts which are seen to mark its progression towards complete collapse. This provides a defining theme and, given Vichy's intrigues and ministerial 'comings and goings', imposes a rigid sense of continuity. Decline is highlighted in the very chapter headings and subdivisions which are employed in the book. They are: 'Chapitre I, Au lendemain de l'armistice'; 'Chapitre II, De Montoire à la chute de Laval'; 'Chapitre III, L'année Darlan' (1941); 'Chapitre IV, Le retour de Laval' (1942); 'Chapitre V L'agonie de Vichy'. Here, the history of Vichy is organised around its development from the armistice question to the ominously entitled 'L'agonie de Vichy', stage. The linear pattern of descent is further emphasised through the paratextual device of a prefatory citation from Hitler's *Mein Kampf*. The quotation given at the beginning of the chapter is used to construct Vichy's destiny out of the mouth of its vanquishers. The quote reads,

> History has demonstrated on numerous occasions that peoples who have surrendered their weapons, without being entirely forced to, prefer to agree to worse humiliations and demands rather than trying to alter their fate through a new call to arms. This is very human behaviour. As much as possible, an informed conqueror will only impose his demands on the vanquished in successive stages (Adolf Hitler, *Mein Kampf*).[12]

By employing the words of Hitler, Madaule anticipates how the Vichy regime was to be marked by successive humiliations. Once Pétain had accepted defeat, his only course was towards further subjugation. Rhetorically this underlined the structural guidance implicit in the sequence of chapter headings.

In the detailed treatment of Vichy's fall two years are emphasised as having been qualitatively different steps towards decline. The two critical moments in the longer process are 1940 and 1942. A number of examples of the notion, or plays on it, can be drawn from the depictions of these years. For instance,

the creation of Vichy in 1940 is marked out as the beginning of an illegiti-
mate governance which held little hope of any meaningful national recovery.
Madaule categorically states that the Vichyite compromise with Nazi
Germany meant that a genuinely French revival would have to have come
from outside France. The following argument captures the dilemma which
Jacques Madaule linked to the Vichy government in 1940:

a) Hitler did not only send troops to France, but also propagandists and a
complete conception of the world, which, whatever one thinks, was considered to be universal. Under such circumstances, how could one hope for a
truly French renaissance to be achieved?[13]

b) The remark denies the regime any contribution to the revival of French
life. Vichy c.1940 (from the vantage point of 1949) is portrayed facing a bleak
future of failure and collapse. In addition, 1940 is also identified as the beginning of several other routes towards dishonour. These include the loss of its
moral-political worth, notably because of the creation of its own anti-Semitic
laws. This retrospective version of 1940, consistent with Cattaui's and several
other Gaullist sources, indicates that once the armistice had been accepted
Vichy was bound to move closer to nazism and thus wither away.

By the time Madaule treats 1942 the reader has already been made aware
that Vichy was a bastard state. However, the account makes 1942 the final
beginning of the end. The first words which follow the title 'Chapter IV
Laval's Return' are explicit, 'Henceforth, Vichy's collapse began'.[14] Indeed, the
further debasements of 1942 are described as the consequences of increased,
rather than new, collaboration. Episodes, such as the return of Laval, the occupation of the Free Zone and the powerful influence of French fascists, such as
Doriot and Déat, are taken as the natural outcomes of earlier decisions.
Madaule declares that, in the light of these events, it is futile to comment
further on Vichy. He argues that the regime had lost all power and authority:

a) If, by the close of 1942, the French Empire had been completely liber-
ated (with the exception of Indochina and Tunisia) the metropole, including
Corsica, remained under the yoke. From this date on, one can disregard the
acts and gestures of the Vichy government.[15]

b) It was only Beuve-Méry and Dunoyer de Segonzac's Uriage project for
the creation of an elite school of Catholic personalist reflection which Madaule
excluded from the global decline. This deviation from the dominant tone of
interpretation is exceptional. For instance, in his account Madaule described
their achievement as having been: 'an admirable accomplishment conducted
without concern for official doctrines and certainly not for the policy of
collaboration'.[16] It is neither the time nor the place to discuss the role of the
Uriage project and its relationship – though we may note that Madaule has
been loosely associated with its teachings. Moreover, in the nineteen thirties he
had been a major contributor to Emmanuel Mounier's journal, *Esprit*. Here is
one plausible explanation for the discursive rescue of Uriage from the otherwise dominant retrospective characterisation of falling Vichy fortunes.[17]

In *Trente ans* what Vichy discursively loses in its fall, de Gaulle and War

Gaullism are shown to have guarded and protected throughout a continuous, inevitable ascent. Thereby, in contrast to the representation of Vichy's precipitous fall, the portrayal of de Gaulle and the Free French is a narrative of magnificent rise. Once more the point of departure is the issue of response to the defeat of 1940. Thus, it is de Gaulle's refusal to surrender which is constructed as the signal for national revival. This is shown to continue from the 18 June 1940 onwards, through the optimistically described 'first fruits' of the movement to the military triumph of Bir-Hakeim (1942). Each stage in de Gaulle's career, from his break with Vichy to his triumphant parade down the Champs Elysée (1944), is portrayed in a tone which indicates the continuity of his, and by implication the nation's, revival. Of course, in reality the history of the Free French was far more turbulent, problematic and complicated than the interpretation reflected. Thus, the commonly held Giraudist position of anti-Gaullist resistance, combined with a continued sympathy for Pétain and military support for the American war effort, was ignored. Amongst the many allusions to the theme of rise, renewal and revival the depiction of the Bir-Hakeim tank battle is exemplary. Madaule wrote,

> The garrison was completely encircled, but they held their ground. On the 9 June a major assault was repelled. However, on the same day, the British command instructed Koenig to leave the position. This meant breaking the siege. The extraordinary feat took place on the nights of the 10 and 11 June. On the 15 June, Koenig announced in his dispatches that 'the French had won a victory at Bir-Hakeim.' De Gaulle himself declared that 'when, at Bir-Hakeim, a ray of renascent glory touched her soldiers, the world once more recognized France.'[18]

The decision to quote de Gaulle, and the vocabulary which is used is indicative. 'Glory', 'renascent' and 'once more recognized', each phrase signifies the spirit of a revival through military triumph. In addition the quotation underlines that the Gaullist tank battle represented a victory for the French nation, in the words of de Gaulle, 'le monde a reconnu la France'. The association between Gaullism and France is established. Ultimately, the two are once more fused together in Madaule's depiction of the Liberation of Paris. In the representation of this genuine crowning glory, de Gaulle and France are shown to have returned home and ushered in a new period of better history. An era of national revival had been forged. Conversely, notions of decline, humiliation, and Vichy are rhetorically banished, or as Madaule almost casually commented, French history had taken 'a decisive turn'.[19]

George Cattaui's biography of de Gaulle's life and times created a similar portrayal of the War years. Once more 1940 and Vichy are associated with a process of decline, whilst the rise of de Gaulle is taken to be the symbol of a new, reinvigorated France. Cattaui's lyrical style and the biographical form in which he is writing make this a different text to the Parias collection. Nevertheless, the opposition of rise and fall, so evident in the earlier example, is repeated. Instead of citing a second series of supporting illustrations from either side of the pattern, I offer the following passage from *CDG* which incorporates both themes and exemplifies how the two characterisations were frequently used to create an overall comparative effect. The quotation is from the centre of the Cattaui biography; it primarily describes the events which preceded de Gaulle's famous 18 June 1940 BBC radio broadcast and his subsequent transmission of the 23 June 1940. The second message was one of the first in which the leader of the Free French commented directly on the new Pétain government. Cattaui recounted:

> Nevertheless, the Bordeaux government accepted servitude at the hands of the enemy. Pétain sought to justify his own actions; he claimed that there was no alternative. He deluded himself that, despite the harshness of their fate, the French people could recover, even under the German yoke. In the face of these official statements, on the radio in London a voice rose up. Not unknown to the 'old soldier' it was his former secretary from the Conseil Supérieur....Through de Gaulle's prophetic words, it was France herself, from the very depths of her History, who spoke and confronted the future. In response to the call the numbed people came out of their stupor, understood their condition, regained possession of themselves and were true. A metamorphosis was wrought.[20]

Pétain was thus challenged by the recognisable voice of his interwar colleague, de Gaulle. This portrait raises a number of points. Clearly, as in the previous case, one can identify both of the dominant themes. Echoes of Madaule's construction of Vichy as a paralysed state held 'under the yoke' are to the fore. Here, de Gaulle is constituted not only as a personification of the nation but specifically of national revival as well. He is, almost literally, cast as the fulcrum of a return to a destiny of glory. The critical factor which reverses the decline is constituted as de Gaulle's first radio broadcasts, which of course we now know were listened to by only a very limited audience. Examine the choice of language, 'a voice rose up', 'from the very depths of her History', and so on. This is a similar vocabulary to that which was used by Madaule in his treatment of the Bir-Hakeim tank battle. Moreover, the quotation illustrates how the two sides of the rise–fall theme functioned together. Again Vichy could not legitimately rally the nation whilst it was itself under Nazi control. Comparatively, the course of Vichy's degradation is all the more pathetic for de Gaulle's rise. On the other hand, the Free French, Gaullism, and national recovery are endowed with greater honour in the light of their opponents' failings. To this extent the rise–fall themes are inseparable. Indeed, one finds it hard to imagine the use of one set of images without any reference to the other. Whilst the events which are being reconstructed occurred at the same time, from June 1940 to the Liberation, the Gaullist presentation works on the basis that the revival followed the episode of decline, essentially a synchronic progression. Vichy collaboration and Gaullist resistance had coexisted.

The retrospective portrayal tended to characterise these political choices as being chronologically separate episodes, the latter replacing the former.

To review, much of the *Trente ans* and *CDG* texts formulated their versions of the War around two simple but effective images. The pattern of national decline and revival allowed each of the writers to associate sets of positive and negative images to the appropriate camps. Vichy is labelled in its very essence as part of a fall in national fortune. This was then equated with many other images and sub-themes. Conversely, the notions of rise and renewal were used as a peg with which to confer honour, military strength, and national legitimacy on de Gaulle's actions. Taken cumulatively the pattern can be seen to represent a consistent type of mythopeic discourse in which history was reorganised and presented in terms of its highly negative or highly positive impact on the nation's destiny. Symbolically resonant to those who believed it to be true, this version of the War was without doubt also perceived to be a grave fabrication by the many French citizens who continued to believe in Philippe Pétain's innocence, as well as in the role of the Vichy regime as a protective shield.[21] Equally, the orientation was very different from the manipulation of the conflict found in French Communist Party literature, such as in the pages of Maurice Thorez's popular autobiography, *Fils du peuple*.[22] Briefly, they viewed it as the culmination of their antifascist campaigns of the interwar years. Nevertheless, the rise–fall myth appears seductive and plausible to a British observer whose own cultural understanding of the Second World War to an extent probably reflects the Gaullist patterning of history in which episodes of terrible military and political failure are replaced by spectacular triumphs. In this incarnation of the rise–fall interpretative grid, one can imagine the British representation of the War beginning with the policy of appeasement, leading to defeat at Dunkirk but then suddenly moving into a stage of national revival, attributed to Churchill's rather than de Gaulle's leadership.

The Gaullist rise–fall interpretation of the French War experience is an example of political myth-making. That is to say, the narrative of French history's pendulum-swing between national failure and triumph was an account of history told with a political purpose. As noted above, the narrative was either supported and reproduced by those who considered it to be broadly true, or it was identified as a falsehood by those who interpreted the War on the basis of different ideological assumptions. On the simplest level, the myth functioned to promote de Gaulle and to attack those who could be identified with Vichy. The idea that the nation was either in the process of a terminal decline, or its opposite, allowed Gaullist commentators to valorise positively or negatively the political circumstances which were associated with each trajectory. Notably, this meant a focus on de Gaulle 'the leader' which suggested that only through his actions had the nation successfully changed course from the dangers of decline to the heights of victory. The Fourth Republic, the present, was cast on the cusp: either an era of continued revival or a return to submission and decline. In this context, the recent past demonstrated a model for the future of France. Implicitly, the message indicated that for recovery to move forward de Gaulle would have to return to power. After all, the history of the Occupation period repeatedly illustrated that it had been the general who had provided the catalyst for that national reinvigoration.

Due to the consistency of its use, one can begin to see the rise–fall device as a fixed story-type, open to be reused to interpret other aspects of the French past, or future. Indeed, working as a generally cyclical philosophy of history, the rise–fall pattern lends itself to employment from a wide range of ideological viewpoints: one can compare the rise–fall myth as a central theme of Gaullist historiographic thinking with other well-known story-type categorisations of contemporary political myths, such as conspiracy myths, foundation myths, eschatological myths or the myth of the saviour. These have been presented in the theoretical outlines by Girardet and the political scientist Henry Tudor.[23] That is not to say that the rise–fall story of the War was the only ideologically marked interpretation which Gaullists used to discuss the past and, in so doing, to talk about the present. Rather, it was a dominant story-type, most frequently employed by the historians.

Perhaps the primary function of the rise–fall War myth, as developed by Madaule and Cattaui, was the creation of a new sense of Gaullist national identity. The account provided national reassurance after the collective trauma of the 1940 débâcle and the Occupation. By showing that the national defeat at the hands of the Third Reich had in fact been the end of a period of national decline, and by implication also the beginning of a period of renewal, the myth allowed the French to consider the War as part of a generally positive experience. It also concealed the complex history of Franco–German collaboration. Notably, it served to obfuscate French reactions to the Vichy government. As is now well documented, particularly thanks to the American historian Robert Paxton's ground-breaking publications on the subject, most Frenchmen in the summer of 1940 were Pétainist and had hoped that the Vichy regime would be a successful force, at least after Britain and Germany had declared a ceasefire.[24] Furthermore, between the heroism of Gaullist rising national fortunes and the decline of the Vichy regime there was little discursive space for the inclusion of those who had adopted a pro-Pétain stance whilst also supporting de Gaulle. Moreover, the pattern excluded the common possibility of shifts in intellectual reaction away from initial collaboration and towards resistance, though this was the route actually taken by many living in occupied France in response to the military development of the War. Cumulatively, the Gaullist imposition of the rise–fall myth created the perception that the nation had uniformly conducted itself with honour. The War was no longer identified as a stain on French history. Instead, fulfilling a similar role to the accounts of the heroism of the infantrymen which had circulated both during and after the First World War, the Second World War was now classified as a valuable part of the national heritage. In the systematic history of de Gaulle's revival and Vichy's ignoble decline, Frenchmen were offered the opportunity to believe that the 1939–45 period had been no less honourable than any other exhibit from the civic past.

The Gaullist presentation of the War, which offered the French a noble image of themselves, was not based on a repression or complete omission of the history of the Vichy regime's activities. The rise–fall myth was far more sophisticated than the simple propaganda it is sometimes mistaken for. Madaule's treatment of Vichy was broadly comprehensive, and even included a relatively detailed discussion of its anti-Semitic legislation. Of course, chapter and verse on French complicity in the Holocaust was not exposed. However, rather than concealing the Vichy past, the twin notions of the rise and fall interpretation demonstrated to the French how they could best understand it. As Pétain's regime was represented in almost constant deterioration and subsequently compared with the images of improvement associated with Gaullism, readers could make their own choice as to which of the two elements of French history were genuinely part of the nation's heritage. On this subject, Henry Rousso has argued that much of the Gaullist retrospective manipulation of the War was centred on an 'attempt to exorcise the year 1940'.[25] Evidence from historiography published at different stages during the Fourth Republic suggests that this was not the Gaullist strategy. In the *Trente ans* text, and Cattaui's *CDG*, the decisions of 1940 were a focal point, being the date from which Vichy's descent and Gaullism's ascendancy originated and could be first identified. The rise–fall myth served to order often relatively detailed historical facts – about both collaboration and resistance – into the well organised narrative pattern. Through this construction it was implied that Gaullist resistance had been the exemplary choice in 1940. Vichy was discussed by Gaullists throughout the 1940s and 1950s, albeit generally being framed within the parameters of the rise–fall narrative.

Despite the regularity with which Gaullists used the rise–fall myth to reinterpret the events of the Occupation, and put the past in its place, the storytype was not a uniquely Gaullist, or even a post-Second World War, invention. In fact, when one reviews the discourse of those who were sympathetic supporters of Vichy France, at least during the lifetime of the regime, one finds that they also sometimes showed the propensity to simplify historical progression into a division between decline and renaissance. By way of a conclusion, it is interesting to note that many among the Vichy governmental and military elite, who Madaule and Cattaui would later condemn as being instrumental members of a course of inexorable national fall, were themselves fascinated with the idea of reviving France. But, rather than looking exclusively to the French past for their historical precedent they were to turn to the history of the new European hegemon, Germany. The beginning of the nineteenth century, 1806, and the recovery of Prussia after the Battle of Jena was the oft-repeated historical paradigm amongst the upper echelons of collaboration. Robert Aron's testimony as both witness and chronicler describes the dominant historiographic mood during the early Vichy years. The quotation speaks for itself.

After the Battle of Jena, Prussia, destroyed by an intractable victor, did she not conspire to revive and re-take her place among the victorious states? Why could France not achieve as much in 1940? This comparison became an obsession in Vichy. As the former member of parliament, Paul Creyssel, declared 'For example, when one visited Du Moulin de Labarthète one saw a book, or two, on his table, one knew that they were studies devoted to Prussia after Jena, by Vidal de la Blache or Lavisse. When one met General Huntziger, one knew that he was reading the same literature. This was the subject of their conversations. It was only ever a question of Metternich'.[26]

Notes

1 I should like to thank my colleagues Christopher Flood and Noel Parker for their valuable comments on earlier drafts of this chapter. Research was financially supported by a scholarship awarded by the University of Surrey.
2 Raoul Girardet, *Mythes et mythologies politiques*, Paris, Editions du Seuil, 1986.
3 Henry Rousso, *The Vichy Syndrome: History and Memory in France since 1944*, translated by Arthur Goldhammer, London, Harvard University Press, 1991.
4 Charles de Gaulle, *Mémoires de guerre I. L'Appel, 1940–1942*, Paris, Plon, 1954; Charles de Gaulle, *Mémoires de guerre II. L'Unité, 1942–1944*, Paris, Plon, 1956; Charles de Gaulle, *Mémoires de guerre III. Le Salut 1944–1946*, Paris, Plon, 1959.
5 Jacques Soustelle, *Envers et contre tout I. De Londres à Alger 1940–1942*, Paris, Robert Laffont, 1947; Jacques Soustelle, *Envers et contre tout II. D'Alger à Paris*, Paris, Robert Laffont, 1950.
6 Louis-Henri Parias (ed.) *Trente ans d'histoire: de Clemenceau à de Gaulle*, Paris, Editions Saint Andrea – Nouvelle Librairie de France, 1949; Georges Cattaui, *Charles de Gaulle*, Paris, Editions Universitaires, 1956.
7 Edmond Michelet, 'Trente ans d'histoire', *Carrefour*, 11 May 1949, p. 8; Adrien Dansette, 'L'Histoire et le photographe', *La France Catholique*, 17 June 1949, p. 2.
8 Cattaui, *Charles de Gaulle*, back cover advertisement.
9 Cattaui's writings which are directly associated with Gaullist cultural politics include: Georges Cattaui, *Charles de Gaulle*, Paris, Portes de France, 1944; 'De Gaulle – le traditionaliste et le novateur' in Parias, *Trente ans d'histoire*, pp. 413–17; 'Remontrance à Machiavel', *Liberté de l'esprit*, 1949, June, no. 5, pp. 116–17; 'Un choix délibéré', *Liberté de l'esprit*, 1950, June–July, no. 11/12, pp. 125–6; *Charles de Gaulle*, Paris, Editions Universitaires, 1956; *Charles de Gaulle: l'homme et son destin*, Paris, Librairie Arthème Fayard, 1960.
10 Jean Charlot, *Le Gaullisme d'opposition*, Paris, Arthème Fayard, 1983, pp. 139–41.
11 Philippe Burrin, 'Vichy', in Nora, P. (ed.) *Les Lieux de mémoire*, vol. 3, *Les France*, part 1 *Conflits et partages*, Paris, Gallimard, 1992, p. 338; Nora, P., 'Gaullisme et Communisme' in Nora, P. (ed.) *op. cit.*, p. 369; Christopher Flood, *Political Myth: A Theoretical Introduction*, New York, Garland, 1996, pp. 195–234.
12 Madaule in Parias, *Trente ans d'histoire*, p. 226.
13 Ibid., p. 219.
14 Ibid., p. 246.
15 Ibid., p. 251.
16 Ibid., p. 239.
17 For Madaule and Uriage see, John Hellman, *The Knight-Monks of Vichy France: Uriage 1940–1945*, Montreal, McGill-Queens University Press, 1993, p. 115. Madaule's autobiography, *L'Absent*, Paris, Gallimard, 1973, makes no reference to either support for, or opposition towards, the Uriage project.
18 Madaule in Parias, *Trente ans d'histoire*, p. 262.

19 Ibid., p. 280.
20 Cattaui, *Charles de Gaulle,* pp. 59–60.
21 Extreme right-wing writers and Vichy apologists constructed the Occupation in very different ways from as early as 1945. See for example, Alfred Fabre-Luce, *Au nom des silencieux,* Paris, L'Auteur, 1945; Louis Rougier, *Mission secrète à Londres,* Paris, Cheval ailé, 1948; Jacques Benoist-Méchin, *Soixante jours qui ébranlèrent l'Occident,* Paris, Albin Michel, 1956, for instance.
22 Maurice Thorez, *Fils du peuple,* Paris, Editions Sociales, 1949; an account produced by ghostwriters.
23 Girardet, *Mythes et mythologies;* Henry Tudor, *Political Myth,* London, Pall Mall, 1972.
24 Robert O. Paxton, *Vichy France: Old Guard New Order 1940–1944,* New York, Columbia University Press, 1972.
25 Rousso, *The Vichy Syndrome,* p. 72.
26 Robert Aron with the collaboration of Georgette Elgey, *Histoire de Vichy 1940–1944,* Paris, Arthème Fayard, 1954, p. 254.

Further reading

The following short bibliography recommends some of the key texts in the fields of the history of Vichy France, Gaullism under the Fourth Republic, French Historiography, the collective memory of the Second World War and the theory of political myth.

Robert Aron, *Histoire de Vichy 1940–1944,* Paris, Arthème Fayard, 1954.
Jean Charlot, *Le Gaullisme d'opposition,* Paris, Arthème Fayard, 1983.
Christopher Flood, *Political Myth: A Theoretical Introduction,* New York, Garland, 1996.
Robert Gildea, *The Past in French History,* London, Yale University Press, 1994.
Raoul Girardet *Mythes et mythologies politiques,* Paris, Editions du Seuil, 1986.
Pierre Nora (ed.) *Les Lieux de mémoire,* 3 vols, Paris, Gallimard, 1984–92
Robert O. Paxton, *Vichy France: Old Guard New Order,* New York, Columbia University Press, 1972.
Henry Rousso, *The Vichy Syndrome: History and Memory in France since 1944,* translated by Arthur Goldhammer, London, Harvard University Press, 1991.
Henry Tudor, *Political Myth,* London, Pall Mall, 1972.

17 Dividing the past, defining the present

Historians and national identity in the two Germanies

Mary Fulbrook

Writing in the shadow of Auschwitz, historians in the Federal Republic of Germany and the German Democratic Republic could hardly present 'Apologias for the Nation-State'. The predominant tradition of 'Borussian' historiography which had, in the nineteenth and early twentieth centuries, played a key role in constructing and celebrating a sense of national destiny, representing unification under Prussian auspices as the culmination of German history, was clearly discredited. In the light of the 'German catastrophe', there were only a few alternatives: to view the Third Reich as the result of an essentially tortuous, distorted pattern of development intrinsic to the long sweep of German history, hence colouring as negative what had previously been seen as positive; or to reject the recent past as an accident, an aberration, a 'spanner in the works' of national destiny; or to rethink and develop new paradigms for the interpretation of the past.[1] In any event, the relationship between the nation's history and its historical conceptualisation had clearly become infinitely more problematic.

'Overcoming the past', or understanding the origins of the Third Reich in the longer term context of German history, was not the only problem. In a divided nation, split up into hostile and opposing states under the western and communist spheres of influence in the Cold War, history became closely connected with processes of constructing new, opposing, identities. The common past of the two German states became reinterpreted into very different histories, and history was – to greater or lesser degrees – deployed as a weapon in the game in which each side sought to represent itself as the 'better Germany', the true heir to all that was good in German history. Conversely, on both sides attempts were made – again to varying degrees – to represent the other German state as a continuation of all that was bad in recent German history.

Given that historians in the two Germanies had the same past to interpret, and yet were seeking to contribute to the construction of very different presents, the character and role of history in the two Germanies provides a very interesting case study of the relations between history and nation building. A naïve – or even a theoretically non-naïve but nevertheless to some extent optimistic! – view of professional history would wish to distinguish it from both myth and memory. Such an approach would wish to suggest that the recourse to empirical evidence, the requirement of some degree of empirical adequacy, would render the writings of professional historians at least somewhat more accurate, even 'true', as a construction or intellectual representation (not simple reflection) of the past 'as it actually happened'. (There are of course some views of history, from a postmodernist perspective, which would deny the possibility of such a degree of empirical adequacy.)[2] The existence of a 'real world out there' – even if we can only investigate it and represent it through forms of discourse, linguistic concepts – should provide some baseline limiting the degree to which history can be instrumentalised for political purposes.

The case study of historians in the two German states provides an opportunity to reflect a little more deeply on the political role of history both in principle and in practice. History in the GDR was very often condemned, from a western perspective, as merely a politically distorted 'legitimatory science' in the service of the leading communist party, the SED, while the notorious West German *Historikerstreit* of 1986–7 revealed, if nothing else, that even would-be objective Western conceptions of history were intimately related to political programmes and sympathies. History has always been a contentious matter on both sides of the Wall.

This chapter argues that, while the historiography of both East and West Germany was politically coloured, there are differences in the degree, character and extent of this coloration. It is oversimplistic to assume that 'political bias' is simply a matter of grotesque distortion, sins of commission and omission, in the blatant interests of a dictatorial state. There are various levels at which the question of 'political coloration' must be addressed, if we are to develop a more differentiated view.

In surveying aspects of history writing in the two Germanies, this chapter seeks both to present a more complex picture of the relations between historiography and national legitimations than is provided by simplistic (and symmetrical) Cold War depictions of 'objective truth' versus 'political distortion', and to make some more general observations on the character of history as an academic discipline and a social and political endeavour in processes of identity construction.

The external political context

There was a clear difference between the two German states in terms of the conditions under which certain individuals were or were not able to become practising members of the historical profession, and were or were not able to undertake and publish certain sorts of research.

The constraints in the GDR were directly political, although the degrees and character of the political pressure varied over time. In the early postwar years, a variety of historical perspectives were still able to be voiced. As in all other spheres, increasing Stalinisation after 1948 implied a tightening of control over historians and their publications. Alexander Abusch's *Der Irrweg einer Nation* (first published in 1946, although written while in Mexican exile), which saw the roots of nazism in the long sweep of German history rather than in European capitalism–fascism more generally, was condemned by the Central Committee of the SED in 1951. In the course of the 1950s, non-Marxist historians were progressively discriminated against, and many took the opportunity of the still open border in Berlin to flee to the West. At the 1958 Trier Historians' Congress, East German historians broke with the all-German *Verband der Historiker Deutschlands* and founded the new GDR-based *Deutsche Historiker Gesellschaft*. At the same time, SED leader Walter Ulbricht took a great personal interest in the political implications of historical pronouncements, for example criticising the historians' theses on the occasion of the 40th anniversary of the 1918 revolution. A great amount of effort was devoted to the enactment of celebrations on the anniversaries of prominent historical figures or events which could be appropriated in the task of building a new historical consciousness anchoring the GDR. Only those historical interpretations which supported the official party line could be promoted.

Starting already in the 1960s, but much more evidently in the 1970s and 1980s, there appeared to be a degree of muted relaxation with respect to both topics and approaches in historical writing in the GDR. There were certain political and institutional preconditions for these developments. Increasing political control over the institutions of higher education and advanced research in the GDR, combined with *Kaderpolitik* (personnel selection and control policies), led to an increasing reliability and internalised subordination of professional historians. The central control of research through dedicated research institutes with five-year plans determining research topics and resources, both human and financial, led to progressive bureaucratisation and control of historical production. The passage of generations, as only those young people who had conformed sufficiently to proceed to university degrees came through the system, contributed to the easier, more 'hands off' control of historical writing. Would-be historians who found they could not quite make the concessions required to engage in politically *brisant* areas, such as twentieth-century history, sought refuge in the more remote periods and places of history. A number, of course, failed to don the appropriate alibis of conformity and found themselves denounced to the Stasi, potential careers cut in shreds.[3]

The great doyens of East German historiography, such as Jürgen Kuczynski and Ernst Engelberg, were able to write with sufficient theoretical finesse and empirical richness to be rewarded with critical acclaim even from sceptically orientated Western scholars. Research institutes, such as Kuczynski's, which were separate from the teaching duties of universities, could be allowed a slightly greater degree of freedom of manœuvre in choices of topics and interpretations. Works ranging from Kuczynski's magisterial studies of the history of the working classes and of everyday life, or the kinds of social history practised by Jan Peters and Hartmut Zwahr, among others, through to the biographies of significant historical figures such as Frederick the Great and Bismarck, by Ingrid Mittenzwei and Ernst Engelberg respectively, suggested that at least some of East German historiography was able to wriggle free of the dogmatic straitjackets imposed by a politically ordained Marxist-Leninist framework. The great 'tradition/legacy' debate of the 1970s inaugurated an opening up of all aspects of the past for analysis and appropriation. Key dates such as the 500th anniversary of Luther's birth in 1983 were accompanied by an apparent rethinking of previous historical judgements, such as the importance of Luther's theology as an ideological precondition for the Peasants' War. In both topic and theoretical approach, a degree of pluralisation appeared to have been taking place in East German historiography. Note, however, the word 'appeared' – we shall return to this issue below.

Despite the apparent relaxations of the last decade or so of the GDR's existence, there was still very close political control of East German historiography. The politically ultra-reliable, the so-called *Reisekader*, could travel to the West, attend international conferences, be exposed to and engage with a wider range of publications and debates. The politically less reliable but still conformist could undertake more limited research and publishing under the watchful eye and at the behest of their superiors. The political implications of every historical interpretation were still evaluated carefully, with paranoid attention to potential public impact, at the highest levels of the political elite, as evidenced by Erich Honecker's close personal interest in the preparations for the 750th anniversary of Berlin. While academic historical accounts might have been less obviously distorted than in earlier years, the public presentation of history – from multi-authored general volumes through to museums, memorials and anniversary celebrations – was clearly subject to vigorous processes of political control and instrumentalisation.

All of this was grist to the mill of western historians of a Cold War mentality, who could point gleefully to the political biases inherent in any Marxist-Leninist version of history produced under the conditions of 'actually existing socialism'. True, some Westerners were more open-minded than others: historians such as Hans-Ulrich Wehler and Jürgen Kocka maintained a real interest in the work of East German contemporaries such as Jürgen Kuczynski, while the American scholars (of German extraction) Georg Iggers and Konrad Jarausch sought to make available to the West some of the empirically most fruitful and least ideologically constrained of East German historical scholarship. On the whole, however, the majority of West German historians were content to remain in relative ignorance of the work of their East German counterparts, simply assuming that East German historiography was intrinsically distorted by the obvious political constraints under which it was produced.

The implicit assumption on the part of many Westerners was that the situation in the West was quite different: under conditions of democracy and pluralism, anything was possible. The record of development of West German historiography suggests that this belief in the open society was at least a shade naïve. The majority of the West German historical profession in the 1950s was conservative, both politically and methodologically. Only a tiny handful of those who had been forced into exile in the Nazi period on political or 'racial' grounds even contemplated returning. While there was a minority of individuals interested in social history (Werner Conze, Theodor Schieder, Martin Broszat), the majority were predominantly traditional diplomatic and political narrative historians. The extraordinarily promising developments of the early twentieth century, such as the historical sociology of Max Weber or the critical theory of the Frankfurt School, had been effectively submerged or diverted, to reappear in new guises on the other side of the Atlantic.

It took the 'Fischer controversy' over the origins of the First World War, in conjunction with the rapid expansion of the universities and the explosion of generational and cultural conflicts of the 1960s, to begin to disrupt the comfortable conservative consensus of the West German historical profession. Nevertheless, even with the institutionalisation of new directions in history, such as the societal and structural 'Bielefeld School' in the 1970s, powerful mechanisms operated against a complete pluralisation of the West German historical profession. The political designation of certain university chairs, the career structure with its inbuilt system of patronage, and its seemingly endless apprenticeships and dependencies, to some extent militated against any easy institutionalisation of proliferating radical and subversive approaches to history. All the same, by the 1980s – with a degree of belatedness – West German historiography was characterised by a plurality of perspectives and debates, with divergent paradigms and approaches ranging from feminist history through the history of everyday life and historical anthropology to new culturalist and postmodernist approaches.

For all this pluralisation, it cannot be argued that history was in some way 'objective' and apolitical in West Germany. Strenuous attempts were made in the 1980s by West German Chancellor Helmut Kohl, assisted by historians such as Michael Stürmer and Andreas Hillgruber and the philosopher–historian Ernst Nolte, to shape popular historical consciousness in the interests of 'normalising' the German past and constructing a new national identity, through the selective presentation and reinterpretation of the past in museums and exhibitions as well as articles and books. It was this trend which precipitated the *Historikerstreit* of 1986–7. The difference in the external politicisation of history in West and East Germany was not that western history was in some way 'pure' and politically irrelevant, but rather that the political implications of alternative views could be fought over openly and energetically in the public sphere in the West, while only that which was acceptable to the dominant political party could hope to see the light of day in the East.

History as an intrinsically political enterprise

Within this broad framework, what sorts of approaches were developed by historians to the conceptualisation and interpretation of German national history?

While it is clear that historical research and publications were directly subjected to political direction and control in the GDR, it cannot be immediately assumed that historical writing in the Federal Republic was entirely apolitical or 'objective'. The ways in which historical writing in both states was intrinsically and implicitly politically coloured can be seen in a number of respects.

Topic selection

First of all, there are biases evident in which topics are chosen for exploration and eventual publication, and how they are related together to form broader historical pictures of the past (to which we shall return in a moment). Foregrounding certain topics at the expense of others which are partially or entirely neglected is an intrinsically honest mechanism for selective forgetting. We are not talking here of wilful distortion or suppression of the truth, but rather a reconstitution and highlighting in the public domain of certain elements and aspects of the past, which then contribute to the formation of at least published, articulate historical consciousness (although there are a multitude of other influences on popular historical consciousness).

Take the example of resistance to Hitler. In West Germany in the early decades, particular attention was paid to the conservative resistance to Hitler, as embodied in the July Plot of 1944, which was deemed to provide some kind of honourable national tradition, an illustration of a 'better Germany'. Along with a rather idealised view of the German army as untainted professionals protecting the fatherland, German national honour could in some sense be salvaged. The mirror image of this in the German Democratic Republic was the massive concentration on communist resistance to Hitler, providing the key founding myth of the GDR as the 'antifascist state'.

It was only in the 1960s and 1970s that historians in West Germany began to pay more serious attention to other aspects of resistance and opposition, opening up both new research areas and new debates on conceptualisation of resistance and opposition. The work of scholars such as Martin Broszat (with his colleagues at the Munich Institut für Zeitgeschichte collaborating on the *Bayernprojekt*) and Hans Mommsen played key roles in this development, which was rooted in the wider paradigm shifts towards social history evident at this time. Such an opening up of both area and approach was even more belated and partial in the GDR, with the 1944 plotters only being accorded official recognition in the late 1970s and 1980s.

Similarly, take the question of Hitler's victims. Curiously, we find a strange similarity in East and West in the 1950s, where neither side wished to devote much attention to the Holocaust or the racial character of Nazi persecution. 'Victims of fascism' in the GDR were characterised by nationality rather than 'race', and were in general demoted in comparison with active (and generally communist) 'antifascists'. In the West, historians in the 1950s tended to consider that the Holocaust was best left to 'Jewish historians'. Both these tendencies shifted in the course of time. In the West, the Holocaust increasingly became a major focus of attention, with ever more lively debates over competing paradigms for explaining its genesis. In the East, the focus remained a little fuzzy, distorted by preconceptions into which it had to be fitted. Historians such as Kurt Pätzold, for example, finally conceded the existence of popular anti-Semitism in the Third Reich only to reassert the old shibboleths which interpreted this as essentially a form of false consciousness serving to dupe the poor German people and disguise the true class character of fascist repression.

Both these historiographical tendencies had their counterparts in other modes of representing the past. The exhibitions and memorials to the Nazi period in the GDR were slanted to emphasise the role of the heroic (mostly communist) antifascist resistance fighters, and the eventual 'liberation' by the Red Army, with a remarkable downplaying of racial aspects of Nazi oppression. The racism of the Nazi period was fully acknowledged in the West, but vicarious mourning for the erstwhile victims was accompanied in many quarters by a somewhat forced 'philo-Semitism' combined with a partially repressed grieving for, or over-emphatic insistence on remembering, the German casualties of the War and its aftermath. In both cases, there were fractured memories, dissonances between officially ordained memories and popular collective memory.

The emotive character of historical writing

As we have just seen, an inescapable fact of writing history is that of emotive tone. It is just about possible to adopt a 'dry-as-dust' approach, at the risk of alienating any but the most devoted small circle of readers. Historians consciously engaged in processes of identity building are directly concerned with arousing sympathy, evoking emotional responses in readers. History, in explicit or more muted ways, then tends to be written in terms of heroes and villains, heroic battles, defeats and victories. Passions are aroused, identifications actively sought. Even when political mobilisation of readers is not the explicit aim (which it was in the GDR, but not – or not always – in the Federal Republic), it is hard for individual historians to disguise their personal sympathies or to evade more general cultural evaluations and prejudices of which they may be less consciously aware. These general remarks apply with a vengeance to the intrinsically emotive topic of the Third Reich.

Even in what was for the most part would-be 'objective' West German history, the Third Reich was the one period of history for which an emotional tone was almost prescribed: it was virtually mandatory to condemn Hitler's 'terror-regime' (*Schreckenherrschaft*, or *Gewaltherrschaft*), and very often condemnation took the place of explanation. The effective evasion of explanation, and the implicit alibi of condemnation, was in part what gave rise to Broszat's plea for 'normalisation', for treating the Third Reich like any other period of history (not to be confused with the Stürmer/Nolte/Hillgruber meaning of 'normalising' the past).

No one would dispute that Hitler is a prime candidate for the category of historical villain. Yet again, we must look at the way in which specific emphases are inserted into a broader historical picture. In West Germany, a focus on Hitler and a relatively small gang of evil henchmen, as evident in the work of popular journalistic historians like Joachim Fest, aroused an understandable public interest. Fascination with Hitler was apparent at the time of the *Hitler-Welle*, the wave of Hitleriana (including films such as Syberberg's) which ironically coincided with the expansion of social historical approaches to the Third Reich in the 1970s. Without wishing to suggest that any of this focus actually distorted the facts of historical record, it has to be pointed out that it implies a wider picture: namely, that the vast mass of the German people were effectively innocent victims, dupes seduced by an evil genius and his close associates. The criminalisation of the few was accompanied by the implicit exoneration of the many.

However, implicit exoneration was not necessarily enough. Andreas Hillgruber's explicit call, in his essay on the 'destruction of the German Reich', for 'empathy' with the Germans and the soldiers on the embattled Eastern front, rather than with the inmates of concentration camps whose suffering was prolonged and whose deaths were multiplied by the extension of the War, provides an illustration of this point. This was one of the key texts (along with Nolte's pleas for 'normalising' the past) which served to unleash the *Historikerstreit*, provoking a very hostile reaction from left-liberal scholars such as Hans-Ulrich Wehler and the philosopher Jürgen Habermas.

One might imagine that Max Weber's concept of 'interpretive understanding' of a wide variety of standpoints would be of relevance in this connection. From a Weberian perspective, one cannot explain human actions without seeking to understand the meanings of action and the actors' motives – however reprehensible they may at first blush appear. The extraordinary success of Daniel Goldhagen's book on *Hitler's Willing Executioners* may in part be explained by the way in which the spotlight is directed onto the motives of the perpetrators, rather than – in the infinitely more sophisticated research of writers such as Hans Mommsen – adopting a largely passive voice with respect to things that 'were done to' the victims without anyone apparently 'doing the doing'.[4] In any event, it can be said in general that emotive tone with respect to West German history remained a clearly unresolved and intrinsically contentious issue.

As far as GDR history-writing is concerned, the position is in some respects simpler, but similarly problematic as far as general historical pictures are concerned. It is simpler insofar as an explicit goal of history in the GDR was precisely 'to gain insights from the battles of the past and to draw inspiration from them to meet today's and tomorrow's challenges', in the words of GDR historian Heinz Heitzer.[5] The problem was that the designation of class heroes and villains, who lacked in individual character, was not always entirely successful in terms at least of popular resonance. The political message was so blindingly obvious, the propagandistic element of most historical accounts intended for popular consumption so blatantly transparent, that it failed to achieve its intended effects. As Ernst Engelberg ruefully noted in 1964, tales of class heroes could seem just a shade dull, a little less than inspiring, in comparison to the more sophisticated psychology and lavish productions of Western historians.[6] It was for this reason, Engelberg felt, that even GDR historians should concentrate on the 'great men' of history – if only in order to undermine their erstwhile power of domination.

But the focus on great men was to backfire in the 1980s. The resurrection of German heroes such as Frederick the Great and Luther, helpful though this may have been in terms of tourism and foreign currency, merely served to underline the all-German past of the GDR – and its common heritage with the West. Despite the fact that, since the conclusion of *Ostpolitik* in the early 1970s, the GDR had officially adopted a class theory of the nation, claiming that there were not only two German states but also two German nations, East Germans were being given a very different message in their historical consciousness. The message for Honecker – which he failed to learn – was that it is unwise to seek to be emotive when you cannot control the emotions aroused.

Concepts, interpretative frameworks and 'historical pictures'

More fundamental, perhaps, is the way in which the entire past was conceptualised. The inherent politics of history is most evident in the choice of concepts and their insertion in broader interpretative frameworks. It is only possible here to introduce a few brief examples to indicate the character of the problem in both western and GDR historiography.

The concept of 'totalitarianism' has been much discussed in this context. It provided West Germans in the 1950s with a very useful Cold War device for equating the Third Reich with communism. Thus, to be against communism meant one was against totalitarianism – and therefore, logically, one must be pro-democratic and hence anti-Nazi. It meant, too, that totalitarianism, in both right- and left-wing guises, was more a function of modern mass society in general than of German history in particular. It thus nicely exonerated both millions of Germans, and the German national past, in one fell swoop. The political implications were clear, and by the 1960s were being hotly debated among Western historians. The concept was eventually to a large extent discredited for empirical as well as theoretical and political reasons in the 1970s and 1980s, with the development of a more sophisticated conceptual vocabulary for interpreting the Third Reich (in terms, for example, of the 'polycratic' state), although some scholars still clung on to it in one form or another. Nevertheless, it has enjoyed an extraordinary resurrection in the 1990s with respect to the categorisation and condemnation of communist regimes. It exemplifies the ways in which an apparently innocent category for analysing the past embodies within it not only a set of empirical criteria (the list of attributes which qualify a regime to be classified as an exemplar of the concept) but also an intrinsic political loading and a tendentious insertion into a broader framework of historical–political interpretation.[7]

Marxism–Leninism has of course a much more explicit philosophy of history into which the Nazi period, and the subsequent GDR, could very easily be slotted. On this view, the Third Reich arose less out of any peculiarities of *German* history as such, but rather was part of the *pan-European phase of fascism*, a political form characteristic of monopoly capitalism in crisis. The GDR, having overthrown capitalism, and hence the socioeconomic preconditions for the political form of fascism, was clearly poised to enter and develop a higher stage of history leading eventually to the ultimate stage of pure communism. The motor of history, in this schema, was class struggle and revolution. There was a clear teleological thread running through, from lower, less advanced, to higher and better historical stages.

Historical writing in the GDR had to be fitted, in one way or another, into this general framework. In some of (what this author considers to be!) the best East German history-writing, concepts such as 'late feudalism' simply took the place of the theoretically more neutral choice of straight dates ('eighteenth century'). 'Class struggles' eventually, in the works of intelligent historians of the calibre of Jürgen Kuczynski, came to be viewed less in wooden terms of heroic faceless puppets and were approached with some sophistication, recognising the need to see class struggles in terms of those above as well as those below. In some works, however, theoretical presuppositions presented an insurmountable barrier to the recognition of the real implications of the empirical record – as in Pätzold's wilful distortions of the meaning of popular anti-Semitism.[8]

Writing the nation?

Historians delude themselves if they think they can, single-handedly, create nations. If a nation is an imagined community, it takes a lot more than a few abstruse, or even well-written and popular, history books to install it in the heads of millions of participants in the nation. National identities are constructed and institutionalised through a range of factors, including common memories, practical experiences, and a sense of common destiny (often in adversity). Nor is historical consciousness – which is but one element in national identity – based solely, or sometimes even at all, on the writings of professional historians. In the modern world, films such as *Holocaust* and *Schindler's List* have done more to bring representations of the Holocaust into the consciousness of Germans than have the outpourings of a generation of excellent (and less excellent) historians. Topographies of memory and sites and celebrations of commemoration, also colour and shape popular historical consciousness. The struggles over history museums, anniversaries and memorials, in both East and West Germany, bear witness to the extent of resources, in time and money, that politicians believe it is worth devoting to the cause of constructing whatever is deemed to be an appropriate historical consciousness and sense of national identity.

These topics range beyond the scope of this volume, however. Let me conclude with a few general theses about history-writing and the nation in the two Germanies.

History-writing in the GDR was in some negative senses a partial success from the point of view of the regime. It was partially successful in that it prescribed the conceptual framework in which people thought.[9] Thinking is of course an individual activity, but it is too a cultural and collective enterprise, in that we think through the inherited language we inhabit. If one thinks of the Third Reich in terms of fascism and left-wing antifascist resistance – and one is simply not exposed to other modes of conceptualisation and interpretation – then this is simply the way the world appears to be. There may be suspicions of propagandistically determined emphases and absences, but no means of knowing what these are. So there may be a degree of scepticism, but not basic disagreement.

In other respects, however, GDR history backfired. In the early decades, a degree of popular memory was – however partial and repressed – at odds with the official accounts. Once the SED began to open up the whole of German history for inquiry, there was exposure to broader themes, questions, frames of reference, which might serve to underline common Germanness with the West and resonate with pan-German sensitivities and identifications.

History was and remained a keenly political matter in the West. For all the greater degree of empirical openness, and for all the possibilities of public debate and disagreement, interpretative paradigms in the West remained highly politically sensitive.

'Nation' is also an intrinsically contested concept. There are many possible definitions of the concept of nation. In the case of the GDR, official policy with respect to the German nation changed in mid-stream, but with little effect on popular consciousness. In the case of the Federal Republic, a variety of attempts to harness history to the construction of a 'normal' national identity were met with vigorous rebuttal. To explore the resonance of these debates with the varieties of popular historical consciousness and senses of identity would go beyond the scope of this chapter.[10]

These conclusions do not mean that the political coloration of history should lead one into a total relativism. There are degrees of empirical adequacy, degrees of political instrumentalisation and – yes – distortion. While no historical account can claim to provide the 'whole truth' in some mimetic fashion, nevertheless there are some representations which approximate better to what we know of the real world through its historical traces than others. The only way in which such adequacy can be improved is through collective and open debate, unconstrained by political appropriation, or, worse, political direction, in which the desired conclusions precede the investigation. History is a human endeavour which can only flourish where a degree of freedom of thought and speech exists.

Notes

1 To some extent, these alternatives appeared sequentially, with the 'spanner in the works' version enjoying its heyday in the 1950s, the inverted *Sonderweg* claiming supremacy in the late 1960s, to be challenged by alternative paradigms in the 1970s and 1980s; but to some extent, however, these variants have overlapped and continue to coexist in a variety of versions.

2 This is obviously not an appropriate place to embark on an extensive discussion of theories of history. For a critique (from a perspective of 'practical realism') of the relativism implicit in much postmodernist writing on the nature of history, see for example Joyce Appleby, Lynn Hunt and Margaret Jacob, *Telling the Truth about History* (New York, London, W.W. Norton, 1994).

3 This has led to much bitterness in the post-*Wende* purge of the East German historical profession and its alleged renewal; many who had been excluded entirely from any sort of career in the GDR felt they had been unjustly denied a second chance after the *Wende*, while former apparatchiks were being given undeserved chances to continue their careers so long as they were not too politically tainted by having served as Stasi informers. The controversies over recent German history (such as the attacks on the Potsdam Institute) pursued by members of the *Unabhängige Historkerverband* can only be understood in the light of this background of personal bitterness and animosity.

4 Daniel Goldhagen, *Hitler's Willing Executioners. Ordinary Germans and the Holocaust* (London, Little, Brown and Co., 1996); for a revealing collection of reactions on both sides of the Atlantic, see Julius Schoeps (ed.) *Ein Volk von Mördern?* (Hamburg, Hoffmann und Campe, 1996).

5 Heinz Heitzer, *GDR: An Historical Outline* (Dresden, Verlag Zeit im Bild, 1981; translation of 1979 original), p. 7.

6 Ernst Engelberg, *Der umfassende Aufbau des Sozialismus und die Aufgaben der Historiker* (Berlin, Akademie Verlag, 1964).

7 I have discussed this issue at greater length in my article on 'The Limits of Totalitarianism: God, State and Society in the GDR', *Transactions of the Royal Historical Society*, 6th series, vol. vii, 1997.

8 See particularly Kurt Pätzold (ed.) *Verfolgung, Vertreibung, Vernichtung* (Leipzig, Verlag Philipp Reclam jun., 1983), p. 19.

9 It could be argued that the exposure to and impact of Western television for most of the GDR population should have modified the success of the regime in this respect. However, the point being made here is that, although people may not have instantly trusted and believed what they read in the GDR's official versions of history, they were not sufficiently exposed to (or able to participate in) active debates over alternative views to be able to develop explicit and articulated alternative forms of historical consciousness.

10 I explore these questions further in a book on *German National Identity after the Holocaust* (London, Polity Press, 1999).

Further reading

GDR history-writing

See generally: Alexander Fischer and Günter Heydemann (eds) *Geschichtswissenschaft der DDR*, vol. I, Berlin, Duncker and Humblot, 1988; A. Dorpalen, *German History in Marxist Perspective. The East German Approach*, London, 1985; Jan Herman Brinks, *Die DDR-Geschichtswissenschaft auf dem Weg zur deutschen Einheit*, Frankfurt and New York,

Campus Verlag, 1992; Konrad Jarausch (ed.) *Zwischen Parteilichkeit und Professionalität. Bilanz der Geschichtswissenschaft in der DDR*, Berlin, Akademie Verlag, 1991; and the very critical views of Hermann Weber, *Aufbau und Fall einer Diktatur*, Cologne, Bund-Verlag, 1991, Part III, 'Geschichtsschreibung – Instrument der SED-Diktatur'.

For a few examples, see Alexander Abusch, *Der Irrweg einer Nation. Ein Beitrag zum Verständnis deutscher Geschichte*, Berlin, Aufbau Verlag, 8th edn, 1960 (original 1946); Jürgen Kuczynski, *Die Geschichte der deutschen Arbeiterbewegung*, Berlin (East), Akademie, 8 vols, 1966; *idem.*, *Geschichte des Alltags des deutschen Volkes*, 1981; Ernst Engelberg, *Bismarck*, 2 vols, Berlin, Akademie Verlag, 1985, 1990; Ingrid Mittenzwei, *Friedrich II. von Preussen. Eine Biographie*, Berlin, VEB Deutscher Verlag der Wissenschaften, revised edn, 1982 (original 1979); Kurt Pätzold and Manfred Weißbecker, *Hakenkreuz und Totenkopf*, Berlin, VEB Deutscher Verlag der Wissenschaften, 1981; and for a selection of short pieces by often less well known social historians, Georg Iggers (ed.) *Marxist Historiography in Transformation*, Oxford, Berg, 1991.

West German historiography

In the first two decades after the War, see: Winfried Schulze, *Deutsche Geschichtswissenschaft nach 1945*, Munich, Oldenbourg, 1989; and Ernst Schulin and Elisabeth Müller-Lückner (eds) *Deutsche Geschichtswissenschaft nach dem zweiten Weltkrieg (1945–1965)*, Munich, Oldenbourg, 1989.

In the interests of space, I am taking only the example of the *Historikerstreit* as an illustration of the politicisation of history in the West. Key short texts are reprinted in '*Historikerstreit*', Munich, Piper Verlag, 1987, available in English translation by James Knowlton and Truett Cates, *Forever in the Shadow of Hitler?*, New Jersey, Humanities Press, 1993; see also Andreas Hillgruber's essays in *Zweierlei Untergang: Die Zerschlagung des deutschen Reiches und das Ende des Europäischen Judentums*, Berlin, Siedler, 1986. For critical commentaries, see: Hans-Ulrich Wehler, *Entsorgung der deutschen Vergangenheit?*, Munich, C.H. Beck, 1988; C. Maier, *The Unmasterable Past*, Cambridge, MA, Harvard University Press, 1988; Richard J. Evans, *In Hitler's Shadow*, London, I.B. Tauris, 1989.

18 A neglected question

Historians and the Italian national state (1945–95)

Roberto Vivarelli

In recent years a number of works have appeared about the decline of the Italian national state, if not the end of Italy herself. The titles speak for themselves: *Se cessiamo di essere una nazione* (*If we Cease to be a Nation*), *Italia nazione difficile* (*Italy. Difficult Nation*), *Finis Italiae* (*Italy's End*), *La morte della patria* (*Death of the Fatherland*).[1] It is not my task to review the content of these works. However two things must be pointed out. First the fact that the phenomenon which these works describe has nothing to do with the more general tendency proper to our times of a decline of national feeling, which has been gradually fading away since the end of the Second World War. Second, that there is something peculiar in the sudden discovery by Italian historians of a fact already quite evident for a number of years and whose origins go back to the particular events which took place in Italy between 1943 and 1945, and to the collapse of the fascist regime.

Actually the end of the War in Italy marked a drastic rejection of national feeling. Since then, the lack of affection for national memories and the neglect in which the national flag and every national symbol are kept are sufficient evidence of this phenomenon. It would seem indeed that in Italy the end of fascism also meant the end of the national state. But why was that? And why have historians been so tardy in recognising the fact?

In a nutshell, the question was whether there was continuity or discontinuity between the Italian national state created by the Risorgimento and fascism. If there was continuity, fascism was right in claiming to represent the national tradition. Therefore the fall of fascism implied the end of the national state. If, instead, there was no continuity and fascism did not have the right to present itself as the heir of the Risorgimento, then the end of fascism should simply give way to a restoration of the national state whose tradition fascism had usurped.

As soon as Mussolini came to power, antifascist historians perceived perfectly the terms of the question and its seriousness. Gaetano Salvemini was the first to point out how drastic a break with the previous political tradition had been wrought by the advent of Mussolini. Salvemini's contribution is particularly significant since before the War he had been a harsh critic of Italian political life. Later on the task of denying a continuity between the national tradition and fascism was taken up by a number of historians, especially Benedetto Croce, Adolfo Omodeo and Luigi Salvatorelli. In their common attempt, some particular topics were singled out to oppose the claims of fascist propaganda: namely Cavour's work and its legacy, the way Italy was governed in the fifteen-year period after unification (the period of the so-called *Destra storica* – historical right), and the First World War. I will not examine in detail the many contributions of these historians. It is sufficient to remember that in one of these works, Salvatorelli's *The Risorgimento: Thought and Action*, published between 1943 and 1944 (a crucial moment), fascism was defined as *anti-Risorgimento*.[2] But after 1945 things changed drastically and not only on the political scene. Generally speaking, the works of these historians and their concerns were rapidly forgotten.

In those years there was of course a certain confusion in the political life of Italy. At the end of the War the head of state was the same king who had opened the way to Mussolini's government. A year after, Italy became a republic but in a very peaceful way. The new republican constitution could very well represent the same set of values which ostensibly had ruled Italy before fascism. In other words, from a formal point of view nothing prevented considering the new republican state as the continuation of the old liberal state, which would have preserved the identity of the Italian national state. Actually things were very different. As a matter of fact the new political forces which were going to rule Italy from now on in no way considered themselves heirs of the Risorgimento tradition, i.e. the national tradition, as far as their main components were concerned (namely socialists and communists on one side, Catholics on the other). As a result, on the political scene only minority groups tried to pick up the thread of national history and to present themselves as the followers of the old national state. They did not score any significant success, and this explains why, in Italy, national feelings rapidly faded away.

If we now turn to the historians, who are supposed to be the custodians of common memories, we can easily see that since 1945 their work largely reflects what was going on in the political scene. There is a real gulf between the generation of historians active before the War and the one which emerged after 1945. The issues to which they were addressing their attention were the same, namely the meaning of the Risorgimento, the nature of the national state, the continuity between such a state and fascism. The answers they gave were very different not only because of a profound ideological diversity but because of a very different *état d'esprit*. The older generation viewed with great anxiety the decline of a national tradition which they felt as their own; the new generation was looking in different directions. Communists and Catholics had at least one thing in common: they were moved by values which transcended national frontiers. How right they were in rejecting the national tradition and casting no more than a scornful eye on the values it had represented is another question. The fact remains that for this new generation of historians the decline of the Italian national state was a question not worth any special attention.

In the first years after the War, the change among historians was not imme-diately perceptible. Gaetano Salvemini re-examined extensively the question of whether pre-fascist Italy was a democracy.[3] He gave a very balanced answer stating that it was a democracy in the making. In so doing Salvemini substan-tially revised his judgement about Giolitti, which previously had been particularly severe. Arturo Carlo Jemolo published in those years a basic work on the relations between church and state in Italy since 1848.[4] In it Jemolo made clear the presence in the Italian state of a genuine liberal tradition. And in 1951 Federico Chabod published a splendid work, which only nominally dealt with foreign policy.[5] In fact Chabod's work was an analysis of the European public spirit around 1870, and against this background he offered a portrait of the whole Italian ruling class, in which the men of the right appeared much more in tune with the values of a European liberal tradition than the men of the left. Fascism, as Chabod's interpretation was suggesting, had more direct links with some of those political forces which opposed Cavour's policy, than with those forces which had picked up Cavour's legacy. Other works in this vein could be quoted. All these voices however were soon isolated. The trend of studies that was gaining strength in those years, and that soon became overwhelming, was very different. Very shortly after the end of the war historians seemed to divide themselves along party lines and to dedi-cate most of their time to tracing the history or the pre-history of the party in which they militated. In such a view the national tradition could find no place.

Gradually the very term Risorgimento disappeared. In studying the period before 1861, the year of the unification, special attention was given particu-larly to the men of that party, the so called *Partito d'Azione* (Action Party), who had opposed Cavour's policy and who, though in very vague terms, had wanted an Italian state different from the one which came into existence. In studying the period after 1861 special attention was given to all those political groups which, from the left as well as from the right, formed an opposition to the national state. Very soon most of the works concerning Italy between 1861 and the fascist period could in fact be divided into two categories: the history of the working-class movement (*movimento operaio*), or the history of the Catholic movement.

In support of this general trend a strong contribution came in the late 1940s with the publication of Gramsci's *Quaderni* (Notebooks). Here I am not concerned with Gramsci's actual thought. If I were, I would advise great caution when using personal notes taken down under very special circum-stances and certainly not meant for publication. What I am talking about here is the way Gramsci's notebooks were used to spread the thesis that the Risorgimento had been a failed revolution. Actually, Gramsci's work and in the same years the work of another communist scholar, Emilio Sereni, turned the attention of historians to the countryside and the situation of the peasants. From here a wide-ranging discussion originated about the condition and timing of an Italian Industrial Revolution. Important as this issue was, it soon moved attention away from the political results of national unification to the economic results. And more and more the Risorgimento, as the process through which the national state was created, lost all meaning. 'Fine del Risorgimento?' ('The End of the Risorgimento?' in which a question mark was purely rhetorical) was the title of a long essay by a communist historian, Ernesto Ragionieri, published in 1964.[6] It was a long review of the many publications which appeared around 1961, the centennial of the Italian unification. By this date, the new trend of studies was dominating the field, and the tune was set by younger historians like Ragionieri himself, Giampiero Carocci, Gastone Manacorda, Rosario Villari, Paolo Spriano or, on the Catholic side, Gabriele De Rosa, Fausto Fonzi, Pietro Scoppola, to mention just a few.

The prevailing tendency was increased after 1968, a devastating date in the civil life of my country. From then on every existing criticism addressed to the history of the national state was made more radical in substance and more aggressive in tone. More particularly a most rabid attack was moved against whoever and whatever represented any form of moral as well as material support in favour of the one event which summarised the history of the national state, the First World War. After this campaign whatever had been left of a national feeling (and it wasn't much) was wiped out and taunted as a very shameful feeling.

All this amounts to saying that during the first period of its life the Italian republic, though ostensibly a national state, was not given any support as such by Italian historians. Instead, by their work they kept showing that between the new institutions and the national tradition there was no continuity whatsoever. In so doing a big question remained open, to which I will come back shortly: on what historical foundations is the Italian state based?

Against this mostly uniform background of historical studies stands, in virtual isolation, the work of a great scholar, the late Rosario Romeo. His first book, published in 1950, examined the Risorgimento in Sicily.[7] Though he did not underrate the shortcomings of the unification, Romeo pointed out why it had to be considered a very positive achievement. Later Romeo moved to study economic history and gave a significant contribution to the discussion about the industrial revolution in Italy.[8] Then, from the beginning of the 1960s – during the same years when criticism against the national state and its makers was becoming more and more common among historians and more and more harsh – Romeo insisted on moving against the current. First he reconsidered in a series of essays the whole course of Italian history from the Risorgimento to fascism.[9] In so doing he pointed out the many positive results, denying a continuity between that course and fascism, whose origins he indicated in the War. Later on Romeo started working on a large biography of Cavour (a very significant choice), the first volume of which appeared in 1969, the third and last in 1984.[10] Based on thorough and painstaking research, but also animated by a most genuine civic passion, Romeo's work stands out as a superb vindication of Cavour's greatness. In his work Romeo was also reaffirming the soundness of those values which had supported the creation of the Italian national state. Aside from his main work, Romeo also contributed a large number of articles, in journals and newspapers, taking issue with many of his colleagues and fighting those trends most fashionable among many historians. His work was not only an open defence of the national state created by the Risorgimento, but also a defence of national history from the unification to the First World War. It can very well be said that Romeo was continuing the same line of interpretation, and the same battle, advanced during the fascist period by those antifascist historians whom I have already mentioned.

In his solitary fight Romeo had no illusions. He was not supported by any faith that the national tradition could be recovered, by any hope that a national state could be restored. On the contrary he was convinced that with the end of the War and the end of fascism the Italian national state had also come to an end. Not because fascism was right in claiming to represent the national tradition, but more simply because in the general history of Europe the values that had formed that tradition had come to an end.

In a way, as we can see, it could be said that between Romeo's line of thought and the views of those historians who in recent years have lamented the end of the Italian national state, there is a substantial agreement. But if these historians had taken Romeo's work in due consideration their 'discovery' would have been no surprise (and it is remarkable how little attention Romeo's work has received in general). In fact, the fate of the Italian national state after 1945 has been so far a most neglected question. To answer that question, which is in many ways quite crucial since it concerns the foundations of the Italian republic, I suggest that proper attention must be given to what happened in Italy between 1943 and 1945. Some new studies have already moved in that direction, but we still have a long way to go.

Notes

1 G.E. Rusconi, *Se cessiamo di essere una nazione*, Bologna, Il Mulino, 1993; G. Galasso, *Italia nazione difficile. Contributo alla storia politica e culturale dell'Italia unita*, Firenze, Le Monnier, 1994; S. Romano, *Finis Italiae*, Milano, Scheiwiller, 1994; E. Galli della Loggia, *La morte della patria. La crisi dell'idea di nazione tra Resistenza, antifascismo e Repubblica*, Roma-Bari, Laterza, 1996.
2 L. Salvatorelli, *Pensiero e azione del Risorgimento*, Rome, Einaudi, 1944; English translation, *The Risorgimento: Thought and Action*, New York, Harper & Row, 1970.
3 G. Salvemini, 'Fu l'Italia prefascista una democrazia?', *Il Ponte*, 1952, pp. 11–23, 166–81, 281–97.
4 A.C. Jemolo, *Chiesa e Stato in Italia negli ultimi cento anni*, Torino, Einaudi, 1949.
5 F. Chabod, *Storia della politica estera italiana dal 1870 al 1896: Le premesse*, Bari, Laterza, 1951; English translation, *Italian Foreign Policy: The Statecraft of the Founders*, Princeton, NJ, Princeton University Press, 1996.
6 E. Ragionieri, 'Fine del 'Risorgimento'? Alcune considerazioni sul centenario dell'unità d'Italia', *Studi Storici*, 1964, vol. V, pp. 3–40.
7 R. Romeo, *Il Risorgimento in Sicilia*, Bari, Laterza, 1950.
8 R. Romeo, *Risorgimento e capitalismo*, Bari, Laterza, 1959.

9 R. Romeo, *Dal Piemonte sabaudo all'Italia liberale*, Torino, Einaudi, 1963; *L'Italia unita e la prima guerra mondiale*, Roma-Bari, Laterza, 1978.
10 R. Romeo, *Cavour e il suo tempo*, 3 vols, Bari, Laterza, 1969, 1977, 1984.

Further reading (suggested by the editors)

R.J.Bosworth, *Explaining Auschwitz and Hiroshima*, London, Routledge, 1993, especially Chapter 6.

R.J.Bosworth, 'Italian Foreign Policy and its Historiography', in R.J. Bosworth and G.Rizza (eds) *Altro Polo: Intellectuals and their Ideas in Contemporary Italy*, Sydney, Frederick May Foundation for Italian Studies, 1983.

G.Bussino, *L'identità dell'italia. Le ricerche di Rosario Romeo (1924–1987) tra storiografia e impegno politico*, Université de lausanne, Faculté des Sciences Sociales et Politiques, 'Cours, séminaries et travaux', no.16, 1995.

C.Cassina (ed.) *La storiografia sull'Italia contemporanea*, Pisa, Giardoni, 1991.

P. Ginsborg, *A History of Contemporary Italy*, London, Harmondsworth, 1988. An acclaimed historical introduction to the period.

C. Levy, 'From Fascism to Post-fascism: Italian Roads to Modernity', in R. Bessel (ed.) *Fascist Italy and Nazi Germany*, Cambridge, Cambridge University Press, 1996.

G.Sasso, 'Rosario Romeo e l'idea di 'nazione'. Appunti e considerazioni', in G.Pescosolidi (ed) *Il rinnovamento della stroiografia politica. Studi in memoria di Rosario Romeo*, Rome, Istituto della Enciclopedia Italiana, 1995, pp.113–43.

Part VII

Contemporary trends

The end of the Cold War in 1989 had major repercussions on the historiographies of all the countries discussed in this volume. Julian Jackson examines efforts in French historiography to lay to rest the demons of the past. Through a discussion of attitudes to the Vichy period, French identity, immigration and the bicentenary of the Revolution of 1789, he shows that these issues remain as divisive as ever. Jackson focuses in particular upon the views of centre-left historians, and upon the ambiguities of the Jacobin nationalist tradition, which permits on the one hand the inclusion of all individuals within the 'neutral' framework of the nation, yet forbids collective public displays of difference.

The renaissance of the German variant of the national narrative following reunification in 1990 is traced by Stefan Berger. Distinguishing broadly between a self-styled 'new right', traditional liberal-conservatism and leftist attempts to recapture the concept of the nation, Berger asks where a possible renationalisation of German historiography leaves the historical profession at the end of the twentieth century.

Just as German historians intervened in debates over the Nazi past in the 1980s and again in post-reunification debates on national identity, so Italian historians have been heavily implicated in debates over the meanings of the 'First Republic' (1948–94) and the experience of fascism and the Resistance. As Carl Levy demonstrates, historiographical accounts are intertwined with contemporary politics. Following the collapse of the postwar, Christian Democratic-dominated republic, nationalist and revisionist historians found themselves with greater political influence. Levy suggests that the re-reading of the 1940s may have smoothed the rehabilitation of the right-wing *Alleanza Nazionale* and investigates the extent to which the shared values embodied in the constitution have been undermined or reinforced by the cross-cutting historical disputes of the 1990s.

19 Historians and the nation in contemporary France

Julian Jackson

In 1988 three distinguished French historians co-authored a book with the subtitle: 'the end of French exceptionalism'.[1] Their argument was that, after two hundred years, the cycle of division opened by the French Revolution was over. The French could now live at peace with themselves, and no longer quarrelled significantly about their history. But it quickly emerged that the politics of consensus would spawn new problems in which interpretations of the national past would play a central role.

Historians, Vichy and memory

At the heart of the debate is the memory of Vichy. The problem is not a refusal to 'confront' the Vichy past. For twenty years information about Vichy has poured out endlessly, and the public has displayed a morbid fascination for the subject. In his book *The Vichy Syndrome* (1987) Henri Rousso analysed the disintegration in the 1970s of the Gaullist myth of France as a nation of resisters and the way in which Vichy had become a national obsession. Recently Rousso co-authored, with Eric Conan, another book, *Vichy, Un passé qui ne passe pas* (1994), arguing that this obsession has become unhistorical by focusing excessively on Vichy's anti-Semitism. This is a contrast with the Liberation when collaborators were tried for intelligence with the enemy, and the Jewish issue was so subsidiary that Xavier Vallat, Vichy's Commissioner for Jewish Affairs, argued in his defence that he was indeed an anti-Semite but an entirely French one and therefore not a collaborator. For Rousso, the contemporary focus on the persecution of the Jews – what he calls 'judeo-centrism' – has distorted the history of the period by making anti-Semitism more central to Vichy than it was and neglecting the fate of the regime's other victims: communists, resisters, freemasons. The desire to repay a moral debt to France's Jewish population leads to anachronism if one forgets that in 1945 most Jewish survivors wanted to be considered not as Jews but as French citizens,[2] and recent historiography, while not denying the *regime's* anti-Semitism, has highlighted the solidarity towards Jews displayed by the French *people*.[3]

The Vichy obsession is kept alive by the decision in 1964 to make 'crimes against humanity' imprescriptible. This makes it possible still to try people who escaped condemnation in 1944–5. Thus we have had the trials of Klaus Barbie (1987), Paul Touvier (1994) and Maurice Papon. Each trial offers the prospect that it will exorcise the demon, but fails to do so: the past still refuses to go away.

The trial of Touvier, a local leader of Vichy's infamous *Milice*, was intended to perform an exemplary role as the first prosecution of a Frenchman for 'crimes against humanity' – that is, atrocities against the Jews. But since the definition of crimes against humanity required they be committed 'in the name of a state practising a policy of ideological hegemony' – that is an Axis power – to convict Touvier it became necessary to prove that his offences had been committed at the behest of the Germans, and this involved underplaying the *Milice*'s autonomy of the Germans, and its links to Vichy – that is to say its Frenchness.[4]

The fiftieth anniversary of the *rafle du Vélodrome d'hiver* – the arrest on 16–17 July 1942 of over 12,000 Jews in Paris by the French police – also caused problems of interpretation. The anniversary witnessed an outpouring of emotion, and in 1993 the government made 16 July a day of commemoration of the persecution of the Jews. But as Rousso points out, the *rafle*, despite French cooperation, was not inspired by Vichy whose complicity was more in the logic of its collaboration policy than its anti-Semitic policy, which aimed at exclusion rather than extermination. To confront France's own anti-Semitic demons it might have been more appropriate to select the anniversary of the Jewish Statute of October 1940 which, although lacking the dramatic horror of the *rafle*, was an entirely French initiative. As it was, this anniversary went almost unnoticed.

Before the decision to make 16 July a day of commemoration, the anniversary of the *rafle* had aroused controversy after 200 public figures petitioned the President of the Republic to 'proclaim officially' that the 'French State of Vichy' was 'responsible for persecutions and crimes against the Jews of France'. President François Mitterrand refused on the grounds that the Republic could not assume responsibility for the crimes of Vichy. He rejected any analogy with Willy Brandt's assumption of responsibility for German crimes, arguing that the French *nation* had not been implicated. Mitterrand also adopted the Gaullist argument that legally the Vichy regime – the 'so-called' State as de Gaulle called it – had never existed. A Gaullist ordinance of August 1944 had affirmed that de Gaulle's Free French had incarnated the continuity of the Republic since 1940. As the socialist Jean-Pierre Chevènement noted, in defence of Mitterrand's position, the petitioners' logic made de Gaulle a 'deserter' and the resisters 'terrorists'. What made it difficult to accept this argument from Mitterrand, however, were the simultaneous revelations, authorised by him, about his own Vichy past.[5] What were Mitterrand's motives in allowing these revelations? Was it, Stanley Hoffmann asks, a desire for reconciliation – 'by revealing the complexity of his own journey he wished to show the vanity of absolute judgements'? – or was it a way of exorcising de Gaulle's ghost – by telling the French: de Gaulle was an exception, 'he wasn't really like us, but you, my friends, were very much like me'?[6]

In either case Mitterrand failed. The French may no longer accept the epic Gaullist version of the past, but this did not make them ready to accept the more realistic Mitterrandian one. The paradoxes are legion: the paradox that although de Gaulle has never been more revered in France, his version of the past has never carried less conviction; the paradox that Mitterrand, a lifelong anti–Gaullist with some indulgence for a Vichy past which was partly his own, employed a Gaullist interpretation of that past in order to avoid accepting responsibility as French President for it; the paradox that in July 1995 it was a Gaullist President, Jacques Chirac, who conceded the gesture Mitterrand had refused three years earlier, thereby legitimising an interpretation of Vichy which undermines the Gaullist one.

Perhaps Chirac's action will eventually contribute to appeasing the Vichy demons. But for the moment it remains difficult to fit the pieces together and construct, in Charles Maier's phrase, a 'masterable past'. When Conan and Rousso appeal for a less obsessional approach to Vichy their motive is not to excuse the past, but to plead that if memory is elevated into a duty, it must also be more historical. They end their book by asking:

> does the duty of memory give one the right to carry out a perpetual trial of the war generation? Has this obsession not become for our generation a substitute for the urgent issues of the present – or even worse a refusal of the future?

Historians and the identity of France

These problems recall Renan's remark in his 1882 lecture *Qu'est qu'une nation?*: 'forgetting, even indeed historical error, are a necessary factor in the creation of a nation, and thus the progress of historical studies are often a danger for nationhood'.[7] Thus the Vichy 'syndrome' is part of a wider crisis of national identity in France. For one critic, the collapse of any agreed version of the Vichy past has destroyed the 'intelligibility of the world in which the French people believed they lived'.[8] For Rousso the debate over Vichy offers 'warning signs about the future of French identity'.[9] National identity has been since the mid 1980s one of the current obsessions of French politics.[10]

One striking example of this was the publication in 1986 of the first volume of Fernand Braudel's *L'Identité de la France*. That the leading representative of the *Annales* school should in his twilight years renounce the Annaliste contempt for purely national history and produce a massive exploration of France's past is itself significant; so is the enthusiasm with which the book was greeted; so, even more, is the self-consciously elegiac tone which pervades it; so, most of all, is the mystically nationalist tone, reminiscent of Michelet. Thus for example Braudel's definition of his notion of identity:

> the shaping of France by its own hand, if not the living result of what the interminable past has deposited, layer by layer….In sum a residue, an

amalgam, a thing of additions and mixtures…a process, a fight against itself, destined to go on infinitely. If it were to stop, everything would fall apart. A nation can have its *being* only at the price of forever searching for itself, for ever transforming itself in the direction of its logical develop-ment, unceasingly testing itself against others and identifying itself with the best, the most essential part of itself.[11]

Braudel is not the only proponent of the *nouvelle histoire* to succumb to the temptation to return to national history. The 1980s saw a huge outpouring of multi-volume collective histories of France, mostly in traditional narrative mode, which would not have looked out of place at the end of the nineteenth century and recall the once decried histories of Seignobos and Lavisse.[12] In the preface to the three-volume history he has edited, Georges Duby notes that the aim was to 'concentrate our discourse on politics. I have not hesitated to linger on certain events…through the event we touch life itself'. Even Braudel whose contempt for the event was legendary now accepted the idea of the 'long-event, that is an event with long term consequences annexing itself to itself a period superior to its own duration'.[13] These developments are part of a revolution in French intellectual life involving a rejection of the previously dominant Marxist and structuralist positions. Another feature of this is the new fashion for biography even by historians particularly associated with *Annales* (Ferro on Pétain, Le Goff on St Louis). The seemingly inex-haustible public thirst for history and the ever-swelling ranks of biographies – everyone from Vercingetorix to Pompidou – suggests that an intellectual trend has converged with a social need. In his survey of French intellectual life since 1980, Olivier Mongin talks of the 'consecration of the historian'[14] and suggests that historians have filled the void created by the disappearance of the engaged intellectual in France.

The *nouvelle histoire* has not entirely surrendered to the sirens of narrative history. This is not true of one of the most remarkable historical publishing projects in France since the War, the seven-volume series *Les Lieux de Mémoire*, edited by Pierre Nora between 1984 and 1992. A team of historians, deploying the most sophisticated approaches of cultural history, have decoded national festivals, monuments, memorials, songs and books, peeling off the layers of meaning and the accretions of myth that constitute the landscape of national memory: Descartes, the Eiffel Tower, the Tour de France, Joan of Arc, the café, Paris, Gauls and Franks, Proust, the 'Marseillaise' – these are among 'sites of memory' visited. In itself the new vogue for 'memory' is symptomatic. The 1974 manifesto for *la nouvelle histoire*, of which Nora was one of the inspirations, made no mention of the theme of memory. Ten years later the theme had become one of the most distinctive features of French historiog-raphy. This resonates perfectly with the insatiable thirst in France today for national celebrations and commemorations – from the tercentenary of the Edict of Nantes (1985) to the fifteen-hundredth anniversary of the baptism of Clovis (1996). Nora noted ruefully that what he conceived as 'kind of counter-commemorative history' aiming to 'avoid the risk of celebration...to objectify the system of national history and decompose its elements' has been absorbed into the commemorative process it sought to demystify: *les lieux de mémoire* had become a *lieu de mémoire*.[15] But it is also true, as Stephen Englund has noted, that the demystification was often more apparent than real with many contributors succumbing to a personification of the Nation as an 'eternal representational given...projected back on to fifteen centuries of French history' – for example, the essay characterising a chronicler's praise for Charles VII's reconquest of Normandy in the fifteenth century, as the first 'discours de 14 juillet'.[16] Nora's project thus bears some resemblance to the teleological nationalism of Lavisse.

In his introductions and prefaces to the volumes, Nora's tone is suffused with an evocative and metaphorical language of melancholy nostalgia.[17] In his first volume he noted that while pre-modern societies live *within* memory, and make no distinction between past and present, in modern societies this unmediated experience of remembering is broken and it becomes necessary to create representations of a past which is no longer spontaneously recalled: thus 'what we refer to as memory is not really memory but already history'. The *lieux de mémoire* are 'moments of history torn away from the movement of history, then returned; no longer quite life, not yet death, like shells on the shore when the sea of living memory has receded'. The historian's relationship to them is that of a lover afflicted no longer by the 'obsessive hold of passion' but 'the true sadness of no longer...suffering from what one had once suffered from for so long, nor to understand any longer with the reason of the heart but only of the head'.

In his final volume Nora is more pessimistic. He notes the 'disappearance of the unitary framework of the Nation-State...and the dissolution of the national myth which linked future tightly to past'. Reflecting on France's commemorative fever, Nora suggests three reasons for it. First, in the mid-1970s, after thirty years of economic growth, the French became conscious of the social transformation which had occurred: the peasantry, a defining constituent of French identity, had almost disappeared. Second, the discrediting of Marxism destroyed the idea of revolutionary change which had been so important in French political culture: as a recognisable present dissolved into an irretrievable past, so too disappeared any eschatological hope for the future. Finally, de Gaulle's retirement in 1969 was the end of the Gaullist epoch, an epic adventure which had tried to persuade the French that they counted more in the world than, in their hearts, they probably knew they did – 'the definite interiorisation of the idea that France had passed from being a great power to being a medium one'. We return to the problem of living in a post-Gaullist present. As Nora says: 'Few eras have experienced such a questioning of the coherence and continuity of its national past....We formerly knew whose sons we were,...today we are the sons of no one, and of everyone'.

For Nora the 'three key words' of the 'contemporary consciousness' are identity, memory and *patrimoine* (heritage). *Patrimoine* is a key concept because in his final reflections Nora diagnoses the transition from a national memory to a 'patrimonial memory'. 1980 was declared the first year of the *patrimoine*, but the notion, originally quite restrictive, has become almost infinitely extensible, 'a splintered system, composed of disparate commemorative languages.... There is no longer a commemorative super-ego, the canon has disappeared'. The impulse now comes from below, from 'the depths of civil society', whether in the celebration of some local worthy or the creation of a regional folklore museum. This degenerates, at its worst, into an ahistorical fetishisation of any vestige of the past.

One could view this as a fruitful democratisation of the notion of *patrimoine* or a meretricious attempt to counterfeit a past to compensate for the collapse of other vectors of identity, but Nora sees a more insidious danger: the past is no longer 'representative of a collective overall identity of the social body in its entirety, but it now constitutes sectional identities'. Once the state renounces its role of ensuring a balance between sectional memories and national ones, and allowing individuals to 'negotiate the modalities of their adherence and the extent of their investment in this collective framework', a breach is opened up into which have flooded the narrow xenophobia of the Front National and the disintegrating multiculturalism of the antiracist organisation SOS-racisme.

Immigration and multiculturalism

Immigration thus emerges as an essential component of the contemporary obsession with identity. Considered historically, the present situation is not as novel as it seems. Previous waves of immigration (Italians, Jews, Poles) also aroused antagonisms and yet they were ultimately absorbed. What makes people resist this historical message is that immigration is absent from France's historical self-image. As Gérard Noiriel, one of the pioneering historians of the subject, remarks, immigration was a 'non-lieu de mémoire'. Noiriel contributed an article on 'Français et immigrés' to Nora's final volume, but its relationship to the overall project is not evident. Noiriel also offers a trenchant critique of Braudel's *The Identity of France* whose chapter on France's population structure more or less stops in the seventeenth century, and treats immigration in a few hasty final pages. Noiriel attributes this to Braudel's holistic conception of French history – seeing France as a person à la Michelet – and to the tradition of the geographer Vidal de la Blache, an important influence on the *Annales* school, which sought the deep permanent features of France over the epiphenomenal. For Braudel, the French nation was essentially formed by the start of industrialisation. In this view the last century of immigration hardly counts.[18]

And yet, as Noiriel notes, without immigration France's population size in 1990 would hardly have been different from 1900. Indeed since America started to impose immigration restrictions in the 1920s, France's population has been more changed proportionally by immigration than America's although in America, unlike France, immigration remains an essential part of the culture's self-definition. A major reason why historians wrote immigration out of the national story was the prevailing concept of the French nation, what Michelet called France's 'universal receptivity...the intimate fusion of races which constitutes the identity of the nation'.

The classic formulation was that of Renan, developed after 1870, in response to German claims for Alsace-Lorraine. In place of the ethnic (objective) conception of the nation, Renan offered a voluntarist (subjective) one. The nation was a 'daily plebiscite'. France's nationality code of 1889 was a mixture of *ius sanguinis* and *ius soli*: children born in France of foreign parents became French at the age of 18 providing the child had resided in France for the previous five years. This was more 'liberal' than the German nationality law of 1913 based on race, but less so than the American one bestowing automatic citizenship on anyone born in the United States with no other stipulation. Thus French law assumed future citizens had become French culturally before becoming so juridically. In America the census asked questions about ethnic origin; in France this was unthinkable. There was no equivalent to the American notion of second generation Italian-Americans or Irish-Americans. In French Republican tradition, questions of origin, belief or custom were confined to the private. As Clermont-Tonnerre said when the Jews were emancipated in 1791: 'One must refuse everything to the Jews as a nation and grant everything to them as citizens'. France's secular school system was an apprenticeship in citizenship inculcating the universalist values of the Republic into generations of schoolchildren. 'Frenchmen' were not only made out of 'peasants' but also immigrants. France was the Republic One and Indivisible.

Although the Jacobin conception of the nation has been an obstacle to a history of French immigration – and possibly also gay or feminist history where the pioneering work in the history of private life in France was by Philippe Ariès, someone from an antirepublican background – in recent years immigration has become one of the growth areas of French social history.[19] What is new about the current debate on immigration in France is that it centres not only on immigrants defined juridically as such, but also on second generation North Africans who will become, or already are, French citizens. But they are viewed by much of the population as unassimilable. There are circumstantial reasons for this: the memory of the Algerian war; the supposed difficulties of assimilating non-European and non-Christian populations; the fear of Islam; and the declining influence of the communist party, trades unions and church as agents of integration. But most important of all is the fact, to quote Nora again, that 'Renan's nation is dead and will not return'.[20]

An explicit link between the dissolution of at least one part of the national myth and France's current malaise was made by the sociologist Paul Yonnet in his *Voyage au Centre du malaise français*.[21] Yonnet's thesis is that the antiracist movement in contemporary France, particularly SOS-racisme, had undermined

French national identity by celebrating cultural and ethnic diversity. He blames the post-1968 historians for subverting existing accounts of France's past, what he calls the 'Roman national', through their concentration on Vichy anti-Semitism – what Yonnet calls an 'excess of anti-anti-Semitism'.[22] These were not the elucubrations of a crank. The book was published by the celebrated publishing house of Gallimard and discussed seriously in *Le Débat*, one of France's leading intellectual journals, and edited by Pierre Nora.[23] And if one removes from Yonnet's tract the tendentious remarks about Vichy historiography, the issues he raises are important.[24] Does the Jacobin republican model still function as a matrix of identity and instrument of assimilation?

The 'Affair des foulards'

In de Gaulle's Fifth Republic, the republican consensus has never been more total. This is part of the problem. The function of republican iconography in the nineteenth century was to defend a contested institution by creating a republican culture around it. Once the institution was no longer contested, the enterprise lost its urgency and capacity to mobilise.[25] For this reason, perhaps, it became a subject of interest for historians – as in the first volume of Nora's *Lieux de mémoire* or Claude Nicolet's *L'Idée républicaine en France* (1982). But after the socialists turned their back on Marxism, and the abortive dawn of 1981 turned into the hedonistic individualism of the 1980s, republican imagery became a means of staking out a left-wing identity and reactivating a vocabulary of civic responsibility. The Minister of Education J.-P. Chevènement, previously the leader of the most important Marxist current of the Socialist Party, tried to reintroduce civic values into schools and make children learn the 'Marseillaise'. He celebrated a 'republican patriotism' founded in 'the affirmation of a specific national identity which for the past two centuries has been an integral part of the values of the Republic'.[26] Although ostensibly directed against the xenophobic nationalism of Le Pen, this rhetoric also targeted another strand within the socialist left in the 1980s – the so called 'droit à la différence' celebrated by SOS racisme.

This debate tended to become polarised around an oversimplified dichotomy between the American and French models of democracy: multiculturalism, on the one hand, the Indivisible Republic, on the other. [27] The issue crystallised in the Affair of the Muslim Headscarves at the end of 1989 when three schoolgirls were sent home for wearing the Muslim headscarf (hijab) and thereby defying the secular tradition of the republican school. Within a week the Affair was headline news. It was replete with ironies: the right, which five years earlier had defended the independence of private Catholic schools against the state, now rediscovered the virtues of secularism; SOS-racisme modified its multiculturalism. This was insufficient for the philosopher Alain Finkielkraut who condemned an unholy alliance of Jews, Catholics, Muslims and antiracists turning the republican school into a juxtaposition of tribes with Lebanon at the end of the road.[28] He signed a petition denouncing the Munich of the republican school.[29] As for the socialists, they were thrown into turmoil. When did secularism become intolerance? When did tolerance become Balkanisation?

The most apocalyptic contribution came from the ex-leftist Régis Debray who drew a distinction between what he called democracy and the republic: between America and France, a society of communities and a society of citizens, individualism and egalitarianism, consumerism and austerity, the particular and the universal, amnesia and memory, Berlusconi and Jules Ferry.[30] Debray's sophistical antitheses were easily dispatched by the historians Jacques Julliard and Jacques Le Goff, but they too were conscious of what Julliard termed a 'regression to tribalism'. For Le Goff, Chevènement's ambitions for civic education were desirable and this had to be provided by historians or 'French identity will suffer the grave consequences one can see in America or Germany'.[31]

The bicentenary of the Revolution

It was especially poignant that this Affair occurred in 1989: the issues at stake resonated with the debates on the bicentenary of the Revolution.[32] The historian who dominated the bicentenary was François Furet. His first assaults in the 1960s on the canonical view of revolution had attacked the so-called *dérapage* of the Revolution – its skidding out of control between 1789 and the Terror in 1793 – but his later position was that 1793 was contained in the 'internal logic' of 1789. This interpretation was bound up with Furet's repudiation of the his communist past: 'the Gulag', he wrote in 1978, 'requires us to rethink the Terror'.

Furet's critique lent respectability to more radical attacks on the revolutionary legacy which started with his link between the Revolution and twentieth-century totalitarianism. This became most explicit in the debate over the Vendée. What was striking about 1989 was the way the Vendée moved from being a local memory – a 'counter-memory' in Nora's series – to a central one. A decisive role in this process was played by conservative historian Pierre Chaunu who popularised the notion of the Vendée as a genocide: 'the greatest carnage perpetrated on French territory in 20 centuries' equal to the Gulag and the Khmer Rouge's. For some conservatives this link between twentieth-century genocide and the Vendée connected with unease about the rewriting of the Vichy period. Why if the 'holocaust' of French Catholics was buried by the collective memory should so much anguish be exercised on the fate of the French Jews? One Gaullist criticised historians for digging up Vichy anti-Semitism which 'a healthy instinct of national unity had pushed the French to bury in the recesses of their collective memory'.[33]

All this suggested that the debate over the Revolution was very much alive and offered the left the opportunity to counterattack. But the right was only able to pre-empt the debate because the left no longer knew what it was defending. A few years earlier there would have been no problem. After the left's victory in 1981, the premier Pierre Mauroy let it be known he had a portrait of Camille Desmoulins in his office. But after the socialists shifted to the right in 1983, this kind of confidence was replaced by uncertainty. Nor were the historians of the left any help. One line adopted by Jacques Julliard was that no choice need be made about what was being celebrated. People could select what they wished from the Revolution: 'as historian', he wrote, 'I have the duty to take it all; as citizen I have the right to choose'. Whereas in the past it was the left that defiantly claimed the Revolution as a block, now the right chose to do so, and pushed the left on to the defensive. Even the *marxisant* historian Michel Vovelle argued that, although it was impossible entirely to separate 1789 and 1793, the Revolution should be celebrated not as a block but as a whole, full of dynamic contradictions. The emerging left-wing view was to celebrate the theme of rights not the Republic or the nation. It was even proposed to change the sanguinary words of the 'Marseillaise' to 'words of love'.

Some left-wingers rejected this pusillanimity. The dissenters included Debray and Chevènement; and also the PCF which stressed the values of the Republic against the rising tide of Europeanism. The historian who steered a middle course between Vovelle and Furet, rights and Republic, 1789 and 1793, was Maurice Agulhon. Although not a historian of the Revolution, Agulhon's work on nineteenth-century Provence, and on republican iconography, has had the Republic as its central thread. Agulhon was an unrepentant defender of the Jacobin tradition whose tendencies towards centralising uniformity he believed had been exaggerated.[34] In his inaugural lecture to the Collège de France he noted the 'national consciousness of our country is going through a crisis' haunted by the decline of her power and the phenomenon of immigration. The dilemma was how to reconcile 'objective history' and 'the teaching of a civic-national history'. France had always been pluri-ethnic and the liberal universalism of 1789 'has been our melting pot'.[35] Deploring the decline of republican culture in favour of multiculturalism, Americanisation and economic individualism, Agulhon hoped the bicentenary could be an exercise in civic education. Despite his preference for celebrating 1793 (democracy) over 1789 (individualism), in the current climate he advocated a consensual approach concentrating on rights: 1989 should be directed against the Mullahs of Teheran.[36]

How in the end was the bicentenary celebrated? For a long time the preparations were dogged by bad luck: the first two organisers appointed by Mitterrand died prematurely, and their successor, the historian Jean-Noel Jeanneney had little time to organise his own projects. The celebrations started slowly and to general public indifference. The key moment was to be 14 July, whose organisation was confided to Jean-Paul Goude, a star of the French advertising world, known more for his videos than his interest in history. The *pièce de résistance* was a parade down the Champs Elysées with floats representing different cultures. As television the event was a spectacular success, and the press unanimously hailed a triumph (despite dissenters from the right reminding Goude that 'France is not black' and from the left deploring hollow advertising images).

But what did it all mean? Solidarity with the oppressed of the world? A hymn to multiculturalism? The truth is that the parade succeeded by sidestepping questions about the meaning of the Revolution, and despite the Goude extravaganza there was a sense that the bicentenary had been an anticlimax. To the extent that it is acquiring the texture of a major historical moment, it is as historians reflect upon it and plot its relationship to France's contemporary concerns. Already a team of researchers is working on a massive history of the bicentenary, already the archives of the bicentenary organisation are open, already historians have written at length on it – 300 pages from Pascal Ory,[37] 900 from Stephen Kaplan – and thus in the remembering, in memory, the bicentenary acquires the accretions of significance which it never had at the time – as if France's future is fated to become an endless series of memories of memories, in which Nora's *Lieux de Mémoire* become themselves a *lieu de mémoire*, Rousso's *Vichy Syndrome* becomes itself a Vichy syndrome, creating a postmodern maze of self-reflection, an infinite gallery of mirrors, in which as the new millennium approaches the French search to discover who and what they are.

Notes

1 François Furet, Jacques Julliard and Pierre Rosanvallon, *La République du centre: la fin de l'exception française*, Paris, Fondation Saint-Simon, 1988.

2 Annette Wieviorka, *Déportation et génocide: Entre la mémoire et l'oubli*, Paris, Plon, 1992.

3 Renée Poznanski, *Etre juif en France pendant la seconde guerre mondiale*, Paris, Hachette, 1994; Asher Cohen, *Persécutions et sauvetages: Juifs en France sous l'Occupation et sous Vichy*, Paris, Editions du Cerf, 1993.

4 Henry Rousso and Eric Conan, *Vichy, Un passé qui ne passe pas*, Paris, Fayard, 1994, pp. 109–72.

5 Pierre Péan, *Une Jeunesse française: François Mitterrand 1934–1949*, Paris, Fayard, 1994.

6 Stanley Hoffmann, *French Politics and Society*, 1995, Winter, vol. 13, no. 1, pp. 4–16.

7 Ernest Renan, *Qu'est qu'une nation?*, Paris, Presse Pocket edition, 1992, p. 41

8 Paul Yonnet, *Voyage au Centre du malaise francais: l'anti-racisme et le roman national*, Paris, Gallimard, 1993, p. 254.

9 Conan and Rousso, *Un passé qui ne passe pas*, p. 9.

10 Alain Touraine, *Le Monde*, 13 May 1990.

11 Fernand Braudel, *The Identity of France*, vol. II: *People and Production*, London, Harper & Row, 1990, quoted by Perry Anderson in *London Review of Books*, 9 May 1991, p. 7.

12 For example Jean Favier (ed.) *Histoire de France*, 6 vols, Paris, Fayard, 1984–88.

13 H. Coutau-Begarie, *Le Phénomène nouvelle histoire*, Paris, Economica, 1989, pp. x–xii.

14 O. Mongin, *Face au scepticisme: les mutations du paysage intellectuel ou l'invnetion de l'intellectuel democratique*, Paris, Editions la Decouverte, 1994, p. 43.

15 The quotations in the rest of this section come from Nora's contributions to the *Lieux de mémoire* volumes unless otherwise specified.

16 S. Englund, 'The Ghost of the Nation Past', *Journal of Modern History*, 1992, vol. 64, pp. 299–320.
17 See also Nancy Wood, 'Memory's Remains: *Les Lieux de mémoire*', *History and Memory*, 1994, vol. 6, pp. 123–47; Olivier Mongin, 'Une Mémoire sans histoire?', *Esprit*, 1993, March, no. 180, pp. 102–13.
18 Gérard Noiriel, *Le Creuset français*, Paris, Seuil, 1988, pp. 50–67.
19 For example: Noiriel, *Le Creuset français*; Patrick Weil, *La France et ses étrangers*, Paris, Calmann-Lévy, 1991.
20 Pierre Nora, *Les Lieux de mémoire*, tome 3, *Les Frances*, vol. 3 *De l'archive à l'emblème*, Paris, Gallimard, 1992, p. 1,009.
21 Paul Yonnet, *Voyage au Centre du malaise français: l'anti-racisme et le roman national*, Paris, Gallimard, 1993.
22 Yonnet, *Voyage au Centre du malaise français*, p. 291.
23 *Le Débat*, May/August 1993, vol. 75, 116–44.
24 Tony Judt, *Times Literary Supplement*, 9 July 1993.
25 Joel Roman, 'La Fin du modèle républicain', *Esprit*, 1990, September, vol. 164, pp. 67–79.
26 Jeremy Jennings, 'Liberalism, Nationalism and the excluded', *History of European Ideas*, 1992, vol. 15, pp. 499–500.
27 Olivier Mongin, 'Retour sur une controverse: du 'politiquement correct' au multi-culturalisme', *Esprit*, 1995, June, no. 212, pp. 83–160
28 *Le Monde*, 17, 21 and 25 October 1989.
29 *Nouvel Observateur*, 2 November 1989.
30 *Le Nouvel Observateur*, 30 November 1989. See also Régis Debray, *Que vive la République*, Paris, Éditions Odile Jacob, 1989.
31 Jacques Le Goff, 'Derrière le foulard l'histoire', in *Le Débat*, 1990, January–February, vol. 58; Julliard in *Le Nouvel Observateur*, 26 October 1989 and 7 December 1989.
32 There is a thorough study of the Bicentenary debate in S. Kaplan, *Adieu '89*, Paris, Fayard, 1993, vol. 89.
33 Kaplan, *Adieu '89*, p. 851.
34 Maurice Agulhon, 'Plaidoyer pour les Jacobins', *Le Débat*, 1981, June, vol. 58, pp. 21–33; Maurice Agulhon, 'Plaidoyer pour la Republique une et indivisible', *L'Histoire*, May 1992, vol. 155, pp. 16–23
35 Maurice Agulhon, 'Politique et mentalités en France contemporaine', *Annales ESC*, 1987, May–June, vol. 42, no. 3, pp. 595–610.
36 Maurice Agulhon, 'Faut-il avoir peur de 1989?', *Le Débat*, 1984, May, vol. 13, pp. 27–37.
37 Pascal Ory, *Une Nation pour mémoire. 1989–1939–1989: Trois jubilés en France*, Paris, Presses FNSP, 1992.

Further reading

On memories of Vichy and Occupation: H. Rousso, *The Vichy Syndrome: History and Memory in France since 1944*, London, Harvard University Press, 1991; H. Rousso and E. Conan, *Vichy, Un passé qui ne passe pas*, Paris, Fayard, 1994; forum on 'The Vichy Syndrome', in *French Historical Studies*, vol. 19, 1995; S. Farmer, *Oradour: arrêt sur mémoire*, Calmann Levy, Paris, 1994; A. Finkielkraut, *Remembering in Vain: the Klaus Barbie Trial; and Crimes Against Humanity*, New York, Columbia University Press, 1992; R. Golsan (ed.) *Memory, The Holocaust and French Justice: The Bousquet and Touvier Affairs*, Hanover, NH, University Press of New England, 1996.

On contemporary historiography: G. Noiriel, *Sur la 'crise' de l'histoire*, Paris, Belin, 1996; R. Rémond (ed.) *Être historien aujourd'hui*, Paris, Erès, 1988; O. Mongin, *Face au scepticisme: les mutations du paysage intellectuel ou l'invention de l'intellectuel démocratique*, Paris, Découverte, 1994. Pierre Nora's *Les Lieux de mémoire* series comprises seven volumes: P. Nora (ed.) *Les Lieux de mémoire*, vol. I: *La République*, vol. II: *La Nation*, vol. III *Les Frances*, Paris, Gallimard, 1984–92. For a critique see S. Englund, 'The Ghost of the Nation Past', *Journal of Modern History*, 1992, vol. 64, pp. 299–320; and 'History in a Late Age', *French Politics and Society*, 1996, vol. 14, pp. 68–77; N. Wood, 'Memory's Remains: *Les Lieux de mémoire*', *History and Memory*, 1994, vol. 6, pp. 123–47.

On the history of immigration; G. Noiriel, *Le Creuset français*, Paris, Seuil, 1998; P. Weil, *La France et ses étrangers*, Paris, Calmann-Lévy, 1991. On the integration of immigrants in contemporary France: D. Schnapper, *La France de l'intégration: sociologie de la nation en 1990*, Paris, Gallimard, 1990. On the *Foulard* affair: F. Gaspard and F. Khosrokhavar, *Le Foulard et la République*, Paris, La Découverte, 1995.

On the Revolution bicentenary: S. Kaplan, *Adieu '89*, Paris, Fayard, 1993; Pascal Ory, *Une Nation pour mémoire: 1989–1939–1989. Trois jubilés en France*, Paris, FNSP, 1992.

20 Historians and the search for national identity in the reunified Germany

Stefan Berger

In 1989 the Berlin Wall fell amidst scenes of celebration and statements such as 'we are today the happiest people in the whole world'. A Freiburg historian, Ernst Schulin, asked prophetically whether the enlarged Germany would witness a 'renaissance of attempts to endow Germans with national identity'.[2] I would like to suggest that the discourse of national identity has been taken up by three groups in the reunified Germany: first, a self-styled 'new right' – sometimes referred to as the 1989 generation – which has attempted an ambitious redefinition of German national identity along nationalist lines; second, more mainstream liberal-conservatives who have also argued that 1990 should be regarded as a significant watershed in that it urges Germans to return to an alleged 'normality' of the nation-state; and third, left-liberal historians who had given up on the national principle before 1989 but have rediscovered it since. After discussing the very different notions of national identity within these three broad camps, I will conclude by asking whether the attempted renationalisation of German historical consciousness will have a lasting impact on future historiographic agendas.

The new right and its old agenda of historiographic nationalism

In 1994, two journalists of the conservative daily newspaper *Die Welt*, Heimo Schwilk and Ulrich Schacht, edited a volume entitled *The Self-Confident Nation* which was widely reviewed as the latest programmatic challenge of the new right to the existing German national identity.[3] Historians were prominently represented in this volume: Brigitte Seebacher-Brandt described sentiments of love for one's fatherland as the return to European normality. Michael Wolffsohn called for a return to an unaggressive 'inward nationalism' which would allegedly allow Germans to face the huge domestic and foreign policy tasks of the future. Klaus-Rainer Röhl identified the roots of German self-hatred in the antifascist tradition of the left and Anglo-American re-education programmes after the Second World War which, in his view, brainwashed the German people into various forms of 'national masochism'.

Ernst Nolte's critique of Western liberalism, which he sees developing into 'liberism' (*Liberismus*), was bound up with apocalyptic scenarios. The liberal principles will 'kill the nations and after the end of a gigantic population move it may well kill humankind'.[4] Karlheinz Weißmann portrayed the concept of a 'civil society' as the last utopian straw of the left. The nation, he insisted, is the only form of community which can constitute a strong enough identity to overcome the domestic and foreign policy difficulties which lie ahead of Germany. Demands for a strong state were combined with the alleged need to recognise the necessity of warfare in international relations. Last, but not least, Rainer Zitelmann pleaded for a new democratic right in Germany, which would, in his view, fill the vacuum created by the other parties. To date, the book on the 'self-confident nation' is probably the most complete statement of the new right's world view. What is most striking is the messianic undertone: 1989–90 is perceived as a major opportunity to end the alleged intellectual hegemony of the 1968 generation in Germany. The attempted renationalisation of German identity is closely linked to a redefinition of the self-understanding of the old Federal Republic.

Vergangenheitsbewältigung or coming to terms with the national socialist past is once again, as in the 'historians' dispute' of the mid-1980s, seen as the major stumbling block for a return to 'healthy' national identity. Hence, new right historians, like Zitelmann and Weißmann, have reinterpreted the history of national socialism. Essentially misusing a call by Martin Broszat in 1985 to 'historise'[5] the Nazi past, they are interpreting nazism as a consciously modernising dictatorship aimed at the creation of a welfare state and greater equality of opportunities.[6] Almost thirty years ago Ralf Dahrendorf and David Schoenbaum had already argued that nazism had unconsciously destroyed the social fabric of the old pillarised Germany, where sections of the population had been locked into 'social mileus' according to class and religion. Thereby, they had unwittingly paved the way for a successful German republic after 1945.[7] Zitelmann, Weißmann and others now emphasise that the modernising elements of the regime were a conscious strategy which should stand in the centre of understanding the Nazi dictatorship. In this interpretation the Holocaust and all the criminal energies of the regime get sidelined and, although not denied, are barely mentioned. Weißmann's 500-page textbook on National Socialism devotes a mere ten pages to the Holocaust and allows not a single victim to be heard.[8] The very fact that Weißmann could publish this volume in the prestigious *Propyläen Weltgeschichte* series was due to a secretive little plot involving the author and the then-commissioning editor of Ullstein, Zitelmann. Hans Mommsen, who was initially under contract to write the volume (he had already contributed the volume on the Weimar Republic in the series), saw his contract withdrawn. Zitelmann apparently did this without informing either the general editors or any of the other authors of the series.

If the history of Nazi Germany is rewritten so as to allow a more positive reception of national traditions, the new right can hark back into history to re-establish an identity which suddenly appears much less problematic. According to Ernst Nolte, Bismarck's unification of Germany appears in line with 'the highest degree of historical necessity'.[9] The new Germany would be well-advised, in Weißmann's view, to recognise that 'surprisingly it has much in common with the Bismarckian Reich'.[10] For Weißmann, the historiography on Imperial Germany has lost its direction by following the heresy of the *Sonderweg* paradigm with its false allegations that the demise of the Weimar Republic was linked to certain peculiarities in nineteenth-century German history.

If the relativisation of Nazi crimes allows a more carefree view of Germany's nineteenth-century history, and in particular a more positive reassessment of Imperial Germany, the comparison of the 'two German dictatorships' further helps to move the memory of National Socialist barbarity from its central place in German national identity. The renaissance of the totalitarian paradigm in scholarship on the GDR and Nazi Germany lends itself to equate the communist and the Nazi dictatorships. Several authors have recommended a return to the anti-totalitarian consensus of the 1950s, for, as they argue, it allows for a clearer perception of the inner relationship between nazism and communism. The surprising revival of the totalitarian paradigm (revealed many times over as a key term in the Cold War western arsenal of ideological weapons with which to beat the West European left) in post-reunification Germany has indeed led to wild comparisons of Honecker with Hitler, of Stasi and Gestapo, of Bautzen and Auschwitz, and of the Soviet internment camps of the post-Second World War era and the Nazi concentration and annihilation camps. Weißmann, for one, has left little doubt about the political usefulness of the totalitarian paradigm. The equation of the communist with the National Socialist dictatorship will, in his view, reveal the victory of left-liberal historians in the *Historikerstreit* of the mid-1980s as a pyrrhic victory.[11] A second *Vergangenheitsbewältigung*, new right historians have argued, will deflect from the Nazi past, whilst conveniently laying the blame at the door of a foreign power. The 'second German dictatorship', the GDR, has already been portrayed as a mere 'Soviet protectorate'[12] which was alien to the traditions of German national history. The condemnation of the GDR – which in some accounts almost appears as demonisation – thus goes hand in hand with a redemption of German national history.

If the collapse of the GDR in 1989 can be interpreted as the convincing victory of liberal market capitalism over illiberal state communism, then the new right has stopped short of endorsing the traditions of the old Federal Republic. Instead it finds fault with its identity, especially with its lack of national self-confidence due to an alleged excessive *Vergangenheitsbewältigung* in the wake of the 1968 student protest movement. Since 1990, book-length studies have sought to undermine the argument that Germans shoved their past under the carpet after 1945.[13] The rejection of the national principle, the new right has argued, has led to the formulation of 'artificial' surrogate identities, such as 'postnationalism', the 'state-nation' or 'constitutional patriotism'. In particular the westernisation of the FRG has been singled out for criticism by the new right. According to them, westernisation amounts to an 'alien identity' which was instilled into the German people after 1945. Ever since, they have argued, it had become a 'quasi-religion' which could neither be questioned nor discussed in the old FRG.[14] Only the events of 1989–90, in this view, have reminded the Germans of their *Mittellage* which allegedly predestines Germans to act as a bridge between East and West. Notwithstanding the fact that the ideologies of *Mittellage* and geopolitics more generally have been discredited by its social Darwinist, imperialist and racist connotations as well as by its direct functionalisation under National Socialism to justify Hitler's search for *Lebensraum* in the East, new right historians have revived geopolitics to explain the 'tragic' history of the German nation-state in the nineteenth and twentieth centuries, to criticise its 'enforced' westernisation after 1945 and to provide strategic plans for the future of the reunified Germany which is routinely portrayed as the new 'superpower' in Europe. Reunification, as Weißmann amongst others has argued, has shifted Germany's geographic position in Europe eastwards. It moved closer to its Prussian past and away from its 'artificial' westernisation after 1949. Hence one of the central tasks of the new Germany will be the economic rebuilding (a term often used as a thinly veiled euphemism for colonisation) of Eastern Europe which takes precedence over any deepening of the western European Union. Anti-Maastricht and anti-European sentiments have been encouraged by the new right, whilst they have also called for a more independent foreign policy by the new German 'superpower'.

The triumphalism of the liberal–conservative mainstream

It is over the issue of redefining the identity of the old Federal Republic that the new right has failed by and large to rally the more traditional liberal-conservative historians around them. Whilst liberal–conservatives have also argued very widely that the nation should be perceived as the 'normal' form of organisation for societies, this normality, in the words of Patrick Bahners, 'has become a western one after 1945'.[15] Liberal–conservative historians have remained committed to the idea of ever closer European union and they are adamant that any greater foreign policy role by the new Germany should be carefully in line with its western partners. Michael Stürmer explicitly warned against questioning the westernisation and western integration of the old Federal Republic.[16] For Karl Dietrich Erdmann, the European dimension was one of the most importance differences between 1871 and 1990. For sure, he agreed with the new right that German historical consciousness needed a good dose of renationalisation, but this, he insisted, had to be in line with the commitment to ever closer union in Europe.[17] Germany remains, as Wolf Gruner has argued, 'the motor of European unity'.[18]

Furthermore the attempts of the new right to relativise the horrors of the Nazi regime are not endorsed. Ernst Nolte has, if anything, become even more of an outsider amongst professional historians. And yet, at times, the line between the new right and the liberal-conservative mainstream has become blurred. So, for example, there is widespread agreement between the two camps about the rejection of an allegedly one-sided, political-educational approach to history (denounced as *Volkspädagogik*). The latter is accused of having produced various forms of 'anti-Germanism' and 'anti-anticommunism' over the past three decades. Since the fall of communism, conservative historians have chimed in with new right demands to end the 'fixation' with the German *Sonderweg* and the Nazi past. Instead representatives of the liberal-conservative mainstream have condemned the GDR in no uncertain terms. Thus, the director of the powerful *Institut für Zeitgeschichte* in Munich, Horst Möller, has argued that the SED dictatorship should in many ways be seen as 'more efficient' than the Nazi dictatorship. In his view, the mechanisms of power and repression were far more developed in the GDR and the SED drove far more people into exile than the Nazis. Overwhelming parallels between the two regimes, he maintained, will make comparisons within the paradigm of totalitarianism both necessary and fruitful.[19] Already the comparison of dictatorships (*Diktaturenvergleich*) has become the catchword of the day, and the financially powerful *Volkswagenstiftung* was quick to announce plans to finance a major new project on the comparison of Nazi Germany with the GDR.[20] In the light of such comparisons, Hans-Peter Schwarz has speculated with obvious glee that, in the medium term, the focus of attention will at long last shift from the Nazi period to the GDR, thus relieving Germans of their 'neurotic guilt complex'.[21]

Equally, liberal-conservatives have rediscovered the merits of geopolitics. For Schöllgen, the 'tragedies' of German history are all – in one way or another – related to its geographic position in the middle of Europe. For the new Germany, which Schöllgen also perceives as a superpower, it will be paramount to consider this *Mittellage* when formulating a new self-confident and self-interested foreign policy.[22] And Hans-Peter Schwarz already dreams about a renewed German hegemony over the countries of *Mitteleuropa*. Germany, he argued, will help their economic development and their integration into the EU and NATO, but, of course, 'everything has its price' – and the price for the smaller nations of Central Europe is to support the new superpower Germany on the stage of international politics.[23] Liberal-conservatives have been engaged in various ways in the continuing search for positive national identity which will underpin the new-found nation state in the twenty-first century. With reference to the glowing example of the nineteenth-century Prussian historians, Hans-Peter Schwarz has already called on fellow historians to stop playing the 'reunification melody with muted trumpets'.[24] Germany, Christian Meier has argued, is suffering from *dementia transitoria* which will only be overcome by the renationalisation of German identity which will provide 'the basis for German self-confidence'.[25]

Left-liberal historians and the discourse of national identity

Left-liberal historians tend to distance themselves from all such attempts to renationalise German historical consciousness. A critical reception of the traditions of the first German nation-state between 1871 and 1945 will, they insist, continue to be as important as the centrality of the Nazi period for any future German identity, if the second German nation-state is going to be a happier affair than the first one. Whilst the recreation of more traditional nationalist myths by historians is widely rejected, some left-liberal historians, like Jürgen Kocka and Heinrich August Winkler, have argued that the revolution of 1989 marks an ideal opportunity to redefine the concept of the nation in line with a democratic and liberal state. Taken by surprise by the strength of national feeling in the former GDR and in the whole of Eastern Europe in 1989–90, Kocka conceded that the nation-state was more firmly rooted in Germany than he had previously thought.[26] It would, according to him, remain 'the normal form of political organisation of European societies'.[27]

In contrast to their position in the mid-1980s, some left-liberal historians have concluded after 1990 that it may be worthwhile fighting over the content of national identity now that the nation has been unexpectedly recreated. Yet it is important to recognise that their concept of the nation is ultimately incompatible with the concept of the new right. Building on the traditions of the old Federal Republic, they want to tie any national identity closely to the liberal-democratic and 'Western' understanding of the nation. This would involve in particular changing the country's 1913 citizenship law which clings to an ethnic definition of citizenship. Several centre-left historians such as Kocka or Bernd-Jürgen Wendt have explicitly denied the first German nation-state, created by Bismarck in 1870–1, any model status for the reunified Germany.[28] Hans-Ulrich Wehler's keenly awaited third volume of his magisterial *Deutsche Gesellschaftsgeschichte* modifies a whole range of his erstwhile conceptual and theoretical positions, yet the one organising theme of the volume is still Imperial Germany's 'special conditions' (*Sonderbedingungen*) which set it apart from other West-European nations and created the conditions in which radical fascism could succeed in the early 1930s.[29] In the light of such critical perspectives on the first German nation state it became quite fashionable amongst the centre-left in Germany to denounce the very term 'reunification' and instead they opted for the term 'unification' to make it absolutely clear that there was no bridge connecting the new post-1990 Germany to the Kaiserreich of the nineteenth century.

Furthermore Hans Mommsen – amongst a whole range of other left-liberal historians – has forcefully rejected the thesis that the National Socialist regime attempted a conscious modernisation of Germany pointing instead to the politically right-wing implications of thus 'historising' the National Socialist period.[30] As far as the debate about the GDR legacy is concerned, left-liberal historians have at times contributed to what amounts to a total destruction of the profession in East Germany, and they have occasionally chimed in with the ongoing demonisation of GDR history. Yet, as far as the revival of the totalitarian paradigm is concerned, they have also, by and large, rejected its usefulness for any deeper understanding of the GDR, and in particular they have denounced its political functionalisation in debates about contemporary national identity.[31] In line with the western orientation of the old Federal Republic, left-liberal historians have been adamant in their defence of moves towards further integration and democratisation of the EU. They have rejected in particular the talk about the new Germany as the new European 'superpower'. Any return to the classical nineteenth-century concept of nation-states would, according to them, spell danger for the European continent at large. Yet at the same time the attempt by some left-liberal historians to jump onto the bandwagon of the 'national identity' discourse has led to a downgrading of concepts they used to champion. Ideas of postnationalism, constitutional patriotism and the state nation are all viewed with increased scepticism after 1990. And some, like Heinrich August Winkler, who in the *Historikerstreit* of the mid-1980s still argued against a renationalisation of German identity, have now called on their fellow Germans to end their 'postnational *Sonderweg*' and return to the 'normality' of a 'post–classical nation state'.[32]

Conclusion

What are the prospects for a successful renationalisation of German historical consciousness?

Where does this scenario leave German historiography? The most recent events in 1995 and 1996 point to an increasing marginalisation of the new right. Weißmann's book on nazism did not find any significant support amongst professional German historians. The Ullstein and Springer publishing houses have distanced themselves from extreme right-wingers like Zitelmann and the publisher Herbert Fleißner.[33] Furthermore, the new head of Ullstein, Wolfram Göbel, publicly announced in July 1996 that he would seek to give a more liberal image to the publishing house. In fact, the notorious textbook on National Socialism written by Weißmann has been withdrawn after massive protests from within the historical profession, and Hans Mommsen is now once again under contract to write a new volume for the series. The exhibition on the complicity of the German Wehrmacht in the horrendous crimes against humanity committed during the Second World War (organised by the Hamburg-based Institut für Sozialforschung) attracted much criticism from centre-right politicians such as Peter Gauweiler (CSU) and MP Erika Steinbach (CDU) at almost every stop of its tour through all major German cities. The criticism focused on the alleged one-sidedness of the exhibition. There were also totally unfounded allegations that some of the photographs shown were forgeries. Those like the CDU-member of parliament, Alfred

Dregger, who served as an officer in the Second World War, see this exhibition as a direct attack on the honour of the German soldier. However, despite such criticism, it has been a major success, attracting 130,000 visitors across Germany by February 1997 and initiating a debate in which there seems to be a relatively broad consensus about the criminal energies unleashed by the Nazi regime within the army and German society at large.

An even broader public debate erupted in 1996 over Daniel Jonah Goldhagen's book *Hitler's Willing Executioners*. Whilst few historians in Germany had anything positive to say about the scholarly merits of this book, the fact that the German translation quickly reached the top of the *Spiegel* bestseller list, and that the audiences in the televised public debates organised with Goldhagen seemed to side with the American against his German colleagues, can be interpreted as signs that many in the new Germany were unwilling to follow the pied pipers of Hamlin from the new right. In fact, as Wolfgang Wippermann in particular has pointed out, any attempted 'normalisation' of German history through the back door of historisation or modernisation has been profoundly disturbed by the Goldhagen debate.[34] Finally, the new right remains completely marginal in university history departments across Germany. Wehler and Michael Schneider have both written powerful indictments of the new right and their various strategies for redefining the identity of the reunified Germany.[35] At the 1996 *Historikertag* in Munich, the new chairperson of the German Historians' Association, Johannes Fried, emphasised that the historical profession had a duty to engage critically with political debates in contemporary society rather than to retreat into the academic ivory tower.

Even the arch-conservative journalists of *Die Welt* rebelled against the head of the new right in Germany and prevented Zitelmann from taking over editorial responsibility for the paper's section entitled *Geistige Welt*. In the end, he had to be content with the much smaller *Ressort Zeitgeschichte*. When, on the occasion of the 50th anniversary of the end of the Second World War, the new right attempted to put forward its own version of events, by and large depicting 8 May 1945 not as liberation from German fascism but as defeat for the German nation with long-term catastrophic consequences – in particular the loss of the German East, – this found very little resonance amongst the wider German public. They published a call 'Against Forgetting' (*Aufruf gegen das Vergessen*) in the conservative German daily *Frankfurter Allgemeine Zeitung* which excluded the memory of the Nazi victims and instead generously incorporated the memory of Germans as victims of the Second World War.[36] However, even one of the signatories, the right-wing CDU politician Alfred Dregger, under pressure from the mainstream of his own party, finally decided to stay away from a rally planned by the new right, and the whole affair ended with a whimper rather than with the intended big bang. By 1995 Zitelmann could portray himself and the new right as victims of West German political correctness. For a short period after 1989, he argued, there had been a window of opportunity for the emergence of a new right. However, the left-liberal mainstream closed ranks and by 1995 it had re-established its old hege-mony.[37]

If the new right more and more resembles a kind of lunatic fringe without much impact on the historical profession, the question still remains whether liberal–conservatives will actually attempt a serious redefinition of German historical consciousness. Historians like Klaus Hildebrand, Hans-Peter Schwarz or Horst Möller have both the intellectual clout and the academic position that is missing on the new right so far. They share some of the views of the new right; they have at times defended members of the new right, like Zitelmann, in public. Yet, on the whole, they seem to have been embarrassed by the new-right initiatives which perhaps were going too far too soon. In the next few years, it will become clearer, what their own position *vis-à-vis* the renationalisation of historical consciousness in Germany will be. It is interesting in this respect that one of the most recent attempts by a represen-tative of the liberal mainstream of German historiography, Hagen Schulze, to present an overview of the whole of German history has been described as 'having good prospects of becoming the favourite history booklet of the Kohl generation…the *Zeitgeist* which demands soothing identity is served with some tasty nibbles'.[38] By playing down the more unpalatable aspects of German history, Schulze finds himself arguing for an allegedly healthy return by Germans to 'normal' national identity. Will such 'normality' become the new guiding star of professional historical research in the reunified Germany?

The multitude of controversies on national symbols, memorials and museums in the reunified Germany is also highly indicative of the importance of debates on historical consciousness and national identity. There was, for example, the debate on the German capital, in which historical reasons were given by both opponents and advocates of Berlin becoming the new old capital of Germany. Especially the latter argued for the establishment of a new national centre which would further the re-establishment of national tradi-tions and consciousness. There was, in 1991, the widely publicised reburial of the coffins of the Prussian kings Frederick Wilhelm and Frederick the Great in a midnight ceremony, attended, amongst others, by Chancellor Helmut Kohl. The same year also saw the restoration of the Quadriga on top of the Brandenburg Gate. Furthermore, there were vigorous debates on whether to change the national anthem or not, and on the question of which days were particularly relevant to national remembrance. The project of rebuilding the Berlin Palace was supported in 1993 by many important public figures from different political camps. Part and parcel of the renationalisation of German architecture, liberal–conservative historians like Michael Wolffsohn and Christoph Stölzl have argued in favour of the restoration of the Imperial Palace as a national symbol. Clearly, the ongoing debates about the renaming of streets in East Berlin – cleansing communists from East German streets whilst retaining many streets in West Berlin named after former Nazis – also takes place within the context of debates about the reconstitution of an allegedly lost national identity. The positioning of an enlarged *Pietà* by Käthe

Kollwitz in the centre of the *Neue Wache* in Berlin, which serves as the national memorial of Germany since 1993, has been denounced by Reinhard Koselleck and others as a further example of the hypocritical identity-building that is going on in Germany today. As they have pointed out, Kollwitz's *Pietà* blurs the necessary distinction between the victims and the perpetrators of the Nazi dictatorship. The image of the suffering mother bemoaning her dead son (fallen as a soldier) and the inscription which simply reads 'To the victims of war and tyranny' ignores German responsibility for two world wars in the twentieth century, for the Holocaust and unprecedented crimes against humanity. In addition, by choosing a visual image which stands in a Christian tradition, this national memorial totally excludes the memory of German Jews.

Furthermore, the depiction of German history in two new museums – in Bonn (*Haus der Geschichte* which deals with post-1945 history) and Berlin (*Deutsches Historisches Museum*) – tends to fix national images and thus homogenise national historical consciousness by presenting millions of visitors with highly selective visions and symbols of the national past. Whilst millions are spent on national museums, there is an apparent shortage of public funds for institutions which preserve memories less easily adaptable to any renationalisation of German identity, such as the planned permanent National Socialist Documentation Centre and the Museum for the History of Jewish Life in Berlin. Finally, the ongoing debate about a central Holocaust memorial in Berlin and, more specifically, the way it would attempt to visualise genocide, also underlines the ongoing struggle over what should be included in, or excluded from, the collective memory of the nation and how such memory shall or shall not be fixed in the national consciousness.

Notes

1 The quotation is from a speech made by the then Mayor of West Berlin, Walter Momper, on 10 November, 1989. Cited in Petra Schulz and Bianca M. von der Weiden, *Die deutsche Sozialdemokratie 1989/90, SDP und SPD im Einigungsprozeß*, Munich, Forschungsgruppe Deutschland, 1997, p. 216.

2 Ernst Schulin, 'Schlußbetrachtung', in *idem* (ed.) *Deutsche Geschichtswissenschaft nach dem zweiten Weltkrieg (1945–1965)*, Munich, Oldenbourg, 1989, p. 275.

3 Heimo Schwilk and Ulrich Schacht (eds) *Die selbstbewußte Nation: 'Anschwellender Bocksgesang' und weitere Beiträge zu einer deutschen Debatte*, Frankfurt am Main, Ullstein, 1994.

4 Ibid., p. 160f.

5 I suggest replacing the term 'historicise' by 'historise' to avoid confusion between two very different concepts. On the one hand, 'historicism' describes a notion, criticised and rejected by Karl Popper, that history develops towards a particular end according to predetermined laws. On the other hand it refers to a concept, prominent amongst nineteenth-century German historians, which understands all political order within its own historical context. Hence I propose to use the term 'historicism' only for Popper's concept and to introduce the term 'historism' for the German *Historismus* (in contrast to the German *Historizismus*).

6 Central texts are Rainer Zitelmann, Eckart Jesse and Enrico Syring (eds) *Die Schatten der Vergangenheit. Impulse zur Historisierung des Nationalsozialismus*, Frankfurt am Main, Ullstein, 1990; Rainer Zitelmann and Michael Prinz (eds) *Nationalsozialismus und Modernisierung*, 2nd edn, Darmstadt, Wissenschaftliche Buchgesellschaft, 1994.

7 Ralf Dahrendorf, *Gesellschaft und Demokratie in Deutschland*, Munich, Piper, 1965; David Schoenbaum, *Hitler's Social Revolution*, New York, Weidenfeld and Nicolson, 1966.

8 Karlheinz Weißmann, *Der Weg in den Abgrund. Deutschland unter Hitler, 1933–45*, Berlin, Propyläen, 1995.

9 Ernst Nolte, *Lehrstück oder Tragödie? Beiträge zur Interpretation der Geschichte des 20. Jahrhunderts*, Cologne, Böhlau, 1991, p. 103.

10 Karlheinz Weißmann, *Rückruf in die Geschichte. Die deutsche Herausforderung. Alte Gefahren – Neue Chancen*, Frankfurt am Main, Ullstein, 1993, p. 77.

11 Ibid., p. 48.

12 Ernst Nolte, 'Die fortwirkende Verblendung', *Frankfurter Allgemeine Zeitung* (hereafter *FAZ*), 22 February 1992.

13 Manfred Kittel, *Die Legende von der 'Zweiten Schuld'. Vergangenheitsbewältigung in der Ära Adenauer*, Frankfurt am Main, Ullstein, 1993; Christa Hoffmann, *Stunden Null? Vergangenheitsbewältigung in Deutschland 1945 und 1989*, Bonn, Bouvier, 1992. Interestingly, both were financed by postgraduate grants from the CDU's Konrad Adenauer-Foundation.

14 See especially Michael Großheim, Karlheinz Weißmann, Rainer Zitelmann (eds) *Westbindung. Chancen und Risiken für Deutschland*, Frankfurt am Main, Ullstein, 1993.

15 Patrick Bahners, 'Glück unter Glas', *FAZ*, 16 June 1994.

16 Michael Stürmer, *Die Grenzen der Macht. Begegnung der Deutschen mit der Geschichte*, Berlin, Siedler, 1990, pp. 222ff.

17 Karldietrich Erdmann, 'Die Revolution Mitteleuropas – historische Perspektiven', *Geschichte in Wissenschaft und Unterricht* (hereafter *GWU*), 1990, vol. 41, p. 536.

18 Wolf D. Gruner, *Die deutsche Frage in Europa 1800–1990*, Munich, Piper, 1993, p. 352.

19 Horst Möller, 'Die Geschichte des Nationalsozialismus und der DDR: ein (un)möglicher Vergleich?', in Klaus Sühl (ed.) *Vergangenheitsbewältigung 1945 und 1989: Ein unmöglicher Vergleich?*, Berlin, Verlag Volk und Welt, 1994, pp. 127–38.

20 Edgar Wolfrum, 'Diktaturen im Europa des 20. Jahrhunderts. Ein neuer zeitgeschichtlicher Förderschwerpunkt der Stiftung Volkswagenwerk', *Vierteljahreshefte für Zeitgeschichte*, 1992, vol. 40, pp. 155–8.

21 Hans-Peter Schwarz, 'Ende der Gedenktage', *Die Welt*, 29 June 1991.

22 Gregor Schöllgen, *Die Macht in der Mitte Europas. Stationen deutscher Außenpolitik von Friedrich dem Großen bis zur Gegenwart*, Munich, C.H. Beck, 1992; idem, *Angst vor der Macht. Die Deutschen und ihre Außenpolitik*, Berlin, Ullstein, 1993.

23 Hans-Peter Schwarz, *Die Zentralmacht Europas. Deutschlands Rückkehr auf die Weltbühne*, Berlin, Siedler, 1994, pp. 240–57.

24 Hans-Peter Schwarz, 'Mit gestopften Trompeten. Die Wiedervereinigung Deutschlands aus der Sicht westdeutscher Historiker', *GWU*, 1993, vol. 44, pp. 683–704.

25 Christian Meier, 'Deutschland zwischen der Bonner und der Berliner Demokratie', *Zeitschrift für Politikwissenschaft*, 1994, vol. 41, pp. 561–72.

26 Jürgen Kocka, 'Revolution und Nation 1989. Zur historischen Einordung der gegenwärtigen Ereignisse', *Tel Aviver Jahrbuch für deutsche Geschichte*, 1990, vol. 19, p. 493.

27 Jürgen Kocka, 'Nur keinen neuen Sonderweg', *Die Zeit*, 19 October 1990.

28 Jürgen Kocka, *Vereinigungskrise. Zur Geschichte der Gegenwart*, Göttingen, Vandenhoeck & Ruprecht, 1995, p. 42; Bernd-Jürgen Wendt, 'Die Debatte um den "deutschen Sonderweg"', in *idem* (ed.) *Vom schwierigen Zusammenwachsen der Deutschen. Nationale Identität und Nationalismus im 19. und 20. Jahrhundert*, Frankfurt am Main, Peter Lang, 1992, p. 141.

29 Hans-Ulrich Wehler, *Deutsche Gesellschaftsgeschichte*, vol. 3: *Von der deutschen 'Doppelrevolution' bis zum Beginn des ersten Weltkriegs, 1849–1914*, Munich, C.H. Beck, 1995. Note however, that the term *Sonderweg* (special path) has largely been replaced by the weaker *Sonderbedingungen* (special conditions).

30 Hans Mommsen, 'Noch einmal: Nationalsozialismus und Modernisierung', *Geschichte und Gesellschaft* (hereafter *GG*), 1995, vol. 21, pp. 391–402.

31 Peter Reichel, 'Bitte keine neue Totalitarismus-Debatte!', *Die Tageszeitung*, 4 March 1992; Ralph Jessen, 'Die Gesellschaft im Staatssozialismus. Probleme einer Sozialgeschichte der DDR', *GG*, 1995, vol. 21, pp. 96–110.

32 Heinrich August Winkler, 'Abschied von einem deutschen Sonderweg. Wider die postnationale Nostalgie', *Die neue Gesellschaft/Frankfurter Hefte*, 1993, vol. 40, pp. 633–6.

33 On Fleißner see Hans Sarkowicz, *Rechte Geschäfte. Der unaufhaltsame Aufstieg des deutschen Verlegers Herbert Fleißner*, Frankfurt am Main, Eichborn, 1994.

34 On the Goldhagen debate in the context of the attempted renationalisation of German identity after 1990 see Wolfgang Wippermann, *Wessen Schuld? Vom Historikerstreit zur Goldhagen-Kontroverse*, Berlin, Elefanten Press, 1997; several of the key texts in the debate have been collected in Julius H. Schoeps (ed.) *Ein Volk von Mördern? Die Dokumentation zur Goldhagen-Kontroverse um die Rolle der Deutschen im Holocaust*, Hamburg, Hoffmann & Campe, 1996.

35 Hans-Ulrich Wehler, *Angst vor der Macht? Die Machtlust der neuen Rechten*, Bonn, Friedrich-Ebert-Stiftung, 1995; Michael Schneider, '*Volkspädagogik von Rechts. Ernst Nolte, die Bemühungen um die "Historisierung" des Nationalsozialismus und die "selbstbewußte Nation"*', Bonn, Friedrich-Ebert-Stiftung, 1995.

36 'Gegen das Vergessen', *FAZ*, 7 April 1995.

37 Rainer Zitelmann, *Wohin treibt unsere Republik?*, Berlin, Propyläen, 1995, p. 7.

38 Hagen Schulze, *Kleine deutsche Geschichte*, Munich, C.H. Beck, 1996; for the trenchant critique of this book see Volker Ullrich, 'Die neue Normalität. Das historische Hausbüchlein für die Kohl-Generation', *Die Zeit*, 4 October 1996, p. 29.

Further reading

For an attempt to put the renationalisation of German national identity post-1990 into a longer-term historical perspective see: Stefan Berger, *The Search for Normality. National Identity and Historical Consciousness in Germany Since 1800*, Oxford, Berghahn, 1997; see also Christhard Hoffmann (ed.) *One Nation – Which Past? Historiography and German Identities in the 1990s*, special issue of *German Politics and Society*, 1997, vol. 15, no. 2; Mary Fulbrook, *The Presence of the Past: National Identity and German History*, London, UCL, 1996; Ian Kershaw, 'Germany's Present, Germany's Past', *The 1992 Bithell Memorial Lecture*, London, Institute for Germanic Studies, 1992. More specifically on the post-1989 scenario see Stefan Berger, 'Historians and Nation-Building in Germany after Reunification', *Past and Present*, 1995, no. 148, pp. 187–222; Stefan Berger, 'Challenge By Reunification: The "Historical Social Science" at Era's End', *Tel Aviver Jahrbuch für deutsche Geschichte*, 1996, vol. 25, pp. 259–80; for direct and indirect responses to my own criticisms see Richard J. Evans, 'After Reunification', in *idem*, *Rereading German History 1800–1996. From Unification to Reunification* London, Routledge, 1997, pp.234–47; and Jürgen Kocka, 'Defending Social History – German

Historians and the Nation', *Tel Aviver Jahrbuch für deutsche Geschichte*, 1997, vol. 26, pp. 507–16; compare also Harold James, 'Germans and their Nation', *German History*, 1991, vol. 9, pp. 136–52; Peter Pulzer, 'Unified Germany: A Normal State?', *German Politics*, 1994, vol. 3, pp. 1–17; Bernd Weisbrod, 'German Unification and the National Paradigm', *German History*, 1996, vol. 14, pp. 193–203; Wolfram Wette, 'Sonderweg or Normality? The Discussion of the International Position of the Federal Republic', *Debatte*, 1996, vol. 4, no. 1, pp. 9–20; Heinrich August Winkler, 'Rebuilding of a Nation: The Germans Before and After Reunification', *Daedalus*, 1994, vol. 123, pp. 107–27. On attempts to reinterpret the Third Reich in a more favourable light see Karl Heinz Roth, 'Revisionist Tendencies in Historical Research into German Fascism', *International Review of Social History*, 1994, vol. 39, pp. 429–55. On Goldhagen see Hans-Ulrich Wehler, 'The Goldhagen Controversy: Agonizing Problems, Scholarly Failure and the Political Dimension', *German History*, 1997, vol. 15, pp. 80–91. On the usefulness of a totalitarian paradigm compare: Ian Kershaw, 'Totalitarianism Revisited: Nazism and Stalinism in Comparative Perspective', *Tel Aviver Jahrbuch für deutsche Geschichte*, 1994, vol. 23, pp. 23–40. On the prospects for a future left-wing historiography which transcends the national paradigm compare Stefan Berger, 'The Rise and Fall of "Critical" Historiography? Some Reflections on the Historiographical Agenda of the Left in Britain, France and Germany at the End of the Twentieth Century', *Europa. European Review of History*, 1996, vol. 3, pp. 213–32.

21 Historians and the 'First Republic'

Carl Levy

The 50th anniversary of the Liberation and the end of the Second World War came at a particularly momentous period in Italian history. The crisis of the early 1990s was associated with the questioning of Italian unity by the Northern League and the dissolution of the old party system leading to debate about the role of the heirs of Italian fascism and communism in the newly emerging system. In 1994, Italy's most right-wing postwar government was elected, led by Silvio Berlusconi. For the first time since 1945, an heir to historic fascism, Alleanza Nazionale, was part of a European national government. Although the government was short-lived, it saw the progressive acceptance of the former MSI into the mainstream of Italian politics, challenging the principles of the antifascist postwar settlement. The fact that Berlusconi exploited anticommunist rhetoric to win his victory and that a substantial proportion of the Italian electorate still distrusted the postcommunist democratic party of the left (PDS) reflected the importance of anticommunism, as well as antifascism, to the postwar material constitution. In 1996, nevertheless, Italy finally experienced an alternation of government from right to left, and although the PDS was still denied the premiership, given the continuing strength of anticommunist prejudice, it was the backbone of the government.

During the 1980s, historians had anticipated many of the debates surrounding these developments. In 1987 Renzo De Felice had urged that Italian fascism be placed in a larger, less emotion-laden context, and that the law forbidding the re-establishment of the PNF be repealed. The Italian debate was fought out in parallel to its more famous German cousin, the *Historikerstreit*, and to its later episode following unification. This debate, in which historians have been involved in both historiographical and acutely political interventions, is the main theme of this chapter.

According to Richard Bosworth, under De Felice's leadership, 'Italy had experienced a paradigm shift about the meaning of the 'long Second World War' which was almost the exact reverse of that experienced in Britain and West Germany in the 1960s, and France in the 1970s. In Italy the conservative empire struck back and effortlessly won acceptance for the sort of historical interpretations which had got Hillgruber and Stürmer into so much trouble in the FRG. In Italy, it seemed, the right has won the 'historians' quarrel'.[1] The collapse of the postwar Italian party system seemed to offer nationalist and/or revisionist historians the opportunity to consolidate their victory. However, whilst the scope for political intervention seemed greater when the short-lived Berlusconi government charted a more Eurosceptical and nationalist foreign policy such a prospect was probably illusory. It is not clear that De Felice's school is as monolithic as was presumed before his death in late 1996. Since then, two journals have replaced *Storia Contemporanea*, and a third is rumoured. Indeed, it is not at all clear that De Felicean revisionism did win such a victory in the 1980s and 1990s. The debates over the collapse of the fascist regime, the Resistance/civil war of 1943–5 and the origins of the 'First' Republic reveal a far more nuanced outcome. On the one hand, the fascist republic of Salò is no longer anathematised; on the other, analysis of the importance of the Resistance and the role of the PCI is becoming more objective.

The crisis of the nation–state, and the contested patriotisms of the PCI and Salò

The historical issues debated in the 1990s were the communists' role in the Resistance, the nature of Salò, and the more general relationship between patriotism and the Italian nation–state after 1943. The debate was cast in such a manner as to affect the concurrent struggle over the significance of the 'First' Republic and the position of the postfascists and postcommunists in the so-called Second Republic.

Since the publication of Claudio Pavone's magisterial oral cum social historical account of the 1943–5 period, the Resistance has been accepted as being simultaneously a patriotic, class and civil war by most historians.[2] Hitherto, the civil war view of the Resistance in Italian historiography had long been associated with neofascist apologias for the Salò republic. The recognition that Salò generated appreciable support from the population of Northern Italy and that one of the key aspects of the Resistance was a battle between Italians, and indeed that sometimes the choices of choosing one side or the other were accidental and not deeply ideological, helped generate a more mature account. Yet, if for some the choice of sides was influenced by accident and expediency, it is also true that ideology influenced both sides of this civil war. As Tobias Abse reminds us, the legacy of the Spanish Civil War also shaped the consciousness of overtly ideological participants.

In debating the Resistance legacy, a number of interlinked issues were raised by Ernesto Galli della Loggia, Gian Enrico Rusconi and other historians.[3] First, that whilst all democrats are by definition antifascist, not all antifascists, i.e. communists, were democrats. Second, to what extent did the postwar settlement of 1945–8 destroy a sense of citizenship in Italy by replacing the nation–state with the state of the parties: the *partitocrazia*? Third, to what extent did the *partitocrazia*'s 'consociational' consensus-seeking continue the practices of the *Partito Fascista Nazionale* (PNF)?

The PCI and national identity

Whilst the left made some use of these very complex and cross–cutting arguments, they were quickly translated into newspaper debates and journal articles by politicians and historians on the right. The issue of the non-equivalence of antifascism and democracy struck at the communists' role in the formation of the Republic. De Felice, Colletti, Sechi and Rusconi questioned the sincerity of Togliatti's acceptance of the democratic rules of the game. Archival evidence recently unearthed in Moscow by Aga-Rossi and Zaslavsky suggested that Togliatti's cooperative, constitutional politics, signalled by the 'Salerno U-turn' (*svolta*), did not mean that the communists abandoned the quest for an Italian people's democracy.[4] Second, all these historians queried the interpretation of the communists' role in this period as being independent of Moscow. Indeed, Soviet archive evidence was employed to show that Togliatti's independent and therefore patriotic line had been crafted by the Russians. The extent to which this meant that the PCI was therefore unimportant for the establishment of a constitutional democracy will be addressed shortly. Here I take up the issue of the fate of the Italian nation-state after 1943.

The debate was shaped by the question of when and how the Italians lost their sense of nation-state, a historiographical question linked to the Italian obsession with modernisation. Rather than stressing strictly economic or sociological issues, authors as various as Lanaro and Sapelli have explained that missed or botched modernisation resulted from the failure to integrate Italians into the postfascist Italian nation-state.[5] In the early 1990s the questioning of the legacy of the Resistance intersected with the rise of the Northern League. Thus, the waning of the Resistance tradition and the rise of Northern separatism were jointly placed in the context of a debate over whether a revived Italian nationalism could preserve the unity of the Italian state without undermining the liberal democratic and social welfare principles of the constitution.

These concerns were similar to those exhibited in German intellectual circles, as outlined by Stefan Berger in this volume. Whilst some historians argued for a refounding of civic life upon the virtues of ethnic nationalism and conservative national histories, others, constitutional patriots, following Habermas's suggestion, argued that national history should be placed within universal values of tolerance, pluralism and human rights. In the Italian context, Rusconi was central not only because his recent books concentrated on national disunity in the 1990s and the legacy of the Resistance, but also because as a Germanist he had introduced the Italian public to the *Historikerstreit*.

Rusconi felt that, although much of the Resistance tradition was mythologised and the constitution flawed, modern Italian democracy could still find much worthwhile inspiration in them. However, Rusconi also insisted that the history of the modern Italian nation-state still had to be grounded in the specifics of an ethnocultural Italian nationalism. The argument in Italy had a different tone from that in Germany. Whilst German unification raised questions about that country's position and nature as a great power, the rise of the League seemed to threaten the very existence of Italy as a nation-state.

One of the most spirited and beautifully written rebuttals of Rusconi's ethnocultural nationalism was Maurizio Viroli's monograph. Viroli uses the experience of the Resistance, and indeed the oral and written testimony in Pavone's text, to argue that patriotism rather than nationalism should be the glue to hold the Italian nation-state together. An example of a patriot, Viroli wrote, was the liberal socialist opponent to Mussolini's regime, Carlo Rosselli (on whom, see Philip Morgan in this volume), who argued that 'we are traitors to the fascist *patria* because we are loyal to another Italy'.[6] Therefore, Viroli adds, 'that love of country is a generous commitment that has nothing in common with nationalism'.[7] Using testimony from Pavone's work, Viroli demonstrates how civil society was awakened in the Committees of National Liberation. Participants would suddenly find a brooding Roman cityscape transformed by their antifascist patriotism. In the defence of liberty in one's own locality, patriotism and love of country are rekindled. Unlike Rusconi, Viroli argues that an ethnocultural Italian who embraced corruption or tyranny could not be a patriot. Therefore civic solidarity, civic responsibility and the tolerance of difference within Italian society in the 1990s could find a grounding in this reading of the Resistance.

Nevertheless, both writers share certain principles. Both Rusconi's and Viroli's interpretations of antifascism and the Resistance suggest that, however flawed, the mass organisations of the Resistance were the key to the birth of a democratic Italian nation-state. By contrast, Ernesto Galli della Loggia defends a return to the values and history of the traditional nineteenth-century conception of the nation-state. This polemical debate gave birth to a series of historical studies which investigated how Italians' sense of the nation-state shifted during the liberal, fascist and republican periods. In a carefully written exposition, Emilio Gentile argued that the crisis in the Italian nation-state could be traced back to the 1930s.[8] If Fascism had arisen as a movement in defence of the Italian nation-state, its attempt at creating a totalitarian society meant that the fascist party-state had become the nation. This, as Gentile demonstrates, upset the fascists' conservative nationalist allies. By confusing 'the myth of the nation with the myths of the totalitarian state, Fascism polluted the national patrimony of the Risorgimento, and contributed to the decadence of the national State in the collective consciousness of Italians'.[9] Rather differently, Renzo De Felice and Galli della Loggia argued that it was the collapse of the Italian state during 'the 45 Days' following Mussolini's fall which had a lasting impact on the relationship between state and nation, discrediting older, monarchical and military forms of national consciousness. Subsequently, moreover, permanent disunity had been built in to the state by the antifascist unity myth, discussed below.

The 45 Days have recently been the object of interesting empirical study. Giuseppe Conti's study of Italian army morale shows that desertion became significant only after 25 July 1943, albeit during the Anglo–American invasion of Sicily from 10 July soldiers had deserted in large numbers to protect their homes – sometimes clashing with German troops.[10] However, Abse notes that the discontent caused by the heavy bombing of the North (which according to Conti worried soldiers stationed elsewhere) and the massive workers' strikes in Milan and Turin in March and April of 1943, preceded the invasion of Sicily.[11] Unlike Britain or Germany, aerial bombing undermined the legitimacy of the Mussolinian regime. Indeed, Aurelio Lepre identifies this bombing as provoking the collapse, in December 1942, of the myths of the *Duce*, the 'proletarian nation' and the state.[12] The 45 Days might not, after all, be so significant for the collapse of identification by Italians with the Italian nation-state. Attachment to the fascist nation-state might even have been quite superficial when Italy entered the War in 1940. Elena Aga-Rossi's concise but detailed account of the 45 Days adds weight to Gentile's contention.[13] She concludes that the king, Badoglio and the traditional military elites did not prepare for a German invasion by closing the Brenner Pass or issuing firm orders to defend Rome in tandem with the Americans because they feared their own people. The monarchist and military elites seemed more frightened by chaos and communism than the looming German seizure of the Peninsula. Yet, as Richard Lamb has argued, a successful defence of Rome would have legitimised the monarchy and probably saved Italy from the harsh provisions of the postwar peace treaty.[14]

This leads us back to the question of the Italian nation-state. Fascism failed to nationalise the masses and to bridge the gap between *paese legale* and *paese reale*. If we follow Gentile's argument, fascism undermined the credibility of the state forged from the Risorgimento. The army and the monarchy lost any connection with the people of their own nation-state. Whereas Pavone and Simone Neri Serneri still argue that it was the Resistance (in fits and starts) that reclaimed national patriotism, its contestation or at least demythologisation has led to a more critical view of the PCI's role in the Resistance.[15]

The postwar period presented a great challenge to the communists. Whether or not Togliatti's moderate line was Stalin's creation, during the hostilities the communists could promote themselves as a national patriotic force. The Resistance was against the *Nazifascisti*, implying that all patriotic Italians were in battle against the Germans and their antinational stooges. The Resistance was a patriotic war, indeed the continuation of the Risorgimento. However, even before the War ended the communists encountered problems because, as Rusconi notes, many of their followers felt the Resistance was a class-based settling of accounts. Thus in the Po Valley, local landlords rather than just the identifiable officials of Salò were considered traitors. Much has been written recently about the 'triangle of death' – the area in the Emilia Romagna where mass executions of class enemies were supposedly carried out by partisans in 1945–6. This allegation was used in polemical newspaper articles in the early-1990s in order to question the communists' democratic legitimacy. The detailed and scrupulous analysis of postwar unofficial purges by Onofrio has shown both that more executions occurred in Piedmont, and that the number killed has been overestimated.[16] Crainz has also shown that the acts of violence in the Po Valley were tied less to communist party policy than the peasant culture of vendetta.[17] Indeed, the Russian archives reveal that leading Italian communists voiced their disquiet to the Russian Ambassador in Rome about incidents of partisan banditry. Nevertheless, in a very hostile survey Salvatore Sechi argues that the communists' attitude towards the nation was entirely instrumental. During their sectarian periods in the middle 1920s or early 1930s the communists had dismissed the legacy of the Risorgimento as a prologue to fascism.[18] Even during the Popular Front era and the Resistance, the communists always considered Marxism-Leninism and Stalinism as more significant for modern politics than the Italian national legacy. The support the *Garibaldini* gave Tito in Venezia Giulia and the hostile sectarian party line resumed after 1947 confirmed, for Sechi, the purely instrumental patriotism of Togliatti and the PCI.

Renewed interest in the Resistance and national unity has also led to re-evaluation of one of the products of the 45 Days, the Salò republic.

Salò and the Italian nation-state

If Pavone's account of the Resistance made the concept of civil war intellectually respectable, Lutz Klinkhammer's path-breaking account of the Salò republic, based on German archives, has given some evidence of the extent to which Mussolini's republic was not merely an auxiliary police force of the Germans, but had some leeway in deciding its own policy. Klinkhammer argues that the polycratic nature of policy-making in the Third Reich had unintended effects when transferred to Italy after September 1943. First, Hitler considered Mussolini a friend and ideological soulmate. Therefore Mussolini's Republic was an 'occupied ally', in the position neither of Vichy France nor certainly of Poland and the East. Second, Hitler's orders were extremely vague, so conflicting organisations and institutions interpreted them to increase their own power in Italy. The chief rivals were the army and the Foreign Office. The former sought a harsh occupation policy but von Ribbentrop and the Foreign Office were more flexible, even bolstering the sovereignty of Salò in order to outmanoeuvre the army's quest for control. Thus, although Ambassador Rahn was successful in retaining a direct relationship with Mussolini's government and his prefects, the victory was not one of humanitarianism in Italy over the monstrous policies reserved for the East.

Attempts to deport or recruit over a million Italian labourers to the Reich were also limited by other clashes of interest between the German occupiers and by the shifting objectives of policy-makers. Thus Saukel originally sought to dismantle Italy's northern industrial base and ship it to the Reich. However, by early 1944 transport systems were so disrupted by Allied bombings, that policy shifted to working with northern industrialists to increase productivity for the benefit of the German war effort. This policy included a certain amount of leeway towards meeting the economic demands of workers in northern factories. But at the same time Saukel and Todt attempted to get voluntary or forced labour to work on German fortifications in Italy and/or be deported to Germany to fill gaps in labour there. These drives for labour were largely unsuccessful due to lax enforcement by their Italian allies.

Whilst Klinkhammer's account derives from the perspective of the conflicting needs of the German occupiers, in the final eighth tome of his massive biography of Mussolini (entitled, *The Civil War*), Renzo De Felice emphasises the initiatives taken by Mussolini rather than his reactions to German orders. Although at the time of writing this tome was yet to be published, a short book-length interview with De Felice was released before his death.[19] De Felice appeared to argue that not only were many key actors in Salò patriotic nationalists and not Nazi puppets, but that Mussolini's own actions may be explained in a similar manner. I have said appear, because throughout his enormous biographical enterprise it has been difficult to follow the twists and turns in De Felice's argument. In particular, it is hard to discern the *Duce's* position because one is never certain if De Felice's biography is an account of Mussolini or of Italy under fascism. The wartime volumes compound the problem: one is now not sure if the last volumes are about Mussolini, Italy and the Second World War, or Mussolini, Italy, the Second World War and the world. De Felice never seems to invoke the good liberal principle of individual responsibility – it is always very difficult to ascertain whether Mussolini is ever responsible for his actions.

De Felice's account of the Salò republic argues that Mussolini accepted his position in order to prevent Northern Italy experiencing the Polish variant of occupation. Certainly in 1943 Goebbels had stated that the betrayal of the Italians meant that Italy had sacrificed its right to be counted amongst the civilised states. De Felice also argues that the various military units of the Salò republic were not all at the beck and call of their Nazi ally. Indeed, he argues that Borghese and the Decima Mas were Italian nationalists having little in common with Italian fascism, and he points to their role in Venezia Giulia in protecting Italian territory from Tito's partisan army at the end of the War. He also points to links between Borghese and unoccupied Rome. It might be true, as Pavone demonstrates, that units of the Resistance, the RSI and the Germans engaged in a three-way game of temporary truces between 1943 and 1945, but it doesn't seem plausible that Mussolini saved northern Italy from the fate of Poland. If one uses Klinkhammer's evidence, whatever margin of independence Mussolini possessed was highly constricted and largely the unintended artefact of bureaucratic wars between quarrelling German interest groups. With the Germans increasingly pressed, the RSI was a useful, if at times timidly independent partner: saving manpower for pressing demands on the Eastern Front.

Evidence of Mussolini's own initiatives are few and far between. Indeed there are several sources which seriously undermine De Felice's thesis. First, parts of Italy were indeed treated to a 'Polish' policy. The Reich effectively annexed the Pre-Alps and the Adriatic Coast: Cossack and Caucasian allies were allowed to settle in Friuli and their Croat partners were allowed to take back Zara and the Dalmatian Coast once Badoglio signed the truce. Second, by April 1944 the German army was given *carte blanche* in its activities against the Resistance. This included operations entailing the wholesale execution of 'guilty villages' and the mass forced evacuation of certain areas. Third, Mussolini's policy of the socialisation of northern industry was consistently blocked by the Germans. Fourth, Mussolini had no power to prevent the harsh treatment of the 600,000 Italian troops interned by the Germans in the Reich. Fifth, Mussolini never condemned the massacre of Italian troops by the Germans in September 1943 in Yugoslavia, Greece, the Aegean or Albania. Rather, in one case where Mussolini did have some margin of power he may not have exercised it. Michaelis and Steinberg have contrasted the largely successful attempts of the Italian army in shielding Jews from the Final Solution in their occupation zones in France, Yugoslavia and Greece to the full complicity of the German army in the Final Solution.[20] It is also argued that Mussolini attempted to shield as many Jews as possible in Italy after 1943. Racialist fanatics were only able to deport 9,000 to Auschwitz. However, according to Klinkhammer, Rahn was little concerned with this policy and he believes Mussolini could have swayed policy here and saved more Jews had he so wished.[21]

The net result of a more nuanced account of the RSI and the Resistance has been both to question the patriotic *bona fides* of the communists and to re-evaluate the position of combatants of Salò. However, the other major parties' contribution to the construction, or destruction, of the nation-state have not been forgotten. Ada Ferrari has presented, in particular, a nuanced account of the Christian Democrats' attitude to the nation-state in the immediate postwar era.[22] Before, 1947–9 and the emergence of the Cold War, it was far from clear where their leadership placed the Italian nation-state in the international system. Although De Gasperi promoted the American position and the American model of the secular political party, left-wing and integralist opponents mounted major challenges to the peace treaty and NATO membership, invoking a neutralist Catholic nation as an alternative attractive to a significant part of the electorate.

Such antinational Catholicism returns the discussion to the continuities between the Resistance and the post-1948 *partitocrazia*. Thus, whilst Neri Serneri can still present the Resistance as a form of radical social and democratic catharsis, a significant portion of the population in the countryside and in the urban centres of the North was either ambivalent, cautious about, or hostile to its message. Much attention has been concentrated on *attendismo*: the behaviour of the fence-sitters who tried to survive as best they could. The Resistance and Salò, it is argued, were the product of active minorities. The majority awaited a postwar settlement of the sort embodied in the triumph of catch-all, Christian Democratic anticommunism which redeployed the fascist regime's mechanisms of consensus-patronage, etc. whilst accepting the communists and the left within the political nation symbolised by the 1948 constitution. The population of the 'First Republic' identified with parties rather than the Italian nation-state the demise of which the political elites thought it expedient to ignore. This argument, however, conflates several issues in order to score points in a debate specific to the early 1990s. It is best to examine precisely what were the boundaries between *attendismo*, the Resistance and the active supporters of Salò.

Roger Absalom demonstrates that the peasants in the Northern country-side were prepared to shelter escaped Allied POWs, disbanded Italian soldiers or others fleeing conscription into the Salò's armed forces or forced labour for the Germans.[23] However, they were hostile to, or suspicious of, the Resistance drawing them into conflict with the Germans or their Italian allies. One must also be careful of periodisation: once the Germans and their Italian allies embarked on policies of collective punishment from 1944 many peasants did mobilise against them. But even then they might only wish to defend their property or the safety of their own valley.

Evidence of direct support for Salò is also available, helping explain how the Resistance and Salò mobilised equal numbers of combatants in 1944. Thus, administrative mismanagement in the South had led to economic chaos and disenchantment with the Allies whereas in the North the urban economy was managed efficiently enough to keep inflation and privation within acceptable bounds. This meant that Mussolini's drive for national reconciliation, using sympathetic priests to lure partisans out of the hills and Giovanni Gentile to build bridges to the intelligentsia, was not completely unsuccessful. Indeed, it has been argued that Gentile's assassination was ordered by the communists to undermine these attempts. The position of the church was ambiguous, however. Bishops and chaplains were found blessing both sides of the civil war amongst the Italians. Moreover, Pietro Scoppola has noted a more difficult to detect form of passive resistance by men and women in the North.[24] Thus, whilst Mussolini could be openly cheered and mobbed in the streets of Milan as late as December 1944 it is hard to evaluate the importance of this event. Abse notes that during the 45 Days there was no spontaneous movement to reinstate Mussolini and his regime, nor was there a discernible fascist resistance to the Allied occupation of the South. In the end Mussolini's regime in the North relied on a fickle, pragmatic and frightened urban constituency.

Antifascist resistance and the origins of the republic of parties

The ambiguities concerning popular attitudes to Salò and the Resistance have been invoked to explain a connection between the *partitocrazia* and the death of the Italian nation-state. The focus of attention is the relationship between the emergent mass parties and the nation-state between 1943 and 1948. The revisionists see the Christian Democrats, communists and socialists as the culprits who established the *partitocrazia* and undermined the nation-state during the 'First Republic' and have refocused attention on the lost moderate alternatives to the suspect internationalism of both communism and Catholicism. The moderate liberal leader and banker of the Resistance, Pizzoni, has been noted by De Felice, whilst the radical liberals in the Action Party have been the target of bitter criticism by Galli della Loggia, accused of being dupes of the communists and utopian intellectual advocates of an impossible form of participatory democracy which could not overcome the apathy of the *attendisti*.

The contested legacy of the communists and their CLN allies leads us back to the assumption that there were connections between the antifascist Resistance, the constitution and the *partitocrazia*. The contention of the revisionists has been that a cosy cartel was created which allowed the communists a share of influence in the party state. Their major opponents, the Christian Democrats, allowed the profile of the nation-state to erode because of their Catholic internationalism and integration into NATO and the EC. Thus, the nation-state and civic virtue were squandered.

Much recent historiography can be employed to reveal the factual weaknesses of this polemical search for connections between the Christian Democrats and the creation of the 'antinational' *partitocrazia*. The *partitocrazia* relied upon a promiscuous mixture of private and state capital which guaranteed patronage to clients. However, the political conditions required to permit it to flourish were the product of shifts within Christian Democracy in the 1950s, the ensuing centre-left governments of the 1960s and the governments of national solidarity in the 1970s. Moreover, albeit the rules of game for postwar liberal democracy were embedded in the constitution of 1948 jointly agreed by the antifascist grand coalition so that one can say that a constitutional patriotism arose from the Resistance, this is not the same as claiming that a *partitocrazia* already functioned during the Resistance or in the immediate postwar era.

Unlike divided Germany, where 'antitotalitarian' Germany faced 'socialist' Germany, the Italian national heritage was contested in the 1950s by left and centre-right within one state. During the height of the Cold War the Resistance was ignored by the Italian state which, naturally suspicious of the left's ex-partisan veterans' organisations, more often tried Resistance fighters for alleged crimes than the combatants of Salò who, as Christopher Duggan has recently noted, were instead treated to the pensions due to combatants of a sovereign state.[25] Meanwhile, the Christian Democrats practised a form of 'protected' democracy which ejected communist mayors from their offices and leftist workers from their jobs. Despite this, a form of national popular patriotism could still be respectable in postwar Italy, unlike in Germany, given that Italian armed forces fought alongside the Allies and that the Resistance succeeded in tying down a considerable number of German troops in the North, with the sacrifice of at least 50,000 Italian lives. The constitution, moreover, resulted from a popularly elected constituent assembly, and its republican form resulted from a popular referendum.

If the Italian communists played a far more constructive role in shoring up their republic than their French counterparts in this period, it does not mean that the relationship between the parties was cosy. In 1943 and again after Togliatti's near-assassination in 1948 insurrection seemed on the cards, but the party cooled the hotheads. For a long time, popular left-wing sentiment awaited the call to arms. At the same time, the stay-behind Gladio force, sponsored by the USA to counter a Soviet invasion, became the kernel of forty years of right-wing subversive activities in the Italian security forces.

The emergence of the centre-left, as Di Loreto demonstrates, saw a re-evaluation of the Resistance.[26] Indeed the event that set off the crisis surrounding the 1960 Tambroni government started when the MSI chose to hold its national conference in Genoa, a city awarded a collective gold medal for services rendered to the Resistance. Furthermore, historians of the 'First Republic' have recently noted how fascism and antifascism became a touchstone for much of the politics of contestation in the 1960s and the opening to the PCI in the 1970s. Not only did the right-wing strategy of tension and the electoral surge of the MSI in the early 1970s make the Resistance a live political issue, but the imagery of the Resistance was adopted by some of the left-wing terrorists of the 1970s, although perhaps not as neatly as some conservative commentators believe.

While the revisionists insist on drawing connections between the Resistance and *partitocrazia*, they fail to emphasise the continuities between fascism and the Republic. But not only did the juridical legacy of Mussolini's regime govern labour, family and personal laws well into the 1960s, his judges and policemen were still very present. Mariuccia Salvati has also shown how the promises of social welfare found in the constitution of 1948 were foreshadowed by discussions of a 'material constitution' amongst fascist jurists in the 1930s.[27]

But there were differences as well. Whilst the Christian Democrats inherited state enterprises from fascism, it used them to modernise the economy, opting for integration in the liberal global capitalist order that ensured unprecedented prosperity for millions of Italians. With all the weaknesses of Italian policy-making within the EC's institutions noted by Paul Ginsborg, it is probably also right to agree with Frederico Romero that European integration rescued, rather than, destroyed the Italian nation-state.[28]

Like Germany's 'Basic Law', the Italian constitution envisaged a democracy founded on political parties. But the fundamental difference between the German (or French) case and the Italian was the latter's lack of a fair and efficient public administration. This meant, as Salvati notes, that the parties (primarily the Christian Democrats), acted as mediators between state and society. The *partitocrazia* was not a product of a putative consociationalism which was most certainly absent during the tense, conflictual Cold War 1950s, but more the unintended byproduct of the failures of the civil service inherited from the past. The major reforms forced on the parties in the 1960s and 1970s rendered all too true the slogan 'politics are everywhere', legitimising the parties' sharing out colonised segments of civil society. The *partitocrazia* was the product of the non-alternation of government and of the secular weakness of the Italian administrative elites.

Conclusion

Vigorous historical debates in the 1990s have addressed the question of the continuities between the collapse of the fascist regime, the 'First Republic' and the fate of the Italian nation-state. The civil war period and the immediate postwar era were employed in these debates to draw attention to the PCI/PDS's imperfect past on the one hand and, in parallel if contrary fashion, to the possibility of re-integrating many, if certainly not all, of the memories of participation in, or indifference to, the Salò republic on the other.

Thus, Italians were asked to accept Neri Serneri's evaluation of the Resistance as an experience that educated large minorities of the population in the methods and significance of democratic civic life, but also not to overlook that murderous revenge and vendetta could not be justified in the name of the struggle for democracy. They were also asked to learn that to deny the possibility of indifference towards, and even positive memories of, Salò was to fail to understand the many different things Salò had been to different people, and that such repression of memories hindered the country's reconciliation with itself and hence its political integration. Equally, the parallel vilifications of negative memories of the Resistance on the one hand and of the PCI on the other hindered the creation of a political culture and a set of institutions able to provide government in the interests of a diversified national community. Nevertheless, the recognition was growing that, even though half a century ago many people fought on different sides for different ideals, many of the heroic myths of that period were also common tragedies. After fifty years of parliamentary government it was commonly accepted that, at last, democracy had been consolidated in Italy – after a long and difficult transition. And yet a legacy of mutual suspicion lingered on, adding to the difficulties of building a constitution intended by reformers to facilitate a politics based on government alternation and tolerance.

Notes

1 R. Bosworth, *Explaining Auschwitz & Hiroshima. History Writing and the Second World War 1945–1990*, London, Routledge, 1994 (paperback edition), p. 140.
2 C. Pavone, *La guerra civile. Saggio storico sulla moralità nella Resistenza*, Turin, Bollati Boringheri, 1991.
3 E. Galli della Loggia, *La morte della patria. La crisi dell'idea della nazione tra Resistenza, antifascismo e Repubblica*, Roma-Bari, Laterza, 1996; G.E. Rusconi, *Se cessiamo di essere una nazione. Tra ethnodemocrazie regionali e cittadinanza europea*, Bologna, Il Mulino, 1993; *idem, Resistenza e Postfascismo*, Bologna, Il Mulino, 1995.

4 E. Aga-Rossi and V. Zaslavsky, 'L'Urss, il Pci e l'Italia: 1944–1948', *Storia Contemporanea*, 1994, vol. XXV, no. 6, pp. 929–82.

5 S. Lanaro, *Storia dell'Italia Repubblicana. Dalla fine della grande guerra agli anni novanta*, Venice, Marsilio, 1992; G. Sapelli, *L'Italia inafferrabile. Conflitti, sviluppo, dissociazione dagli anni cinquanta a oggi*, Venice, Marsilio, 1989.

6 M. Viroli, *For Love of Country. An Essay on Patriotism and Nationalism*, Oxford, Clarendon Press, 1995, p. 162.

7 Ibid., p. 168.

8 Emilio Gentile, 'La nazione del fascismo. Alle origini della crisi dello Stato nazionale in Italia', *Storia contemporanea*, 1993, vol. XXIV, no. 6, pp. 833–87.

9 E. Gentile, ibid., p. 886.

10 G. Conti, 'La crisi morale del '43: le forze armate e la difesa del territorio nazionale', *Storia Contemporanea*, vol. XXIV, 1993, no. 6, pp. 1,115–50.

11 T. Abse, 'Italy', in Jeremy Noakes (ed.) *The Civilian in War. The Home Front in Europe, Japan and the USA in World War II*, Exeter, University of Exeter Press, 1992, pp. 104–25.

12 A. Lepre, *Storia della prima repubblica. L'Italia dal 1942 al 1992*, Bologna, Il Mulino, 1992.

13 E. Aga-Rossi, *Una nazione allo sbando. L'Armistizio Italiano del Settembre 1943*, Bologna, Il Mulino, 1993.

14 R. Lamb, *War in Italy 1943–1945. A Brutal Story*, London, John Murray, 1993, and Harmondsworth, Penguin, 1995.

15 C. Pavone, *La guerra civile*; S. Neri Serneri, 'A Past to be Thrown Away? Politics and History in the Italian Resistance', *Contemporary European History*, 1995, vol. 4, no. 3, pp. 367–81.

16 N.S. Onofrio, *Il triangolo rosso (1943–1947)*, Rome, Sapere, 1994.

17 G. Crainz, 'Il conflitto e la memoria. "Guerra civile" e "triangolo della morte"', *Meridiana*, 1992, vol. 6, no. 13.

18 S. Sechi, 'Togliatti e la questione nazionale: un pretesto per la legittimazione', *Storia contemporanea*, 1993, vol. XXIV, no. 6, pp. 983–1,039.

19 I should like to thank Professor MacGregor Knox for his assistance in helping me to follow contemporary debate on this subject.

20 M. Michaelis, *Mussolini and the Jews: German–Italian Relations and the Jewish Question in Italy 1922–1945*, Oxford, Clarendon Press, 1978; J. Steinberg, *All or Nothing: The Axis and the Holocaust*, London, Routledge, 1990.

21 L. Klinkhammer, *L'Occupazione tedesca in Italia 1943-1945*, Turin, Bollati-Boringhieri, 1993.

22 A. Ferrari, 'Democrazia cristiana e idea nazionale: la memoria e il progetto', *Storia contemporanea*, 1993, vol. XXIV, no. 6, pp. 887–926.

23 R. Absalom, *A Strange Alliance: Aspects of Escape and Survival in Italy 1943–45*, Florence, Olscki, 1991.

24 P. Scoppola, *La repubblica dei partiti. Profilo storico della democrazia in Italia (1945–1990)*, Bologna, Il Mulino, 1992.

25 C. Duggan, 'Italy in the Cold War Years and the Legacy of Fascism', in C. Duggan and C. Wagstaff (eds) *Italy in the Cold War. Politics, Culture and Society 1948–58*, Oxford, Berg, 1995, pp. 1–24.

26 P. Di Loreto, *La difficile transizione. Della fine del Centrismo al Centro-Sinistra 1953–1960*, Bologna, Il Mulino, 1993.

27 Mariuccia Salvati, 'Amministrazione pubblica e partiti di fronte alla politica industriale', in *Storia dell'Italia repubblicana. Volume primo. La costruzione della democrazia. Dalla caduta del fascismo agli anni cinquanta*, Turin, Einaudi, 1994, pp. 413–534.

28 F. Romero, 'L'Europa come strumento di nation-building: storia e storici dell'Italia repubblicana', *Passato e presente*, 1995, vol. XIII, no. 36, pp. 19–32; P. Ginsborg, 'L'Italia e l'Unione europea', *Passato e presente*, 1996, no. XIV, no. 37, pp. 85–92.

Further reading

J. Jacobelli (ed.) *Il fascismo e gli storici oggi*, Rome/Bari, Laterza, 1988.

C. Levy, 'From Fascism to 'Postfascists': Italian Roads to Modernity', in Richard Bessel (ed.) *Fascist Italy and Nazi Germany. Comparisons and Contrasts*, Cambridge, Cambridge University Press, 1996, pp. 165–96.

MacGregor Knox, 'The Fascist Regime, its Foreign Policy and its War: An "Anti-Antifascist Orthodoxy" ', in *Contemporary European History*, 1995, vol. 4, no. 3, pp. 347–65.

N. Tranfaglia, *Labirinto italiano. Il fascismo, l'antifascismo, gli storici*, Florence, La Nuova Italia, 1989.

G. Spadolini (ed.) *Nazione e nationalità in Italia. Dall'alba del secolo ai nostri giorni*, Rome/Bari, Laterza, 1994.

Part VIII

Conclusion

22 Historians and the nation-state

Some conclusions[1]

Kevin Passmore with Stefan Berger and
Mark Donovan

Few historians have been as honest as Augustin Thierry: 'In 1817, motivated by the burning desire to contribute to the triumph of constitutionalism, I set about searching in history books for proofs and arguments that would support my political ideas'.[2] When representative government became a reality in 1830, Thierry, as Ceri Crossley shows, preached that the new regime represented the reconciliation of monarchy and nation, and therefore the fulfilment of French history. Contemporary historians have been more reluctant to make the nation-state the subject and object of history, but the use of the national past to legitimise (or delegitimise) particular governments and regimes remains as widespread as ever. Inevitably, the contributors to this volume must be seen in the same light, most obviously in the sharply differing perspectives of Roberto Vivarelli and Carl Levy on recent Italian historiography.

It is, of course, far from novel to suggest that historians are motivated by political agendas; for forty years this has been the starting point of the history of history. Nevertheless, the very familiarity of the assumption suggests that re-examination might be worthwhile, for often evidence of nationalist or other forms of bias have provided sufficient grounds to dismiss all historical writing as distorted. Thus, Antoinette Burton has recently argued that British historians are participants in a 'disciplinary project' designed to 'enculturate' educated citizens in general and university students in particular into the nation-state. The historical establishment therefore fears that practitioners of postmodern studies have undermined the unity of national history.[3] Underlying this hostility to postmodernism, Burton suggests, is a nostalgia for the days when the nation-state was uncontaminated by decolonisation. Furthermore, she argues that *any* evocation of the nation-state 'naturalises' it, and that even postcolonial theorists have not avoided this danger. Worse still, she fears that she might herself have 'let the nation in through the back door' – and she does indeed make some rather essentialist statements about British historiography. By her own account, we might ask whether she too is possessed of a residual hankering after the conceptual security supposedly represented by empire.

This kind of critique is the logical result of an approach that confines itself to the extraction of metaphors used by historians, and which unhelpfully assimilates all historical writing to the same nationalist and racist discursive system. The emphasis in the present volume, in sharp contrast, is upon the diversity of historiographical nationalism. The contributions make clear that the nature of historical writing cannot be fully understood in isolation from the nation–state, but also that the nation–state represents only one of a number of influences upon historians. This volume amply reveals the connection between ideas of national history and social class, whether in Ranke's view that the critical method represented an extension of the common sense of the German bourgeoisie, or in the conviction of English historians from Froude to Trevelyan that the study of medieval constitutions would prepare their students for careers in the civil service and government. This elitism was, of course, masculine, as is evidenced by Macaulay's indignant rejection of the notion that he wrote for 'female boarding schools' and in his desire to 'open a school for men'. Although gender is outside the scope of the present volume, one could also point to Bonnie Smith's discussion of the relationship between masculinity, nationalism and the notion of the autonomous historical subject in early twentieth-century France,[4] or to Joan Wallach Scott's demonstration of the gendered nature of E. P. Thompson's 'free-born Englishman'.[5] Historical writing must be understood in the context of these multiple axes of social differentiation, each of which conditions the others: class constructs politics; politics constructs gender, and so on. The result is that there is a multiplicity of historiographical nationalisms (or antinationalisms), which changes over time, and which is constructed in particular historical contexts. These nationalisms, moreover, are differentially related to the distribution of power in a given society. Historiographies are, as Burton insists, necessarily positioned in relation to the nation–state, but in conflicting ways.

This accent on diversity casts light on two further problems. First, it leads us to the question of how far historical writing 'legitimates' the nation–state: are historians, as Burton suggests, engaged in a project designed to socialise the masses? This volume does indeed provide abundant evidence that historians endorsed particular regimes and participated in attempts to ground the nation–state in popular consciousness. Yet the failure of some states – East Germany, as described by Mary Fulbrook, is the best recent example – to secure mass support, in spite of intense use of history for political purposes, suggests that such efforts are not always successful. Partly this is because the ruling class itself rarely agrees on the vision of history it wishes to propagate (because the complex interaction of class, gender, religion, etc. divides it too).[6] As for historians themselves, the diverse and contradictory nature of their views, the complexity and narrowness of much scholarly work, and the fact that historians must compete as purveyors of history with popular myths, oral traditions, newspapers, television and films, all militate against the view that they are the vectors of a *successful* legitimatory project. Even where historians do reach a popular audience, it cannot be assumed that their works will be interpreted in the intended manner. Because historical writing does not play a major role in shaping the views of the masses does not mean that it is unimportant. Historians are perhaps most significant in influencing the ideas of the ruling classes, or rather parts of them, for it is often forgotten that along with academics more generally, historians themselves constitute a privileged interest group. The profession is not therefore simply a transmission belt for a dominant ideology, for it also defends its own special interests: without necessarily calling into question their value as a means of making sense of historical evidence, the techniques used by historians constitute a form of professional closure. Historians will therefore invest dominant views of the past with their own intonation, and will do so in response to the intrinsic demands of their methodologies, their own professional interests, and in the context of wider social and political struggles.

The second question regards comparison. This book has shown both the variety of historiographies within individual states and the ambiguity of historiographical traditions – for example we find that the Italian liberal tradition, French republicanism, English Whiggism and even the Rankean legacy in Germany were uncertain in their views of the state as the agent of national history. This volume also demonstrates the extent of international cross-fertilisation, ranging from the well-known impact of the German critical method on historians in the rest of Europe to the less familiar influence of the Whigs upon Ranke, revealed by Patrick Bahners. These two points call into question the whole notion of national peculiarities, and more specifically make it difficult to explain, say, the accommodation of so many German historians to nazism as the logical product of a national historiographical tradition. This does not mean that there are no significant differences between national historiographies. But rather than look for such distinctions in the supposed logic of traditions, we should seek them in the different ways in which ideas common to more than one state were combined together in particular contexts. We must also examine the relationship of the various historiographical schools to the distribution of social and political power within individual states.

Varieties of historiography and national peculiarities, 1870–1945

One of the central themes of the book is the question of whether there has been a German conception of the nation that is distinct from the British, French and Italian. Those who take the view that there was such a difference argue that Germans define the nation in terms of biological descent, whereas one could become French, British or Italian simply by a decision to embrace the political ethos of the nation-state within which one resided. German nationalism was therefore particularist and exclusive, while British, French and Italian nationalisms were assimilationist and inclusive. In another version of the same argument, it is Germany and Italy that are said to depart from the norm, in that both are said to have been resistant to the identification of nation and democracy.

Georg Iggers accepts that until 1945 many German historians preached the superiority of their own conception of inner freedom within an authoritarian polity (*machtgeschützte Innerlichkeit*) over the facile liberty of French democracy. He also agrees that there was much continuity in the profession during the Weimar period, and that few historians had much difficulty adapting to Nazi rule. But, Iggers continues, the barrier between German and European conceptions of the nation was not watertight. The nationalism of the *Kaiserreich* mixed aristocratic militarism with a liberal imperialism that would have been recognisable in Britain, France and Italy. It could, in fact, be argued that in late nineteenth-century Germany there were two versions of the Rankean legacy – one conservative, the other more liberal. Both agreed that the object of politics was to maximise the advantages of the state, seen as the expression of an historically evolved *Volk*, in the inevitable conflict between nations. Both also replaced Ranke's optimistic view of history as the development of Protestant states with a more pessimistic view of international politics based on a Darwinian struggle for existence. The attention of present day historians has most often been focused upon conservative neo-Rankeans such as Max Lenz and Erich Marcks, who feared that socialism, parliamentarianism and Catholicism would weaken the state internally. Alastair Thompson's contribution to this book directs our attention to liberals such as Meinecke and Delbrück, who felt that the state would be strengthened by granting parliament a greater role in government and by less repressive policies towards socialists and national minorities. The liberals were, moreover, supported by the growing power of the liberal press and public opinion. Liberals avoided attacking the state or the Kaiser openly, concentrating their fire upon the government. But their practical policies towards socialism and national minorities would, if implemented, have fundamentally altered the character of the German state, shifting it away from repression towards a more constitutional monarchy.

Thompson's analysis represents, in many respects, an extension of the arguments of Geoff Eley and David Blackbourn to the historiographical sphere.[7] Amongst other things, Eley and Blackbourn argued that from the 1890s Germany had developed an increasingly important 'public sphere', and that this was accompanied by a silent parliamentarianisation of German political life, to the point that governments were obliged to tack between the demands of the parliamentary parties and a Kaiser who had no liking at all for constitutional government. This would explain why liberals like Delbrück were sometimes able to use public opinion to fend off administrative attempts to discipline them. Especially relevant in the present context is Eley and Blackbourn's view that the differences between British and German historical development have been exaggerated. As the latter puts it, 'the German experience constituted a heightened version of what occurred elsewhere', and that what makes the German case distinctive was 'a particular combination of elements' (the expansion of capitalism, rampant materialism and cultural pessimism) also found elsewhere. This view allows for the diversity of historiographical nationalisms within states. Divisions among Wilhelmine historians over whether state-power was best maximised by strengthening parliament or by authoritarianism were paralleled, as we shall see, by the disagreement among British historians as to whether or not the defence of Empire required curbing of parliamentary power. German historians, of course, supported a more aggressive foreign policy than did their British counterparts. But this bellicosity can be explained by the fact that they resented exclusion from the scramble for Empire, while British historians feared the potential loss of Empire.

Blackbourn's view that Germany was not so different from the rest of Europe is lent support by the fact that even progressive French, Italian and British historians were not wholly antipathetic to exclusionary nationalism. Ethnic views of history can be detected in the writings of early nineteenth-century democratic federalists like Carlo Cattaneo, the subject of Martin Thom's chapter in this volume. Against pro-Piedmontese and Mazzinian centralists, Cattaneo defined Italy not as Latin, but as the product of ethnic diversity. Yet he also saw the Italian aristocracy as foreign usurpers and identified the nation with the allegedly 'Gallo-Roman' cities rather than the barbarous 'Germanic' countryside. In France, republican historians, taking their cue from the liberal theorist of 'race war', Amédée Thierry, insisted that the origins of the French nation lay in the egalitarianism of *Gaulois* opposition to the Romans.[8] French republican nationalism may have been politically ambiguous too, as is evidenced by the example of Ernest Lavisse, professor at the Sorbonne, and author of primary school history textbooks that sold in millions. Lavisse is often seen as the epitome of progressive nationalism. In fact, he had been a late convert to the Republic, having until the late 1870s been a Bonapartist. His nationalism was not based on reason but on a categorical imperative. He shared with *fin de siècle* right-wing nationalists a sense of national decline, a belief in tradition, a cult of the soil and the dead, and the same religious sense of unity and duty. But he differed from the right politically, for whereas neo-royalists like Charles Maurras called upon a restored monarchy to gather together the people in defence of *la patrie*, Lavisse expected the Republic to perform this task of national representation.[9] The fact that Lavisse allied mystical nationalism with republican politics illustrates clearly the difficulties involved in relating his writings to political practices. The example also highlights the paradoxes of a republican tradition that theoretically welcomes anyone into the national community, yet which also insists on the indivisibility of the nation, and which may therefore be ambivalent towards cultural diversity – a point to which we shall return.

In Britain too, political radicalism contained notions of ethnicity. E.A. Freeman, Regius Professor of History at Oxford from 1884 to 1892, combined Gladstonian liberal-nationalism with a philological racism.[10] Freeman, in an argument that shared something with the views of French republicans, held that the origins of the democratic English constitution could be found in the Teutonic invasions of the fifth century. He went further than

his French counterparts in interpreting national history in terms of the realisation of a vaster Aryan project. The primary purpose of his *The Norman
Conquest* (1867–9) was to demonstrate that the constitution had remained
unchanged since early medieval times, and that, for example, the English
language had not been 'Frenchified' by the conquest. Freeman also professed
assimilationist views, denying that any nation was racially pure, and defended
the rights of subject peoples in the Balkans against the Turks. Yet he held that
race could still be the central element in the determination of national character and institutions so long as this core was not swamped. The races most
closely related to the English were the Saxons and Americans. Yet his view
that America would be 'a grand land if every Irishman would kill a Negro and
be hanged for it', together with his anti–Semitism, suggests that he regarded
some inhabitants of the latter country as more assimilable than others. If the
jury remains out on the question of whether Freeman's racism was 'liberal'
[*sic*] or of a more exclusive variety, his example does suggest the difficulty of
drawing a sharp line between assimilationist and frankly racist nationalism in
the late nineteenth century. Comparison becomes even more problematic
when it is borne in mind that some historians in Germany displayed negative
stereotypes of Jews, yet also admitted the possibility of absorption into
national culture – Herman Oncken, for example, described the historian
Gustav Mayer as Jewish, yet 'a product of the mark, not an import'.[11]

The idea of race underpinned conservative nationalism in Britain too. The
view of William Stubbs (Regius Professor at Oxford from 1866 to 1884) that
the polity developed by the German race on English soil was the purest
product of their primitive instincts was part of the intellectual furniture of the
great majority of Victorian historians. For Stubbs, the British had a sort of
racial capacity for development towards freedom and representative institutions. But as Stuchtey points out, other British historians participated in the
antiparliamentarian mood of the late nineteenth century. Indeed, it would
seem that there were two versions of the Whig view of history, the one identifying the national mission with parliament, the other with the state or
monarchy – just as the Rankean tradition in Germany could be interpreted in
different ways. Thus F.W. Maitland looked to the monarchy, arguing that
parliament had represented a royal court of law rather than a deliberative
assembly. J.R. Seeley (Regius Professor at Cambridge from 1869 to 1895),
inspired by the example of the Prussian reformer Stein, held that 'history is
not concerned with individuals except as members of a state'.[12] Seeley felt
that historians had placed too much emphasis on the development of constitutional liberty in the eighteenth century, and instead regarded the seizure of
colonies as the key to national development. Seeley, like many Prussian historians, posited the primacy of foreign policy. Another Tory, J.A. Froude (Regius
Professor at Oxford from 1892 to 1894), hoped that 'without the sacrifice of
eventual authority' the sterile parliamentary struggle of parties might give way
to a system that allowed a 'longer and more secure lease of power'. 'The great
interests of the Empire', wrote Froude, 'cannot remain at the mercy of parlia-

mentary intrigues, or the transient gusts of popular opinion'.[13] Although much more measured than Thomas Carlyle, who had praised despotism and condemned representative institutions in his life of Frederick the Great (published in 1858–63), Seeley and Froude were not a million miles from German liberal-conservatives like Droysen and Treitschke, who had moved from the liberal opposition in the 1860s to become supporters of Bismarckian power-politics.

In interwar Britain there was a marked retreat from the racism and antiparliamentarianism that characterised many late-Victorian historians, partly because of a reaction against ideas regarded as 'German'. Moreover, liberal internationalism seems to have been strengthened by the creation of the League of Nations. R.G. Collingwood criticised pre-1914 liberals for having combined liberalism in domestic politics with power-state principles in international politics.[14] Nevertheless, pre-war attitudes did not completely disappear. Collingwood regarded British Imperialism, since it involved the rule of the more over the less civilised, as morally superior to the German variety, which was directed at European conquest. Even Collingwood's denunciations of the alleged predilection of Germans for statism and bellicosity sometimes implied the assumption of a German national character. George Macaulay Trevelyan, as Stuchtey shows, stressed the role of heroic individuals such as Lord Grey and John Bright in fighting for liberty and representative government. But Trevelyan also believed in the unvarying nature of the English character. 'We would', he wrote, 'feel at home' among the Anglo-Saxons. Trevelyan was an uncompromising believer in the view that British imperialism was the carrier of civilisation, and with it came the supposition of the inferiority of subject peoples. His views of the Irish, as expressed in his *British History in the Nineteenth Century* (1922), involved the usual contrast between the irrational Irish and rational English. Charles Stewart Parnell, leader of the Home Rule movement in the late nineteenth century, was said to possess a 'strange and solitary mind' that was the product of a mixture of English character with more 'mysterious' forces. His intellect was powerful but 'almost completely uneducated' (in spite of the fact, revealed in a footnote, that Parnell had studied at Cambridge). Parnell's force of character permitted him to dominate the Irish masses – 'an eloquent and emotional race'. But at the end of his career, the fires which had 'blazed beneath' ultimately 'burst out in wild destruction'. There is little in this book to suggest that Trevelyan had much faith in the capacity of the Irish to govern themselves.[15] If old assumptions about national character survived as a sub-current in Trevelyan's writings, he nevertheless identified British destiny with parliament. In 1938 he wrote that the 'glory' of the Revolution of 1688 lay in the fact that by making a firm choice in favour of parliamentarianism, it had secured a national power that was greater than that of the unlimited monarchy of France. On balance, he concluded, this choice remained commendable in the face of the still more formidable absolutist governments of the 1930s.[16]

There was, in fact, a more general retreat from the anti-parliamentarianism of the late nineteenth century, and indeed from politics in general, on the part of British historians. Doubtless the belated expansion of professionalism in the interwar years was one of the reasons for the reluctance of historians to pronounce on political issues. There is little sign of overt sympathy for fascism or nazism. But there were, again, ambiguities in the liberal–conservative tradition. On the liberal side, Powicke's appeal for historical writing based on 'feeling' rather than the minutiæ of documentary study had something in common with Carlyle, with the Nazi *Volksgeschichte* movement and with pro-Vichy historians in France. In the context of the 1930s his description of Edward I as a 'self-made king' was as likely to remind his readers of Mussolini as of the liberal ideal of the self-made man. Meanwhile the idealism, nostalgia for medieval monarchy and Wagnerian overtones of Powicke's *England in the Thirteenth Century* recalled the work of the German romantic conservative, Ernst Kantorowicz.[17] Another example of liberal uncertainty was H.A.L. Fisher, who on the one hand endorsed a Whig view of history updated to include colonial self-government and democracy, yet on the other regarded poverty as eugenically desirable, and regarded the education of the poor as not necessarily worthwhile. This eugenicism might explain why the fascist sympathiser Douglas Jerrold signed him up to write his *History of Europe* in 1931. On the conservative side there was C. Oman, an admirer of Carlyle, who wrote in 1939 that a third 'great man' might well succeed Frederick the Great and Bismarck as creators of modern Germany.[18] Of course, British historiography was not protofascist. The point is rather that the Whig tradition, which remained dominant in the interwar period, possessed diverse possibilities, and the precise emphasis depended on context and the preferences of the individual historian.

In this respect comparison with France is instructive, for here too the liberal–conservative historiographical tradition was equivocal. The difference was that, throughout the life of the Third Republic, the establishment of an antidemocratic conservative regime was a real possibility, and so the political shifts of liberal-conservatives were more evident. As Stuart Jones demonstrates, Hippolyte Taine's concern to defend liberty against democratic mediocrity led him to espouse an elitist marriage of 'brains and birth' and to preach the revival of intermediate communities, a synthesis that later made his thought attractive to the far right. For comparative purposes it might be added that Taine admired aspects of British liberalism, including the views of historical development espoused by Macaulay and Burke. Taine argued that human history was the product of the intersection of race (one of the scientific certainties that according to Taine's positivism gave meaning to human history), physical and social environment and 'moment'. The third factor permitted human intervention, but only so long as reform went with the grain of the first two conditioning factors.[19]

Insofar as Taine's political views can be unravelled, it would seem, argues Jones, that he hesitated between moderate republicanism and constitutional monarchism. In this he was not untypical of some strands of liberal-conservatism in the Third Republic (especially in its Orleanist version). In the absence of restoration many of these conservatives reluctantly accepted the Republic. Like the British Whigs, they idealised representative government, but some never quite reconciled themselves to democracy − the 'law of number' as they sarcastically put it. This is perhaps why in the 1930s many such conservatives, perhaps because they were more buffeted by domestic unrest, and more directly threatened by Hitler than their British counterparts, became increasingly authoritarian. The largely amateur historians associated with this strand of conservatism − as Gordon shows, most professionals resisted the Vichy agenda[20] − participated in this mood. Daniel Halévy, for example, took on many of the themes of the far right. He interpreted the history of the Republic in terms of the influences of the occult power of freemasonry, and borrowed wholesale from the nineteenth-century anti-Semite, Édouard Drumont. After 1940 Halévy became an uncritical admirer of Marshal Pétain's Vichy regime. In his *Trois Épreuves, 1814, 1871, 1940*, he attributed the defeat of 1940 to 'alcoholism, the declining birthrate and the influx of non-natives'.[21] Halévy's support for Vichy lends support to Robert Paxton's view that the Vichy regime owed something to the French liberal-conservative tradition.[22]

Before leaving France, it is also worth noting that, as in Britain, it was difficult in the 1930s, and even more so during the Occupation, to draw the line between assimilationist nationalism and biological racism. Georges Montandon, discussed by Bertram Gordon, illustrates this point. Montandon, an anthropologist by training, argued that, although the French did not constitute a race in the classic sense of the term, there was a distinctive '*ethnie*' based on the convergence of several races, and that there was a French racial 'type'. Like the nineteenth-century left, Montandon interpreted the conflicts of the French Revolution in racial terms, yet identified with the supposedly German-Gallic aristocracy rather than the revolutionaries. Montandon also distinguished two biologically distinct Jewish racial types. In 1942–4 his 'ethnoracial examinations' had the power of life and death for those held in the Drancy transit camp. Montandon's works were cited by the amateur historians Georges Soulès and André Mahé who endeavoured, during the Occupation, to reinterpret the French past in racial terms.[23]

The difficulties inherent in any effort to distinguish sharply the historiographies of France and Britain on the one hand from Germany and Italy on the other are compounded by the diversity of historiographical endeavour in the Nazi and fascist regimes, and in particular by the continued influence of conservative nationalism in both. In Italy, Mussolini admired the work of the pre-war historian Oriani, who stressed the role of the people in making the Italian nation.[24] As Martin Clark shows, the Education Minister, Cesare De Vecchi (a royalist), saw the Risorgimento as the work of the monarchy. Gioacchino Volpe, the main subject of Clark's chapter, occupied a sort of median position, regarding national unity as the work of both state and nation. His *History of Fascism* depicted Mussolini's movement as one of several interventionist groups that worked together with the state to remake Italy.

Volpe, then, would seem to epitomise the mixture of suspicion of, and attraction to, fascism felt by elitist liberal-conservatives across Europe. Volpe's position of qualified support (especially of fascist foreign policy) contrasts most obviously with the attitude of the high priest of liberal-conservative opposition to fascism, Benedetto Croce – but even the latter admired Mussolini's invasion of Abyssinia.

In Nazi Germany, as Hans Schleier shows, the greater strength of the Nazi Party within the regime meant that purges of the German historical profession were much more extensive than in Italy. Nevertheless, conservative nationalists remained influential here too. Although historians agreed on the priority of the national idea, there was no consensus on how to write history. Some historians had since the 1920s espoused a more populist form of nationalism, in which blood and race became the moving force of history (*Volksgeschichte*). Those who held such views openly despised facts and objectivity and praised irrationalism, feeling and intuition. The contempt of the Nazis for the 'bloodless objectivism' of the historical establishment perhaps explains why many professional historians, even pro-Nazis, rejected the more extreme racial theories promoted by the regime. Mainstream historians certainly endorsed the Nazi regime, but from a perspective that remained essentially conservative and state-centred. The impact of nazism was more evident in choice of subject (war, negative portrayals of British and French history, the study of Germans outside the *Reich*, for example). The history of Prussia continued to be written in the old style. Another view of Nazi nationalism was provided by the one-time left-liberal Fritz Rörig, the subject of Peter Lambert's contribution. Rörig, historian and admirer of the Hanseatic towns, opposed Nazi identification of the *Volk* with the peasantry; instead he saw the Nazi regime as a means of regenerating the German bourgeoisie, and he added to his work the notion of the *Volk* as a racial entity. Rörig's Protestant and bourgeois vision of German history differed sharply from the views of the Catholic historians recently discussed by Oded Heilbronner, who endeavoured to reinterpret Nazism as a resurrection of the aristocratic Holy Roman Empire.[25]

Comparison

In his Berlin bunker in 1945 Hitler passed his time reading Thomas Carlyle's biography of Frederick the Great, dreaming perhaps that British troops would come to his aid against the encircling Red Army. Hitler's interest in Carlyle does not prove that the latter's work was protofascist – after all Carlyle had also been read by British Labour Party leaders. What it does show, however, is the extent to which historiographical currents spilled across national boundaries, the plurality of intellectual currents within states, the difficulty of reading political attitudes from historical texts, and consequently the problems inherent in any attempt to reconstruct 'national' genealogies for Nazism or any other ideology. My intention in making these points is not to show that potentially genocidal impulses could be found everywhere in Europe, or to dissolve away all differences between national historiographies. On the contrary, my aim is to show that the relationship of ideas to action can only be elucidated by very close attention to historical context and more precisely by relating nationalism to other sources of social power. Most of the approaches to national history detailed in this book can be found in one form or another in all of the countries considered. What really mattered was their relative strength and above all the distribution of power.

The first important point is that before 1914 there was much overlap between British and German historiography, the differences being to some extent explicable in terms of contrasting international positions. Only after 1918 did historians in the two states clearly part company, and then not completely. The reason was the impact of military defeat and social crisis upon a nationalistic German historiographical profession. British historians experienced no equivalent radicalisation, and, indeed, there was a certain reaction against 'German' historical ideas. Insofar as British and French historians participated in the ambient antiparliamentarianism of the 1930s, they leaned towards a more elitist form of conservatism that was not especially inclined to undermine the established regime. The case of France, however, shows that once authoritarian regimes came to power, many liberal–conservatives were more than happy to endorse the new status quo. Yet the existence of 'bridges' between ideologies does not mean that they will necessarily be crossed. Even in Germany, conservative historians still had a choice, admittedly unenviable, between unemployment and accommodation to the regime.

It is also vitally important that democracy and pluralism possessed deeper roots in Britain and France than in Italy and Germany. This does not mean that the longest tradition of democracy will preserve a nation from racist extremism, as the seemingly inexorable rise of the French National Front demonstrates. But the pluralism or otherwise of a society does at a given moment have a significant impact on the influence of competing historical interpretations. A comparison of the attitudes of historians to national minorities in Britain and Germany, discussed by Benedikt Stuchtey and Alastair Thompson respectively, will illustrate this point. Historians of both moderate left and right agreed that national minorities were, for the time being at least, temperamentally unable to govern themselves. In both countries historians were divided between qualified sympathy for, and hostility to, subject nations. In Germany the liberal historian Delbrück took up the cause of Alsatian and Danish minorities, but since the liberal left was entirely excluded from power, he had no impact upon governmental or state policy. Indeed, his efforts to invest the ideal of the *Reich* with liberal meanings involved an implicit recognition that a frontal attack was not possible, and that conservatives could not easily be displaced from their hold on state power. In Britain, on the other hand, the alternation in power of Liberal and Conservative governments provided access to the corridors of power for a wider range of historians. Lecky's justification of limited home rule for Ireland greatly influenced Gladstone and had significant influence on the framing of his Home Rule

Bills. Figures like Froude or Seeley could not monopolise academic positions. Nevertheless, there can be no doubting that British historiography placed itself at the service of imperial conquest and might, in other circumstances, have contributed to a different pattern of domestic politics, just as some liberal-conservatives in Italy and France sympathised with the fascist and authoritarian regimes respectively.

The historiographical persistence of the nation-state after 1945

The decline of nationalism in historiographical circles after 1945 has often been exaggerated. It is certainly true that racist and aggressive nationalism declined, and had already been in retreat in Britain and France long before 1945. But liberal, and sometimes conservative, forms of nationalism remained strong. There were common tendencies across Western Europe, such as the view of conservative historians in France, Italy and Germany that their respective authoritarian regimes were 'parentheses' in the normal course of national history. Differences in the strength of nationalism depended on context; especially the degree to which the historical profession was opened up to pluralism. Germany saw the least change in this respect, for many pro-Nazi historians were able to keep their posts. The fortunes of nationalist historiography also depended on the nature of antifascism within each state. In Britain a nationally conditioned historiography was strengthened and spread to the left by the myth of the 'people's war'. In France too, thanks to the involvement of Gaullists, socialists and communists in the Resistance, nationalism influenced the historiographies of both right and left. In Italy, in contrast, the ideal of the Resistance remained a monopoly of the left. In Germany, the Resistance itself had been much weaker, but its ideals were still used to buttress the entrenched power of conservative historians in West Germany and of the communist regime in the East. Since the 1960s historians all over Europe have increasingly made some other principle of difference, such as class or gender, the focus of their work. Yet the national framework continues to condition their writing, sometimes openly, sometimes more subtly.

Mary Fulbrook's comparison of historical writing in East and West Germany illustrates especially well the relationship between historical writing and the nation-state. Both 'Germanies' sought to appropriate for legitimatory purposes what they regarded as positive aspects of the past. West German historians devoted much attention to the conservative resistance to Hitler, while in East Germany the focus, inevitably, was upon the communist resistance. In both East and West the historiography of the other was dismissed as biased and political, although in fact there was a conformist majority and a dissenting minority in each. In both countries too, valuable work was done — within the limits of the questions asked. The crucial difference, argues Fulbrook, was that in East Germany only those historians who toed the official line could easily publish and disseminate their work, whereas in West Germany, especially after the opening up of the historical profession from the 1970s, there was a genuine pluralism.

Even in West Germany, however, the national framework remained central for opposition historians. Fritz Fischer's contention that Germany was almost solely responsible for the outbreak of the First World War could be seen as even more excessively Germanocentric than the view he opposed – Fischer had, after all, grown up within mainstream German historiography, and was not a representative of the 'new generation' of the 1960s. Fischer's assumption of a German 'special path' has been erected into an elaborate historiographical system by figures such as Hans-Ulrich Wehler and Jürgen Kocka. For these historians the misfortunes of German history are the result of the anachronistic influence of the 'pre-industrial elites' (chiefly the Prussian aristocracy), which had united the country under Bismarck's leadership in 1866–71. Their antimodern ideas were accepted by the bourgeoisie and inculcated into the masses through education and conscription. But the inevitable modernisation of German society increasingly threatened the power-base of the pre-industrial elites. In order to defend their position they launched a world war in 1914, and were responsible for giving Hitler the Chancellorship in 1933. Only in 1944, when the War was almost lost, did the traditional elites break with Hitler. This, however, was the beginning of the end of their power. The failure of the Stauffenburg plot to kill Hitler in 1944 led to purges of the officer class – an aristocratic bastion. Then communist East Germany deprived the old elites of their land. The way was therefore free for Germany to become a liberal-democratic society. This interpretation (the target of Eley and Blackbourn's critique – see p. 284), shares the Whiggish assumption of a normal pattern of historical development towards the democratic nation-state.

In different circumstances, the same persistence of the national framework can be seen in Italy, the main difference being that the Resistance ideal was largely monopolised by the left. Roberto Vivarelli's argument that the nation-state, with the exception of the work of Rosario Romeo, ceased to be a positive frame of reference for postwar Italian historians is over-stated. Vivarelli's own view that the Risorgimento cannot be blamed for fascism, and that it was a positive event in which the roots of the Republic can legitimately be found, was in fact quite influential in Italian historiography. This view was, of course, famously espoused by Croce and others, who saw fascism as a 'parenthesis' in national history. Left-wing historians, it is true, combined nationalism with universalism (Catholic or communist), but then so had the Risorgimento state. And far from rejecting nationalism, left-wing historians sought to counterpoise a democratic national historiography to the elitist liberal view of the past. As Philip Morgan points out, the Rosselli brothers had in the 1930s sought to lay the foundations of a democratic *national* historiography. After 1945 left-wing historians located this democratic patriotism in the Resistance. Italian Marxism, based on a domestic hero of iconic status, Antonio Gramsci, was especially nationalist. Gramsci, as interpreted by the communist leader Palmiro Togliatti, saw the task of the left as completion of the 'failed' bourgeois revolution represented by the Risorgimento.[26] The Gramscian interpretation of the Italian past closely resembles the views of Fischer, Wehler and Kocka in Germany. We find the same emphasis on the incompleteness of national unity as it had been achieved in the nineteenth century, and the same assumption that the democratic nation-state is a necessary stage in historical development. But whereas in Germany the completion of national unity resulted from the action of the state (i.e. the destruction of the old aristocracy by Hitler and the communists), in Italy the 'second unification' was brought about by popular resistance to fascism.

In France, in contrast, a nationalist Resistance myth could be claimed by both left and right, Gaullists and communists. This is perhaps why Marc Bloch's call for a historiography that would focus on spatial units larger or smaller than the nation-state: the region or the 'civilisation' was only partially followed in postwar France. Even though *Annales* history became the orthodoxy of large sections of the centre-left historical establishment, the nation-state was not entirely displaced as a framework of analysis. Bloch had shown a great interest in the historiography of other European states, yet to this day French scholars still carry out relatively little primary research on other countries. Braudel, at least, took up the challenge of studying 'civilisations' in his *Mediterranean World in the Age of Philip II* (1949), whilst others have studied Atlantic civilisations. But they have been exceptions to the rule. More often the regional study has been the preferred framework of French historical writing. Yet regional history is often interpreted in the light of the traditional timescales and conflicts of national French politics. And indeed, this framework is defined by the political history that has maintained an unbroken hold on the enormously influential Institut d'études politiques – formerly the École libre des sciences politiques, which Taine had helped to found.

The dominant figure at this institution is the moderately conservative René Rémond. His brilliant *La Droite en France de 1815 à nos jours*, first published in 1954 and revised in 1963 and 1982, describes the essence of Gaullism as 'the alliance of democracy and nationalism'.[27] We cannot help but be reminded of the claim by the historians of the July Monarchy that the Orleanist regime had reconciled nation and monarchy. Rémond's book also represents an attempt to divest the Gaullist state of any affinity with fascism (regarded as inherently unFrench) and with the Vichy regime. The latter was seen as the result of an upsurge, due to the trauma of defeat, of a 'traditionalist' mentality in the French people. And precisely because it was traditional, the ideology represented by Vichy was bound in the end to be eliminated by the onward march of progress. Thus, in a version of the 'parenthesis' idea, Rémond frees the postwar right, and indeed the French nation, from the taint of Vichy.

Rémond's positive attitude towards the Gaullist state is shared by a broad spectrum of the historical profession, including many pro-socialist historians. The authors of the final volumes of the *Nouvelle histoire de la France contempo-*

raine see presidential democracy almost as an historical necessity. Indeed, there is a tendency to assume that the problem with the Third and Fourth Republics was that they were not the Fifth. Jean-Pierre Rioux, in his two volumes on the Fourth Republic, contends that the Resistance and Liberation had created amongst the French people a desire for national unity in a modern society.[28] Yet the Resistance ideal, Rioux argues, was confiscated by the political parties of the parliamentary Fourth Republic. The parties, since they were concerned only with short-term gain, were incapable of instilling civic duty into the electorate (readers will note a convergence with Italian 'revisionist' historiography). Rioux's leftist sympathies emerge from his interpretation of the government of Pierre Mendès-France (1954–5) as a potential left-wing alternative to Gaullism. But in the end, he argues, only Charles de Gaulle recognised that the basic desire of the French was to be 'governed strongly'. In attributing to the people this collective desire for strong government Rioux demonstrates graphically the assumption of the indivisible nation as historical actor in some areas of French historiography. Thus historiographical nationalism, rooted in the Resistance, has characterised both the moderate right and moderate left in France.

In postwar Britain too, since confidence in the national mission had been reinforced by victory, the nation-state remained a significant framework for analysis, and nationalism in various forms was shared by the four most significant postwar historians, ranging from the Tories Lewis Namier and Geoffrey Elton through the liberal A.J.P. Taylor, to the socialist E.P. Thompson. Since the 1930s Lewis Namier had devoted his historiographical efforts to unpicking the foundations of the Whig view of the English past. But he remained firmly attached to English institutions, and replaced Whiggism only with a view in which progress came about through the pragmatic 'fixing' beloved of Tories, rather than through high-minded liberal idealism – democracy for the English, he said, had been a fine art rather than a doctrine. During the late 1940s Namier vaunted the superiority of the 'territorial' English definition of the nation over the ethnic German view. Namier therefore contributed to the genesis of a school of postwar British historiography that studied continental countries in order to understand 'what went wrong', and implicitly measured their pasts against the British ideal.

Namier's anti-Germanism was passed on to A.J.P. Taylor. The crux of the latter's *The Origins of the Second World War* (1961) was that 'the problem with Hitler was that he was German'. Taylor's assumption of a timelessly aggressive German character would have been recognised by the French nationalists of the 1930s with whom, as Peter Schöttler points out, Marc Bloch had taken issue. Of course, Taylor's anti-Germanism was harnessed to a liberal view of international relations, evident above all in his participation in the campaign for nuclear disarmament – a reminder that there is no automatic connection between nationalism, even where it is based on a belief in national character, and right-wing politics.

The case of the socialist E.P. Thompson, another campaigner against nuclear weapons, reinforces the point that nationalism may be harnessed to progressive politics. Thompson's activism in the peace movement was underpinned by a commitment to socialist internationalism. Yet Thompson, who had served in a tank regiment during World War Two, refused to accept that internationalism should consist in 'lying prostrate' before French Marxism. Failure to translate foreign traditions into our own terms, said Thompson, would lead to 'evacuation of the real places of conflict within our own intellectual culture, as well as the loss of real political relations with our own people'. This, he continued, made him a 'socialist internationalist speaking in an English tongue'.[29] Thompson's defence of the 'free-born Englishman' was directed both against the rigidities of Stalinism and at the anonymous bureaucratic technicians of the Cold War. R.J. Bosworth argues that both Taylor and Thompson perceived a special role in the world for the humanitarian values of English history and culture.[30]

Thompson used national intellectual currents as a means to communicate with a wider public and to mobilise the power of English nationalism for left-wing purposes. But the logic of critical history is also important in ensuring that the national framework conditions historical writing less overtly. Critiques of historiographical orthodoxy inspired by class or gender perspectives have to position themselves in relation to existing problems and debates, which are often centred on national issues. This is all the more true because one of the central tasks of labour history has been to explain why movements in particular countries 'failed' to devise successful strategies for the capture of state power. This generated endless debates about various 'national exceptionalisms', all of which crumble away when the assumption of a 'normal' national development is abandoned.[31] Gender history too has been conditioned by the framework of the nation-state. One reason was that the pioneers of 'women's history' sought to 'recover' the past of women by showing their influence in what were considered to be the most important – read political – historical events. Gender historians rejected this approach as marginalising the concerns of feminists. Their alternative was to integrate the study of 'gender' into mainstream history and in turn to transform it. This often meant demonstrating the gendered nature of traditional objects of historical analysis, including conceptions of national identity.

Finally, the growing interest in Western European national minorities, from the Catalans to the Bretons and Welsh, has ensured that the nation-state remains an important historiographical issue. There is no space in this essay to examine the enormous amount of work on this topic. Where the history of these minorities has been written by nationalists, it will hold few surprises for readers of this volume. John Davies accepts that 'Welshness' can be expressed in many different forms. But as Chris Williams points out, his work retains the core assumption that history must be understood in terms of 'national characteristics'. Davies writes of the resistance of 'Wales and its attributes' to predictions of imminent oblivion which go back to Tacitus in AD 100. 'This book', he concludes, 'was written in the faith and confidence that the nation in its fullness is yet to be'. In other words, the nation constitutes the subject of the historical process, and its realisation in the nation-state represents the end of history.[32]

Others have seen Welsh identity as a more elusive object of analysis. Dai Smith is distrustful of the notion of a unitary Welsh past or present. His work demonstrates what he sees as the 'culturally distinctive human experience of South Wales', based on coal mining and a shared popular culture.[33] For his nationalist critics, Smith is representative of the English-speaking political establishment's disdain for Welsh-speaking Wales. But of more relevance in the present context is that Smith's work does not altogether eliminate the national framework. Rather his view that there are multiple forms of Welshness brings national identity into relationship with other sources of social differentiation, and therefore avoids the danger of 'essentialising' it. For historians such as Smith, national feeling has existed in certain historical conditions, but this does not mean that it must necessarily do so, that there has ever been a singular national experience, or that a nation-state distils the essence of something present within each of its citizens.

A 're-nationalisation' of the past?

Thus the national framework, and sometimes a frankly nationalistic one, retained considerable vigour after the Second World War. Nevertheless, there can be no doubting that since the 1960s there has been a considerable shift away from the narrative political history that was previously dominant. It is in this context, of a comparatively recent retreat of historiographical nationalism, that the calls for 'renationalisation' of the past examined in the essays by Stefan Berger, Julian Jackson and Carl Levy must be seen. The targets of the historiographical right, as Burton suggests, are chiefly women's and labour history and postcolonial studies. There are shared themes in this history, especially concerning reassessments of the impact of fascism on Europe, anti-Marxism, and the belief that liberal historians have been soft on communism, and often these developments are seen as undermining the unity of the nation-state. But closer inspection reveals that calls for a return to political history extend well beyond the right, while not all conservative historians have been nationalist in a straightforward sense. In fact, such is the diversity and quantity of contemporary historical writing, that conservative historiography itself has been fragmented. Conservatives have not simply sought to re-establish the political history of the nation-state as a point of reference, but have often accepted elements of the new historiographies, and have incorporated a view of Europe into their work.

These complexities are particularly clear in Britain. In some cases historians have called for a return to the past. Roger Kenyon's *The History Men*, published in 1983, represents a celebration of the medieval and early modern constitutional and political Whig history of the late-Victorian and interwar periods.[34] Kenyon endorses Geoffrey Elton's view that the state is the motor of national progress and the guarantor of liberty. He also adheres to the

Whiggish conviction that it is the duty of historians to teach lessons. Indeed, history constitutes an essential training for statesmen [*sic*]. Historical training would permit politicians to predict, albeit on a modest scale, the results of social processes and of their own actions. Kenyon also shares some of the less reputable aspects of the Victorian historiographical tradition, in that he is unable to discuss Lewis Namier without constant reference to his Jewish 'racial' origins – a point which reminds us that certain universities have represented one of the few places in British society where 'Jewishness' is recognisable and regarded by some as worth remarking upon. Kenyon's lament for the supposed decline of medieval and British history constitutes a reaction against what he sees as the 'inanities of women's history', the 'infestation' of African history, the influence of sociology (a degree which he associated with toilet paper), vaguely sociological core courses with titles such as 'Themes in Modern History', and joint degrees with biology.

Kenyon's rejection of just about every historiographical development since the social history of R.H. Tawney in the 1930s was not, however, typical of those who opposed Marxism and feminism. Opposition to historiographical Marxism led in some quarters to an appeal for a return to political history. This was most evident in the study of the French and English Revolutions, where British historians were in the forefront of efforts to show that great events need not have great causes.[35] As far as the French Revolution is concerned, the nation-state has been assumed as the framework of analysis. But if the political purpose is anti-Marxist, there is little or no evidence of a nationalist agenda. The historians concerned have usually been part of the liberal left, and they have been as ready to engage in social analysis as their opponents. In the case of the English Revolution, the most important revisionist historian, Conrad Russell, focuses on high politics, yet places the Revolution in the context of a European reaction against absolutism, and also insists that the civil wars were part of a 'British problem' affecting the relations of England, Scotland and Ireland. Russell, a liberal peer, reflects his party's preoccupation with administrative devolution within the British state. In the 1990s historians of a more right-wing bent have engaged in a campaign against Marxist 'determinism' (a defunct horse, if ever there was one). But the results are not necessarily nationalist. For example, Michael Burleigh is motivated by anti-Marxism, regards gender history as a 'tired academic fad', and hints of his attitude to the history of British minorities emerge from vaguely dismissive references to 'Celtic squiggles'. Yet he seems more concerned to defend a European idea of progress against the notion that it was responsible for nazism than to write traditional Anglocentric history.[36]

The European dimension of some contemporary conservative historiography emerges more clearly still from Norman Davies's *Europe: A History* (1996).[37] Davies's debt to the English tradition of historical writing arises from his dislike of 'unreadable academic papers' and his preference for the 'poetic' style of Thomas Carlyle. And like his master A.J.P. Taylor, Davies concentrates on the kings, battles and politics of traditional narrative history.

Davies shares with conservative historians across Western Europe a dislike of the supposed reluctance of liberal historians to condemn the crimes of Stalinist Russia. But as Neil Ascherson argues, Davies is more original in using anti-Marxism as a means to unite Eastern and Western Europe – a cause which, as Michael Burleigh points out, sometimes 'tips over into surprising indulgence towards, for example, wartime Axis collaborators'.[38] For Davies Russia is an inherently expansionist and oppressive power (just as Germany was for Taylor) – the antithesis of the humane values of the putative new Europe. It could be added that Davies's views are close to those in the British Conservative Party who regard the integration of the new democracies of Eastern Europe into the European Union as more important than the drive towards monetary union. Davies's European Union, like his historical Europe, is a Europe of nation-states – although there are some hints that he could also live with a Europe in which Britain would be divided into its constituent parts: a sort of 'Europe of Singapores', perhaps.

Similar diversities and ambiguities mark the moves to 'renationalise' the German past discussed by Stefan Berger. Those historians sympathetic to the new right wish to restore pride in nationality, which they regard as having been undermined by antifascism. Rejecting the old conservative idea of a 'parenthesis', they integrate both the Bismarckian Reich and the Nazi state (the latter as a modernising and egalitarian force) into the national story. The postwar 'westernisation' of Germany within NATO and the European Union is regarded as a temporary diversion from Germany's Central European mission. The liberal-conservative 'establishment' shares some of the new right's hostility to antifascism, but it opposes relativist approaches to Nazism. It seeks to reconcile the alleged imperatives of Germany's position in Central Europe with its membership of the European Union and NATO. The German left, on the other hand, would seem to be divided. Some, like Berger himself, fear 'any attempt to provide historical legitimacy to forms of national identity'. Others, in recognition of the strength of national feeling revealed by reunification, seek to redefine the nation in liberal-democratic terms. They postulate the normality of the nation-state, yet give it a different practical meaning to the conservatives, as is evidenced in their participation in the campaign for reform of the 1913 citizenship law.

Carl Levy describes a parallel movement for the renationalisation of the Italian past. It can be seen above all in Renzo De Felice's calls for a 'less emotional' treatment of fascism and in reassessments of the nature of the Resistance. Emilio Gentile argued that the Italian national idea first entered mass consciousness through fascist mass mobilisation rather than through the Resistance; De Felice himself endeavoured to rehabilitate the Salò republic; others contended that since the Resistance was an affair of active minorities, it had given birth to a regime of parties rather than a democracy of citizens. Levy, a convinced opponent of revisionism, highlights research demonstrating that fascism failed to nationalise the masses, and that it gave birth to a constitutional patriotism. In the historiographical field, he argues, the victory of the right has been less complete than some have thought it to be. This, perhaps, reflects the fact that although anticommunism remains significant in Italy, it is now commonly accepted that Italy is, and should remain, a democratic state. Nevertheless Levy's essay reaffirms the point that the nation–state is a contested concept, for historians of both left and right have attempted to give it their own meaning.

In France, contrary to appearances, political history never really went away, and, as we have seen, there is a broad consensus among historians that the Gaullist state has solved the problems of French history by reconciling the nation with authority. This is accompanied by a tendency to assume that the people, and indeed the nation, is a given, and explains why, as Julian Jackson shows, so many historians would seem to fear the dissolution of stable reference points. Explicitly right-wing historians remain relatively uncommon in French history departments, and only in the case of Emmanuel Mousnier is political purpose evident in practical historical writing.[39] In France, even more than in Germany and Italy, historians of the left and centre have been concerned with the alleged dislocation of national identity. Henry Rousso argues that obsessive concern with Vichy has led to the portrayal of the French under the Occupation as exclusively Pétainiste. Pierre Nora fears that the fragmentation of identity, fostered in part by the multiculturalists of SOS-racisme, has opened breaches that have been exploited by the National Front. For Jackson, the preoccupation of these historians with the question of identity derives from the ambiguity of the republican tradition. It is liberal in the sense that it welcomes any *individual* into the national community so long as s/he leaves behind other identities or confines them to private life. But by the same token, republicans are suspicious of the *public* display of alternative collective identities.

Jackson's arguments remind us once again that national historiographies contain diverse potentials, and suggest too that connections between historiographical nationalism and politics in a wider sense are far from straightforward. The fact that historians and politicians are worried about the fragmentation of French identity does not seem to have prevented the assimilation of second and third generation North African immigrants into French society, while the current boom in French rap music would suggest that, in some quarters at least, multiculturalism is an accepted reality. The fact that left-wing German historians are less fearful of the breakdown of national identity than their French counterparts may not tell us much about the general social and political context. Indeed, the status of 'guestworkers' in Germany is considerably more precarious than that of immigrants in France, who can, at least, hope for citizenship.

Conclusion: objectivity, politics and the nation–state

The contributions to this volume confirm amply that since the invention of the nation–state in the late eighteenth century, historians have been unable to ignore it. Some have propagandised actively on its behalf; some have sought to undermine it. Others have endeavoured to make class, gender or some other axiom the focus of their work, without being able to escape the subtle conditioning of the political framework within which they work. But if historians are inescapably conditioned by their national context, just as they are by class, gender and ethnic attitudes, this happens in an enormous variety of ways, with radically different political consequences.

Furthermore, the inescapably politicised nature of their work does not always invalidate the work of historians. The bias evoked in this volume has been most evident in the *questions* asked by historians – when and where did the nation originate? what are its chief characteristics? and so on. As historians we cannot avoid this form of subjectivity, for our starting point must always be with something in which we are interested. Nevertheless, certain kinds of questions are more susceptible of being answered than others. Since particular nation-states and forms of national feeling are historical facts (not, of course, inevitable or natural facts), the question of their origins is in principle one that can be answered. The notion that nation-states are based on biologically pure races has, on the other hand, been falsified beyond reasonable doubt. Yet questions relating to 'national characters', 'national cultures' or 'ethnic groups', which have often replaced discredited biological ideas, are impossible ever to pin-down or define – hence their attraction. These latter ideas have incited some of the more absurd speculations detailed in this volume. Here lies one of the crucial differences between the two historians evoked at the beginning of this chapter: Augustin Thierry and Carl Levy. The former drew upon the science of romantic philology in order to root national character in an ahistorical zone where it was not subject to analysis; the latter takes contemporary national feeling as an observable fact (to be treated in the same way as a manifestation of feminism or socialism), accepts that it is a contested phenomenon, and seeks to explain its origins in the Italian Resistance. Many (though not all) of the questions posed by Thierry, however, are 'unfalsifiable' – since the relationship between race and national history is defined so nebulously that it is impossible to conceive of any kind of evidence that could refute his arguments.

This brings us to bias in the use of evidence. Nazi historians dismissed scholarly conventions altogether. The use of the critical method has been inconsistent: Freeman, for example, proceeded first by reading the Saxon account of an event, and then the 'Norman perversion' of it. Properly applied, however, the rules of evidence permit us to distinguish between the relative value of particular interpretations, even where they originate in nationalist bias. Some of the historical works discussed in this volume we would dismiss altogether since they derive from questions that are unfalsifiable (even though these works may be internally systematic and present a mountain of 'evidence'); in other cases we would evaluate how well the evidence deployed substantiates the hypotheses put forward (not how well the account *reproduces* reality). In other words, bias is inevitable, including nationalist bias, but some answers to particular questions are better than others.

Concern that the dissolution of all forms of identity in contemporary society will lead, in the end, to chaos has led some centre-left historians, especially in France and Germany, to attempt to capture the nation-state for themselves. Such fears may be unfounded, for there has never been a time when the nation-state has been unchallenged, or even where those who did accept it have agreed on its meaning. Indeed, the implicit assumption that societies need some kind of common identity if they are to remain stable may be erroneous, for in spite of the demonstrable lack of consensus, even within the ruling classes, that characterises all societies, chaos has not usually resulted. The fact that most people normally do little (consciously at least) to undermine the social and political arrangements in which they find themselves does not mean that they have 'interiorised' the core values of a particular society. Rather it signifies that the likely costs of resistance outweigh the rewards gained through conformity, however meagre they might be. If extreme nationalism were to triumph again in any of the states of Western Europe it would not be because common identities actually had broken down, for such a consensus has never existed, but because certain groups *believed* that it was necessary to impose a common identity on the rest of society, and had managed to secure the political power necessary to attempt to realise this impossible dream.

Notes

1   In writing this essay the authors benefited from the helpful advice and criticism of Garthine Walker, Peter Coss and Chris Williams.
2   Cited in Olivier Dumoulin, 'Histoire et historiens de droite', in J.-F. Sirinelli (ed.) *Histoire des droites en France*, 3 vols, Paris, Gallimard, 1993, vol. II, pp. 327–98.
3   Antoinette Burton, 'Who Needs the Nation? Interrogating British History', *Journal of Historical Sociology*, 1997, vol. 10, pp. 227–48.
4   Bonnie Smith, 'Historiography, Objectivity and the Case of the Abusive Widow', *History and Theory*, 1992, vol. 31, pp. 15–32.
5   Joan Wallach Scott, 'Women in the *Making of the English Working Class*', in Joan Wallach Scott (ed.) *Gender and the Politics of History*, Oxford, Oxford University Press, 1988, pp. 68–90.
6   Here I am following Nicholas Abercrombie, Stephen Hill and Bryan S. Turner, *The Dominant Ideology Thesis*, London, Unwin & Hyman, 1980.
7   David Blackbourn and Geoff Eley, *The Peculiarities of German History: Bourgeois Society and Politics in Nineteenth-Century Germany*, Oxford, Oxford University Press, 1984.
8   Dumoulin, 'Histoire et historiens de droite', pp. 347–8.
9   Pierre Nora, 'Lavisse, instituteur national: Le "Petit Lavisse", évangile de la république', In *Les lieux de mémoire*, vol. 1 *La République*, ed. Pierre Nora, Paris, Gallimard, 1984, pp. 247–89.
10   M.E. Bratchel, *Edward Augustus Freeman and the Victorian Interpretation of the Norman Conquest*, Ilfracombe, Sockwell, 1969; C.J.W. Parker, 'The Failure of Liberal Racialism: A.H. Freeman', *Historical Journal*, 1991, pp. 825–46.
11   Deutsche Staatsbibliothek Berlin, Nachlaß Hans Delbrück, Oncken to Delbrück, 14 April 1916.

12 Quoted in John Kenyon, *The History Men: The Historical Profession in England since the Renaissance,* London, Weidenfeld and Nicolson, 1980, p. 172.

13 J.A. Froude, *Short Studies on Great Subjects,* London, Longmans, Green & Co., 1893, pp. 346–7.

14 Parker, *The English Historical Tradition,* p. 123.

15 G.M. Trevelyan, *British History in the Nineteenth Century, 1782–1901,* London, Longmans, Green and Co., 1922, pp. xiv, 350–52, 406–412.

16 G.M. Trevelyan, *The English Revolution 1688–1689,* Oxford, Oxford University Press, 1954, first published in 1938.

17 On Powicke see Clanchy, 'Inventing Thirteenth Century England'; on Kantorowicz's sympathy for the far right, and perhaps even qualified sympathy for the Nazis, see Norman F. Cantor, *Inventing the Middle Ages: The Lives, Works and Ideas of the Great Medievalists of the Twentieth Century,* Cambridge, Lutterworth, 1991, pp. 94–8.

18 Parker, *The English Historical Tradition,* pp. 128, 132, 150.

19 Michael Biddiss, 'Hippolyte Taine and the Making of History', in Nicholas Atkin and Frank Tallet (eds) *The Right in France,* London, Tauris, 1997, pp. 71–87.

20 The question of the attitude of professional historians to Vichy is not, however, quite closed, for we still lack answers to some of the questions asked of German historians by Hans Schleier. Did the attitude of historians towards Britain and Germany change during the Occupation? What was their view of Empire?

21 Muel-Dreyfus, *Vichy et l'éternel féminin,* pp. 28–30.

22 Robert Paxton, *Old Guard and New Order 1940–1944,* New York, Morningside, 1972.

23 On Montandon see also Pierre Birnbaum, *'La France aux français': histoire des haines nationalistes,* Paris, Seuil, 1993, pp. 187–98.

24 Clark discussed Oriani in his paper presented at the 'Apologias for the Nation-State' conference, but, owing to lack of space, not in the published version.

25 Oded Heilbronner, ' "Aber das Reich lebt in uns". Katholische Historiker unter dem Nationalsozialismus', *Tel Aviv Yearbook for German History,* 1996, vol. 25, pp. 219–31.

26 A. Ballone, 'Una proposta didattica', in G.N. Modona (ed.) *Cinquant'anni di Repubblica italiana,* Milan, Einaudi, 1996, pp. 267–91, pp. 288–9.

27 The most recent edition is *Les Droites en France,* Paris, Aubier, 1982.

28 Jean-Pierre Rioux, *La France de la Quatrième république,* 2 vols, Paris, Seuil, 1980–3.

29 E.P. Thompson, 'The Peculiarities of the English', 1965, in E.P. Thompson, *The Poverty of Theory,* London, Merlin Press, 1979, p. 37.

30 R.J. Bosworth, *Explaining Auschwitz and Hiroshima,* London, Routledge, 1993, pp. 45–52.

31 See Stefan Berger, 'European Labour Movements and the European Working Class in Comparative Perspective', in Stefan Berger and David Broughton (eds) *The Force of Labour,* Oxford, Berg, 1995, pp. 245–63.

32 John Davies, *A History of Wales,* London, Penguin, 1994, p. 686; Chris Williams, 'Searching for a New South Wales', *History Workshop Journal,* 1996, vol. 41, pp. 266–74;

33 Dai Smith, *Aneurin Bevan and the World of South Wales,* Cardiff, University of Wales Press, 1993.

34 Kenyon, *The History Men,* especially pp. 254–5, 270–87.

35 See, for example, William Doyle, *Origins of the French Revolution,* Oxford, Oxford University Press, 2nd edn, 1988, pp. 35–6.

36 Michael Burleigh, 'A Political Economy of the Final Solution? Some Reflections on Modernity, Historians and the Holocaust', *Patterns of Prejudice,* 1996, vol. 30, pp. 29–41; Michael Burleigh and Wolfgang Wipperman, *The Racial State,* London,

Edward Arnold, 1993; Michael Burleigh, 'Dressed by Genoese, Throttled by Croats', *The Independent on Sunday,* 13 October 1996.

37 Norman Davies, *Europe: A History*, Oxford, Oxford University Press, 1996. My interpretation relies heavily on Neil Ascherson's review in *The London Review of Books*, 23 May 1997.

38 Burleigh, 'Dressed by Genoese, Throttled by Croats'.

39 Dumoulin, 'Histoire et historiens de droite', pp. 372–81.

Index